Strategies and Styles

The London Business School
Centre for Business Strategy Series

The London Business School Centre for Business Strategy was established in 1982 as a centre for the study of strategic and competitive processes in modern business. An independent body, the Centre draws on research expertise from a variety of disciplines to examine issues of central importance in both mature and high-technology industries. This series presents the findings and implications of the Centre's research through a combination of original case-studies and conceptual analyses. Each book is carefully written to draw out practical implications for senior executives.

STRATEGIES AND STYLES

The Role of the Centre in Managing Diversified Corporations

Michael Goold
and Andrew Campbell

Basil Blackwell

First published 1987
Reprinted and first published in paperback 1989

Basil Blackwell Ltd
108 Cowley Road, Oxford OX4 1JF, UK

Basil Blackwell Inc.
432 Park Avenue South, Suite 1503
New York, NY 10016, USA

British Library Cataloguing in Publication Data

Goold, Michael
  Strategies and styles: the role of the
  centre in managing diversified corporations.
  1. Conglomerate corporations—Management
  I. Title   II. Campbell, Andrew
658'.046   HD2756
    ISBN 0–631–15829–4
    ISBN 0–631–16846–X Pbk
Library of Congress Cataloging in Publication Data
  Goold, Michael.
    Strategies and styles.
    Includes index.
    1. Conglomerate corporations. 2. Diversification
  in industry. I. Campbell, Andrew. II. Title.
  HD2756.G66 1988 658'.046 87-12151
  ISBN 0–631–15829–4
  ISBN 0–631–16848–X (pbk.)

Typeset in 10 on 11 pt Times
by Cambrian Typesetters, Frimley, Surrey
Printed in Great Britain by
Billing & Sons Ltd, Worcester

For
E. B. G.
and
A. E. C.

Contents

Acknowledgements

We have been working directly on this book for the past three years. Indirectly, however, we have been grappling for much longer with the question of the role of the centre in large firms. This means that we have benefited from many influences in developing our thinking. We are grateful to colleagues, past and present, at the London Business School, at The Boston Consulting Group (BCG) and at McKinsey; to numerous clients with whom we have worked on these issues; and to many others with whom we have debated our conclusions.

Although we cannot list all the individuals who have helped us, there are some specific acknowledgements we want to make. At the London Business School we would single out John Stopford, who was Director of the Centre for Business Strategy during most of the work on the book, and who encouraged us to focus on the issue of how the centre adds value to the business units; and John Roberts, Research Fellow in the Centre for Business Strategy, whose own research ran in parallel with ours, and who pressed us constantly to avoid oversimplifying problems. John's influence is most evident in our discussion of the tensions in the corporate role. Ian Mackenzie, another BCG alumnus, worked closely with us in some of the field research, and James Lyle, Hugh Woolhouse, Judith Waters, Matthew Bishop and Bryan Rimmer all provided valuable background analysis at different stages in the work.

We clearly could not have undertaken the work at all without the cooperation and support of the 16 companies. We are grateful to them not only for research access, but also for helping to shape and test our thinking through a series of meetings, seminars and presentations. They have been more than the subjects of the research: they have been true collaborators.

We probably owe our greatest debt, however, to the members of the Council of the Centre for Business Strategy. The whole Council, but particularly Trevor Chinn, Dick Giordano, David Plastow, David Sainsbury and David Walker, helped us gain access to the companies in our sample, criticized and challenged our thinking, and provided a never-ending source of encouragement by their enthusiastic interest.

Lastly we would like to praise Kathryn Duff and Hayley Bell who typed and retyped draft after draft of our manuscript, remaining cheerful and resilient throughout.

Despite our many debts, the responsibility for the views presented in this book remains, of course, our own.

M. G.
A. C.

1

Introduction

This book is about the management of large, diversified companies. It deals both with conglomerates like Hanson Trust, which operates in several unconnected industries, ranging from bricks to batteries, and with industrial giants such as Cadbury Schweppes, which has remained in essentially two related industries, soft drinks and confectionery, but has many separate businesses within these industries. Since the war diversified giants such as these have come to dominate industry in all the major Western economies.

The importance of diversified companies is evident from their high and rising share of industrial production. In 1950, 75 per cent of the 200 largest companies in the UK derived the bulk of their sales from a single business. The proportions were similar in other developed economies. By the mid 1980s these figures had altered dramatically: now only 35 per cent of large firms concentrate on a single business. This change follows precedent in the United States and is reflected in all the main European countries.[1] It must represent one of the most rapid and profound shifts in industrial structure ever witnessed.

Some experts feel this trend towards diversity has gone too far. In the United States, in particular, pundits are exhorting businessmen to 'stick to the knitting'. Yet the merger boom of the 1980s has simply reinforced the movement towards increasing size and diversity. As a result, it is no exaggeration to argue that the economies of the developed world now depend crucially on the performance of large, multibusiness, diversified companies.

As firms diversify, they move away from being functionally organized towards a divisional structure, in which responsibility is pushed down to business unit and profit centre managers.[2] In large companies there may be as many as five levels of general managers – the profit centre (the lowest level where profit is measured), the business unit (often consisting of two or three profit centres), the division, the group and the corporate headquarters. Strategies are set and implemented at the sharp end, in the profit centres or business units. But there also needs to be a role for the higher levels and, in particular, for the corporate centre.

Given the involvement of several organizational levels and of many different individuals, the strategic decision-making process becomes highly complex and subject to many influences. Our work unravels these influences.

- What is the role of each level of management in the decision-making process, and, in particular, how do corporate and divisional managers influence business unit strategy?
- How does the process blend broad vision, corporate goals, detailed market knowledge, the results of strategy analysis, and the aims and aspirations of the members of the management team?
- What part does 'strategic planning' play? How much planning is done, and is it useful?
- How is commitment generated? What objectives matter most, and how are they established? Do they follow from, or precede, strategy?
- What facilitates good strategies? What gets in their way? Why do some companies get locked into unimaginative or unsuitable strategies, while others go from strength to strength?

In management textbooks the answers to such vital questions may seem straightforward. In practice, the picture is far less clear.[3] We can illustrate the complications and ambiguities with an account of a review meeting that we attended late in 1984.

Strategy in the Making

The meeting concerned the strategy for a smallish subsidiary of a large and diversified company. Around the table sat the subsidiary's managing director and its marketing director, together with the chairman, the finance director and the planning manager from the division of which the subsidiary formed a part. The topic under discussion was the launch of a series of new products.

The subsidiary had recently been acquired for £20 million. It held a 3 per cent share of a market dominated by three industry giants. The strategy being proposed by the subsidiary's marketing director was to become a 'niche innovator' – to bring out new products to slot into niches too small to attract the attention of the giants. In this way the marketing director believed he could increase share to around 5 per cent or beyond. A strategy of this sort had already been operating with some success for the past 6 months.

The marketing director argued that the strategy would build on advantages which the subsidiary possessed: greater experience in launching new products, better ability in managing low volume products, a more innovative marketing team. These advantages, however, were now under attack from the divisional planning manager, and were beginning to look less than convincing. The planning manager referred to the results of a consulting study. The study had concluded that the niche innovator strategy was unlikely to be defensible against the industry leaders. Soon the competitors would strike back, and the subsidiary's success would then evaporate. He also pointed out that even if the marketing director's strategy worked according to plan, the cash flow did not turn positive for another 5 years. He questioned whether the investment of £5 million in machinery, product development and advertising could be justified.

Despite his planning manager's arguments, the divisional chairman seemed to support the strategy. He acknowledged the force of the planning manager's comments and suggested that the subsidiary's managing director review the points that had been raised. But he claimed to see benefits for other parts of the division in going ahead. The mood of the meeting appeared to be in favour of proceeding as planned.

After leaving the room, we discussed the outcome with the subsidiary's marketing director. He seemed confident that the strategy would be continued, despite the criticisms that had been voiced. His observations were candid: 'We're all emotionally committed already. In fact, quite a bit of the new equipment has been purchased. The division chairman needs the growth we can offer, and I know the corporate CEO backs us.'

It emerged that, when the subsidiary was being acquired, both the corporate chief executive officer and the divisional chairman had supported the acquisition because of its potential for growth. The CEO, who believed in providing bold and visionary leadership, had seen the subsidiary as the basis for big new initiatives. The division chairman saw the acquisition as an opportunity to grow, at a time when most of his division's businesses were mature. Together they had pushed the acquisition through a somewhat sceptical board. Ever since, the subsidiary managing director had felt under pressure to live up to the expectations of his superiors.

The consulting study, commissioned immediately after the acquisition, had therefore proved an embarrassment. It had been much less optimistic about the growth prospects, and had suggested a strategy that would focus on raising the profitability of existing products. But by the time the report was received a major new flexible manufacturing line had already been ordered. Furthermore, the first new products were doing well in test market.

Confident in their own assessment of the market opportunity, aware of the sentiments at corporate and divisional level, and bowled along by the momentum of events, the subsidiary's management team had discounted the consultant's report. They had decided to steam ahead at full throttle, modifying their plans only by drawing out somewhat the time scale over which the strategy could be expected to pay off.

When we probed the marketing director further, he admitted some concern with the strategy, but remained convinced that they should go ahead: 'Basically, it comes down to backing your market judgement, and I reckon we know this market about as well as we can. Without the CEO's support, I suppose we might think again. But he's as convinced as we are that this is the right way to go. At least if we're wrong, we're all in it together.'

This example captures the complexity of the influences on managers as they decide on strategy. It also demonstrates the importance of the relationship between the centre and the business. Because the centre signalled that it wanted, even expected, an ambitious growth strategy, the subsidiary managers knew their plan would get a favourable reception. A less aggressive plan would have needed to be extremely well argued to receive approval.

Yet the subsidiary managers also knew that the plan was risky. The division planner's comments and the consultant's report were evidence for this. In many companies the risk would have caused the subsidiary managers to have been cautious: to have talked their bosses' ambitions down to safer levels. They didn't do this because they knew that failure of the plan would not destroy their careers. By recognising that 'we're all in it together', the marketing director was pointing out that the responsibility for the plan was shared further up the hierarchy. For him the plan was ideal. It gave him the opportunity to demonstrate creativity in marketing and product development. If it succeeded, he would be the architect of success. If it failed, the mud would not stick to his reputation.

The centre's influence was, therefore, a result not only of signalling to the subsidiary managers that a growth strategy was needed, but also of communicating that the risk of failure would not be borne by the subsidiary alone. This was vital both in guiding strategic thinking and in structuring expectations about the consequences of success or failure.

In the event the plan worked well for 18 months. The new products were a success, volume and profit grew, and return on capital, though low, was bearable. Then problems occurred. Volume declined, some new products failed, profits fell and return on capital became unacceptable. But both the managing director and the marketing director had by now been promoted into other parts of the company. A new team were faced with pushing through a cost reduction plan.

It could be argued that this was an example of bad decision-making. The logic of the strategy analysis was not confronted, and the management team allowed a sort of 'group think' to guide their judgement. Indeed, the planning meeting appeared to be a sham because the decision had effectively already been taken once the new equipment was ordered. On the other hand, the decision process achieved a high degree of commitment to the strategy. Despite its riskiness, the strategy was enthusiastically implemented and achieved some big successes in the first year and a half. Given that the division was looking for growth, the results were, on balance, satisfactory, and the decision process may not have been inappropriate.

More importantly, this story describes the kind of situation encountered regularly in large companies. It serves to bring out the variety and ambiguity of the influences that shape strategy. Informal understandings work alongside more formal processes and analyses. The headquarters' agenda becomes entwined with the business unit agenda, and both are interpreted in the light of personal interests. The sequence of events from decision to action can often be reversed, so that 'decisions' get made retrospectively to justify actions that have already taken place.

Our task in this book will be to create some order in this apparently chaotic scene. It will be to seek an improved understanding of the reality of corporate decision processes.

The Role of the Centre

Our particular focus will be on the role of the corporate centre. This is because the centre defines the approach a company takes to making decisions. It determines planning procedures, hurdle rates, control processes and organization structures. It steers strategy by influencing managers in the business units, by supporting one investment rather than another, and by making acquisitions or divestments. Most essentially, it establishes the atmosphere, the culture, in which lower level managers propose and implement strategy.

Despite the importance of corporate headquarters, there are few accepted theories or useful prescriptions for how it should operate.[4] There is no clear consensus on the right role for the centre. Moreover, there are doubts about the value the centre creates. When is the centre's influence beneficial, and when is it merely an expensive overhead? What advantages, if any, does membership of a large group confer on the individual businesses within it? Time and again in our interviews these themes recurred. They are vital issues not only for corporate management but also for those working at divisional or business unit levels.

These questions emerge into the public arena at a time of major takeover bids. Over Christmas 1986 and throughout January 1987 the British industrial community debated the advantages and disadvantages of the bid by BTR for Pilkington. Pilkington, a family-led business for more than 100 years, is the world's leading glass-maker. It invented the float glass technology in the 1950s, and is one of the few companies in Britain that can claim to lead the world in both technology and market share. BTR is Britain's most successful conglomerate. Formed in 1934 out of the British arm of an American tyre company, BF Goodrich, it has built its success around a particular management philosophy. By applying the approach to larger and larger acquisitions, BTR has outperformed all but two other quoted UK companies in terms of return to shareholders in the period from 1974 to 1986.

Anthony Pilkington, chairman and chief executive of the glass company, stood for long-term strategies. He argued that investment in plant and technology was the key to business success. He underlined the importance of a global strategy and of the willingness of managers to make investments for strategic reasons, even though financial returns might be uncertain. The centre's role was to promote and reinforce these strategies. Sir Owen Green, BTR's chairman, accused Pilkington of spending too much on research and of following a global strategy that constrained the actions of managers in each country. He believed that Pilkington could substantially increase current profits without losing world position. 'Only a radical change in the culture at Pilkington can restore it to long term profitability,' he claimed. At BTR, the centre sees its role much more in terms of motivating managers to stretch for increased profitability than in terms of guiding long-term strategies.

In the event, Pilkington's share price rose to a point where Sir Owen Green withdrew his bid. This can be seen as a vote from shareholders in favour of the long-term policies of existing management.

In a similar battle a year earlier, shareholders voted the other way. Hanson Trust, another successful conglomerate, was competing with United Biscuits for control of the Imperial Group. Sir Hector Laing, the chairman of UB, claimed that he could turn the combined food companies into a world-beater. He envisaged investing in China, Brazil and Indonesia, to build world food brands that would rival Coca Cola or MacDonalds. Lord Hanson, the chairman of Hanson Trust, rested his case on the simpler claim that Imperial was badly managed. He argued that he could come close to doubling profits from the Imperial companies.

In this case the Imperial shareholders voted for Hanson Trust. They have since seen their company broken up: the head office has been closed, large parts of the business have been sold, and strong controls have been imposed on the remainder of the company. But the financial returns to the Hanson strategy have been excellent.

In both these cases the role of the centre was crucial. Anthony Pilkington, Sir Hector Laing, Sir Owen Green and Lord Hanson all have different philosophies about how large, multibusiness companies should be run. Moreover, these differences have deep roots. They are born out of years of successful practice. Differences of opinion about the right way to run a diversified company therefore become all the more acute; but too often these crucial questions are debated with little real understanding of what the different management approaches entail, and of what other approaches are available. Predictably, the resulting arguments generate more heat than light.

We feel that a fuller account of what different corporate headquarters do, how they work, and what issues they face is needed. Even senior corporate managers know remarkably little about how their counterparts in other organizations function. And they devote too little time to the question of whether their performance would improve if they copied some of the practices of other companies. Outside this circle there is widespread public ignorance concerning the role of the corporate centre. Not surprisingly, this has bred suspicions and misconceptions, which a wider sharing of experiences will help to eliminate.

Research Approach

Our work has involved research with a cross-section of leading British firms. We approached companies that are widely regarded as successful, state-of-the-art organizations, seeking a working relationship that would give us access to corporate, division and business level managers. The 16 companies who agreed to participate in the research are listed in table 1.1. In these companies we carried out open-ended interviews with between 5 and 20 senior managers, in almost all cases including the chief executive. We asked questions about the management approach and about particular decisions. We discussed strategy, management philosophy and individual personalities. We attended management meetings. We also collected information on the formal aspects of the planning and decision-making processes, and on the financial and strategic results achieved by these companies.

Table 1.1 The 16 participant companies

Company	Main activity	Sales 1985 (£m)	Rank in *Times 1000*
BP	Oil	47,156	1
ICI	Chemicals	10,725	4
GEC	Electricals	5,222	14
Imperial	Tobacco, food, drinks	4,919	15
BTR	Diversified	3,881	18
Hanson Trust	Diversified	2,675	33
Courtaulds	Textiles and chemicals	2,173	45
STC	Electronics	1,997	48
BOC	Gases and healthcare	1,901	54
Cadbury Schweppes	Confectionary, soft drinks	1,874	56
UB	Foods	1,806	60
Tarmac	Construction	1,536	72
Plessey	Electronics	1,461	76
Lex	Distribution	1,041	110
Vickers	Engineering	611	159
Ferranti	Electronics	568	169

Source: *The Times 1000, 1986–87* (Times Books Limited, 1986).

It is from this mix of opinion and fact, of detailed descriptions and broad impressions, that we have developed our conclusions about the role of corporate headquarters and how it adds value to the subsidiaries.[5] Our hundreds of pages of interview notes are full of stories, anecdotes and quotes. By using these throughout the book, we hope to recreate in part our fascinating experience in researching these companies.

Strategic Management Styles

When we began our work we expected to find a 'right answer': to be able to describe the best role for corporate headquarters. We hoped to be able to identify how the centre should add value to the businesses, what sort of relationship it should have with business unit managers, and how it should manage the process for making strategic decisions. We expected to be able to define 'good' strategic management. But as we went further into the research we found successful companies that managed strategy in very different ways.

At one extreme we found companies such as BTR, GEC, Hanson Trust and Tarmac, who believe in

— limiting the activities of the centre to a few essentials, such as approving or rejecting proposals and appointing managers;
— giving as much responsibility as possible to the managers in charge of the business units: the centre does not interfere in the thinking of these managers, other than to replace those who fail;
— setting tough targets for profit and insisting that managers meet them: failure to meet budget in these companies can be tantamount to resigning.

This style was summed up well by a Tarmac group managing director:

> In Tarmac we have a highly decentralized type of operation. We [the centre] are not going to be able to make detailed operational decisions, so these need to be done at the operating level. Only if the business units have got a high degree of autonomy are you going to get the commitment to perform. If you pull the responsibility away from the operating unit, you lose control rather than gain it. We want the mechanism for driving creativity and performance.

The power of the drive for performance was expressed by a BTR division head who stated: 'I'd give up £10,000 a year of salary to be able to be sure at the beginning of the year that I will be ahead of budget, at the monthly meetings when we review performance against plan.'

At the other extreme, we found companies such as BOC, Lex and STC, who

— believe the centre should have a leadership role, giving direction to business units, and helping to develop strategies that support the corporate objectives;
— expect the centre to be involved in major decisions and to coordinate plans between different units in the group;
— emphasize the value of strategic, long-term planning;
— set targets mainly in terms of progress against competitors and seek motivation from a shared commitment to these goals.

This philosophy was encapsulated by a senior executive who stated:

> It's a charade to pretend in this era of corporate democracy to decentralize this right and responsibility [i.e. to be involved in strategy decisions] widely

into the organization. Down at the business level there are two or three decisions that make or break a business. Do you really want to leave the business alone to make these?

Between these polar opposites we encountered a variety of intermediate styles. Since there were successful companies operating under each style, we began to doubt whether any single, universal approach to central management would emerge as superior. The recognition that there might be different but valid corporate management styles led us to formulate some more specific questions.

1 What different management styles are there and how should they be classified?
2 What kind of results are achieved by the different styles? Are some more successful than others?
3 Why do different styles exist? Why have successful companies not been able to converge on a single right style? Are there any common pitfalls that cause companies to be less effective?
4 Do all the management styles add value to the businesses being managed, and if so how?
5 What determines the style a company adopts? Do different business environments require different styles? How does a company's style affect the way it builds its portfolio?
6 Are there any universal right ways of handling strategy?

We believe the conclusions presented in this book have important implications for the way that large, multibusiness firms should manage themselves.

Overview

In chapter 2, as a prelude to reporting on our own research, we lay out and review some of the main opinions on the role of the centre that have been put forward by other writers. By identifying the key issues and establishing some of the main responsibilities of the centre, we provide the starting points for our work.

Chapters 3 to 8 then address the first two questions raised above, namely what different management styles are there and what results do they achieve? The discussion is largely descriptive, setting out to record the way in which companies make decisions and the results that they achieve.

Chapter 3 lays the conceptual foundations, and introduces the framework we have developed to capture our detailed findings. The framework identifies eight different styles of strategic management. The styles are defined in terms of two major dimensions:

1 The degree to which the centre influences strategy formulation in the business units (planning influence).

2 The type of control imposed by the centre against results achieved (control influence).

In chapters 4 to 7 we describe in some detail the nature of planning and control influence under each style, illustrating the discussion with examples from the companies we researched. These chapters contain detailed descriptions and comparisons. They are probably best used as a source of reference, and as support for our more general conclusions.

The most popular styles are those that we have termed Strategic Planning (high planning influence, flexible controls); Financial Control (low planning influence, tight financial controls); and Strategic Control (low planning influence, tight strategic controls). Other styles are less popular because they have drawbacks that make them less suitable as the predominant approach. The three main styles lead to different strategies and different results.

- **Strategic Planning** companies push for maximum competitive advantage in the businesses in their portfolio. They seek to build their portfolios around a small number of 'core' businesses, often with coordinated, global strategies. The style leads to a wide search for the best strategy options, and tenacious pursuit of ambitious long-term goals. But decisions tend to be slower, reaction to poor performance is less decisive, and there is less ownership of strategy at the business unit level. Financial performance is typically strong with fast organic growth, but, from time to time, setbacks are encountered. Companies with this style were BOC, BP, Cadbury Schweppes, Lex, STC and UB.
- **Financial Control** companies focus more on financial performance than competitive position. They expand their portfolios more through acquisitions than through growing market share. The style provides clear success criteria, timely reaction to events, and strong motivation at the business level resulting in strong profit performance. But it can cause risk aversion, reduce concern for underlying competitive advantage, and limit investment where the payoff is long term. Although financial performance in these companies has been excellent, with rapid share price growth, there has been less long-term, organic business building. Companies with this style were BTR, Ferranti, GEC, Hanson Trust and Tarmac.
- **Strategic Control** companies balance competitive and financial ambitions. They support growth in strategically sound and profitable businesses, but rationalize their portfolios by closing down or divesting other businesses. The style focuses on the quality of thinking about strategy, permits businesses to adopt long-term strategies, and fuels the motivation of business unit managers. But there is a danger that planning processes can become superficial and bureaucratic, and that ambiguous objectives can cause confusion, risk aversion and 'political' manoeuvring. Strategic Control companies have achieved profitability improvement and share price recovery, but have seen less growth and

fewer major initiatives. Companies with this style were Courtaulds, ICI, Imperial, Plessey and Vickers.

Chapter 8 provides a brief summary and distillation of the main features of each style, and of the results achieved. From comparing the styles in this way, we conclude that there is no one best way to manage strategy: a variety of styles exist, each with characteristic advantages and disadvantages.

In chapter 9 we focus on the reasons why different styles exist. We conclude that the styles follow from fundamental tensions that are always part of the role of corporate management. These tensions result from incompatible objectives that are each separately desirable. It is, for example, not possible both to provide strong leadership from the centre and to encourage entrepreneurial freedom for business unit managers; nor can corporate management both establish severe sanctions for failure to reach targets and push for innovative strategies that respond flexibly to changing circumstances. We describe five tensions of this sort, which force central management to make choices and trade-offs. The different strategic management styles exist because each represents a different balance between these tensions.

In chapter 10, we identify 12 common pitfalls into which all companies are liable to fall, regardless of style. Unlike the tensions, these pitfalls are avoidable, and we suggest ways in which companies can negotiate them.

In chapter 11 we take up the vital question of whether and how the centre adds value to the businesses in the portfolio. We conclude that each style can and does add value in different ways; but also can and does subtract value in different ways. This balance of advantage and disadvantage is a reflection of the choice of emphasis in terms of the tensions referred to above. We believe that a clearer view of the trade-offs and choices involved in each style will lead to more effective management of large diversified companies.

Chapters 12 and 13 discuss the match between business circumstances and management style. We argue that the style the centre adopts for a particular business unit should be a reflection of the nature of the business, and of the management and financial resources of the company. Crucial factors are:

1 The diversity of the portfolio of which the business unit is part.
2 The linkages between the unit and other businesses in the portfolio.
3 The size and payback of investments.
4 The stability of the competitive battle facing the business.
5 The personality of the chief executive.
6 The skills and experience of senior managers.
7 The degree of financial stress on the organization.

A mismatch between business circumstances and corporate style damages effectiveness.

Given the need to match corporate style and business circumstances, we also consider different ways of building and managing a diversified portfolio of businesses. There appear to be three viable options. The first concentrates on a few 'core' business areas; the second accepts greater diversity and manages it by supporting different management styles in different parts of the company; the third concentrates on a single style and adjusts the portfolio to ensure that all the businesses in it are manageable with this style. Each of these strategies can work well, but each involves some compromises.

In chapter 14 we look briefly at four of the world's best managed companies – IBM, GE, Matsushita and Hewlett-Packard. These companies have management systems that fit our models and they face the same difficulties in trying to balance competing objectives. Overall, however, they appear to do a particularly good job of balancing the tensions. They appear to be aware of the strengths of their styles and effective at reducing the weaknesses.

Finally, in chapter 15 we summarize our overall findings, and draw out four ideals that distinguish those companies whose strategic decision-making processes are most successful. These are:

1 Matching style to business circumstances. Our research has led us to the conclusion that the choice of strategic management style, and its fit to corporate circumstances, is a major determinant of a company's success. We believe that many companies could improve their performance by more explicit attention to matching their style, their organization and their portfolio of businesses.
2 Understanding the business. The level of knowledge needed varies according to the style adopted, but in all cases central managers need to be willing to get close enough to each business to be able to add value. A superficial knowledge can be more dangerous than no knowledge at all.
3 Openness and mutual respect. A free exchange of information and views is necessary to make any style work effectively. Mutual respect between business managers and the centre is a precondition for open and constructive communication. The people at the centre must have confidence in the managers of the units. In turn, unit managers must trust and respect their bosses. Anything less than mutual respect leads to ritual behaviour that takes up time and provides no benefit.
4 Energy and common purpose. The most successful companies strive to create a shared commitment between all levels of management to work together to get things done. In some, this comes from the charisma of the leader. In others, it is due to the clarity of the objectives. In all cases, it is necessary to work to build a shared energy for action.

All companies should aim towards these ideals.

Reader's Guide

Many readers of this book will not have time to sit down and read it from cover to cover. We have therefore tried, at the cost of some repetition, to make each chapter largely self-contained so that it should be possible to dip into the book on a selective basis. We would also like to give some guidance on how to get to grips with our main messages most efficiently.

Practising managers will want to gain a clear understanding of the main points of our argument, before using this book as a source of ideas and information. We suggest they read chapter 3, chapter 8 and chapter 15 first. These chapters summarize our overall conclusions. They should then read chapters 9, 10, 11, 12, and 13, which amplify these conclusions and draw out their implications. Finally, chapters 4, 5, 6, 7 and 14 can be used as a reference guide, providing detail on how the companies we have researched manage their strategic decision making process.

Professional or academic readers will want to understand the nature of our study, its relationship to previous work, and the strength of the data we have to support our conclusions. They should start with chapter 2 and chapter 3, followed by Appendix 4. The remainder of the book can be taken in the order of the chapters, although we would warn even the hardened reader of academic books that chapters 4, 5 and 6 will be slow reading since they include a wealth of detailed material. Chapter 6 is probably the easiest of these three, because it describes the simplest style – Financial Control. The reader may prefer to start with chapter 6 before tackling the other two.

Notes

1 Writing in *Long Range Planning* for October 1982, Derek Channon gives the following data for the largest 200 firms in the UK:

	1950	1960	1970	1980
Percentage of companies which are:				
Single business	35	21	11	9
Dominant business	41	41	30	26
Related businesses	20	31	50	47
Conglomerate businesses	4	7	9	18

(Definitions: single business – not less than 95 per cent of sales from one basic business; dominant business – 70–95 per cent of sales from one major business; related businesses – less than 70 per cent of sales from any single business, but relationships between businesses; conglomerate businesses – sales distributed amongst a series of unrelated businesses such that no one accounts for 70 per cent or more of sales.)

The trend to increasing diversity amongst large UK companies is unmistake-able. Similar trends are reported for the United States by Richard R. Rumelt in *Strategy, Structure and Economic Performance* (Division of Research, Harvard Business School, 1974); for France by Gareth Pooley Dyas in 'The Strategy and Structure of French Industrial Enterprise'; for Italy by Robert J. Pavan in 'The Strategy and Structure of Italian Enterprise'; and for Germany by Heinz T. Thanheiser in 'Strategy and Structure of German Industrial Enterprise'; the last three works are all unpublished doctoral dissertations, Harvard Business School, 1972.

2 See Alfred D. Chandler Jr, *Strategy and Structure* (MIT Press, 1962). This phenomenon will be discussed more fully in chapter 2.

3 A number of writers have sought to bring out the complexity of the management task, and the fact that decision-making seldom follows a simple rationalist paradigm. See, for example, Graham T. Allison, *Essence of Decision* (Little, Brown, 1971); Chris Argyris and Donald Schon, *Organizational Learning: a Theory of Action Perspective* (Addison-Wesley, 1978); John Kotter, *The General Managers* (The Free Press, 1982); Henry Mintzberg, *The Nature of Managerial Work* (Harper and Row, 1973); Noel Tichy, *Managing Strategic Change* (John Wiley, 1983). The present book complements these accounts by concentrating on the diversified firm, and on the ways in which relationships between different levels in the organization influence strategic decisions.

4 When we asked senior corporate managers in our participant companies what books, articles or theories they personally found useful in fulfilling their responsibilities, a very short list emerged. Portfolio planning techniques are used in some companies, but are regarded, at best, as a useful aid rather than a complete guide. Tom Peters and Robert Waterman's *In Search of Excellence* (Harper and Row, 1982) was cited by some chief executives, although it was not seen as targeted on the particular problems of corporate management in diversified companies. Otherwise, there seemed little that had proved of practical value to senior managers.

5 Appendix 4 provides a fuller description of our research methodology.

2

The Role of the Centre

Our focus in this book, as we indicated in chapter 1, is on the role of the corporate centre in strategic decision-making. What are the distinctive tasks of the centre in strategy? How do the centre and corporate strategy relate to the business unit manager and business strategy? These are vital questions, given the trend to diversity in major companies.

But we need to do more than describe the role of the centre. We must also try to pin down whether and how the centre adds value to the businesses in its portfolio. We need to know what the centre does that cannot be done by the financial markets or the business units. We need to understand why this intermediary role exists. The rapid increase in diversification that we have witnessed suggests that the corporate centre can and usually does create value. If it did not, single business firms would be able to outcompete the subsidiaries of diversified groups, which would be weighted down with corporate overheads, from which they derived no corresponding benefit. Over time, one would then expect to see a trend away from diversification rather than towards it. The fact that diversification is instead becoming more and more widespread is therefore strong evidence that the centre does have an important role.

But this is a rather general viewpoint, and does little to reassure the sceptics. They argue that the trend to size and diversity simply reflects the desire of boards to insulate themselves from the risks inherent in any individual business. Through diversification, boards can hedge their bets and rely less on particular businesses or industries; but they add nothing to the effectiveness of their subsidiaries. There is also the suspicion that part of the drive for growth reflects corporate megalomania – the quest for power over more and more people and assets as an end in itself.

As evidence to support these views, we can cite the increasing popularity of management buyouts, which are seen as liberating operating management from central control; and the emerging trend for corporate raiders in the United States and the UK to acquire diversified groups and break them up. Amongst our research companies, both BTR and Hanson have sympathy with this view. They are known for drastically reducing the central staff in the companies they acquire, and for restructuring and selling off substantial parts of their portfolios. Hanson gave redundancy notices to 250 headquarters staff within 3 weeks of the acquisition of Imperial; and within a few months it had sold Courage, Golden Wonder and the Hotels and Restaurants division, three important businesses in the Imperial portfolio.

The academic research that has been done on the performance of diversified firms does little to resolve the argument. In the early 1970s Dick Rumelt, then a Harvard doctoral student, contrasted the performance of a sample of Fortune 500 companies in the US, classified into the categories of single business, dominant business, related businesses and conglomerate/unrelated businesses. He concluded that 'related business' diversification produced somewhat better results than other diversification categories.[1]

Since Rumelt, many studies have been done, some supporting and others refining his conclusions.[2] As more data has emerged, especially data extending beyond 1980, the force of Rumelt's conclusions has been weakened. It appears that the mix of industries in which a company competes explains much of the difference in results that Rumelt attributed to diversification strategies. Taken together, these studies imply that there are no significant differences in performance between diversified and undiversified firms.[3] On the one hand, this indicates that the centre of a diversified firm adds no special value to its subsidiaries. On the other hand, the evidence does not discredit the diversified company. The net effect of diversification seems to be broadly neutral.

Yet the logic of Rumelt's conclusion, that diversification into related areas will be more successful than diversification into unrelated areas, still seems intuitively sound. So researchers are now focusing on new definitions of 'relatedness', such as diversification around a single skill, as suggested by Peters and Waterman,[4] or diversification within a 'dominant strategic logic', as suggested by Prahalad and Bettis.[5] But despite a wide base of research, there is as yet little evidence to support any strong statements about the advantages or disadvantages of diversification.

At the level of specific decisions, the evidence is more negative. John Kitching surveyed acquisitions in both the United States and Europe, and concluded that they often failed to fulfil prior expectations.[6] For example, about 50 per cent of acquisitions of European companies by US multinationals were rated as 'failures or not worth repeating'. Michael Porter, of Harvard Business School, has researched 2,000 acquisitions made by 33 US companies since 1950. On average about half have subsequently been divested.[7] Ralph Biggadike looked at a sample of diversification initiatives, whether by acquisition or greenfield investment, and found that typically they were highly unprofitable, at least during their early years.[8] On average, pre-tax return on investment from these diversification moves was −78 per cent in their first two years; and it was not until year seven that a break-even was achieved. It would appear that corporate managers generally underestimate the difficulties of entering new business areas: the grass is by no means always greener.

Faced with this conflicting evidence, we can have sympathy for the managing director of a newly acquired subsidiary, who has just been told by corporate HQ about the procedures for 5-year planning, capital appropriations, annual budgeting, monthly reporting and daily cash control to which he must now conform. It is clear that life from henceforth will be more complicated; what is less clear is what benefit he will derive from the efforts involved. What is desperately needed is an account of how, whether and when the subsidiary *is* better off as part of a larger company than as an independent entity.

Why the Divisional Structure Evolved

To cast light on this question, we need to understand how the divisionalized, diversified firm has evolved. A good starting point is to review what other writers have said on these topics. What emerges from the literature is that there are reasons for the existence of a headquarters that takes on the role of intermediary between the business unit and the financial markets. The centre's contribution revolves around its ability to help the business units *plan* and *control* their performance. But some observers have voiced doubts about precisely how the role should be discharged, and have pointed to conflicts between an active central role and the whole idea of decentralized responsibilities. These are themes to which we shall return throughout the book, using our research data to cast fresh light on these familiar dilemmas.

The Chandler Model

In 1962 Alfred Chandler, the leading Harvard business historian, published his seminal book *Strategy and Structure*.[9] It describes how four major US firms (Du Pont, General Motors, Standard Oil of New Jersey and Sears, Roebuck) changed from a functional structure to a divisional structure. Chandler argues that in each case it was the strategies for growth and diversification that these companies employed which pushed them away from their functional organizations and towards a decentralized, divisional form. Under this form there was, for the first time, a clear separation between divisional management, who enjoyed considerable autonomy over day-to-day decisions, and central management.

Chandler's work is important because it is the first description of the emergence of the divisional structure, and because it explains why a divisional structure proved to be more effective for these companies. Chandler's views correspond closely to those expressed by Alfred Sloan, General Motors' long-serving chief executive from 1923 to 1946, in *My Years with General Motors*.[10]

Chandler begins by describing the centre's role in a functionally organized company. Here the centre's role is critical: it sets overall direction, coordinates between functions, provides central services, allocates resources and appraises performance. As the functional departments grow larger, this role becomes increasingly complex.

Chandler describes the role as follows:

> Once resources had been accumulated to permit the exploitation of the national market . . . , each of the four companies developed, over time, a central structure to permit the effective administration and presumably the more profitable employment of those resources. Whether planned or not, the new central office eventually developed three types of duties. One critical role became the coordination and integration of the output of the several functional departments to changing market demands, needs and tastes. This included the coordination of product flow from one functional department to another . . . It also required the maintenance of cooperation between the manufacturing, sales, and development or engineering departments . . . Second, expansion and vertical integration encouraged the growth of auxiliary or service departments in the central office which could relieve the administrative load on the functional departments by taking over more specialized activities. Finally . . . the central office, of course, allocated the future use as well as appraised the present performance of the resources of the enterprise.[11]

Chandler then describes the systems that were created to make this functional structure work:

> The executives at all four companies came to realize, some more slowly than others, that systematic policy formulation and allocation of resources called for carefully defined budgeting and capital appropriations procedures. This planning also required information on future financial and general economic conditions as well as on anticipated market demand.[12]

But, as the four companies grew larger and more diverse, the centre became overloaded. The coordination and management role of the centre was too complex, and it was difficult to devote enough time to the important policy and resource allocation decisions. Where the centre was able to be more detached from the functional departments, it was more successful. But the normal pattern was for the centre to get drawn into operating issues and fail to have the time or the objectivity to set direction and exercise control.

> Even more critical for the present health of the enterprise and its future growth than the creation of central staff offices [i.e. the specialized central services] was the clarification of the duties of the senior executives. They had to be encouraged to concentrate on entrepreneurial rather than operational activities . . . , on broad, long-term planning, approval and coordination, while [each] department's director should handle the more regular and routine activities necessary to keep it running smoothly.[13]

Overload at the centre and the success of managers who detached themselves from operating issues led to divisionalization. General management repsonsibility, the responsibility for running a business, was pushed down to a level below the centre. In turn, the centre focused more on what Chandler refers to as 'policy formulation and resource allocation', something we would now call planning or strategy. Budgeting and capital approval processes were also strengthened to permit central control. And the centre reduced its involvement in coordination, limiting its role to forming links between divisions and leaving the functional coordination to the new general managers.

It was evident that the central role in the divisionalized company was effective. Chandler gives the reasons for its success as follows:

> The basic reason for [the structure's] success was simply that it clearly removed the executives responsible for the destiny of the entire enterprise from the more routine operational activities and so gave them the time, information, and even psychological commitment for long-term planning and appraisal. Conversely, it placed the responsibility and the necessary authority for the operational administration in the hands of the general managers of the multifunction divisions.[14]

By decentralising, the centre was able to focus attention on adding value to the divisions through its planning, appraisal and control activities. The centre in the functional structure had carried out these activities, but had become overburdened with coordination and operating issues. As a result, it failed to plan and control efficiently and objectively.

Chandler's work thus explains why the divisional structure came about and, in general terms, he points to the reason why it has been more successful than the functional structure in companies with diverse businesses. He did not, however, ask whether the centre of a divisionalized company is more effective in allocating resources and exercising control than the outside financial markets. He did not explore whether the divisions would have performed even better if they had been independent.

The Centre versus the Capital Markets

Oliver Williamson filled this gap. He supported Chandler's view that the divisional structure could be more effective than the functional structure, but he also addressed another fundamental question: why should businesses within a large diversified firm perform any better than they would as separate companies, each responding to the pressures of the outside capital markets? In effect, he asked what the centre was doing that could not be done as efficiently by the capital markets.

Whereas Chandler is an observer of management who bases his views on extensive data about the companies he researches, Williamson is a theoretician. Williamson adds no fresh data on the role of the centre, but he pushes Chandler's logic a step further in analysing the value added by the centre.[15]

The essence of Williamson's argument is that the capital markets are inefficient because they lack information. The outside investor needs to evaluate the prospects of a whole variety of firms. Each of these may consist of many businesses. The amount of information available to the investor on each firm and business is limited, and so restricts his ability to dig deep in analysing the firm. Furthermore the firm's interests may be best served by not presenting information that is as full or as informative as it could be. All this means that the capital markets are liable to use broad brush criteria for resource allocation.

This view may seem to ignore the efforts of the armies of investment analysts employed by stock brokers and the major investing institutions such as pension funds. Nor does it mention the detailed reporting requirements demanded by prospectuses for fresh issues of capital. But the main point – that the capital markets must make most of their day-to-day decisions based on limited information – remains valid.

The centre of a divisional organization can stand back from the individual businesses and allocate resources rather as the outside capital market does. But the centre is able to command much more inside information, and to carry out much more thorough analysis than an outsider. Individual business managers, as employees of the firm, can be motivated to provide a fuller and freer flow of information on their activities; and the central staff can carry out checks on the validity of this information. Lastly, the central staff receives more timely reports on results achieved, and so can act more decisively to replace underperforming managers. The centre can, therefore, be more efficient than the capital market at allocating resources. As Williamson puts it:

> Effective divisionalization thus requires the general management to maintain an appropriate distance.

> . . . Optimum divisionalization involves: (1) the identification of separable economic activities within the firm; (2) according quasi-autonomous standing (usually of a profit centre nature) to each; (3) monitoring the efficiency performance of each division; (4) awarding incentives; (5) allocating cash flows to high yield uses; (6) performing strategic planning (diversification, acquisition, and related activities) in other respects.[16]

In addition, Williamson argued that it is the skills of the 'elite staff' attached to the centre that give more control over operating divisions. Their advisory and audit functions reduce the likelihood that 'partisan political input' from the divisions will sway the centre in its strategies and resource allocation decisions.

The Responsibilities of the Centre

Chandler and Williamson together argue that a divisional structure can be more effective than either a functional structure or the capital markets in managing a diverse portfolio of businesses. The centre's role as inter-mediary between the businesses and the financial market is defined as:

- Planning and allocating resources, i.e.
  - setting policy, as a framework for guiding coordination and operating decisions;
  - appraising plans;
  - appraising resource requests.
- Controlling and auditing performance.
- Providing some central services.

Of these tasks, Chandler and Williamson are clear that the provision of central services is of relatively minor importance, while the key functions are *planning* for the future and *controlling* against results. It is around these two categories of activity that we have developed our research. But before we explain our framework, it is useful to look at some other views on these activities.

Providing Central Services

Chandler noted that in a functional structure the centre provides most important services centrally. In the divisional structure many of these were decentralized, but some were retained at the centre.

In theory, there is a strong argument in favour of central services. There should be efficiency gains from sharing services wherever fixed overheads exist, as in the finance, legal and personnel departments, or where skills are scarce, as in research or export marketing. These benefits are captured in the phrase 'economies of scope'. By having a number of companies in the portfolio, the centre can save costs by sharing overheads and improve services by hiring specialist skills.

The idea that these economies of scope are a key factor in favour of diversified firms has, however, been questioned on theoretical grounds by David Teece, a Stanford-based economist. Teece claims that economies of scope do not always favour the diversified firm. He summarizes a lengthy argument as follows:

> the basic conclusion is that economies of scope do not provide a sufficient raison d'etre for multi-product firms. There are likely to be numerous instances where economies of scope can be captured by an economy of specialized firms contracting in the market place for the supply of common inputs.[17]

In other words, firms can often buy in the required services from efficient outside suppliers rather than set them up internally. Indeed, there are few services that a company cannot purchase from outside consultants, professional advisers, bankers and so forth. In Teece's view, economies of scope only favour the diversified firm *if* the separate businesses draw on shared proprietary know-how or on specialized assets. Shared central services alone are not enough. It is necessary that the subcontract alternatives are unable to provide the quality or the assurance of service that would be available internally.

Interestingly, at the same time as Teece has been developing his theoretical critique of shared corporate central services, many large companies have been tending to disband their central staff. The most famous example is General Electric of the United States, long recognized as one of the best managed companies in the world. It went through a 'destaffing' exercise in 1981 which earned its chief executive, Jack Welch, the label 'neutron Jack', because the neutron bomb elimates people but leaves buildings intact. Companies have become only too aware of the danger that the central functions take on a life of their own and grow, without regard to the needs of the businesses they serve. Economies of scope are then defeated by diseconomies of empire. Insisting that each division provide its own services has often resulted in better value for money.

This is not to deny that some services should be provided centrally or that there can be economies of scope in so doing. It does, however, raise a caveat over any blanket belief in the value added by central services and calls for a more careful look at what services should be provided centrally and in what circumstances. In any case it seems unlikely that the economies and effectiveness of central service departments represent the key added value of diversified firms. We will therefore spend relatively little time on this issue in the remainder of the book. We will make observations on the sorts of services typically provided by different types of companies and we will note that the trend is towards smaller, leaner head offices rather than the other way round. We will make our search for corporate added value elsewhere.

The Centre's Role in Setting Strategies

The role of the centre in policy formulation, planning and resource allocation was viewed as critical by Chandler and Williamson. But how these roles should be defined and discharged is less clear.

Alfred Sloan recognized this at an early stage. In 1919 he carried out an organization study for General Motors which began to establish the principle of central policy formulation and decentralized operations. Looking back on this study, he comments as follows:

> The principles of organization in the study thus initiated, for the modern General Motors, the trend toward a happy medium in industrial organization between the extremes of pure centralization and pure decentralization. The new policy asked that the corporation neither remain as it was, a weak form of organization, nor become a rigid, command form. But the actual forms of

organization that were to evolve in the future under a new administration – what exactly, for example, would remain a divisional responsibility and what would be co-ordinated and what would be policy and what would be administration – could not be deduced by a process of logic from the 'Organization Study'.[18]

There is some conflict between centralized influence over strategies and the whole thrust of the decentralized structure. This conflict exists whether we are talking about the establishment of broad principles to guide operating decisions, or about the allocation of resources, or about the review of divisional plans. We will take up each of these topics in turn.

Corporate Missions

The idea that a large firm needs some sort of guiding mission has been put forward by several writers. Writing in the 1950s, Philip Selznick suggested in *Leadership in Administration* that the key function of leadership is to identify the 'distinctive competences' of the organization, and to build on them:

> Leadership goes beyond efficiency (1) when it sets the basic mission of the organization and (2) when it creates a social organism capable of fulfilling that mission . . . [*Institutional leadership*] is not so much technical administrative management as the maintenance of institutional integrity . . . It is a practical concern of the first importance because the defence of integrity is also a defence of the organization's *distinctive competences*.[19]

More recently, based upon interviews with senior managers in 12 large US companies, Gordon Donaldson and Jay Lorsch, two experienced and highly respected Harvard professors, have also emphasized the importance of the centre's beliefs about the organization's distinctive competences.[20] They argue that these beliefs provide a framework for resource allocation decisions and for functional policies, and give a sense of corporate identity. This idea is reinforced by our observation that many chief executives do perceive the need for a corporate identity, so much so that a variety of consulting companies and corporate identity specialists have grown up and prospered by feeding management's appetite for mission statements and corporate identity themes.

But the popular demand for missions and policy statements does not prove their worth. First, the breadth of these statements makes it hard to avoid 'motherhood' and to come up with policies that are genuinely distinctive. IBM, we are told,[21] drives its business forward on three central policies – respect for the individual, devotion to customers and an insistence on excellence in all its activities. These are sound goals, but could surely be applied to any business. Marks & Spencer, one of Britain's few examples of excellence, has more specific guiding principles.[22]

1 To offer our customers a selective range of high quality, well designed attractive merchandise at reasonable prices.

2 To encourage our suppliers to use the most modern and efficient techniques in production and quality control.
3 With the cooperation of our suppliers, to enforce the highest standard of quality control.
4 To plan the expansion of our stores for the better display of a widening range of goods for the convenience of our customers.
5 To foster good human relations with customers, suppliers and staff.

But even these more specific principles could be applied by any ambitious retailer. On the face of it they are just statements of good business practice – motherhood. What the current literature does not tell us is how (and whether) such broad policies impact the organization and why they work effectively.

The second criticism of broad policies and beliefs is that they can be damaging when applied across all businesses in a diversified group. Donaldson and Lorsch point out that beliefs are often rooted in history and change only slowly. Ensuring that they are still appropriate to today's business circumstances is not easy. Lorsch argues elsewhere, in *Managing Diversity and Interdependence*, that superior performance in diversified companies depends upon the ability of each business unit to attune its objectives, strategies and culture to its competitive environment.[23] He acknowledges the benefits of broad policies but brings out the need to balance these with strategies in each business that are tailored to its own circumstances. The centre needs to provide policies and a structure that integrates the divisions into a corporate whole. But, Lorsch maintains, the more different the environments faced by these divisions, the less possible and desirable integrative policies and devices become. The conclusion of *Managing Diversity and Interdependence* is therefore that a balance must be struck between allowing divisions to do their own thing, responding as they see fit to their specific opportunities and threats, and establishing central policies that apply in all business areas. Top management needs to recognize clearly the potential that broad policies have to inhibit business units and to subtract value. It must set that potential against any value that such policies are expected to create.

Broad corporate polices must therefore steer a difficult course between vacuity and specificity. How, and whether, this can be done was an important question for our research. We will describe, for each company, the sorts of policies they espouse, and how these policies effect results. We will also comment on whether and when these policies add value.

Resource Allocation

Williamson championed resource allocation as the role with the potential to add most value when compared to the capital markets. Because the centre has access to more detailed information on plans, projects and people, it can make better allocation decisions. In Williamson's world, the corporate centre possesses a high-powered ('elite') staff, who take a well-informed and critical view on the claims for resources which come to them, and who influence the strategies of the businesses in a rational and objective way.

But this picture of an omniscient and rational corporate centre is unrealistic. Joe Bower, for example, tracks in great detail the capital approval process of one large firm in his book *Managing the Resource Allocation Process*.[24] He points out that corporate reviews are not always thorough and very seldom alter the nature of a proposed project:[25]

> The [corporate] review varied in thoroughness depending in large measure on the extent of the project's controversialism, but always the result of the review was a 'go' or 'no go' response. The definition of a project did not change. In fact, the response was typically 'go' and . . . the last level at which projects were turned down with any frequency was the division.

In reality, the centre often has too little time and too little familiarity with the business units to dig deeply into capital requests. Furthermore, by the time a request reaches the chief executive, divisional and business management are frequently so committed that they put together a justification which is hard for the centre to turn down. It is uncommon in Bower's view (and in our own experience) for the centre to reject formal capital requests.

The process of 'selling' the proposal to the centre can involve a variety of flanking movements or financial adjustments. If business unit managers sense that the mood of the centre is against a proposal that they feel strongly is right, there are many ways of subverting the capital approval process. Bower gives an example concerning a factory chimney. He quotes the perplexed corporate controller:

> I couldn't see what anyone could do with just a chimney, so I flew out for a visit. They've built and equipped a whole plant on plant expense orders. The chimney is the only indivisible item that exceeded the $50,000 limit we put on the expense orders.
>
> Apparently they learned informally that a new plant wouldn't be favourably received, and since they thought the business needed it, and the return would justify it, they built the damn thing. I don't know exactly what I'm going to say.[26]

The 'elite staff' here clearly has difficulty in making rational and objective resource allocation decisions!

We have been involved in many similar, if less extreme situations, where initially unpromising analysis is circumvented. Prices or volumes are adjusted, reductions are made to costs or contingencies, and the attitude is, as one manager put it, 'We will just have to find a way of getting this one through.' These attitudes are by no means universal; but any manager knows that they occur, and that the centre can be fooled, so long as the business has a track record.

Bower concludes that the centre adds little to the substance of capital requests. Instead, he sees its influence arising through the organizational context and processes that it sets. This conditions the thinking of unit managers, and hence influences the sorts of projects that are likely to be proposed.

If Bower is right, and his conclusions are given additional weight by more recent work on corporate culture,[27] then it is the tone or context created by the centre that influences resource allocation just as much as the rational, objective selection process suggested by Williamson. Williamson's argument that the divisional organization makes better decisions than the capital market because of better data and more thorough analysis needs to be broadened to allow for the shortcomings in most capital approval processes, and for the importance of background, cultural factors. Certainly the implication that tone is important matches with our research results.

The ability of the centre to switch cash from less to more promising areas of a portfolio is another resource allocation strength that has been argued in favour of diversified firms.[28] During the past 15 years this idea has received much attention, and a variety of techniques for moving cash around the portfolio has been suggested. The Boston Consulting Group's portfolio matrix, for example, is intended to help corporate managers to achieve a balance in growth, profitability and cash flow between the different businesses in their portfolios. Guidelines for resource allocation, acquisition and divestment are proposed for each of the well-known types of businesses – cash cows, stars, question marks and dogs. A number of other portfolio models with similar purposes have also been put forward.[29]

These models have become widely used by corporate managers. In a 1982 survey, Philippe Haspeslagh, one of the few academics currently focusing on corporate level issues, found that more than 50 per cent of the Fortune 500 now use some form of portfolio planning.[30] But there is less consensus on the value of the portfolio models. Richard Hamermesh has pointed out the dangers of the portfolio models in his book *Making Strategy Work*. The book, an excellent practical guide to the use of portfolio planning techniques, shows the power of cash allocation models. But Hamermesh notes that frequently the models are used naively, resulting in a worse set of decisions than a less structured approach would yield:

> [Portfolio planning's] use can also lead to some unfortunate self-fulfilling prophesies. The most common of these affect mature business units. When these units are labelled cash cows, receive no new investment, and are tightly controlled, the morale and performance of the unit can deteriorate far beyond what was originally anticipated, which in turn can lead to disposal of the previously healthy (albeit mature) business unit. At the same time, unquestioned support and loose control of star businesses can eventually lead to their lower profitability. Neither of these negative outcomes is inevitable, but both need to be recognized and managed if they are to be avoided.[31]

Resource allocation based on portfolio planning principles evidently has drawbacks as well as advantages.

In one of our early research contacts, Graeme Odgers of Tarmac took up a stronger stance and argued against the whole idea of the centre as a rationer of scarce capital resources. He maintained: 'We don't view capital as a scarce resource. Our job at the centre is to ensure we have the finance available to support all good investment projects.'[32] Tarmac's success is evidently not based on selective capital rationing, nor on moving cash from one part of the portfolio to another, but on the quality of the proposals being put forward.

We therefore approached our research knowing that the resource allocation process has the potential to be a major source of central added value, but unsure how far it works in practice. We wanted to determine what sorts of resource allocation processes are currently in use. Even more importantly, we wanted to understand better what processes are most effective.

Planning Reviews

The resource allocation process feeds off the work that the centre does in reviewing the plans of business units. The strategic plans of the businesses provide a background, against which to assess capital budgets, and a means of estimating likely resource needs. But planning also has wider functions. Systematic and thorough reviews of business plans are today widely advocated by academics such as Igor Ansoff[33] and Peter Lorange[34] and by consultants such as The Boston Consulting Group[35] and McKinsey.[36] These reviews allow the CEO and his team to inject their own ideas into business plans and to test the quality of proposals being put up to them. There is a widespread belief in corporate management that, particularly where the quality of business level thinking is weak, this review process is vital.

Chris Hogg, chairman of Courtaulds, told us how he saw the company's situation on becoming chief executive in 1979:

> In the strategic reviews of 1979–80, most group businesses had a hard time: first, in getting and laying out relevant information; and then in believing it. Acting on it was of course more difficult still. Most plans described (imperfectly) the competitors of 2 years back, contrasted with themselves in a year or two's time, assuming a following wind. The habits of thinking widely, fearlessly and straight about the environment, the industry and the competition were largely absent. Effective internal communication of a kind that would really assist strategy-forming was rare and, in some places, positively discouraged. Myths about past successes and competitors abounded. Standards were low. Time horizons were too short. External viewpoints were desperately needed in many areas.

Against this background, the role of the centre in reviewing and testing plans becomes a major task.

But the idea that strategic planning reviews are a panacea for all corporate problems has now been widely discredited. There are rumblings within the corporate sector, suggesting that for all the efforts that go into strategic planning, the results are meagre. BOC in the UK and GE in the United States have both moved away from elaborate planning systems. And there is mounting criticism of formal planning processes.[37] Writing in the December 1986 issue of *Long Range Planning*, Michael Carpenter, then vice president for corporate business development and planning at GE, stated: 'It must be said that the process of strategic planning that most companies use today is not responsive to the strategic management needs of today's business world.'[38]

Indeed, the underlying premise that managers will pursue less than optimal strategies if left to their own devices is peculiar. If business managers are so incompetent, why are they not replaced? And why should we expect central management which is much further from the detail of the business to be able to identify and challenge sub-optimal strategies? The Bower argument on resource allocation would suggest that the centre is poorly placed to take issue with the substance of strategies; and criticisms from business unit level of ill-founded and uninformed corporate reviews are all too common (see chapter 10).

Despite these reservations, we have seen the value of review sessions. But we recognize the need to pin down exactly how and when reviews contribute and how they can be handled to gain maximum effect.

The Centre's Role in Controlling and Auditing Performance

The control and auditing functions of the centre are linked to the planning activities described above. Control and auditing is about what has been achieved and whether the results are satisfactory; planning is about what managers want to achieve. The objective of both sets of activities is the same – to exert influence over managers in the business. As Williamson commented: 'The elite staff attached to the general office performs both advisory and auditing functions. Both have the effect of securing greater control over operating division behaviour'.[39] Audit and control is the necessary follow through to the planning activities of the centre.

But the control process brings with it some dilemmas for the centre: what control measures to choose and how to ensure clear signals of inadequate performance?

The Choice of Control Measures

In 1980 Robert Hayes and William Abernathy wrote an article in the *Harvard Business Review* that captured a growing mood in America. Entitled 'Managing our way to economic decline', the article argued that American business is overmanaged, and that management concentrates on the wrong issues. Part of the blame lies with the control system, which focuses closely on short-term financial measures of performance. Hayes and Abernathy pointed to modern management techniques as the cause of this problem: 'These new principles, despite their sophistication and widespread usefulness, encourage a preference for short-term cost reduction rather than long-term development of technological competitiveness.'[40]

This concern is on the lips of many businessmen today. They claim that the capital markets are driving managers to focus on quarterly earnings statements rather than long-term competitiveness, and that CEOs are passing this pressure on to their subsidiary managers. They argue that the activities of acquisitive conglomerates and corporate raiders prevent managers from making long-term investment decisions.

The dilemma for the centre of a divisionalized company is evident: whether to use controls that are aimed at measuring the long-term or the short-term performance of the business. Or, to put it another way, whether to use profitability and return on capital or market share and new product development as the key control measures.

Inevitably, the centre will use a basket of controls with a different balance for each business. But the choice of whether to slant these controls towards long-term goals or quarterly profit is important. On the one hand, the centre can add value to the business unit by acting as a buffer between the unit and the stock market. The centre can protect the unit from the short-term pressure of the capital market. Yet, on the other hand, a company that is not producing good short-term results may face a hostile takeover bid from a conglomerate whose role is to push the market pressure for financial performance as low down the organization as possible. The balance between short-term and long-term performance measures is an issue to which we shall return throughout this book.[41]

Another dilemma concerning the definition of control measures was recognized by Alfred Sloan. He was unsure how to retain control at the same time as preserving a decentralized structure. 'The general question remained. How could we exercise permanent control over the whole corporation in a way consistent with the decentralized scheme of the organization? We never ceased to attack this paradox.'[42]

As the centre's controls become more and more detailed, the autonomy of the general managers is reduced and the company is less decentralized. As the controls become fewer and more aggregate, autonomy is restored, but the effectiveness of the centre's influence is reduced. Finding a suitable level of detail for control objectives is by no means easy, and this is a topic on which we shall find that different companies hold very different views.

The Need for Clear Signals of Inadequate Performance

We are all familiar with the phenomenon of tunnel vision. In the business world, it means that managers can be too close to their business to see the issues. They can become locked into a strategy and a way of thinking that blocks out alternatives. The idea that business managers get committed to particular courses of action and strategies that are subsequently resistant to change has been widely documented. Henry Mintzberg uses the concept of 'patterns' in strategy to describe this phenomenon; a business's strategy is less a series of discrete, conscious choices, and more a pattern that is revealed through the stream of decisions, the behaviour and the reaction patterns of people in the organization.[43] This strategy pattern is often not fully explicit, and relies on premises that are only partially tested. It evolves gradually, reinforcing policies that have succeeded in the past, and building on the skills and predilections of those who have risen to the top of the business.

Under these circumstances change becomes difficult. Not only is the strategy implicit and hard to challenge, but also personal vested interests will have grown up to protect the status quo. Left alone, a business will seldom alter its prevailing strategy pattern. Danny Miller and Peter Friesen have studied a whole range of different businesses and concluded that strategy patterns change only at times of crisis.[44] Otherwise there is a powerful momentum that carries the organization along to support and reinforce its prevailing strategy pattern, even though that strategy may become less and less appropriate to the business circumstances. In the motorcycle industry firms such as Triumph, BSA and Norton continued to pursue the strategies that had made them profitable in the 1950s throughout the 1960s and early 1970s, despite the fact that they faced a very different competitive challenge from companies such as Honda and Yamaha.

The outside capital market's only option in these cases is to replace the management by takeover, a drastic remedy usually applied only at a late stage. A corporate centre can intervene much earlier, based on superior knowledge of each business's situation, and can create a pressure for change that would not otherwise exist. To do this, however, the centre must have clear control measures that signal inadequate performance. In this way the centre can create the crisis that Miller and Friesen say is necessary to achieve a real change in strategy.

However, the centre is again faced with a dilemma. Should it choose a variety of control measures that can guide the actions of the managers in the business? Or should it control through one or two critical performance measures that will clearly signal the time when the strategy should be changed. With a spread of strategic and financial objectives, the centre can help to steer a business along a path that achieves both strategic progress and adequate financial performance. But a combination of objectives means that the strategy is only likely to be changed when both strategic and financial targets are being consistently missed. In most cases the signals will be mixed and therefore less clear.

An alternative control system, relying only on market share or only on return on capital, is likely to provide a clearer signal when the strategy is failing. But its very simplicity means that it will be less easy to ensure an appropriate balance between a range of legitimate goals.

More fundamentally, there are questions concerning the true ability of the centre to challenge tunnel vision, even where objectives are not being met. For central management can, itself, get locked into a tunnel vision of the way forward for the company, so that the probing it does is biased rather than dispassionate.[45] There is nothing worse than a broad, but misguided, corporate vision of the future which is used as a benchmark against which to test all businesses' strategies. And controls that are not based on a minimum level of understanding of the businesses may mistake sound strategies for tunnel vision or incompetence.

The control role therefore does have the potential to bring about valuable changes in business level strategy, but much depends on how it is performed. Is the centre of a divisionalized company really any better at unlocking management teams than the external capital markets? And how can it do this? It was a major purpose of our research to find out more about these vital questions.

Summary

The centre has a potentially valuable role to play in managing the multibusiness company. To exist, the centre must be more effective than the capital markets and more effective than the centre of a functionally organized company. Its main functions are to help plan the business strategies, and to control against results achieved. It is through these two functions that the centre can add value to the business units and cause the multibusiness company to outperform the functionally organized company or the independent business.

But the role of the centre in discharging these functions is by no means clear. This leads to a number of issues and tensions, which cause different companies to see the role of the centre in different terms. The point was amply illustrated in one of our research meetings in a dialogue between Sir Peter Walters, the chairman of BP, and Lionel Stammers, one of the joint chief executives of BTR. Walters made the traditional point that at BP they try to make the main policy decisions at the centre, but to delegate the operating decisions to division managers. Lionel Stammers responded: 'That's interesting. At BTR we do almost the reverse. We delegate decisions on business strategy down to the managers in touch with their markets; but we keep tight control of certain key operating ratios and procedures at the centre.' To understand and explain such radically different views of the role of the centre has been our task in this book.

Notes

1 See Richard R. Rumelt, *Strategy, Structure and Economic Performance* (Division of Research, Harvard Business School, 1974).
2 For an excellent review of this literature, see pp. 3–5 of Robert M. Grant, Azar Jamine and Howard Thomas, 'Diversification and Profitability: a Study of 305

British Manufacturing Companies 1972–84'. Centre for Business Strategy, Working Paper no. 25, December 1986.

3 Ibid.
4 Thomas H. Peters and Robert J. Waterman Jr, *In Search of Excellence* (Harper and Row, 1982).
5 C. K. Prahalad and R. A Bettis, 'The dominant logic: a new linkage between diversity and performance', *Strategic Management Journal*, Nov.–Dec. 1986.
6 See John Kitching, 'Why do mergers miscarry?', *Harvard Business Review* Nov.–Dec. 1967, pp. 84–101, and 'Winning and losing with European acquisitions', *Harvard Business Review*, Mar.–Apr. 1974, pp. 124–36.
7 Michael E. Porter, 'From competitive advantage to corporate strategy', *Harvard Business Review*, May–June 1987.
8 See Ralph Biggadike, *Corporate Diversification* (Division of Research, Harvard Business School, 1979), which examines the experience of a sample drawn from Fortune's top 200 companies in the United States. He gives the following data:

Mean pre-tax return on investment (%)

Established Businesses	21
New Businesses	
Years 1 and 2	(78)
Years 3 and 4	(43)
Years 5 and 6	(5)
Years 7 and 8	5

On average, the payback on diversification comes very slowly, if at all.

9 Alfred D. Chandler Jr, *Strategy and Structure* (MIT Press, 1962). *Strategy and Structure* remains the standard work on the role of the corporate centre, despite the fact that it was written more than 20 years ago, and discusses data from the inter-war period. There have, in fact, been very few more recent empirically based studies of the role of the centre. The reason for this gap in the strategic management literature probably concerns the very considerable difficulty in obtaining access for this sort of work, and the time-consuming nature of the work involved.
10 Alfred P. Sloan Jr, *My Years with General Motors* (Sidgwick and Jackson, 1965).
11 Chandler, *Strategy and Structure*, p. 291.
12 Ibid., p. 293.
13 Ibid., p. 294.
14 Ibid., p. 309.
15 See Oliver Williamson, *Markets and Hierarchies* (The Free Press, 1975). This book, which has become a classic of modern economic theory, examines the rationale for the existence of large companies and concludes that, in certain circumstances, it is more efficient to 'internalize' transactions within a corporate entity than to handle them as open market contracts between independent entities. His discussion of diversification is part of this general approach.
16 Ibid., pp. 148–9.
17 David J. Teece, 'Economies of scope and the scope of the enterprise', *Journal of Economic Behaviour and Organisation*, 1 (1980), pp. 240–1.
18 Sloan, *My Years with General Motors*, p. 55.

19 Philip Selznick, *Leadership in Administration* (Harper and Row, 1957), pp. 135–9.
20 Gordon Donaldson and Jay W. Lorsch, *Decision Making at the Top* (Basic Books, 1983), ch. 5.
21 Buck Rogers, *The IBM Way* (Harper and Row, 1986).
22 *Marks & Spencer*, Harvard Business School case no. 375–358.
23 Jay W. Lorsch and Stephen A. Allen III, *Managing Diversity and Interdependence* (Division of Research, Harvard Business School, 1973).
24 Joseph L. Bower, *Managing the Resource Allocation Process* (Division of Research, Harvard Business School, 1970). Bower's book was based on detailed study of only one US corporation, but his findings will strike a chord with most practising managers. See also P. King, 'Is the emphasis of capital budgeting theory misplaced?', *Journal of Business Finance and Accounting*, 2 (1) (1975).
25 Bower, ibid., p. 65.
26 Ibid., p. 16.
27 See, for example, Terence E. Deal and Alan A. Kennedy, *Corporate Cultures*, (Addison–Wesley, 1982).
28 This is part of Williamson's argument.
29 See Richard Hamermesh, *Making Strategy Work* (John Wiley, 1986).
30 See Philippe Haspeslagh, 'Portfolio planning: uses and limits', *Harvard Business Review*, Jan.–Feb. 1982, pp. 58–73. In Haspeslagh's unpublished doctoral thesis ('Portfolio Planning Approaches and the Strategic Management Process in Diversified Industrial Companies', Harvard Business School, 1983), there is also an interesting discussion of the role of the centre. Haspeslagh discusses operating control, portfolio strategy, interdependence strategy and strategic renewal (elements that have already been identified in this chapter) and puts them together into a particularly demanding role for the centre. He is, however, less critical of whether this role can be effectively discharged, without also encountering some severe downsides. See below, chapter 10.
31 Hamermesh, *Making Strategy Work*, p. 141.
32 The view that companies should not see themselves as rationing capital is widely supported by academics in the field of corporate finance. They argue that the capital markets are willing to supply sufficient funds to support any investment, provided that they can be convinced that it will provide an acceptable rate of return. See, for example, Richard Brealey and Stewart Myers, *Principles of Corporate Finance* (McGraw-Hill, 1981).
33 Ansoff's thinking has evolved from his early stress on formal approaches to strategic planning (see *Corporate Strategy*, McGraw-Hill, 1965) to a more flexible belief in 'strategic management' (see *Implanting Strategic Management*, Prentice-Hall, 1984). Throughout, however, there is a belief in systematic, long-term review of strategies.
34 See Peter Lorange and Richard Vancil, *Strategic Planning Systems* (Prentice-Hall, 1977); Peter Lorange, *Implementation of Strategic Planning* (Prentice-Hall, 1979); Peter Lorange, *Corporate Planning: an Executive Viewpoint* (Prentice-Hall, 1980).
35 See the BCG Perspectives publication series.
36 See, for example, Frederick Gluck, Stephen Kaufman and A. Steven Walleck, 'Strategic management for competitive advantage', *Harvard Business Review*, July/August 1980.
37 See, for example, Karl A. Ringbakk, 'Why planning fails', *European Business*, Spring 1971; R. T. Lenz and Marjorie Lyles, 'Paralysis by analysis: is your

planning system becoming too rational?', *Long Range Planning*, 18, (1985) no. 4; Thomas H. Peters and Robert J. Waterman Jr, *In Search of Excellence* (Harper and Row, 1982).

38 Michael A. Carpenter, 'Planning vs strategy – which will win?', *Long Range Planning*, 19, no. 6, p. 50 (1986).

39 Williamson, *Markets and Hierarchies*, p. 137.

40 Robert H. Hayes and William J. Abernathy, 'Managing our way to economic decline', *Harvard Business Review*, Jul.–Aug. 1980. See also Robert S. Kaplan, 'Yesterday's accounting undermines production', *Harvard Business Review*, Jul.–Aug. 1984.

41 The conventional view of control suggests that long-term objectives and short-term controls need to be integrated together and made consistent. (See, for example, Lawrence Hrebiniak and William Joyce, 'The strategic importance of managing myopia', *Sloan Management Review*, Fall 1986, and John C. Camillus and John H. Grant, 'Operational planning: the integration of programming and budgeting'. *The Academy of Management Review*, 5 (1980), no. 3.) Others have, however, recognized that the feasibility of long-term control is often problematic (see Kenneth A. Merchant, 'The control function of managment', *Sloan Management Review*, Summer 1982), so that balancing the short and long-term becomes hard.

42 Sloan, *My Years with General Motors*, p. 139.

43 See Henry Mintzberg, 'Patterns in strategy formation', *Management Science*, 24 (1978), no. 9, pp. 934–48. Others who have written about this phenomenon include John D. Steinbrunner, *The Cybernetic Theory of Decision* (Princeton University Press, 1974); Daniel Kahneman, Paul Slovic and Amos Tversky, *Judgment Under Uncertainty: Heuristics and Biases* (Cambridge University Press, 1982); Richard R. Nelson and Sidney G. Winter, *An Evolutionary Theory of Economic Change* (Harvard University Press, 1982); P. H. Grinyer and J. C. Spender, *Turnaround: the Fall and Rise of the Newton Chambers Group* (Association Business Press, 1979); The Corporate Consulting Group, *Frogs & Paradigms* (Turning Points pamphlet no. 14).

44 D. Miller and P. H. Friesen, 'Momentum and revolution in organisational adaptation', *Academy of Management Journal*, 23 (1982), pp. 591–614.

45 C. K. Prahalad and R. A. Bettis argue this point in an article entitled 'The dominant logic: a new linkage between diversity and performance', *Strategic Management Journal*, 7 (1986), no. 6, pp. 485–501.

3

Strategic Management Styles:
the Framework

Our research has demonstrated that no single account of the role of the centre is adequate. The activities carried out at the centre, and the ways that central management tries to influence managers in business units, differ greatly between companies. Some managers believe that the centre should be closely involved in the strategies of the business units; others are convinced that the centre should remain detached. Some companies have elaborate planning systems; others none at all. In some companies, discussions on strategy are structured and formal; in others, they are ad hoc and informal.

Capital expenditure limits run from £500 in one company to £15 million in another. The attitude to acquisitions varies. In some companies the centre reacts to proposals made by the divisions; in others the centre initiates and executes major acquisitions two or three times a year. Some chief executives adopt a friendly, encouraging manner, and offer a helpful hand when problems arise; others are fierce, even cruel, applying additional pressure to managers in trouble and insisting that they solve their own problems.

In subsequent chapters we will give details of the management approaches taken by each of the companies in our sample. In this chapter our concern is different. It is to establish a framework for describing the variety of approaches we encountered rather than to give examples and data. The framework is intended to bring out the key differences in systems, philosophy and style that cause a company to choose one strategy rather than another.

To bring out these differences, we focused on the way that the centre influences managers lower down and affects the decisions that they make. Following the work of previous researchers, we defined two dimensions of the centre's influence process – planning influence and control influence. Using these dimensions, we have identified eight different management approaches – which we have called 'strategic management styles' (figure 3.1). We have categorized each of the companies in our sample as having one of these styles (figure 3.2). The rest of this chapter explains the way we

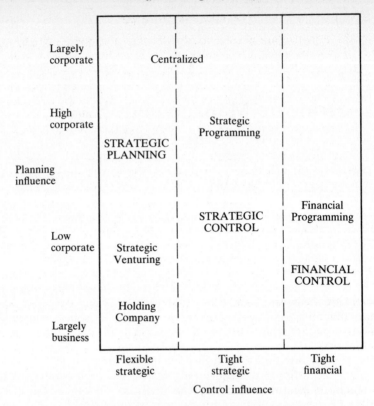

Figure 3.1 Strategic management styles.

have used the terms 'planning influence' and 'control influence' and defines the eight management styles.

Planning Influence

Planning influence concerns the centre's efforts to shape strategies as they emerge and before decisions are taken. It is a measure of the top-down involvement of the centre in major decisions, and of the contribution that the centre makes to the strategy proposals developed in the business units. It is through planning influence that the centre seeks to improve the quality of thinking that surrounds major decisions.

The centre's influence on the proposals made by business managers is a function not only of the objectives that are set and the instructions given, but also of the atmosphere and systems within which the unit managers operate. The organization structure, the review processes, the type of guidance from the centre, the way overlaps are managed and the way scarce resources are allocated all have an effect on the centre's planning influence.

1 Organization Structure

The way the organization is structured will affect the degree of planning influence. If a manager has full responsibility for a business unit, without any constraining overlaps or functional links with other units, he will feel less pressure to seek top-down advice and guidance, and he will be more prepared to fight for his bottom-up point of view. If, on the other hand, there are extensive overlaps, coordinating committees, and dual responsibilities, the unit manager will feel more external influences on his planning decisions.

In BP for example the organization is divided into business streams and geographic areas. It is a matrix. In this way the centre makes sure that business managers and country managers are forced to coordinate and to involve the centre when they cannot reach agreement. This structure gives the centre an opportunity to influence plans as they are being developed. BP's strong functional departments at headquarters also give the centre more planning influence.

2 Review of Plans

In all companies, business units review their plans with the centre. In some companies this review is carried out only on the annual budget. In others, the centre reviews strategic plans as well as budgets. These formal reviews provide an opportunity for the centre to 'give a steer' to the managers in

Strategic Planning
BOC
BP*
Cadbury Schweppes
Lex**
STC**
UB*

* Strategic Venturing
  for some businesses
** Strategic Programming
  attempted, but not
  sustained

Strategic Control
Courtaulds
ICI
Imperial
Plessey
Vickers

Financial Control
BTR***
Ferranti***
GEC
Hanson Trust
Tarmac

*** Trends towards
  Financial
  Programming

Figure 3.2 Company styles.

the unit if they think the strategy being proposed is weak. At the extreme the centre can reject the proposal or issue instructions, but normally the centre limits its involvement to asking probing questions.

Alongside these formal reviews there is continual informal contact between managers at the centre and in the business units. In these discussions the centre is trying to find out more about the business. And the unit manager will be testing the ground on initiatives or projects he wants to pursue. These informal reviews are an important part of the influence process.

3   Strategic Themes

In some companies, the centre has a view of what are (or should become) the 'distinctive competences' of the company as a whole. In the case of Lex Service its philosophy of 'service excellence' is intended to underlie the strategies of all its businesses and to guide decisions on resource allocation and acquisitions. Even though such themes are often stated in the broadest of terms, and allow business units latitude to interpret them in their own way, they can have an important top-down impact on strategy choices. But by no means all companies have explicit themes of this sort.

4   Broad Strategic Thrusts

A related, but separate, type of influence stems from specification by the centre of broad objectives or thrusts for particular business units. After its separation from ITT, STC's central management team developed guidelines for each of its major businesses concerning broad product range goals, market development objectives and competitive position. Although the businesses were free to devise plans to achieve these targets and to propose objectives consistent with them, the guidelines provided a framework for their strategic thinking. The importance of these strategic thrusts varies between companies.

5   Specific Suggestions

Another way for the centre to influence plans is by making specific suggestions. The degree to which central managers refrain from intervening with specific suggestions reflects their commitment to decentralization. But even in companies that profess a high degree of decentralization, central managers will still from time to time make suggestions (e.g. the pricing of a major contract, pack size and design for a particular brand, factory layout etc). These may arise from regular budget or plan discussions, from formal reviews by head office 'experts', or from much less formal conversations. The suggestions may be based on wider central perspectives, external contacts, personal beliefs, detailed knowledge – even pure prejudice. Whatever the basis, they are unlikely to be ignored, and they form part of the top-down influence process.

6   *Management of Overlaps between Businesses*

Central influence in the form of broad thrusts or specific suggestions is exercised particularly where overlaps, links or relationships between businesses or divisions need to be managed. The coordination of functional strategies; cross-supply and transfer pricing between units in a vertically integrated chain; sharing or transfer of expertise; exploitation of a shared resource: all of these overlap issues arose in at least some of the companies we investigated, leading to opportunities for intervention. The extent of overlaps is determined largely by decisions on the divisional and business structure of the company. The degree of influence which the centre exerts, however, is a function of how active central managers want to be in resolving the overlap issues.

7   *Allocation of Resources*

The ultimate and most powerful way in which the centre can influence strategy is through the allocation of resources. By supporting one investment project rather than another, the centre can affect the whole shape of the portfolio.[1] All of the companies exert influence of this type, although in different ways. Some link resource allocation closely to long-term business plans; others adopt a more project-by-project approach. Some give considerable freedom to division managers; others wish to sanction even the smallest expenditures. Some largely react to divisional proposals; others take the lead in sponsoring changes in the portfolio, including acquisitions and divestments. The way the centre allocates resources is, therefore, a critical part of the influence process.

These seven mechanisms are the tools that the centre uses to exert planning influence on the business units. The difference in planning style between companies follows from the ways in which they use these mechanisms.

At one extreme there are centralized companies in which the CEO and his team take all the major decisions. The managers in the business units are not involved in strategy and focus only on operating decisions. At the other extreme, there are holding companies[2] where the centre is wholly detached. Central managers make no attempt to influence the thinking of business unit managers or to shape the proposals put forward.

As we explain in a later chapter, both these extremes have important drawbacks. Successful companies tend to lie somewhere between the extremes, and to mix top-down and bottom-up contributions. Although the precise nature of the centre's planning influence differs in each company, we were able to establish a scale of planning influence, running between companies which push the main responsibility for strategy on to the business units (low planning influence) through to those that believe a strong central role is needed (high planning influence). Two or three companies in the sample are difficult to classify, because they retain central leadership in some areas or over some businesses, but devolve decisions elsewhere. For the rest, it was comparatively easy to rank them in terms of the overall level of the centre's planning influence.[3]

Control Influence

Control influence concerns the way in which the centre reacts to results achieved. Whereas planning influence is about the 'inputs' to decisions, control influence is about the results of decisions – the 'outputs' such as profit or market share. Control influence arises from the targets that the centre agrees with its business units, the way the centre reacts to poor performance, and the frequency with which the centre monitors results.[4] Control influence has its most immediate impact on day-to-day actions – how strategy is implemented. But it can also indirectly influence thinking and choices about future strategies. For example, a manager who follows a risky strategy that fails is likely to interpret his experience very differently depending on whether he receives a bonus that year or not. And his interpretation will affect the choices he makes about strategy in the future. The budget process, the capital appropriation system, and the strategic planning system provide the formal framework for control, which is essentially a linked process of agreeing objectives, monitoring results and applying pressure and incentives.

Agreeing Objectives

The setting of objectives is the first step of the control process. Companies differ widely in how they establish objectives. Sir Hector Laing of UB is reputed to have given the new management team at Wimpy the objective of becoming the 'Marks & Spencer of the fast food industry' – quality food for the average person. Other companies, such as BTR, rely almost entirely on annual profit numbers when setting objectives. There are differences in the precision and detail of targets; the balance between objective and subjective measures; the time frame for achievement; the influence of the centre in proposing and agreeing objectives; the degree of 'stretch' built into objectives; and the emphasis on financial versus non-financial targets. These differences are important to the type of control influence adopted by the centre.

Monitoring Results

All the companies in the research ask their business units to report results monthly, and for some there are weekly reports, ad hoc questions and many informal ways for the centre to check up on how well the business unit is performing. The way in which the centre seeks out performance information, the type of information it asks for, and the arrangements it has for discussing the results with managers are all part of the control process. Some have 2-hour meetings every month between central and business unit managements to review detailed figures on performance versus plan. Others are satisfied with quarterly reports that are seldom, if ever, discussed or commented on by the centre. These differences inevitably cause the managers in the business units to behave differently.

Pressures and Incentives

The follow through on performance achieved is also important. Where bonuses are linked to performance targets, or where careers are at risk, the pressure of the control process is enhanced. Companies such as Hanson Trust and Vickers believe in providing bonuses that can amount to 30 per cent or more of salary. A number of companies link promotion prospects to the achievement of planned targets. But there are also successful firms, such as UB and Lex, that believe in a more flexible interpretation of objectives, and do not tie careers or bonuses to specific performance targets. The reaction of the centre to poor performers varies among companies and is an important influence both on the sorts of strategies that business managers are likely to propose and on the actions they take during the year.

These three activities are the main steps in the control process. By understanding how different companies execute these steps we have been able to define three different control styles

- **Flexible Strategic Control.** Under this approach, financial targets (such as return on sales) and strategic targets (such as market share) are established. However, enforcement is seen[5] by unit managers as flexible, with the centre accepting that there may, from time to time, be good reasons why targets are not met. There is a belief that severe sanctions may be neither appropriate nor possible. As long as the unit is broadly moving in the right direction and as long as the management team are seen to be loyal to the agreed strategy, the centre is satisfied.
- **Tight Strategic Control.** Here, also, objectives cover both financial and strategic targets, and they are established both for one year ahead and for longer periods. Enforcement is, however, perceived to be strict, at least against the annual objectives. Significant rewards (such as bonuses and recognition) are given to those who achieve the targets, and penalties in terms of career progress and close scrutiny from the centre are imposed on those who fail.
- **Tight Financial Control.** With this style, objectives are set primarily in terms of annual financial performance (the annual budget). Once the budget has been agreed, it becomes a contract between the centre and the unit. Variances are discussed monthly and managers are expected to get back on budget before the year end. Performance below budget is considered to be a failure and will affect career prospects and status.

Underlying these three control styles is a scale running from low to high on the amount of attention given to annual budget targets. The flexible strategic control style does not view annual performance as critical, as long as progress is being made in broadly the right direction and as long as the financial health of the total organization is acceptable. The tight strategic control style is more focused on annual financial targets. Managers are expected to meet these targets and are only excused if they can provide good strategic reasons for a lower level of performance. But financial targets are normally set at an achievable level, recognizing that the unit manager may need to balance financial performance with strategic progress. In the tight financial control style the annual budget has centre stage. Profit targets are critical and must be met. It is therefore possible to think of the control styles as forming a scale which measures the 'emphasis given to budgets' and which varies from low to high.[6]

Classification of Styles

Figure 3.1 employs the two dimensions of planning influence and control influence to display different management styles. The figure identifies eight strategic management styles that we encountered during our research. The following summaries define the essence of these styles. Full descriptions are given in chapters 4 to 8.

Holding Company   The centre is largely passive. It has little involvement in business unit strategy development. It generally allows divisions to reinvest their own funds, rather than actively intervening to allocate resources. Control is loose and only sustained non-performance leads to action from the centre.

Centralized   The centre takes the lead in developing strategies, effectively deciding the important issues itself. Business unit managers implement the strategies determined by the centre. The centre's controls are mainly concerned with whether decisions have been carried out, rather than with the results achieved.

Strategic Planning   The centre works with the business unit managers to develop strategy. It establishes extensive planning processes, makes contributions of substance to strategic thinking, and may have a corporate strategy or mission guiding and coordinating developments across the business units. Less attention is devoted to the control process. Performance targets are set in broader, more strategic terms such as 'become the leading supplier' or 'establish a position in'. Annual financial targets are seen as being less important than the longer term strategic objectives.

Strategic Programming   This style is a variant of Strategic Planning. As in Strategic Planning companies, the centre is involved in developing strategies at the business unit level, but in addition it attempts to set clear performance targets and to insist that they are met. The style embraces detailed planning, central sponsorship of strategy and tight control against financial objectives and strategic milestones.

Strategic Control The centre prefers to leave the initiative in the development of plans to business unit managers. The centre does review and criticize the plans, but it uses reviews as a check on the quality of thinking of business unit managers, rather than as an opportunity to give direction. The control process is an important influence mechanism for the centre. Targets are set for strategic objectives (such as market share) as well as financial performance, and managers are expected to meet the targets. Budgets can only be missed when important strategic objectives are at stake. Strategic Control companies combine moderate planning influence with tight strategic controls.

Strategic Venturing In this style the centre delegates the development of strategies to the business units, and makes few attempts to challenge their proposals. Controls are flexible, allowing time for the business units to build a position in the market. But the centre does more than in the Holding Company style. It monitors results being achieved, is willing to intervene if serious problems are emerging, and retains discretion over major resource allocation decisions. The style is similar to that used by venture capital companies.

Financial Control The centre's influence is exercised mainly through the budget process. Corporate management's role in developing strategies is limited, and long-term plans are not formally reviewed by the centre. Instead, the centre focuses on a close review of the annual budget. Profit targets are set when the budget is approved, and careers are at stake if budgets are missed. Financial Control companies combine a low level of planning influence with tight financial controls.

Financial Programming This style is a variant of Financial Control. Although the broad strategic directions are left to the business units, central management in Financial Programming companies will suggest, even dictate, which financial results and ratios can be improved. This is in addition to sanctioning budgets and capital expenditures. It also controls tightly against budgetary objectives.

Figure 3.2 classifies the 16 companies in our research. It is clear that Strategic Planning, Strategic Control and Financial Control are much the most common styles.[7] These styles appear to be the most viable options for managing a large diversified company, and it is on these three major styles that we will concentrate our attention.

The other five styles are less popular amongst our companies. The Centralized and Holding Company styles were adopted by several of the companies in the past, but all the companies have now chosen to move away from these styles because of problems that they bring with them. Strategic Programming has been attempted by certain companies (Lex and STC), but has within it some internal conflicts that make it difficult to sustain. Strategic Venturing is employed for certain divisions or subsidiaries of some of the companies (BP and UB), but is not the dominant style in any company. Finally, Financial Programming is a variant of Financial Control rather than a wholly separate style. We will treat these five minor styles much more briefly than the three major styles in the chapters that follow.

The definitions of the styles are of course idealized. Each company is in some ways *sui generis* and none fully conforms to any single style. Our purpose however is to establish some essential distinctions between approaches and to provide a broad framework within which to discuss our findings.[8] The centre's role in strategic decision-making is too complex and too varied a phenomenon to allow for more precise or scientific forms of description. Furthermore, we believe that our classification captures some vital differences between companies and that companies can be fitted into our scheme without much distortion. We will therefore use this framework to present our findings.

Notes

1 The term 'corporate strategy' is sometimes used to refer to major resource allocation decisions taken at the centre that determine the shape of the overall portfolio. A distinction is then drawn between business unit strategy and corporate strategy (see, for example, Charles W. Hofer and Dan Schendel, *Strategy Formulation: Analytical Concepts*, West Publishing, 1978). Business unit strategy concerns the ways in which each business chooses to compete and seek competitive advantage. Decisions on product-market scope, marketing approach, major investments and organization structures are the essence of business unit strategy. Corporate strategy is about the composition and performance of the overall portfolio of businesses that make up the company. Decisions on acquisitions and divestments, on the balance to seek between different sorts of businesses, and on how to allocate resources between businesses are the prime topics for corporate strategy.

Although we accept this distinction, we believe that corporate management has a role *both* in influencing business unit strategies *and* in establishing overall corporate strategy for the portfolio as a whole. Indeed, we see a strong linkage between business unit strategies and corporate strategy. The strategies pursued by the business units entail decisions on resource allocation between businesses in the portfolio; the results achieved by the business units collectively constitute corporate performance. Corporate strategy is, for the most part, put into practice through business unit strategies.

Even acquisitions and divestments can often be seen as influencing, or following from business unit strategies. UB's decision to buy Terry's, the chocolate company, is a good example. It was clearly a decision to enter a new business; but it was also related to the strategy of the Biscuits division. The acquisition provided synergies in marketing and distribution, and gave the

Biscuits division some additional strategic leverage over competitors such as Rowntree's, Mars and Cadbury's. Moreover, this acquisition arose from a divisional rather than a corporate initiative. The demarcation between corporate strategy and business strategy can become blurred, even in the case of major acquisitions.

Since corporate strategy and results are so heavily dependent on business strategies, we shall focus mainly in this book on how corporate management influences business unit strategies. We shall find that it is through differences in the relationship between the centre and the businesses that the most profound differences in corporate strategy emerge. In chapter 13 we will, however, return more directly to the question of how corporate management builds and designs the overall portfolio.

2 The term 'Holding Company' is used by Oliver Williamson in *Markets and Hierarchies* (The Free Press, 1975). Williamson argues that diversified firms can allocate capital more efficiently than the outside capital market, provided they have appropriate planning and control mechanisms. He refers to firms with such mechanisms as M-form (Multidivisional) enterprises. Divisionalized firms which lack the requisite planning and control mechanisms are referred to as H-form (Holding Company) enterprises.

3 In assessing the level of corporate influence on strategy development, we have focused on the perceptions of business unit management. That is to say, high influence exists only where business unit managers respond to the signals they are receiving; and low influence only where business unit managers feel free from corporate steering. In principle, therefore, corporate management may fail to realize their intentions as far as the level of influence is concerned. In practice, we found a close coincidence between the level of influence that corporate management intend to wield and the level of influence business unit managers perceive them to exercise.

4 'Control' as used in this book therefore relates to the sort of functions discharged by the corporate controller. We do *not* use the term control in the sense of having the power to decide or dispose of events ('I am in control of this business').

5 Again, the key test is the perception of business unit management, though the intentions of corporate management and the perceptions of business unit management tend to coincide.

6 Other control combinations are less feasible. For example, flexible controls almost certainly imply that short-term financial targets exist side by side with broader, longer-term, strategic goals. Equally, long-term goals are unlikely to be cast solely in financial terms; the idea of long-term goals is to provide a balance to shorter-term, often more purely financial targets. This means that an exclusively financial long-term plan will not be seen as satisfactory. And the existence of financial and strategic objectives probably indicates that targets are not exclusively short term. See the table on p. 46.

7 In *Organizational Strategy, Structure and Process* (McGraw-Hill, 1978), one of the most perceptive and useful recent attempts to integrate strategy thinking and the analysis of management processes, Raymond Miles and Charles Snow also stress the way in which certain combinations of strategy, structure, systems, and people go together. They draw distinctions between ways of managing that have some analogy with our Strategic Planning, Strategic Control and Financial Control classifications, although their focus is on the business unit rather than the corporate level. Miles and Snow identify Prospectors (businesses that are constantly seeking market opportunities for new products), Defenders (busi-

nesses that concentrate on optimizing their performance in existing product-
markets), and Analysers (businesses that analyse the changing competitive
environment to determine whether and when to match competitors' new product
or optimization moves). Miles and Snow believe that the whole administrative
context and structure tends to differ between these strategic orientations.
Although the analogy with our conclusions is by no means complete, it is
interesting that they propose two philosophies that are polar opposites
(Prospectors and Defenders) and one which is a combination of them
(Analysers). This is reminiscent of our contrasts between Strategic Planning and
Financial Control, with Strategic Control as an intermediate position.

8 We have identified no style that combines high corporate management influence
and tight financial control; the more involved corporate management are in
strategy decisions, the less able they are to control purely against financial
outcomes. We have also identified no style that aims at tight strategic control,
while remaining highly detached from the taking of strategy decisions. To be able
to establish strategic objectives requires some involvement in the strategy
thinking.

Control Styles

| Objectives | Time frame | Enforcement | |
		Strict	Flexible
Financial	Short-term	Tight Financial Control	Not feasible: 'flexible' controls imply long-term goals
	Short- and long-term	Not feasible: long-term goals imply strategic and financial objectives	Not feasible: long-term goals imply strategic and financial objectives
Financial and strategic	Short-term	Not feasible: financial and strategic objectives imply some long-term goals	Not feasible: 'flexible' controls imply long-term goals
	Short- and long-term	Tight Strategic Control	Flexible Strategic Control

4

Strategic Planning Companies

Senior managers at the centre in Strategic Planning companies believe that they should participate in and influence the development of business unit strategies. Their influence takes two forms: establishing demanding planning processes and making contributions of substance to strategic thinking. In general, they place rather less emphasis on central control. Performance targets are set flexibly, and are reviewed within the context of long-term strategic progress. Participant companies whose strategic decision-making processes showed these characteristics were BOC, BP, Cadbury Schweppes, Lex Service, STC and UB.[1] Brief background descriptions of these companies can be found in appendix 1.

Planning Influence

The belief in Strategic Planning companies that the centre has a vital role to play in the development of business unit strategies was expressed firmly again and again. Dick Giordano at BOC sees the chief executive as 'the principal source of initiative in strategic decision-making'. The philosophy at STC was stated to be to 'centralize strategy and decentralize operations to a number of management companies based along market lines . . . The assumption is that operating managers only look one or two years ahead. The centre must provide the longer-term perspective.' And a senior manager in another Strategic Planning company claimed: 'It's a charade to pretend in this era of corporate democracy to decentralize this right and responsibility [i.e., to be involved in strategy decisions] widely into the organization. Down at the business level there are two or three decisions each decade that make or break a business. Do you really want to leave the business manager alone to make these?'

These assertions illustrate the difference between these companies and the Strategic Control and Financial Control companies, where the emphasis is on devolved responsibility. We will now review in more detail the ways in which the Strategic Planning companies exert planning influence in business unit strategy development.

Organization Structure

The organization structures of Strategic Planning companies are typically less clear-cut than in Strategic Control or Financial Control companies. Although prime responsibility for strategy is located with business management, the structure encourages different levels in the organization, and other businesses or divisions with related or overlapping interests, to put forward relevant ideas. Furthermore, the extent of overlaps between businesses and divisions is often greater than in Strategic Control companies (table 4.1), and changes in organization structure have been used in the Strategic Planning companies to redirect strategic thinking.

Table 4.1   Strategic Planning companies' organization structures (1985)

	Number of divisions[a]	Overlaps between businesses[b]	Number of businesses[c]	Overlaps between businesses within divisions[b]
BOC	4	Low–medium	37	High
BP	11	Medium	11(S)	High
Cadbury Schweppes	4	Low–medium	45(H)	High
Lex	3	Low	9(H)	Medium–high
STC	4	Medium–high	20–25	High
UB	3	Medium	13	Medium

[a] We use the term 'division' for the most aggregated organizational unit whose senior line executive is held profit responsible for results.
[b] Judgemental assessment of degree of overlap in terms of common technologies, resources, markets, skills; and potential for synergies from coordination.
[c] Businesses that submit separate plans, budgets and reports to the centre. (S) indicates that businesses reporting include many strategically separate segments. (H) indicates that businesses reporting are homogeneous single business units.

In BP every important strategy decision is based on a variety of inputs and must go through several review levels. The company was reorganized in 1981, and the centralized, vertically integrated structure in which, for example, Exploration and Production, Downstream Oil, and Gas, were not separately managed profit centres was replaced by some 11 'business streams', or organizational units with worldwide product-based responsibilities. The restructuring is designed to encourage strategic, business-based thinking at a lower level in the company. However, any major proposals developed within a business stream must also be reviewed by geographically based regional or national units; by the board of the business stream, which will include 'non-executives' who represent other parts of the company; by the corporate planning staff; by the executive directors of BP; and finally by the full BP board. Knowledgeable managers at each of these levels, most of them with extensive experience of different aspects of the oil business, can offer different perspectives on the proposal. This process ensures that a multiplicity of relevant views is expressed, and that the assessment of strategy is a balanced one. Sir Peter Walters has also stressed the importance of main board executive directors adopting a corporate perspective in their dealings with businesses that they oversee, and moving away from a more baronial role as senior line executive for their territories.

BOC and Cadbury Schweppes have recently reorganized along similar lines. In both companies an essentially national or regional structure has been superseded by one based on global product responsibilities, overlaid by the geographical dimension. The changes are intended to create more coherent, integrated international strategies in the main global businesses (Gases, Healthcare, Carbon for BOC; and Confectionery and Soft Drinks for Cadbury's). The companies also hope to capitalize on potential cross country skill transfer and strategic interdependence, while still preserving local geographical flexibility and interests. The resulting 'matrix' organiz-ations[2] are complex to administer; but again they ensure that multiple perspectives are brought out. In both BOC and Cadbury's, global coordination is provided by a main board director and is seen as a corporate role, whereas in BP the business stream head reports to a board member.

STC has also undergone major restructuring. Since the separation from ITT, the company has made a number of acquisitions as part of a strategy to shift the balance towards private sector, service-based businesses and away from its traditional base with British Telecom and the Ministry of Defence. To implement this strategy, and to incorporate acquisitions such as IAL (the airport services business acquired from British Airways) and ICL into the portfolio, the centre at STC has established a new divisional structure and defined new product-market scopes for the businesses and divisions. In the early stages of the reorganization, division chairmen adopted a line rather than corporate role. However, it had been intended to appoint new line managing directors for each division, moving the divisional chairmen into the corporate office. This intention had not yet been realized by the time of the management changes in mid 1985. The centre also actively managed the extensive overlaps and connections between the divisions (see below), and within the central team itself, powerful staff departments carried informally defined and overlapping responsibilities. For example, corporate development, business planning, management and social policy, and financial control departments all had to work together on major issues of strategy and structure.

In UB important overlaps exist between a number of the businesses. For example, the food manufacturing companies in the UK all serve the same customers, particularly Marks & Spencer. There is an in-house distribution company that handles the distribution of all the manufactured products. The McVities brand name is used in Frozen Foods as well as Biscuits. The own label biscuit company competes directly with the branded biscuits. A large proportion of the hamburgers used in Wimpys are made by the

Frozen Foods division. It is therefore impossible for these business units to operate entirely independently.

Historically, divisional overlaps have been managed personally by Sir Hector Laing. Even though the main divisions in the UK have been given substantial decision-making autonomy, they operate within the policies and decisions Sir Hector has made about overlaps. His strong leadership has meant that these issues have not been widely debated in the company. Managers have been comfortable following Sir Hector's lead.

However, as Sir Hector has become increasingly involved in the international operations of UB, he has backed away from close involvement in the UK divisions. The structure has therefore begun to change to create a more formal forum for managing the overlaps. Initially a Grocery Committee was set up for the managing directors of the grocery divisions to identify and resolve issues. Then, in 1986, the manufacturing companies were brought under a strong group executive, whose explicit role was to integrate the strategies of the companies.

Lex's organization structure reflects changes in the portfolio, as the company has made major acquisitions in Electronic Component Distribution and divestments in Hotels, US Automotive Parts Distribution and Transportation. But the structure is 'cleaner' than in other Strategic Planning companies. With few overlaps between divisions, most strategic decisions can be taken directly between the business in question and the centre.

The Strategic Planning companies have therefore been active in restructuring their organizations to reflect changes in their portfolios and new strategic focuses. They have established organizations which build in multiple perspectives and divisional overlaps on strategic issues, thereby gaining a greater variety in the views expressed on strategy issues, but sacrificing some clarity on who is responsible for what. This contrasts with the Strategic Control companies, where clear and independent strategic responsibilities are stressed, and where any coordination is provided essentially by the divisional managements to which businesses report. Financial Control companies go further, attempting to define each business as far as possible to need no coordination with others in the portfolio. The Strategic Planning approach is partly a reflection of the nature of the overlapping businesses in which these companies are competing, but also follows from a desire to bring to bear all relevant views in a cooperative approach to decision-taking.

The multiple perspective organization is, however, less of a feature of Lex and UB. It also applies mainly in the core businesses of the other Strategic Planning companies, where there are overlaps between businesses and where there are many senior managers with relevant views and experience to contribute.

Review Process

All the Strategic Planning companies devote considerable effort to the process of developing and reviewing business unit strategy. In this respect they are similar to the Strategic Control companies, although the review processes in Strategic Planning companies generally allow the centre to come to closer grips with the details of strategies being proposed, at least in selected key businesses. The nature of the review process differs among companies.

The review process at Cadbury Schweppes exemplifies a formal, sophisticated, state-of-the-art approach:

December   Guidelines issued by corporate management. Businesses divided into three classes: Full Review, Standard Review, Short Review.

↓

March   Full Review businesses submission that identifies key strategic issues and creates alternative strategy options (some flexibility in time allowed for full reviews). Discussion with corporate management.

Standard Review businesses submission that identifies any major changes to environment in which competing and reports on success in implementing previously agreed strategy. Normally no formal meeting with corporate management.

↓

May   All businesses submit long-range plans, and meet with corporate management to review them. (Full Review businesses may take longer to complete plan; not all Short Review businesses will receive individual reviews with corporate management.)

↓

October/November   Budget submissions and reviews with corporate management for all businesses.

The Cadbury Schweppes planning system shares a number of features with the Vickers process described in the Strategic Control chapter of this book. The key difference is that the Cadbury approach provides the opportunity to give different amounts of attention to different businesses. This selectivity is formally built into the process by grouping the businesses into three classes according to the amount of effort expected to be given to strategy review during the year.

- Full Review businesses are required to undertake a fundamental reappraisal of their strategies. This may entail joint work with corporate staff and/or outside consultants. Although it is intended to treat these businesses within the regular annual cycle, it is accepted that they may be unable to complete the reappraisal within the comparatively short time available. Two or three businesses that are of particular importance, or that face particular issues, carry out Full Reviews each year.
- Standard Review businesses are expected only to update their strategies and plans in the light of developments during the year. Unless significant changes or issues are thrown up by the reviews, the centre normally just endorses a continuation of existing strategy.
- Short Review businesses, which tend to be the smaller businesses in the portfolio and/or those which face few strategic issues of corporate significance, simply concentrate on a shorter version of long-range plans. They do not submit any background strategy analysis.

All businesses follow up their strategy plans with budget plans that are required to be consistent with the agreed strategy.

Central management starts the planning process by issuing comprehensive guidelines to all businesses. The detail varies from one business to another. But the general content is the same for all: timetables, main topics to be considered, analytical methods to be adopted, forms and definitions for presenting results and projections, and specific issues to be addressed. To improve the sophistication of the thinking underlying these reviews, a high proportion of senior managers in Cadbury Schweppes have attended courses in strategic planning and analysis.

The centre sets high store by this review process. It sees it as a way of forcing business management to consider every aspect of their strategies before presenting them, and as an opportunity for the centre to become closely familiar with business unit thinking. Dominic Cadbury told us:

> I do not expect to be involved in the tactics of individual businesses, or in the making of detailed trade-offs in the marketing mix. But I monitor the trade-offs that are made and the tactics that are chosen, and I get closely involved in the discussion of strategic direction and issues. It is the role of the centre to ensure that fundamental re-examinations of strategy take place.

Because of the selectivity built into the process, both the businesses and the centre can concentrate effort on areas where the need is seen to be greatest. This allows more in-depth questioning and review than could be achieved in an across-the-board process. Furthermore, the combination of the relatively homogeneous nature of the businesses in the Cadbury portfolio, and the experience of the chief executive and other corporate managers in running several of them, ensures that corporate questioning can go quickly to the heart of strategic issues in most areas. In the Beverages & Food and Health & Hygiene divisions, which were outside the core areas for the company, the ability of corporate management to pinpoint issues was, however, less. These divisions have now been sold.

This formal process is complemented by frequent informal contacts between corporate management and business management. Thus, although Dominic Cadbury uses the plan review meetings to raise searching questions about the businesses' plans, it is an objective of the head of planning that there should be 'no surprises' at these meetings. In other words, there is sufficient informal prior discussion to ensure that all the major issues will be flagged, that where possible disagreements will be resolved amicably, and that the main items on the agenda for debate are agreed. It is felt that this allows the formal review meetings to take place in a constructive atmosphere and to focus on matters of real strategic importance. Further, the formal process provides a 'constitutional' forum in which different views can be put forward and decisions eventually taken in the light of the cases that have been made. For central management, this helps to 'legitimate' important decisions – the decision to close down the Schweppes Italian business was instanced to us as a case in point – while business management values the opportunity for formal meetings with, and feedback from, the chief executive.

The BP review process bears some resemblance to Cadbury's. It has three phases: strategy review – development plan (5-year projections) – operating plan (1-year budgets and milestones). However, the strategy review is not a yearly affair: the last cycle took 18 months to complete; and no formal selectivity is built into the process.

Many of the most crucial strategic issues in BP turn on decisions on major capital projects. The capital appropriation system is therefore a vital complement to the strategic plan, which provides more of a background for individual capital projects. The multiple perspective organization really comes into its own in the discussion of major capital items. Each major project passes through a number of review levels, both within the business stream and in other parts of the company.

In addition to providing the context for considering capital projects, and a sense of overall business positioning, the strategy plans in BP have been used by the centre to focus attention on external environmental factors that they wished to see addressed more explicitly by the businesses. Thus each business has been required to conduct a 'technology audit' and a 'competition audit', to show how well it was placed technologically, and to identify its main competitors and their respective strengths and weaknesses. After initial reluctance, a number of the businesses established working parties to tackle these topics, and found, to their surprise, that they gained (or at least shared) some useful insights in the process.

In the overall plan review process the questioning-probing role of senior central management is again stressed, and Sir Peter Walters, the chairman, sees his role in terms of 'asking good questions and testing the logic of proposals which are brought up, based in part upon a career's experience in the oil business'. The staff work behind this questioning is, however, extensive, and the size of the corporate planning department at BP, 45 professional staff, is the largest amongst our participant companies.

The size, and product, and geographic diversity, of the company also mean that the review process is a comparatively formal one, and that major decisions have to be handled through the formal processes. However, because these processes are structured to involve a cross-section of managers, the formal meetings provide opportunities for a variety of more informal off-line dialogues. The formal structures in this way facilitate informal contacts. As an example of this at the most senior level, the executive directors meet weekly each Monday. Part of the agenda for these meetings covers specific topics that are formally nominated well in advance (e.g. BP's position in Sweden). But the meetings also bring the executive directors together regularly, and give an opportunity to talk through priority items as they arise more informally.

Review processes of this sort are inevitably time-consuming. Their justification is that they provide a systematic and comprehensive basis for taking very major decisions. On the other hand, unless it can be clearly seen to add value, the formal process does run the danger of imposing too much bureaucracy. In this connection it is notable that dissatisfaction with the return to planning efforts is much higher in the non-oil businesses, where corporate familiarity is lower and hence corporate questioning less well informed, than in the core oil-related businesses.

Lex is a smaller company, with fewer different businesses in its portfolio. Central management can therefore devote more time to becoming closely familiar with the plans of each business. Furthermore, the company has historically had a particularly high commitment to analytical sophistication in planning. Trevor Chinn, the chief executive, stresses the importance of 'raising the level of professionalism in the businesses and asking good questions'. Indeed, it has been suggested that the ability to perform well in the periodic reviews and debates of strategy with the centre is a key criterion in career advancement – and not always linked to broader general management capabilities. 'These occasions revolve around the ability to present a logical and lucid account of your strategy, and to defend the plans being put forward. For many line managers this is an unfamiliar setting. Nevertheless, they are judged by their ability to perform in this context', said one division head.

In Lex, plan reviews went through a period when they were carried out on an 'as needed' basis: frequently and irregularly in the fast moving component distribution business, but less often in, for example, the Volvo Concessionaires business. Now that the portfolio has reduced in diversity, the two core business areas will undertake annual plans, although there will be selectivity in the specific issues that receive attention. Recently Lex has been shifting the emphasis of its plan review process away from analysis and towards implementation. We return to the reasons for this below.

The STC planning system was similar to the Lex system in putting the businesses through rigorous analytical testing of their proposals. But it had a somewhat greater 'top-down' component. Businesses were assigned 'missions' (i.e., broad product-market scopes and directions for strategic development), and were required to develop plans and objectives for fulfilling these roles. We will discuss the nature of these top-down inputs further below.

In UB the review process has less importance. The company's informal entrepreneurial culture downplays documentation and conceptual analysis of strategy issues. Just the same, each division produces a strategic plan of 50–100 pages. The plans are formally presented to the centre in July or August prior to the budgeting process that begins in the autumn.

The main emphasis in the formal planning process is on the capital budget. Comparatively little discussion takes place around underlying strategy or competitive advantage. The main issue is whether the medium-term capital needs of the businesses fit with the amounts of capital the centre can provide. The important strategic discussions between the divisions and the centre occur informally outside the formal planning system.

The BOC approach to strategy review is distinctive. Despite its belief in the importance of the central role in strategy development, BOC is unique among the Strategic Planning (and Strategic Control) companies in having no regular formal strategic planning system. Instead, somewhat as at Cadbury Schweppes, the centre determines which strategies (one or two a year) need a fundamental, formal review, and Intensive Strategy Reviews (ISRs) are carried out in the businesses selected. Business, divisional and corporate management (line and staff), managers from other interested parts of the company and (often) outside consultants, participate in an ISR. The duration of an ISR is flexible; it is determined by the complexity of the task rather than by the demands of a calendar.

In other businesses, strategic thinking is left to the business or divisional management, on the basis that either an agreed strategy is already in place or the priority to determining one is less high. Formal corporate review in these businesses is limited to the capital appropriation system and the budget process; and, every second year, to a mainly top-down exercise to forecast aggregate future financial performance for corporate financial planning purposes. This means that heavy reliance is placed upon informal contacts to provide the centre with a view of progress in implementing agreed strategy and of any changes in the environment that might lead to the need for a revision of strategy (compare Cadbury's Standard Review category). BOC senior managers agree that this approach may risk missing early warning signals of strategic issues: 'The one beauty of the old planning system was that, however horrible it was, it did at least produce a fairly comprehensive flag for issues'. But they feel it is more than justified by really focusing attention on a few key businesses. This allows the centre to immerse itself in these businesses, and to devote enough resources to them to allow old patterns of thinking to be broken and new ideas to emerge. Previously, when BOC ran with a regular annual planning cycle, it was felt that spreading attention thinly across all businesses created form filling and work, but added little value.

Table 4.2 summarizes the review process in the Strategic Planning companies. The formal strategic review process provides the background and determinant of short-term plans and budgets for all businesses. Reviews can, however, also dig deeper on a selective basis, going into much more thoroughgoing detail in key business areas. The importance of extensive informal contacts is also stressed. The Strategic Planning review process not only provides a quality control procedure for business plans; it also gives a framework within which joint corporate–business unit decisions can be hammered out.

Table 4.2 Strategic Planning companies: planning systems

	Plans formally reviewed by corporate management			Link of long-term strategy to detailed plans and budgets
	'Strategy'[a]	'Business'[a]	'Operating'[a]	
BOC	– ISRs Only –		Annually	Yes
BP	Every 2 years	Annually	Annually	Yes
Cadbury Schweppes	Annually	Annually	Annually	Yes
Lex	–	Annually	Annually	Yes
STC	–	Annually	Annually	Yes
UB	–	Annually	Annually	Yes

[a] The terms 'strategy' plan, 'business' plan and 'operating' plan are used in the sense described in the Strategic Control section.

There is, however, some variation between the Strategic Planning companies in how they operate their review processes. Some (BOC, Cadbury's and Lex) are more selective in their formal processes; some (Cadbury's, Lex, STC and UB) believe more in an annual cycle; UB is less committed to formal analysis; and the informal networks have grown up somewhat differently in each company. But the commitment to corporate review of business strategies and plans is common to all the companies.

The advantage of the planning review process in Strategic Planning companies is that it can concentrate enough time to cross the threshold of effort necessary to provide a real challenge to business thinking. The disadvantage is that the process gives less freedom and flexibility to business management, and takes up a great deal of senior management resources. Speedy decisions are less likely under this style of strategy review. It can, therefore, only be justified if a second view of business thinking is deemed to be of high importance. We shall return to this in chapters 10 and 11.

Strategic Themes, Thrusts and Suggestions

It is in their willingness to propose ideas of substance for business unit strategy that the Strategic Planning companies differ most markedly from the Strategic Control companies in exercising planning influence. However, the nature of these ideas, and the way in which they are developed and communicated, differ among the Strategic Planning companies. We look now at each company in terms of how far it proposes top-down strategic *themes* (types of businesses to be in, and types of strategies to pursue across the portfolio as a whole), *thrusts* (broad strategic positioning and objectives to aim for in specific businesses or divisions), and specific *suggestions* (particular ideas for how a business strategy could be improved).

Lex has perhaps the most explicitly articulated strategic themes for the businesses in its portfolio. Central management has decreed that each business should pursue a strategy of 'service excellence', with its underlying message that Lex should operate at the high service end of any industry. In addition, it has published a statement on business ethics (e.g., how the business should be run, how employees should be treated). Both the 'service excellence' theme and the values statement have been discussed at length with senior management and have been promulgated throughout the organization. It is felt that in any given situation there is a range of actions that will be compatible with both concepts, and that therefore the business unit is not unduly constrained in choosing its way forward. On the other hand, certain strategies are ruled out. Trevor Chinn states that 'managers who are not convinced by this approach [service excellence] will probably not find Lex a satisfactory home for their working careers, and businesses that cannot find a profitable strategy with the service excellence concept probably do not belong in the portfolio.'

Lex central management has in the past also been willing to put forward broad thrusts and objectives for the businesses, and detailed suggestions as to how they should be run – a reflection of their close personal interest and involvement in business unit strategies. Many of these central initiatives have arisen from the analytically intensive reviews in the planning process. More recently, Trevor Chinn has been trying to pull back from detailed intervention of this sort, to allow more autonomy to business unit management.

STC has also been prepared to intervene in matters of strategic substance. After the separation from ITT, the central team went through a period of intensive thinking and analysis. The conclusions were that the portfolio was unbalanced and there was a need for radical strategic change. To restore balance to the portfolio, it was decided that three themes should guide STC's development: the need for growth, particularly internationally, in selected businesses; the need to move into service provision as well as product manufacture; and the need to orientate more towards private sector clients and away from the UK public sector, especially the two traditional major customers (BT and the Ministry of Defence). Underlying these themes was the conviction that STC was fundamentally in one linked business area, information technology, and that the various communications and computing technologies were converging. This led to the decision that product-market scopes and the linkages between different parts of the group should be managed centrally.

These themes have provided the basis for establishing the top-down missions or thrusts for each business already described. It was stressed that the mission statements do not specify precise objectives. Nevertheless the role of each business within the total STC strategy clearly implied avenues of development. Finally, the detailed knowledge and involvement of the centre led to more specific suggestions being put forward, either as part of the formal planning process or outside it in informal discussions. It was made clear to us that this approach both required and depended on the focused nature of the portfolio and the level of the centre's knowledge about the businesses. 'The centre must have detailed knowledge of the businesses. Our limited size and diversity allows us to do this. The system works because the debate is about the intellectual quality of the argument. For this approach to succeed, the centre must understand the businesses well – to be able to challenge the management companies on the quality of their cases.'

Sir Hector Laing, at UB, has exerted influence over business strategies in various ways. In the UK Biscuits division, the core of the business, he still has a strong influence both on the broad direction and on the detail of strategy. For example a technical manager explained that it would still be necessary to get Sir Hector's approval if the division wanted to change the recipe of one of the main biscuit products: 'We couldn't decide to use Dutch butter in place of Aberdeen butter without his say-so.' Whether formal approval is required or not, Sir Hector's influence is evident.

In other divisions, Sir Hector's influence is much less detailed, concentrating on broad thrusts and objectives. In Laing's words: 'The job of the chairman is to lay down targets for return on capital, the share of market and things like the product quality. The operating company head then translates these objectives into his strategy.' For example, when Sir Hector acquired Wimpy he charged the chief executive with 'becoming the Marks & Spencer of the fast food business'. Wimpy management chose to compete with MacDonald's in the counter service fast food business. Sir Hector did not influence this decision or interfere with the strategy, except to reinforce his message of high quality products for the mass market. Provided the strategy was consistent with this broad vision, he was willing to back it.

The dedication to product quality is a theme running across UB's businesses that is almost as strong as Lex's 'service excellence' theme. In an encounter with the factory director of Terry's, UB's chocolate confectionery company, Sir Hector produced a high quality Swiss chocolate and asked why UB were not producing chocolates as good as these. When told they were the best in the world, he replied: 'Why? What are we in business for if someone else makes better chocolates than we do?'

Cadbury Schweppes also has a view of the way in which the company should develop overall. Following a major review of strategy in 1977, it decided that the future of the company lay in developing selected strong brands, primarily in confectionery and soft drinks – the 'core' businesses – and in penetrating international, particularly US and European, markets in these businesses. Accordingly, the centre has given systematic support to investment and acquisitions designed to achieve these ends. Another result of the review was the establishment of certain broad objectives for the core businesses (for market penetration, market position and profitability), which have been retained and refined over the subsequent years. The specific details of the strategy are generally left to business unit management. However, we also heard about occasions when senior management made a contribution at the more detailed level, based partly on personal experience in a business and partly on the detailed information provided by the plan review process. For example, suggestions by Dominic Cadbury on the segmentation of the German soft drinks market were found persuasive by business management and subsequently implemented.

BP's influence on matters of strategic substance is somewhat similar to, though less explicit than, Cadbury's. There is a sense of the company's core business lying in the oil and gas area – though in BP the broad strategy has until recently been to diversify away from this core. There are broad objectives for each business, but with more bottom-up influence in their establishment. And the centre's process of detailed questioning and their personal experience can also lead to specific suggestions and actions. Outside the oil business, however, the centre is less able to steer and direct strategy, due to lack of familiarity with the businesses. Here the initiative rests more firmly with business management.

In BOC, corporate influence is exercised through the ISR process, which provides an opportunity for the centre to press for particular strategies or decisions. But there are no broad themes (as in Lex) and no top-down objectives, other than those that emerge from the detailed planning process in response to market opportunity. Central management may also get involved in the detail, either through the capital appropriation system or the budget reviews or on an ad hoc basis. However, once a strategy has been agreed for a business, there is in principle commitment to decentralize decisions to business unit management.

The style and basis of corporate influence on matters of substance therefore differs among these companies. The term 'strategic vision' catches, we believe, some of the flavour of Sir Hector Laing's leadership of UB. In companies such as Lex and BOC the directions favoured by the centre owe more to strategic analysis than to any more visionary insights. In STC the centre provides strong direction, and takes the lead in overall strategy development. In contrast, the BP and Cadbury Schweppes processes embrace more levels and organizational units in a cooperative endeavour to define and develop certain core business thrusts. Although these differences are important in influencing results, the common thread running through these companies is the belief that the centre has a positive role to play in creating business strategy. Thus, the commitment to decentralize strategic thinking to the business level is much less emphatic than in the Strategic Control companies.

There are also differences in the level of substantive influence exercised by central management in different parts of these companies. In general, influence is highest in 'core' businesses, or in businesses that have been selected for some other reason for careful corporate attention. Elsewhere, there may be a more hands-off style, that pushes the initiative for strategy development more squarely on to the business units.

Management of Interdependencies

In the management of interdepedencies between divisions and businesses central management in the Strategic Planning companies is generally more active than in Strategic Control companies. This reflects partly the nature of the businesses, partly the organization structures adopted, and partly the willingness and ability of the corporate level to intervene on matters of substance.

Probably the company that intervenes most in managing overlaps is STC, for reasons already described. In BP, despite trading links between the oil-related businesses, the centre has deliberately pulled back from active intervention. However, there are still aspects of the business that can and do benefit from central involvement – for example, sharing know-how across the group, using regional connections developed in one business stream to advantage elsewhere, and coordinating strategies between businesses on a worldwide basis. At BOC most of the coordination is between different businesses and countries in the two main groups, Gases and Healthcare. However, the group heads are corporate representatives, with seats on the main board, and there are also interdependencies, for example between the Cryogenic Engineering function and the Gases group, which are organizationally separate units.

In Cadbury Schweppes and UB mechanisms to manage coordination issues are not yet fully in place. Business streaming is a recent phenomenon at Cadbury's, and has so far been implemented on a worldwide basis only in Confectionery. However, the intention of the business stream structure is to provide the opportunity for a main board corporate director to provide national and brand coordination in the core businesses. 'When it comes to the core businesses, the centre plays a far more positive role; trying to ensure we are maximizing our opportunities for synergy, making sure we are transferring skills, product knowledge and sharing assets', stated Dominic Cadbury. At UB, many of the interdependencies have been managed by broad policy decisions made from the top. In the future, more active management of interdependencies is likely and this will involve greater coordination between division level managers. Few coordination issues in Lex cut across divisions.

The distinguishing feature of the Strategic Planning companies is therefore a willingness, where appropriate, to try to develop coordinated strategies between divisions, businesses and countries.

Resource Allocation

All the Strategic Planning companies view the allocation of resources as a vital central function. It encompasses the sanctioning of capital investment, closure or divestiture of businesses, acquisitions or new business entries, and senior management appointments in the divisions.

The approach to capital investment sanctioning is similar in each Strategic Planning company. Investments are initiated and proposed from within divisions, but corporate management retains the right to review and sanction investments above a certain level (see Table 4.3). In order to encourage divisional autonomy, the centre allows the business units to spend money at their own discretion, but only in limited amounts. As it happens, all the Strategic Planning companies seem to settle for about the same limits, when expressed as a percentage of the total net assets of each company.

Table 4.3 Strategic Planning companies: limit of divisional authority for capital expenditures

	£m	As % of net assets of company
BOC	1.0	0.05
BP[a]	15.0	0.06
Cadbury Schweppes	0.5	0.07
Lex	0.25	0.08
STC	0.6	0.19
UB	0.25	0.05

[a] Some variation from this figure between different business streams.

For capital expenditures above the divisional authorization limit, a formal capital appropriation system (CAS) runs in parallel with the strategic planning system. Capital investments that have already been identified and agreed in principle in the strategic plan will typically receive a relatively easy passage through the CAS. Indeed, an important way in which the strategic planning process in these companies is seen as valuable for line management is through making the planning and authorization of capital expenditures easier and less of a project-by-project inquisition. On the other hand, 'surprise' items that did not feature in the previous strategic plan will be more closely scrutinized.

The meshing of the CAS with the strategic planning reviews also means that it is easier for central management to assess capital projects for their fit with a business's overall strategy, as well as on the forecast return of each individual investment. It is argued that this helps the centre to take a longer-term view of payback criteria, and to identify and test the assumptions that lie behind a project's justification. Much of the debate on the desirability of major capital items, and on priorities between projects, therefore, occurs in the strategic planning reviews.

Although consistency with agreed strategy is in all cases seen by corporate management as an important criterion in approving a proposal, 'comfort' – the extent to which the centre feels it understands a proposal and has confidence in its sponsoring management team – also plays a role. The personal experience or feel of corporate management, the track record of the business management, the professionalism of the presentation of the supporting case, the amount of informal prior discussion of the proposal, all play a part in building comfort.

It is, in fact, rare for capital expenditures to be rejected by corporate management in the final stages of the formal CAS review.[3] By the time a project has received this degree of divisional and business sponsorship, and after discussion in the strategic planning round, the centre is unlikely to turn it down. Its influence on capital proposals is much more readily exercised through earlier, more informal discussions. The purpose of the formal CAS, therefore, is to see that the divisions and businesses do their homework thoroughly, and to satisfy central management that detailed technical, marketing and financial justifications have been prepared.

Although the initiative for capital investments normally comes from the divisional or business level, there are also important central inputs in the resource allocation process. Corporate management sets priorities between projects, and can block business strategies by deciding not to authorize important capital items. Ultimate strategic decisions in this sense rest with central management. Furthermore, the centre can guide the shape of the total portfolio through resource allocation decisions. In Strategic Planning companies it is not uncommon for corporate management to sponsor capital projects as part of its view of the way forward. This is particularly evident in major acquisitions or new business entries.

Lex, which has seen a particularly high level of portfolio change, provides a good example of the role of the centre in this area. In the late 70s, the corporate group at Lex decided that it needed a new business with growth potential to make use of surplus cash being thrown off by Motor Distribution and by the recent divestitures in Hotels. It was felt that Lex's management skills lay in industrial distribution, and that any new business should be in this broad field. There was also an interest in reducing the reliance of the company on UK businesses, and a desire to expand in North America.

Working with outside consultants, a survey of all possible industrial distribution businesses in the United States was carried out, and a short list of three to four industries drawn up by mid 1979. These industries were then intensively investigated by a team led jointly by the prospective line manager for the new acquisition and the corporate planning director. A year later a proposal had been worked up to enter the electronic component distribution business. It is still felt in Lex that the basic analysis of the industry, the market and the competition on which this proposal rested was sound. Admittedly the proposal did not foresee the severity of the downturn in the industry in 1985; but it did, at an early stage, identify the growth potential of the industry, and point to attractive strategic options for Lex. The close involvement of all members of the central team in pulling together this proposal was vital, both in generating the cooperative commitment to move forward, and in shaping the thinking behind the proposal. In 1981, Lex entered the business via the Schweber acquisition.

In parallel with this analytical search process, the senior managers of the existing businesses were kept fully informed of the development of thinking. There was a series of presentations showing first the need for new growth opportunities, then the sorts of industries on the short list, and subsequently narrowing down to the electronic components move. This led to the gradual building of consensus behind a radical portfolio shift.

Since the initial US entry, there have been further acquisitions, in both the United States and Europe–Hawke Electronics (UK), the David Jamison Carlyle Corp(US), Almac (US), two subsidiaries of Cargill Inc. (US), Panel Electronics (West Germany), Sasco Gmbh (West Germany), E.I.S. (France), Celdis (France), Jermyn Holdings (UK). Once again, the centre has been closely involved in the thinking behind these moves and in the search process. It has actively sponsored the rapid growth and development of the business.

Lex's resource allocation process has therefore involved identifying a new and attractive industry in which the company believed it could build a core business for the future, and systematic sponsorship of investment and acquisitions to achieve this. As we shall see in the Results section of this chapter, similar attempts at radical extensions to existing core businesses or at building new ones have been in evidence at the other Strategic Planning companies.

The acquisitions process at UB provides an interesting contrast to that at Lex. At Lex there was detailed analysis, involvement of management and step-by-step progress. At UB the process is more intuitive, more opportunistic. Much of the strategic analysis for major portfolio moves is carried out in Sir Hector Laing's head. 'I run the business from the nose and from the plants', explained Sir Hector. UB's acquisition of Wimpy restaurants is an example. The move was not part of any UB strategic plan; when Sir Hector heard that Lyons wanted to sell he made the decision to buy the same morning. Another example is UB's acquisition of Keebler: 'We had set our sights on Europe. After a number of attempts, we had just been rebuffed by the French again. Then we discovered that Keebler in the US was for sale. We made a snap decision. We just knew that they were a good buy', explained one senior UB manager.

Corporate influence in the Strategic Planning companies then is geared towards building selected core businesses. This may be a matter of supporting investment in existing businesses, or pushing existing businesses towards more aggressive expansion and related acquisitions. It may also involve a centrally directed search for 'greener pastures', in new industries (such as electronic component distribution for Lex) that offer opportunities not found within the existing portfolio. These initiatives may stem from thorough and systematic analysis, as in Lex, or they may derive from more intuitive insights or personal preferences. The intuitive approach runs the risk of failing to perceive major stumbling blocks. Indeed it was argued in one company that major acquisitions were always liable to be highly risky because their confidentiality precluded any very thorough or wide background research, with the result that the personal preferences of main board sponsors were the main basis for proceeding. But it has also been claimed that the analytical approach does not generate creative new ideas and is by no means infallible in predicting results. It can stand in the way of seizing openings opportunistically, and is liable to be negative. At its worst, analysis can stultify portfolio development.

In this connection, it is worth noting that the Strategic Planning companies make little formal use of portfolio planning techniques[4] in arriving at corporate resource allocation decisions. Some companies, such as BOC and Lex, which have used these techniques in the past, have now moved away from them; and in other companies, for example BP and UB, portfolio balance thinking lies behind resource allocation decisions, but is not a formal part of the process. The Strategic Planning companies appear to feel that portfolio grids do not provide a sufficiently deep understanding of a business's situation to bring out the options it truly faces. They prefer to treat each business on its merits, and to allow options for resource allocation to emerge from the detailed planning process. This has the attraction of avoiding superficiality, and is more consistent with the close involvement of corporate management with business unit strategy. But although it allows more attention to be focused on defining tailored strategic initiatives for each business, it may make tough choices concerning portfolio rationalization less easy to confront.

Control Influence

The emphasis in the Strategic Planning companies is less heavily on control processes. Objectives are, of course, set within the planning process, and performance is monitored. But there is more flexibility in the objectives, and more understanding for businesses that deviate from them.

Agreeing Objectives

The objective-setting process in the Strategic Planning companies emerges from the strategic planning reviews. Strategic Planning companies try to establish short- and long-term targets, and to set financial and non-financial goals. But they find it difficult to identify non-financial targets or strategic milestones that are as precise, as objectively measurable and as widely accepted as financial objectives.

STC saw the setting of both financial targets and strategic milestones as an integral output from the centre's close involvement in the planning process. They believed that adequate milestone measures could be developed – for example, in terms of penetration of new markets, product development goals and so forth. The debate between the centre and the businesses on acceptable objectives could go through as many as three iterations before a mutually agreeable set of targets emerged. It was the centre's intention that these objectives should represent 'fingertip reach'.

In Lex a similarly strenuous discussion of objectives between the centre and the businesses occurred, but Trevor Chinn has now reached the conclusion that detailed non-financial milestone measures are very hard to set. He cites the example of measures of service excellence. These are hard to identify in any comprehensive or quantifiable fashion; liable to be manipulated by management, once they are identified, in an effort to meet the measured target at whatever cost elsewhere; and difficult to relate credibly and precisely to financial performance in a way that will allow trade-offs to be made between 'strategic' and financial objectives. Partly for this reason, Lex's current philosophy stresses a move from 'control to commitment'.

Prior to business streaming, BP found objective-setting hard for all of its vertically linked, oil-related businesses, since profit figures were only available for the total activity. By breaking out separate business streams and making them trade as far as possible at arm's length, each business stream can now aim for a defined and measurable set of objectives. In the core oil businesses, BP is convinced that objectives need to encompass long-term strategic and non-financial variables – and is reasonably content with its ability to specify milestones in a business such as Exploration and Production. Nevertheless, milestone specification problems in the oil business remain, and outside oil the problems of setting strategic objectives are much more intractable.

In BOC the balance between financial and strategic objectives, and the feasibility of establishing strategic objectives, differ between businesses. The objectives for businesses embarking on new growth strategies (e.g., Carbon) may be less financially orientated than those for more mature businesses (e.g., UK Gases) or smaller, more peripheral businesses; while the centre is better able to specify milestones for businesses that have recently undergone an ISR than elsewhere.

The objective-setting process in Cadbury's and UB involves agreement on a strategic direction for a business, but with objectives set mainly in terms of broad financial aggregates to allow business unit management flexibility in the detail of implementation. Cadbury's also have unusually explicit corporate objectives, within which individual business objectives are set. In the 1984 Annual Report, these corporate objectives covered business scope, marketing goals, organization structure and style, as well as financial targets.[5] Again, there is the sense that attempts to define strategic milestones have not met with much success.

Objectives in the Strategic Planning companies therefore emerge from and are linked to the strategy. In this sense, the basic goal is to realize the long-term strategic ambitions that have been agreed, and short-term targets – financial and non-financial – are simply steps along the path to this end. This is very different from Financial Control companies, where budgets and operating plans are seen as contracts between the centre and the business, and regarded as having top priority in their own right. But the difficulty of controlling against long-term strategic ambitions is recognized by Strategic Planning companies, and they therefore seek more specific shorter-term strategic milestone measures to track progress with the strategy. The difficulty of identifying such measures has prevented this search from being wholly successful.

Monitoring Results

In all the Strategic Planning companies mechanisms exist for monthly and quarterly reporting of financial results versus plan, and for narrative summaries of how the businesses' strategies are progressing. At BOC, Lex and Cadbury's the centre has tried to reduce the amount of detail in the regular performance reports. As with the Strategic Control companies, however, there are no regular formal meetings to discuss these control reports. Deviations from plan will be commented upon, but only in exceptional cases. Progress against long-term plans (whether strategic plans or capital appropriations) is less closely checked – if at all.

Probably the most elaborate reporting system in the Strategic Planning companies was in STC. Here each monthly report also covered a rolling look one year forward and one year back. Furthermore, business controllers had a dotted line reporting relationship to the corporate financial controller, which gave them some independence from their direct line bosses. This was intended to ensure unbiased reporting of results. Indeed, business controllers were required to indicate what they saw as 'soft spots' in future projections as they emerged, thereby flagging potential problems for corporate management's attention. Disagreement between the managing director and the controller of a business on the identification of soft spots was not uncommon, and the reporting system was designed to allow both views to be put forward to the centre.

The monitoring process is therefore largely a paperwork exercise in the Strategic Planning companies. There is a full flow of information on results against plan, but the centre does not, as in the Financial Control companies, use face-to-face retrospective reviews as an important part of the strategy influence apparatus.

Action and Incentives

In general, control in Strategic Planning companies tends to be less tight than in either Strategic Control or Financial Control companies. This is not to say that there is no incentive to deliver and no follow-up to non-performance, but that priority in many of the Strategic Planning companies is given to following the broad strategic direction rather than to the achievement of specific objectives. If the centre feels that a business is strategically on track for the long term, it tends to accept deviations from particular goals and milestones along the route. This can be interpreted in two ways: as no more than a realistic attitude to the uncertainties of forecasting in business planning; or as a less rigorous motivation to perform than is found in the control orientated companies.

Both BP and Cadbury's have recently started to tighten control. In BP, new messages from corporate management followed the financial stringency of 1981–2 ('No strategy without profitability', 'No sacred cows'). Business streaming provided the objectives and the information against which to exercise control, and a modest incentive compensation scheme has also been introduced. (Table 4.4 lays out the incentive compensation schemes of the Strategic Planning companies.) Motivation to perform is almost certainly greater today than in the 70s. Yet many of BP's investment projects remain highly risky and very long term; the company finds it difficult to establish strategic objectives, especially outside oil; and the culture continues to stress the building and defence of long-term, global businesses and BP's societal responsibilities. Not surprisingly, motivation to perform against control objectives is set within this wider context.

Table 4.4 Strategic Planning companies: incentive compensation schemes

	Incentive bonus	Basis	Average level (%)	Maximim level (%)	Stock options
BOC	Yes	Judgement	20	40	Yes
BP	Yes	Judgement	< 5	—	Yes
Cadbury	Yes	Actual vs	10	20	Yes
Schweppes		budget RoCE	10	20	Yes
Lex	Yes	Actual vs targeted corporate EPS	15	25	Yes
STC	Yes	Actual vs budget RoCE and other criteria	20	50	Yes
UB	No[a]	—	—	—	Yes

[a] Except on ad hoc basis to achieve specific goals.

The style in Cadbury's is similar, though the business mix is different. The corporate objective for RoCE has been 25 per cent for 8 years, but many of the businesses in the portfolio still fall short of this objective. Although there is an RoCE-based incentive compensation scheme, it does not provide high bonuses, and there appears to be a feeling within the company that it is not very important in influencing behaviour. Although there are ultimate sanctions for non-performance, we did not get the impression, in either BP or Cadbury Schweppes, that managers who failed to hit their targets were in any imminent danger of serious reprisals. This leads to a tendency to over-optimism in long-term forecasts.

Like Cadbury's, UB has a 25 per cent RoCE objective, and yet many of the businesses have been permitted to perform below these standards for long periods. Rather than apply pressure to a business performing below standard, the centre is more likely to be supportive. 'On a number of occasions, in our darkest hours, Sir Hector defended us against the others. He would put us on the spot privately. But in front of the others he would be confident that we would get it right.' Sir Hector himself explained: 'If things are going wrong, you identify with the management and help them out. At these times, control should get more friendly, not more fierce.'

One of the reasons for the flexible way that the centre controls businesses is the long time horizon UB expects for the achievement of results. Sir Hector pointed out: 'We have been in the restaurant business for 8 years. The first 6 were very unprofitable, at least in return on capital measures. I believe it takes about 8 years to build a business.'

UB has stock option programmes for senior managers, similar to many other companies. But there are no performance-related bonuses. Bonuses of that sort would jar with UB's culture, which values family feeling and working for UB above individual effort. The centre has, however, used specific bonuses to achieve special objectives. During the past few years, when UB has been under some cash squeeze, the centre has offered the managers of particular divisions special incentives to reach particularly stretching targets. For example, Foods Division managers were offered a 15 per cent bonus half way through the year if they could reach a certain profit figure by the end of the year.

Control in BOC is rather more selective. Substantial incentive compensation is provided, and the culture is one in which heads are perceived to roll for non-performance. Yet the centre is concerned that strong immediate motivation of this sort may compromise long-term position. Dick Giordano pointed out that, in businesses with long investment cycles (e.g., Gases and Carbon Graphite) even stock options that cannot be exercised for 4 years may in due course come to have an undesirably short-term motivational effect. Difficulties in establishing 'strategic' objectives therefore lead to a situation in which it is difficult for the control process to balance tight enforcement with encouragement of long-term thinking. In BOC businesses the relative emphases on control and strategy appear to vary. Businesses that have embarked on a major, perhaps risky new strategy to build long-term advantage give precedence to pursuing the strategy rather than to achieving budgets. More mature businesses place a heavier premium on delivering profit and cash flow.

Lex and STC differ from the other Strategic Planning companies in having espoused a more unequivocal tight control philosophy. Central managements in both companies sought strict enforcement of objectives to go hand in hand with their high influence on strategy making. In the event, neither company has achieved this aim.

In Lex, businesses such as Transport consistently underperformed, despite frequent management changes, extensive strategy analysis and clear objective setting. It is now believed that, even with the motivation provided by the control process, the commitment to achieve strategic change was not generated. In 1986 the bulk of the Transport business was eventually divested. And in the Electronic Component Distribution business the severity of the trade cycle has led to a rapid swing from boom to gloom, with results either well ahead or behind planned objectives. Lex has therefore abandoned strict enforcement, accepting that in some businesses precise targets cannot be set without prejudicing the achievement of strategic objectives.

At STC the implementation of the major portfolio and strategy changes described above ran into problems in 1985, and was followed not long after by changes in senior management. As these problems began to be revealed by control reports within the company, one may ask why action was not taken at an earlier date within the businesses. The answer appears to be that once a long-term strategy is launched, with support and even initiative from the centre, it is often extremely hard to find short-term actions that will remedy problems and quickly bring results into line with plans. Furthermore, corporate commitment to the strategy, and support for business unit management who are implementing it, militates against any precipitate changes in direction. Hopes that such changes may not be necessary in the long term are liable to prevail over short-term deviations from plan.

Control therefore tends to be less tightly enforced in the Strategic Planning companies than in the Strategic Control or Financial Control group. The philosophy stresses decentralization and performance against targets less clearly, and gives more prominence to strategic directions. Corporate involvement in the strategy-setting process may somewhat impair the ability of the centre to exercise control in a dispassionate and objective fashion. Indeed, it may be seen as undesirable for the centre to be closely involved in a cooperative relationship with the business in setting the strategy, and then ruthlessly detached in follow-up control processes. Furthermore, the bold strategies to which Strategic Planning companies often aspire, through their intrinsic risk and uncertainty, can preclude accurate objective setting. For all these reasons, a general philosophy of more flexible control characterizes the Strategic Planning companies.

Summary of Strategic Planning Characteristics

The common denominators between the companies with what we have termed the Strategic Planning style are therefore as follows:

- Responsibility for strategy development at business level in first instance, but multiple perspectives from different levels and overlapping businesses encouraged.
- Extensive formal and informal plan review processes to raise the quality of business thinking, to allow multiple perspectives to be expressed, and to permit corporate views to influence strategy proposals. Some selectivity between businesses in their application.
- Central management willing to support strategic themes for portfolio development, and particular thrusts or suggestions for individual businesses.
- Centralized attempts to integrate and coordinate strategies across divisions and businesses.
- Centre allocates resources to support agreed strategy, and sets priorities between options.
- Capital projects and new business entries both from business or corporate ideas. Corporate sponsorship particularly important for major new initiatives.
- Long- and short-term goals, and strategic and financial targets, emerge from plans.
- Detailed reporting of performance for each profit centre to central management.
- Flexible control, in terms of incentives and sanctions, for actual performance versus planned objectives. Key concern is with strategic progress.

These are the main characteristics of the Strategic Planning style. There is some variability between the styles of the Strategic Planning companies. Nevertheless, the philosophy of close central involvement in business-level strategy development and of flexible controls is shared between all the Strategic Planning companies. Therefore, although the ways in which this philosophy is implemented vary, we feel that these companies can be viewed as a common group.

In certain businesses, and at certain times, however, the Strategic Planning companies adopt other styles. BP and UB come close to Strategic Venturing in some of their new activities. Lex and STC have attempted to operate Strategic Programming, though with limited success. Until their recent disposals, Cadburys had a more distant relationship to their non-core Beverages & Food and Health & Hygiene businesses than is normal for Strategic Planning companies. And, once having got a strategy for a business in place through an ISR, BOC withdraws to a more Strategic Control role. Moreover, several of these companies (e.g., BOC, UB) have small businesses that are not strategic parts of their portfolios, and are treated on a Financial Control basis.

Results

We will now review the results that have been achieved by the six Strategic Planning companies. Appendix 1, which gives background information on the companies, provides support and detail for many of the points that we make. We will be concerned with financial results, the building and maintenance of long-term competitive advantage and satisfaction within the companies on the quality of the dialogue between the centre and the businesses on strategy issues.

We shall find that the most significant feature of the Strategic Planning companies' performance is the range of major strategic initiatives they have undertaken during the past 5 or 6 years. These companies have set out to create significant change in their portfolios, and in the strategies of several of their largest business units. The evidence is not yet in on which of these initiatives will eventually prove successful and which will fail. Reported financial results during the same period have been mixed. Most are strong companies with good profitability and cash flow from their base businesses. Several have encountered financial setbacks in important areas, which can often be linked to their aggressive strategic ambitions.

Within individual companies, satisfaction with the strategic decision-making process also varies. Where corporate management is knowledgeable about business unit affairs, and where it exercises influence in a cooperative rather than a directive manner, the Strategic Planning style can lead to a mutually satisfying partnership. Where the opposite is the case, the result can be frustrations, resentments and a lack of openness.

BOC

BOC's strategy has been to build a strong worldwide Gases and Healthcare business. It has invested in the development of these businesses and in supportive acquisitions. In Gases, it has made major continuing efforts to improve the performance of the US business; it has acquired businesses, particularly in Japan; and it has invested both in basic cryogenic engineering support and in applications technology. It has also acquired Healthcare companies, and this division has grown rapidly. In addition to these two core areas, BOC has set out to build a major new business, with greenfield investment, in Carbon Graphite Electrodes.

Over the same period, BOC has divested itself of more peripheral or unsuccessful businesses – Computer Services, Food-related Diversifications, Ferrochrome, most of Welding, and a number of other smaller businesses. This rationalization has substantially concentrated the balance of the portfolio.

During the period, the financial performance of the company has been quite good overall though the contributions by different parts of the company have varied. The most notably strong performers have been Healthcare and UK Gases; US Gases has been less profitable; and Welding and Carbon have created a substantial drain.

The company is proud of its strategic achievements, even though it accepts that they may have entailed some financial sacrifice. 'Hanson would have a smaller but more profitable Gases business if he was running this company', claimed Giordano. The highly selective review process is also seen as a marked improvement over more routine planning systems: it has helped both to improve the quality and sophistication of planning analysis and to create strategic change in some key BOC businesses. Selectivity in control, though a less explicit part of the strategic decision-making process, is also defended as being responsive to the needs of different businesses.

This selective Strategic Planning style is not without its shortcomings. First, some businesses do not welcome close corporate attention, since it can entail heavy planning work loads and curtail freedom of action. Furthermore, in the multiple perspective organization managers trespass on each others' territory. As a result, there is a tendency in some businesses to protectiveness and lack of openness. Second, the stress is placed more on information, analysis and logic as a means of attacking strategy problems than on building a consensus for action. Where central or divisional management is adopting a strong lead, this can mean that businesses do not always follow. Finally, corporate involvement in strategy development may undermine the role of the centre in the review process. With hindsight, the centre now sees that there were 'amber lights' flashing around the Carbon Graphite Electrode investment (a decline in world steel demand, low profitability in the steel industry, entrenched competition). However, at the time both the centre and the business persuaded each other to 'fall in love with the proposal' and turn a blind eye to its dangers. This is an occupational hazard in Strategic Planning companies.

On balance, however, BOC is one of the most thoughtful and sophisticated companies in our sample. Its selective approach to strategic management is a well-considered way to try to add value strategically, and has already recorded significant achievements. Its drawbacks relate largely to intrinsic tensions in the corporate role which cannot be avoided under any style (see chapter 9).

BP

BP's achievements are considerable. It has become one of the world's largest oil companies. It has survived the oil shocks of 1973 and 1979 and the cash flow reverses of 1981–2 and has now emerged in robust financial condition. Throughout the past decade, BP's purpose has been to maintain its position in oil, while diversifying the portfolio into other, related business areas.

In aggregate, BP's oil businesses continue to prosper, though this has owed much more to successful exploration than to the relatively unprofitable downstream business. Now that the oil price has fallen, exploration has itself become less profitable. By contrast, the price drop, together with refinery closures and rationalization since 1982, have led to an upturn in financial results downstream. However, the downstream business remains poor in profitability terms.

Success in trying to build new legs for the company has been more elusive. During the 70s and early 80s, BP moved into the chemicals, nutrition, minerals, coal and telecommunications businesses, but few of the diversifications have yet performed well financially, and it is hard to be entirely confident that this is simply a matter of trading off long-term position for short-term results. Indeed, it can be argued that there has been too much tolerance of poor profitability for too long. 'The existence of corporate has meant that the bailiffs have never come', said one business stream manager. There is now some evidence that the company's enthusiasm for diversification is waning, and that it is concentrating more on exploiting its original base in oil. For example, BP has sold its stake in Mercury Telecommunications, and slowed the rate of investment in the Minerals division.

The company's thorough, time-consuming, multiple perspective decision-making process, with its orientation to long-term developments, has many advantages for the oil business. Indeed, BP's ability at one and the same time to support massive long-term exploration investments, and to check and then reverse the momentum of downstream expansion, is a testimony to its effectiveness. But much of the quality of the process depends on the experience of senior managers. Managers in the newer businesses are less happy about central involvement in their strategies – largely because the centre is not sufficiently familiar with these businesses to make what is regarded as a contribution corresponding to the effort involved in going through the strategic planning processes.

The trend in BP since its centralized period in the 70s has been in the direction of more decentralization, more control, improved knowledge of non-oil businesses. In this sense, the issues identified above are already being addressed through changes in emphasis in the strategic decision-making process, which mean that in some respects the style is now moving away from Strategic Planning and towards Strategic Control. It would, however, be sad if these changes away from a style that has built the oil business so successfully were to impair the ability of BP to maintain its position in the oil business into the next century.

Cadbury Schweppes

Cadbury Schweppes' strategy is remarkable for the influence that the major 1977 review still exerts within the company. The establishment of objectives, the elimination of minor brands, the concentration on confectionery and soft drinks as core businesses, the push into the United States and Europe, all date from this exercise, which is still widely quoted within the company. Real changes in strategy thus appear to stem more from single, major, *ad hoc* concentrations of effort than from regular routine work.

The company has indeed succeeded in expanding its international interests. With the exception of North America, where there was a major setback in 1985, the profit trend of these international activities has also shown basic progress being made. The acquisitions of Canada Dry and Sunkist and of a 30 per cent stake in Dr Pepper in the United States, and the formation of a joint company with Coca Cola for the UK soft drinks market, have also reinforced the core business growth thrusts. Meanwhile, the non-core areas in Beverages and Food and Health and Hygiene have underperformed consistently. It is only recently that Health and Hygiene and, now, Beverages and Food have been sold. The Strategic Planning orientation may have assisted the company in defining and supporting its growth thrusts; but it may have inhibited speedy action to turn around the low-performing businesses. Cadbury's basically sound financial position, anchored in the UK and Commonwealth markets for confectionery and, to a lesser extent, soft drinks, has enabled the company to carry the less successful operations.

Strategic decision-making in Cadbury's is now conducted in a generally cooperative atmosphere, and managers at the centre and in the divisions believe that the process works well. As with BP, the exceptions were the non-core businesses, which complained not only of less constructive corporate contributions due to lack of knowledge, but also of constraints on strategic freedom. Corporate management is unlikely to accept growth strategies for businesses designated as non-core. But at the same time, corporate 'commitments' prevent some of these businesses from making closure or exit decisions. These complaints provide another illustration of the difficulties experienced by non-core businesses in Strategic Planning companies.

Despite these shortcomings – the delays in turning round less profitable parts of the portfolio, the problems of the non-core businesses, the shortfall against profit objectives generally – Cadbury Schweppes are one of the few British companies to have built significant international businesses during the past 7 or 8 years. Corporate management has led this effort. The Strategic Planning style of management has facilitated it.

Lex

Major strategic change in terms of portfolio composition has also been a feature at Lex Service. During the 70s the company entered, then subsequently exited from, employment agencies and hotels. New businesses were also acquired in fork truck hire, transportation (largely divested in 1986) and US automotive parts distribution (divested in 1985). However, the most major entry was into the distribution of electronic components in the early 80s. Thus, although the Volvo Concessionaires business has remained the profit mainstay throughout the period, there have been strenuous efforts to find new activities to diversify the portfolio. It is now felt that, despite setbacks in 1985, the Electronic Component Distribution business has the potential, on a long-term and international basis, to fulfil this function. Of the continuing businesses, the Motor business, and particularly Volvo Concessionaires, has been consistently profitably: but some of the other activities, such as Transport, have beeen less successful.

Lex's Strategic Planning process has been built up gradually. A single central management team has been in place since the early 70s. The strongly analytical flavour it has developed over the years, combined with Trevor Chinn's leadership, has contributed to the major portfolio decisions described above. Within the company it is felt that not only was the analysis leading up to the Electronic Component Distribution entry sound, but that the senior management team consensus on the entry was also built successfully.

Despite this, the company has recently embarked upon a new approach to Strategic Planning, under the slogan 'from control to commitment'. It was believed that the centre had become too strategically involved (too 'controlling'). As one division manager put it: 'The process has worked well for the major strategy issues. But it has become frustrating due to a tendency to get into too much detail. Also, it has never been clear enough who is responsible for what in this collaborative approach.' All this reduced ownership of the strategies in the business units, and led to a situation in which excellent analysis appeared to be done, but little action was taken. Now the centre intends to concentrate more on generating 'commitment' to action at the business level, by spreading the strategic debate more widely into the organization, and by holding back at the centre from directive influence in the strategy-making process. Furthermore, as described above, the control reins are being loosened.

How far this programme will be carried by a central management team who have operated a more hands-on style for many years remains to be seen: the parallel top-down 'service excellence' theme seems to work in a somewhat opposite direction. Nevertheless, the intention to shift from control to commitment on the part of one of the most analytically sophisticated and strategically involved corporate management groups in the UK is worthy of note.

STC

The trials and tribulations of STC in 1985 were widely reported in the press, and it is evident that the ambitious strategies of earlier years have not led to the hoped for results. Yet in many ways these strategies were a bold and imaginative response to some pressing strategic problems. It is therefore pertinent to look at the relationship between STC's strategies, its decision-making processes and its results.

Given the analysis that indicated that STC's portfolio after the separation from ITT was fundamentally unbalanced and weak, the company felt that it had no choice but to make major changes. It is a strength of the strategic decision-making process that it was able to state this conclusion openly and then identify initiatives to redress the situation. STC made a series of acquisitions in quick succession, and all the divisions embarked on radical new strategies. Components moved into semiconductors and began to expand internationally; IAL became the core of a new service business thrust; ICL played the same role for private business telecommunications and computing systems.

As it turned out, events did not favour STC. A downturn in the demand for components worldwide, coupled with stiff international competition, depressed profits in Components; tougher buying from BT and a run-down in TXE4 public exchange orders that was more rapid than expected damaged profitability from the core public telecommunications business; and the start-up and transition costs of aggressive entry into private business systems were higher than expected. The combined effect of these setbacks was to stretch the cash position of the company to the limit. It can be argued with hindsight that the company took on too many risky ventures simultaneously, and that it should have concentrated its resources on fewer areas. This approach, however, would have been at odds with the single integrated IT business concept described above.

This sequence of events might seem to condemn STC's Strategic Planning process. It led to too much expansion with insufficient resources, and the corporate controls failed to prevent the crisis. By wresting much of the initiative from the business level, the strategies may have not sufficiently taken into account the detailed realities of specific competitive market places. This is a potential danger of top-down corporate thrusts. Furthermore, there may have been problems, as in Lex, of failing to generate grass roots commitment.

On the other hand, the strong central drives behind these strategies were probably necessary if radical change was to be contemplated. In fact, they were remarkably effective in creating massive change in an old-established company, and moving it in directions which have arguably not been basically discredited. Perhaps STC's starting position was too weak, and its level of resources too low, for its grand design; but at least there was an attempt to take seriously the need to compete internationally in the rapidly changing world of information technology.

Despite the problems of 1985, STC's strategic decision-making process must therefore receive credit for the way it grappled with the company's competitive difficulties. If it had a fault, it lay in not coupling the resulting strategies sufficiently closely to the details of the individual businesses in the portfolio.

UB

UB's strategic style has been highly successful. The company has achieved a remarkable profit and growth record over 20 years and is now a major international biscuits and snacks group. Dominant positions have been built up in the UK, and UB has successfully entered the United States, where it appears to be ahead in the 'cookie' war against the strongest of competitors in Procter & Gamble and Pepsico. Currently the group is building a position in restaurants in the UK. There have been setbacks: an unsuccessful Spanish company, failure to enter Europe satisfactorily, an unhappy attempt to get into frozen foods, and, most recently, the failure to bring off the merger with Imperial. But there has been plenty of action and the wins have generally been bigger than the losses.

Management in the company is, in the main, very satisfied with the way strategy is made. UB's entrepreneurial style is highly praised; Sir Hector Laing's involvement is often appreciated, and speed of decision-making is considered a virtue. Moreover, management has the ability to change the pace when necessary. The closure of the Liverpool biscuit factory was a major trauma for a company priding itself on expansion and on looking after its employees. In these circumstances the decision was taken very slowly and thoroughly, with consultation and discussion at all levels.

Another aspect of UB is its ability to make changes in strategy. In the early 1980s the Biscuit division made an important change in strategy when it refocused on a generic brand name – McVities – and away from the promotion of individual brands. The signal for the change was a small loss in market share. For many companies the loss of share might have gone unnoticed in a market battered by own-branding. However, for UB it was a signal that something was wrong. Management changes occurring at the same time opened the door to new thinking, and a change in strategy was quickly implemented.

But UB's style has drawbacks. The ambition and boldness at the centre led to a cash squeeze in 1983 and 1984. This unexpected cash constraint caused some arbitrary and possibly ill-judged decisions. Advertising budgets in some businesses were arbitrarily cut back half-way through the year, and some prices were pushed up to the point where managers felt the price difference between branded and own-label was too high. The cash squeeze was eliminated with a rights issue and some tighter controls. But the management style had not prepared managers for this type of problem and some damaging decisions may have been made. Like other Strategic Planning companies, UB has also found it hard to manage poor performing divisions. Both D.S. Crawford and Frozen Foods spent long periods providing inadequate returns and failing to make any progress in the market place.

Another drawback concerns the development of managers. While the core biscuit company has provided much of the management talent for UB's ventures into restaurants and frozen foods, UB failed to grow enough general managers. At one point, 30 per cent of senior appointments were from outside. Moreover, Bob Clarke and Frank Knight, the heirs apparent to Sir Hector, are respectively from Cadbury and Colgate Palmolive.

Lastly, the strength of the informal decision-making process may have weakened the formal strategic planning process. For some it is seen as planning for its own sake, with little real discussion about anything other than the financial projections. 'Historically we all produced business plans which were aggregated into a beautiful corporate plan, and they all then filled up the bottom of some filing cabinet', explained one UB manager.

Summary

In summary, Strategic Planning companies have demonstrated the ability to introduce major strategic changes and embark on bold and ambitious strategic moves. Attempts have been made to build strong core businesses, often with integrated global strategies involving the coordination of several different business units. There has been aggressive expansion, both into areas related to existing businesses and into new, greener pastures. It can be argued that without close corporate involvement in a Strategic Planning mode, aggressive strategies of this kind are unlikely even to be proposed, let alone pushed through. 'The pressure to get into the US came from the centre. I had proposed a more modest move, but I went along with the logic of the US pressure. It was a very exciting prospect, but a bit risky and a very big jump', said one business manager.

In the search for optimum strategies, Strategic Planning companies can draw on the experience and wider perceptions of central management. These companies are less likely than Strategic Control or Financial Control companies to fail to get important strategic alternatives on to the table for discussion. On the other hand, the Strategic Planning companies have been less active in closure decisions, although there have been divestments in BOC, Cadbury's and Lex. The Strategic Planning approach is more likely to search for strategies that will improve the performance of unsatisfactory businesses than to move quickly to exit from them.

Strategic Planning is a style in which tight control is difficult, and in which the involvement of the centre can lead to a loss of objectivity. This can lead to high costs in continuing to fund and invest in businesses that are not profitable, and over-ambitious expansion that the company may have difficulty in supporting. These characteristics suggest that the Strategic Planning company, particularly when it is contemplating major risky moves, must have levels of financial strength and reserves that are sufficient to enable it to weather possible reverses.

Other problems faced by Strategic Planning companies include a planning process that is too analytical and time-consuming for some businesses; alienation of business unit management and lack of commitment to strategies that are strongly sponsored by central management; and less development of general management capability down the line. An extreme version of the Strategic Planning style would come close to the Centralised style, and would stifle general management capability at the business level.

To work well, the style requires central management to have close knowledge of the business units. This criterion is most likely to be met in less diverse companies, and in companies where corporate management has personal experience of the businesses. Non-core businesses, or businesses that are not well understood by corporate management, encounter difficulties with the Strategic Planning style.

We conclude this chapter by dealing briefly with two styles, Strategic Programming and Strategic Venturing, that we have encountered in our work with the Strategic Planning companies. No company adopts these styles fully, but Lex and STC have some experience of Strategic Programming, while UB and BP have adopted Strategic Venturing for parts of their portfolios.

Strategic Programming

The conceptual framework introduced in chapter 3 suggests that, in theory, there is a corporate management style, Strategic Programming, that combines high planning influence with tight strategic control. At first sight it may appear that this style gives central management maximum opportunity to add value both in a planning and a control mode. However, we have found no solid current examples of this style amongst our participants, although two of the Strategic Planning companies have attempted it. We believe that this is primarily a consequence of drawbacks in Strategic Programming rather than a reflection on low profile corporate management in the UK.

Amongst our participants, both Lex and STC could be said to have embarked upon a Strategic Programming style; in Lex until the shift from control to commitment, and in STC until problems began to emerge in late 1984 and early 1985. The reasons for these companies abandoning tight control have been described earlier. They relate to the intrinsic difficulty for central management of controlling tightly against the results of a strategy that they have been closely involved in developing, especially with risky and uncertain new strategies; and to the problems of motivating business management when their freedom of movement is closely constrained by the need both to agree detailed strategies and objectives with the centre before the fact, and to be held closely accountable for results achieved subsequently.

It is now accepted in most leading companies that planning should not be confused with forecasting. In today's uncertain business world, the purpose of planning is to help to make good decisions, not to generate spuriously accurate long-term predictions of results. But this distinction between planning and forecasting has implications for the Strategic Programming style. As Lex's director of planning put it: 'We are less concerned with the budget than we used to be. This is on account of the world becoming increasingly uncertain, and businesses such as electronics where the rate of change is so rapid that the budget is quickly outdated by new circumstances.' In fast-changing and complex businesses, forecasts are inevitably fallible, and detailed controls are difficult. The ability to programme the future does not exist. This realization dawned earlier in BP: 'In the late sixties and early seventies, we had a longish flirtation with vast models as an approach to planning, trying to provide an integrated operations and finance view of the total corporation. This involved considerable expenditure and effort, before it was realized that there was no way this approach could encompass the complete requirements of planning for the company.'

Since predictions are not likely to be accurate, if corporate management wishes to control tightly against results or outputs, it is under an obligation to give some discretion over decisions or inputs. In essence, the tight control style implies 'Do whatever is necessary to achieve the following specified results.' Conversely, if corporate management wishes to be involved in agreeing the input strategy decisions, it must accept something more along the lines of 'Follow this strategy, whatever results it may bring.' Only if it believes that the results of a given strategy can be accurately forecast in advance will it be possible to programme both the strategic actions to be taken and the results to be achieved. If a business is new or rapidly growing, or if its strategy is innovative but risky, this is plainly not possible. STC's experiences represent a case in point.

The feasibility of combining high planning and control influence is arguably greater in slower growth, more stable businesses. But there can be difficulties even in more mature situations. Lex, for example, experienced problems in businesses such as Transportation, because the limitations on business unit autonomy led to a lack of commitment to 'agreed' strategies. The perception of the personal risks that accompanied tight control probably aggravated the problems. We have also suggested that similar issues may have arisen in certain of BOC's businesses.

In fact, the Strategic Programming style comes close to Centralized management (see chapter 7). The problems it encounters are similar; it differs from the Centralized style only in degree. Although both Strategic Planning and Strategic Control companies will be tempted to push towards Strategic Programming at certain times and in certain businesses, we do not regard it as a desirable style for long-term management of a corporate portfolio.

Strategic Venturing

The Strategic Venturing style appears to be associated with Strategic Planning. The style involves the same flexible approach to controls and the same willingness of central management to give the business time to build a position in the market. The difference lies in the amount of central influence over the strategies pursued. In Strategic Planning, the centre is actively involved in discussing the strategies, making suggestions, pushing for broad thrusts and initiating supportive activities. In Strategic Venturing, the centre's role is more passive. The centre's faith is vested in the management team and in the market. Little attempt is made to second guess the strategies being pursued by the business. The philosophy is uncomplicated – good management in an attractive market is all you need for good performance.

None of our sample of companies has Strategic Venturing as its main style, although some have parts of their portfolios running under a version of the Strategic Venturing style. Venture capital companies are probably the organizations that come closest to operating this style consistently. Many of the operating procedures of venture capital companies are relevant.

● Fully decentralized organization structure with each business acting as a stand-alone entity.
● No elaborate formal strategic planning processes; but frequent informal contact and planning discussions.
● No themes or thrusts coming from the venture capital company; but frequent suggestions and discussion of issues.
● Resources allocated in large lumps and committed for the medium term, e.g. through term loans and equity.
● Medium-term objectives and targets set, but main energy devoted to the downside – what if we fail to get orders, meet cash targets etc.?
● Frequent monitoring as an education tool and discipline rather than as a tool for motivating or applying sanctions.
● Main effort devoted to getting the right team in place.

From our sample UB is the company that comes closest to Strategic Venturing. For example, the Foods division in UB was run by John Wardell, who was part of the management originally acquired with the Meredith & Drew acquisition. He is an entrepreneur in the same mould as Sir Hector Laing. He built the own-label biscuits and snacks businesses with very little interference from the centre of UB. In fact, Sir Hector intentionally kept the Foods division separate and free from the influence of the Biscuits division. He wanted the own-label activities to have a free run at the branded business. Planning influence from the centre was, therefore, low. A similar approach was adopted in the Restaurants business. Another example from among the Strategic Planning companies is BP. BP has run some of its diversified businesses (Scicon, Minerals) on a relatively loose rein. Central management was involved in the decisions to enter these businesses, and periodically reviews the level of resource allocated to them. But it is much less involved in the development of strategies than in the oil business. There are few other examples of Strategic Venturing in our sample.

It appears that Strategic Venturing fits most easily within an overall Strategic Planning style. This could be because of the nature of Strategic Planning companies. We have seen that the Strategic Planning companies are building businesses focused on a few core industries. If they achieve success, the businesses they have built start to provide large free cash flows. They may therefore look for new business areas to build.

The centre, however, has no experience in the new business. It may be naturally cautious about providing too much planning influence, and give the management team in the new business a relatively free hand with strategy. The centre is also ambitious for the new businesses, and is therefore likely to apply the same flexible controls that it has been using in the core business areas. Strategic Venturing is less likely to be associated with Strategic Control or Financial Control companies because it is hard for these companies to accept the need for flexible controls.

The results of Strategic Venturing are difficult for us to assess because of the limited number of examples we have. In financial terms, UB has had successes and failures. The snacks and restaurant ventures are successes whereas the frozen goods venture has been less successful. BP's new ventures have, in general, not yet paid off.

The main problem with Strategic Venturing for large companies is to know when to stop. Strategic Venturing businesses are often intrinsically risky, and may incur periods of losses before success is established. Some will eventually reach their goals, while others never make the breakthrough. At what point does the centre decide to cut its losses? It is the importance of experience in making this particular judgement that is probably the reason for the current rise in venture capital companies specializing in the Strategic Venturing style.

In summary, Strategic Venturing can nurture new growth opportunities successfully, but is seldom found as the dominant style across the whole portfolio in large UK companies. Low planning influence and flexible control may seem to allow the corporate level too few opportunities to add value, over and above what can be provided by the capital market and the venture capital companies.

Style Changes

Strategic management styles do not remain static indefinitely. Central management approaches evolve to meet changing business circumstances, to reflect the preferences of new members of senior management, and in response to shifting priorities. Table 4.5 summarizes the changes that have occurred with the Strategic Planning companies.

BP and UB have moved away from the more Centralized style of management as their businesses have become more diverse. Both

Table 4.5 Style changes in Strategic Planning companies

	Previous style	Approximate date of change
BOC	Holding Company	late 1970s
BP	Centralized	late 1970s–early 1980s
Cadbury Schweppes	Strategic Planning since mid 1970s	
Lex Service	Strategic Programming	mid 1980s
STC[a]	Strategic Programming	mid 1980s
UB	Centralized	mid 1970s

[a] Strategic Planning style up to mid 1985. Now may be moving towards Financial Control.

companies have sought to delegate more responsibility to managers down the line, in the belief that this will ultimately lead to better decisions and better managers. They have also introduced more formal controls against results achieved than previously. The changes at BP began before Sir Peter Walters became chairman, but have been reinforced under his regime. They were also coincident with a number of new board appointments, and with a period of heavy negative cash flow in the early 1980s. At UB, the corporate style has evolved in anticipation of Sir Hector Laing's eventual retirement and the need to move towards increasing devolution of general management tasks. In both BP and UB the move away from centralized decision-taking is continuing, as is the introduction of tighter controls. Over time these companies may move from Strategic Planning to Strategic Control.

In the section on Strategic Programming we have already discussed the evolution of styles at Lex and STC. In these companies it was the difficulty of tight control coupled with corporate sponsorship of ambitious and risky new strategies that led to the changes. At Lex, the transition from Strategic Programming to Strategic Planning is recent, and it is too early to say yet whether further style changes will follow. At STC, severe financial problems have led to management change, and the style has changed again, away from Strategic Planning and towards Financial Control.

At BOC Dick Giordano has led a move towards greater central influence over strategy, and away from the Holding Company situation. Peripheral businesses have been sold, and the focus of the company has been directed back on to the core areas in gases, healthcare and carbon. This re-ordering of priorities reflected a new perception both of the opportunities and the threats in the core businesses. There appear to be no plans to alter the current style.

Lastly, Cadbury Schweppes' basic style has remained constant for some years, although there are continuing minor shifts of emphasis within it. Currently the company is pressing for somewhat tighter controls and rather more decentralization of responsibility. This has moved the company towards the border between Strategic Planning and Strategic Control.

Long periods of style stability therefore appear to be the exception rather than the rule. Periods of looser control are followed by tightening up, and strong central influence is succeeded by more delegation. But, at the same time, there is evidence in Lex and STC of controls that proved too tight being loosened, and in BOC of too much devolution preceding a higher degree of central influence. A tendency exists to swing between periods of tighter and looser controls and of greater and lesser central influence on strategy formulation. We anticipate further shifts in style in these companies in the future, in the elusive search for the best way to discharge the strategic role of the centre.

Changes in style, however, do not come about painlessly. Managers who have been accustomed to a high degree of autonomy resent attempts by the centre to become more involved in strategic decisions. Conversely, those who have never been asked to think strategically for themselves take time to acquire the skills (and interest) to do so. A strong new chief executive (Dick Giordano at BOC) and/or a period of serious financial reverses (BP in the early 1980s) make it much more possible to overcome these resistances.

The change process therefore appears to involve determined and continued efforts by the chief executive. He needs a clear view of his preferred style, and a willingness to overcome resistance by selective use of incentives and sanctions including senior management changes, repeated public support of new systems and new attitudes, and gradual education in the new skills necessary to make the style work. The acceptance of change is much more ready when visible financial stress exists to reinforce the challenge to old ways of doing things.

Notes

1 The field work for this research was carried out mainly in 1984 and 1985, and our descriptions of the companies refer to this period of time, although we note obvious changes since then. In particular our work with STC was carried out before the management changes in mid 1985. Our analysis of the company therefore refers to the management style and results only up until that time.

2 Matrix organizations involve dual reporting relationships, in which a manager can have more than one 'boss'. The matrix structure is fully discussed in S. Davis and P. R. Lawrence, *Matrix* (Addison-Wesley, 1977).

3 This point, widely recognized by managers in our participant companies, has been documented by Joseph L. Bower in *Managing the Resource Allocation Process* (Division of Research, Harvard Business School, 1970) and by Paul King in 'Is the emphasis of capital budgeting theory misplaced?', *The Journal of Business Finance and Accounting*, 1975. Bower and King both argue that the role of corporate management is to manage the process, the context in which capital investments are proposed, not to act as real decision-makers.

4 For a description of portfolio planning techniques, see Richard Hamermesh, *Making Strategy Work* (John Wiley, 1986).

5 In the 1984 Annual Report, Cadbury Schweppes stated their group objectives as follows:

Group objectives
We have developed the following summary of objectives to guide our management plans and shape our corporate strategy:
Our business objectives
- The Group will concentrate on its principal business areas of confectionery, soft drinks, beverages and food products. Our objective is to maximize the use of existing assets rather than to diversify into unrelated areas.
- In confectionery we at present hold a 5 per cent share of the world chocolate market and are ranked as the fifth largest company in it. We intend to increase that share and to climb the league of international chocolate companies.
- In soft drinks we are currently number three in the market outside the USA, but fifth in the world overall. Our aim is to become the world's leading non-cola carbonated soft drinks company.
- An organization structure based on product streams to encourage the maximum use of our assets on a worldwide basis through product sourcing and effective planning of capital expenditure.

● We will build on the strong personnel traditions of our companies by bringing about greater accountability and decentralization, honest assessment of performance, reward related to our progress as a business, and a management style based on openness and participation.

Our financial objectives

● Earnings per share	– 5 per cent per annum in real terms
● Return on assets	– 25 per cent per annum
● Gearing	– the ratio of debt to equity to be below 50 per cent
● Interest cover	– trading profit to be at least five times greater than interest charges
● Dividend cover	– earnings to cover dividends up to three times

5

Strategic Control Companies

The centre in Strategic Control companies is concerned with business unit planning; but it believes in organizing around independent profit-responsible business units and leaving as much of the initiative to business unit management as possible. It therefore focuses more on establishing demanding planning processes, and on reviewing and criticizing business unit proposals, than on advocating particular ways forward. Strategic Control companies also try to exercise tight control against results achieved, taking into account both financial and strategic objectives. Participant companies whose strategic decision-making processes have these characteristics were Courtaulds, ICI, Imperial Group, Plessey and Vickers.[1] Brief background descriptions of these companies can be found in appendix 1.

Planning Influence

The flavour of planning influence in the Strategic Control companies is best conveyed through the words of the chief executives of these organizations. 'The corporate level', said Sir Christopher Hogg of Courtaulds, 'acts as a detached but sympathetic and knowledgeable 100 per cent shareholder . . . The HQ is not only judging the content of strategic plans. We judge the process, how the plans were put together . . . At the centre our role is to enforce quality standards in strategic thinking and we have a role in helping educate and develop managers.' Sir David Plastow of Vickers expressed a similar point of view: 'The purpose of the planning process is to get facts out on the table and challenge the gut reactions of managers. My role is to establish and structure the process. Although occasionally I will dive into a key decision, for example on acquisitions.' The emphasis is on establishing a process within which business units themselves will come up with improved plans and proposals. The centre has less direct influence than in Strategic Planning companies, but is more involved than in Financial Control companies. We will now describe in more detail how the Strategic Control companies achieve their purposes in planning influence.

Organization Structure

The predominant organizational theme in these companies has been the creation or reinforcement of independent, profit-responsible divisions that can devise their own strategies with little need for coordination between divisions, and that can be held separately accountable for their results. The businesses within these divisions often require coordinated strategies, and this is a prime function for the divisional management level. Nevertheless, the divisions are broken up into profit centre units, which each report separately to the centre. Table 5.1 shows the divisional and business structure for the five companies in question.

Table 5.1 Strategic Control companies: organization structure

	Number of divisions[a]	Overlaps between divisions[b]	Number of businesses[c]	Overlaps between businesses within divisions[b]
Courtaulds	8	Low–medium	30–40	Medium
ICI	20	Generally low	50–60	High
Imperial	3	Low	20–25	Medium
Plessey	3	Medium	20–25	High
Vickers	10	Low	25–30	Medium

[a] We use the term 'division' for the most aggregated organizational unit whose senior line executive is held profit-responsible for results.
[b] Judgemental assessment of degree of overlap in terms of common technologies, resources, markets, skills; and potential for synergies from coordination.
[c] Businesses that submit separate plans, budgets and reports to the centre.

Courtaulds is a good example of the independent profit centre approach. Under Lord Kearton, in the years up to the mid 1970s Courtaulds was run as a vertically integrated organization, with extensive, centrally directed trading links between units. Recently, Chris Hogg has chosen to place greater emphasis on the independence of each business unit. Trading between units is now at arm's length, and each business is required to show a separate profit result. There are getting on for 200 separate profit centres, each of which is free to devise and pursue its own strategy. This is an unusually large number of profit centres, and reflects the commitment of the company to decentralization as well as the nature of the markets in which they are operating. The profit centres are aggregated for management purposes into eight reasonably homogeneous divisions (concerned with clothing, fabrics, spinning, plastics, films, paint, woodpulp and fibres), and the divisional level has a role in coordinating the strategies of the businesses reporting to them. It is, however, notable that in 1985 clothing, fabrics and spinning were combined into a Textile group under its own board; at the same time a greater degree of management coordination was established at top level to explore opportunities for profitable cooperation between the other divisions, which were termed the Chemical and Industrial group.

ICI is structured around a number of UK product divisions, six overseas regions, and a few worldwide product businesses. Divisions that are heavily mutually dependent (for example, Plastics and Petrochemicals) have been combined, and a worldwide business structure has been introduced for products where globally integrated strategies were seen to be important (e.g., Pharmaceuticals). Although there are some needs for coordination, the divisions are now largely independent profit centres. Divisional management play an important role in coordinating the strategies of the separate profit centres within each division. The size of the head office staff has been dramatically reduced, falling from around 1,300 people in the early 1980s to 250–300 by 1986.

Divisional chairmen report to main board executive directors, and for this purpose the divisions are aggregated into five groups. However, the main board director responsible for the group is intended to be a corporate representative rather than a profit-responsible senior line executive. Sir John Harvey-Jones personally stressed this separation of corporate and business responsibilities, in an effort to move away from the establishment of 'baronies'. The baronial problem is a common worry among the companies in our sample. It arises when individual directors begin to take more interest in building or preserving the businesses for which they are personally responsible than in the corporate whole. Locating personal profit responsibility for areas of the company at the level immediately below the main board, and emphasizing the exclusively corporate role of main board directors, is an increasingly popular way of tackling the barons.

Vickers is structured in a similar fashion to ICI and has two main board group heads to oversee its ten quite separate divisions. Previously, these directors also carried personal profit accountability for divisions (or groups of divisions), but now their corporate role is stressed, with primary profit responsibility at the division head level.

Imperial and Plessey are structured around a comparatively small number of divisions, and in each company the profit-responsible senior line executives for the divisions do sit on the main board. In Imperial, there were few points of coordination between divisions to be managed. In Plessey, however, it is less easy to structure the divisions to be wholly self-contained. Decisions taken by the Components division, for example, have a material influence on both the Telecommunications and Defence Systems divisions. But even here there is a strong philosophical commitment to decentralized profit-responsible business units, and such coordination mechanisms as exist (see below p. 93) are overlaid on this basic structure.

There is therefore a uniform belief in decentralized profit responsibility in the Strategic Control companies. Where there are overlaps between businesses these are largely handled at the divisional level, and the structure calls for little involvement by the centre in managing inter-dependencies between businesses. These arrangements are similar to the Financial Control companies, who, if anything, take the independent profit centre emphasis even further. But they contrast with at least some of the Strategic Planning companies, whose structures build in more overlaps between businesses and between levels in the organization. This means that Strategic Control companies may sacrifice potential 'synergies' between divisions, but provide the motivation that goes with devolved strategic responsibility.

Review Process

Each of these companies involve the corporate level in the review of business unit strategic plans and budgets. As part of this process, they employ formal and structured review systems for plans and budgets. The Vickers system is a good example.

In Vickers, there is a basic annual planning cycle that falls into three phases. The first phase is initiated with a set of guidelines from the centre that establishes the background economic (and other) assumptions to be adopted in planning, and identifies in each division the key questions that corporate management wishes to see addressed. Divisions then prepare and discuss with corporate management strategic plans that concentrate on qualitative directions and underlying competitive logic rather than on precise plans or targets. These plans form the basis for the second phase, a more detailed 3-year planning exercise (the business plan) that translates the agreed strategy into action programmes and financial objectives for the medium-term future. The business plan is also reviewed and agreed between the divisions and the centre. Finally, the business plan provides the context for a 1-year operating plan, which constitutes the budget for the coming year, together with detailed action items. The process can be summarized thus:

December/January   Guidelines issued by corporate.
↓

March/April   Strategy plans submitted by all 26 businesses, and discussed with executive committee[2] by Vickers. Narrative only, concerning broad strategy.
↓

May/June   Business plans submitted by all businesses and reviewed/approved by executive committee. Translates broad strategy into 3-year forward projections and action plans.
↓

October/November   Operating plans submitted by all businesses and reviewed/approved by executive committee. One-year budgets and detailed action plans for first year of business plan.

The three-phase review in Vickers is intended to separate the broad discussion of strategy from the more detailed debate over numbers and details, to create a strategy that is realistic by tying it to more specific medium-term plans, and to ensure that the operating plans and budgets are consistent with the agreed strategy direction. There is increasing flexibility in the application of the review process to each division. For example, in divisions where no change is proposed to a strategy that has already been fully analysed and debated in previous cycles, the strategic plan and business plan phases may be comparatively light.

The formal planning system is supplemented by a variety of informal contacts between the centre and business management. Tony McCann, main board member responsible for planning, sees these informal contacts as vital for making the formal process work well. 'The difficult cases are the ones that arrive in black and white, with no alternatives. Nowadays that seldom happens. The chances of the divisional managing director suddenly coming up with a proposal to shut down an area, without anyone having any idea before are remote. The dialogue would be extensive before it arrives.' It is also argued that the existence of a formal review process makes business managers more anxious to sound out the centre informally at an early stage, in order to facilitate the formal discussion that will eventually have to take place.

The purpose of the planning reviews is to challenge the views of business management, and to raise questions that might otherwise be avoided. 'The role of the corporate planning staff is to put ferrets down holes', says David Plastow, the chief executive. And, commenting on his own position: 'I feel a responsibility for helping managers to get their heads up over the parapet and to think more broadly from time to time.'

Table 5.2 lays out the review process in the Strategic Control companies. The number of review steps, the balance between formality and informality, and the extensiveness of plans, analyses and documentation may

Table 5.2 Strategic Control companies: planning systems

	Plans formally reviewed by corporate management			Link of long-term strategy to detailed plans and budgets
	'Strategy'[a]	'Business'[a]	'Operating'[a]	
Courtaulds	—	Annually	Annually	Yes
ICI	—	Every 2 years	Annually	Yes
Imperial	—	Annually	Annually	Yes
Plessey	Annually	Annually	Annually	Yes
Vickers	Annually	Annually	Annually	Yes

[a] The terms 'strategy' plan, 'business' plan, 'operating' plan are used in the sense described for Vickers. Courtaulds, ICI and Imperial combine the strategy plan and business plan reviews in one step.

differ; but in all companies there is a commitment to a corporate review process that requires long-term strategy thinking to be laid out and linked to specific plans and budgets. A two- and three-step formal review process, involving well over 20 units, not to mention extensive informal contacts off-line from the formal review process, represents a major effort.

The corporate role in the review process generally concentrates on probing the commercial logic and consistency of plans proposed. The 'quality control' on business strategies that this represents is seen as essential. Both Geoffrey Kent at Imperial and David Plastow at Vickers made the early introduction of formal strategic planning – in some cases against considerable divisional or business opposition – a high priority during their tenures as chief executive. In part the introduction of the planning system was justified by providing corporate management with a much better data base on which to take its decisions; at Imperial this involved an on-line 'Chief Executive Information System' providing direct access for senior corporate managers to up-to-date plans and results for all businesses. But even more importantly – there are questions about how often Imperial's Chief Executive Information System was actually used – the requirement for each business to lay out in a structured way an appraisal of its business situation, and a rationale for its proposed strategy led to much improved communication between the centre and the businesses, and to new perceptions of opportunities and threats. Being forced by the centre to be explicit about strategies and plans created a useful discipline for the businesses.

The value of the quality control role, however, depends on the sophistication of both business and corporate management thinking. The early planning cycles at Imperial and Vickers were seen as helpful, by both the centre and the businesses, since they were, for the first time, asking basic questions, gathering basic information, making explicit basic issues and choices. Once this groundwork is in place, however, subsequent cycles run an increasing danger of becoming repetitive unless the level of corporate questioning is sufficiently sophisicated to continue to open up new perspectives for business management. This is no mean task in an annual review of upwards of 20 separate businesses, and there are complaints from some businesses in all the Strategic Control companies that the review process degenerates into bureaucracy and paper pushing. This is particularly the case where the balance between formal and informal reviews is weighted heavily towards formality. Maintaining freshness and insight in the review process is a real challenge for corporate management.

Central management in the Strategic Control companies normally uses the review process more for this probing, questioning role than to push a particular corporate view of how businesses should develop. If there are significant corporate worries about the strategy in a particular business, a common response is to suggest the retention of independent consultants for a second view rather than to involve the centre itself in a more detailed investigation. Both Courtaulds and Vickers have made extensive use of outside consultants for this purpose.

The review system for strategy plans and budgets is therefore an important part of the strategic decision-making process for all the Strategic Control companies. There are variations between companies, and between different businesses within each company, in precisely how the process is carried out, but in all cases there is an extensive and time-consuming annual review of strategic plans and budgets. Strategic Control companies are in this respect somewhat similar to Strategic Planning companies. Strategic Planning companies devote even more effort to reviews of strategy, but they tend to be more selective about which businesses receive attention, and less comprehensive in undertaking annual reviews. Financial Control companies, on the other hand, focus their formal reviews exclusively on budgets, and do not believe in formal strategic planning systems.

The Strategic Control review process does ensure that certain minimum standards of information and analysis are met in planning for all businesses. But there is some danger that the system takes up considerable management time, and provides relatively little contribution to a competent and well-informed business management. This is a particular problem if the centre is remote from the detail of the businesses.

Broad Themes, Major Thrusts, Specific Suggestions

A distinguishing feature of these companies is the decentralization of strategy formulation responsibility to divisional or business level. Thus, broad themes, major thrusts and specific suggestions are generally delivered, if at all, in low key. For Chris Hogg the centre's role in Courtaulds should not be directive. On questions of strategic choice, he prefers to do no more than 'create warm air' in favour of certain messages or priorities. Sir John Harvey-Jones (ICI) sees strategy development as a primarily divisional role with the centre in a 'largely reactive' mode. And, in Sir John Clark's (Plessey) view, 'You can't hire a dog and bark yourself'.

There are exceptions to this. Within ICI, for example, there is a preference for shifting the portfolio towards higher added value 'effect' chemicals and towards a more international business spread; and specific initiatives to achieve this have been sponsored by corporate management in electronics, advanced materials and specialty chemicals. In Plessey, the chief executive's office attempts to provide a sense of overall direction for the company, and to manage the linkages between the divisions. In addition, it will occasionally intervene to support a particular initiative – for example, the development of gallium arsenide chips – or to press for cost reductions in selected overhead functions. At Vickers, Sir David Plastow aims to communicate a few broad messages (for example, the importance of international markets, or of quality control in manufacturing) and uses these to condition strategy thinking in the divisions. And in all the companies, corporate management do on occasions intervene directly on specific pet topics. Nevertheless, the intention and philosophy is to leave the substance of strategic proposals and initiatives to business unit management.

Inevitably, this reduces the role of the centre in proactively sponsoring selected strategy directions. But Strategic Control companies argue that there is more to be gained from leaving the strategy initiative firmly with the businesses. We have seen in the previous chapter that the Strategic Planning companies adopt a fundamentally different philosophy on this point.

Management of Interdependencies

The organization structures adopted by these companies have reduced the scope for corporate involvement in managing linkages between businesses or divisions, and in seeking synergy between them. In Imperial and Vickers the opportunities for cross-divisional coordination are few, and little corporate attention is devoted to them. At ICI and Courtaulds, the opportunities may be greater, but in both companies the corporate management teams have been willing to sacrifice some centrally managed synergies to create a greater sense of independence in the divisions and businesses. To this end, where divisions trade with each other, transfer prices are set as far as possible at third party, open market rates, and the relationship is at arm's length. Although the recent cross-divisional initiatives in electronics and advanced materials at ICI, and the creation of the two groupings at Courtaulds, signal some movement away from this position, neither company appears close to adopting a significantly more active role in central management of cross-divisional issues.

Mutual dependencies between divisions are greatest at Plessey, where, for example, the Components division is an important supplier to other parts of the company. For this reason mechanisms have been put in place to handle coordination. A Chief Executive Office, effectively the executive committee of the board, has been established to include senior corporate and divisional management. Its purpose is to ensure coordination across Plessey's activities, as well as to develop the overall direction for the group. There is also a cross-divisional technology coordinating committee. However, the decentralization philosophy remains strong, and the co-ordination process does not yet work well. 'We don't realize the goal of corporate strategy very well. The centre exorts but it doesn't happen. Each business tends to optimize its own return.' The Chief Executive Office has difficulty in adopting the corporate perspective, since its divisional members are concerned to advance their own divisional interests. As a result, decentralized divisional initiatives tend to prevail over corporate coordination.

By structuring for separate profit responsibility, the Strategic Control companies generally avoid the need to manage interdependencies. Where feasible, this undoubtedly fits the overall Strategic Control style. But where businesses in the portfolio do require coordination, the style creates problems for overlap management. Similar difficulties arise for Financial Control companies.

Resource Allocation

As in the Strategic Planning companies, central resource allocation is seen as vital. Furthermore, the formal capital appropriation systems (CAS) in both groups of companies are similar. Business management is expected to identify possible capital requirements in the strategic planning reviews, and to use the CAS simply for more detailed and thorough justification of individual projects that have been approved in principle in the strategic plan; most initiatives come from the businesses; fit with long-term strategic plans is seen as an important criterion; and there is delegated divisional authority for capital spending that falls within the plan to a fairly high authorization limit (table 5.3). The centre is also active in ranking proposed projects, and, where bids for resources exceed what is available, allocating capital selectivity between them. All these points are more fully discussed in chapter 4 on the Strategic Planning style.

Table 5.3   Strategic Control companies: limit of divisional authority for capital expenditures[a]

	£m	As % net assets of company
Courtaulds	1.0	0.12
ICI	5.0	0.08
Imperial	1.0	0.07
Plessey	0.5	0.07
Vickers	0.25	0.08

[a] Authorization limits are generally much lower for items that did not feature in a previous strategic plan. ICI, for example, reduces its limit from £5 million to £200,000.

The main difference in Strategic Control companies is that, since they are less proactive in the strategy review process, capital projects emerge less often from corporate initiatives and ideas than in Strategic Planning companies. Divisions are encouraged to take the lead on capital spending proposals, and are given freedom to make their own choices concerning smaller items of expenditure. It was in this spirit that ICI increased its divisional authorization limit to £5 million per project, and is currently considering raising it further for capital expenditures that are consistent with agreed strategy. The resource allocation process is then mainly a quality control check on business ideas, rather than an opportunity for corporate management to sponsor new directions. There is, however, a strong sense that the centre must be the ultimate judge of priorities and allocator of resources. 'We take the view that the cash belongs to the centre. We fund the businesses in accordance with their plans. But that is something of a change of philosophy, since there did tend to be a view that businesses were allowed almost indefinitely to accumulate their own results and invest out of them', said a Vickers director, contrasting their Strategic Control style with their previous Holding Company regime.

The initiative on major decisions that affect overall portfolio design is also more likely to come from the centre than the businesses. Businesses may put up proposals for acquisitions or new business entries that they believe will fit in with and strengthen their existing strategies, but they are unlikely to suggest closure decisions or radical initiatives. Here, the onus rests more with the centre. 'It's unrealistic to expect me to propose closing down parts of my business. It has to be done at the centre', said a Plessey division manager.

Corporate management needs to take primary responsibility for closing or selling businesses that do not fit with the company's long-term ambitions, or are seen as having low long-term profit potential. Major initiatives in new businesses are also less likely without corporate sponsorship. We shall show in the discussion of the results achieved by the Strategic Control companies that they have tended to be more active in closures and divestments than in major new initiatives. This, again, reflects a corporate style that reacts to business proposals rather than takes the initiative at the centre.

In making resource allocation decisions and reviewing overall portfolio balance, four of the five Strategic Control companies make use (or have recently made use) of portfolio planning techniques. The exception, ICI, makes only informal use of these techniques. The purpose of portfolio planning is to identify variables that will measure, for each business, the attractiveness of the industry in which it competes (e.g. its long-term growth and profit potential) and the strength of its position relative to other competitors (e.g. its relative cost position and product differentiation compared with other companies in the industry). A portfolio grid is then prepared which positions each business on the two major dimensions. According to its positioning in the grid, a business may be categorized as, for example, 'grow', 'maintain', or 'harvest'. Businesses that are competitively strong and are in growing and profitable industries are candidates for growth, while businesses that are in unattractive industries and are competitively weak may be considered for divestment. Both Imperial and Vickers have used portfolio planning to help sort out their portfolios. Businesses with underlying weaknesses have been identified, and exit decisions taken. Businesses with long-term potential are beginning to receive priority in resource allocation. Similar considerations lie behind ICI's closure decisions, and their push into electronics and specialty chemicals.

The attractions of the portfolio planning techniques are that they allow comparisons of strategic positioning to be made across a large number of diverse businesses. They create a first cut at resource allocation priorities using a simple two-dimensional display. Acquisitions and divestments can be assessed for their impact on portfolio balance in these terms. The disadvantages of portfolio planning techniques are that they force a simplication of much complex information, and can lead to glib, superficial or erroneous conclusions if they are used naively. Furthermore, they are better at identifying weak businesses that should be rationalized out of the portfolio than for determining strategies and initiatives that will create strong businesses for the future. In recognition of this, Vickers, which has passed through the initial phase of divestments in its portfolio planning, now places less emphasis on portfolio grid analysis. Portfolio planning techniques are used less by Strategic Planning than Strategic Control companies, and are not employed by Financial Control companies.

   In addition to the allocation of capital resources, there is also an important corporate role in the allocation of management resources. In Strategic Control companies, divisional managing directors are appointed by corporate management. Other senior appointments within divisions are also monitored, with the centre retaining an ultimate right of veto. Where main board executives have responsibility for overseeing a group of divisions (ICI and Vickers), one of their primary tasks concerns management appointments, capabilities and succession.

Resource allocation in the Strategic Control companies is therefore set within an overall strategic context, with corporate management prioritizing and selecting between proposals. This contrasts with Financial Control companies which adopt a more project-based approach, and expect to fund all proposals that meet the corporate criteria. Strategic Control companies have been active in rationalizing and restructuring their portfolios, and have used portfolio planning techniques to aid decisions on strategic resource allocation priorities. The Strategic Control companies, unlike the Strategic Planning companies, have, however, sponsored fewer portfolio building initiatives.

Control Influence

The control processes in these companies are closely linked to the planning processes. While part of the purpose of reviewing and criticizing strategy proposals is to improve the quality of thinking, an equally important intention is to establish objectives against which future performance can be controlled.

Agreeing Objectives

Objectives in Strategic Control companies generally emerge from the detailed discussion of the plans proposed by the business units. The objectives stem from the plans, rather than vice versa. This is not to suggest that the objective-setting process is wholly bottom-up. The initiative lies in the first instance with the businesses, who formulate the plans, rather than with the centre,[3] but corporate management can and do push and probe for alternative objectives as they see fit. The result is usually a compromise that both business and centre can live with.

The planning processes in the Strategic Control companies are designed to generate both long-term plans and objectives, and short-term budgets, action programmes and milestones that are consistent with the agreed long-term strategy. Objectives therefore exist for both the short term and the long term, and are set to take account of strategic goals as well as financial results. Businesses can face a range of objectives, covering a variety of financial and non-financial aggregates and referring to different future time periods. The complexity of these multidimensional objectives is intended to allow a balance to be struck between strategic, tactical and operating considerations, between short- and long-term goals, and between measures of financial profitability and underlying competitive advantage. One attraction of portfolio planning techniques for Strategic Control companies is that they purport to provide measures of strategic position to complement financial results.

In practice, however, Strategic Control companies have found difficulty in specifying non-financial, strategic objectives that are as tangible and credible as financial objectives. Gaining market share, launching a new range of products and improving customer service may be part of the strategy, but precise, measurable targets for these activities are set much less often ('our objectives are to gain share relative to Bayer while remaining profitable'). This is partly because it is difficult to define acceptable and comprehensive objective measures of, for example, customer service; partly because the strategy may call for directional improvement rather than a specific level of improvement; and partly because the trade-offs between different objectives in an uncertain business world render precise forecasting of multiple, interlocking objectives unfeasible. More typically, therefore, precise objectives emerge for certain financial variables, which are set in the light of an agreed strategic direction, perhaps together with some more loosely specified, non-financial strategic milestones.

Furthermore, consistent with the spirit of decentralized responsibility, companies such as Courtaulds and ICI have been moving away from a multiplicity of very detailed and extensive control objectives, and are now focusing on a small number of key targets. Both these companies see the profit and, just as much, the cash flow numbers as vital. Moreover, profit and cash flow objectives are set for whole divisions rather than for individual businesses within the divisions. This leaves greater discretion to the divisions to manage as they see fit and to make trade-offs between businesses reporting to them, provided the divisional bottom line is delivered. Chris Hogg refers to this as 'control to get things done, not to stop them from being done'. It also gives clearer and less multidimensional criteria against which to assess whether performance is satisfactory. For Strategic Control companies this is important, since they set out to enforce control targets tightly.

Objectives in the Strategic Control companies therefore have a dual aspect. They are the outcome of the strategic planning process, and express the agreement reached on the broad way forward. But they are also a contract between business unit management and the centre, and detail what the business undertakes to deliver. It is in finding ways to make agreements on the strategic way forward sufficiently precise to act as the basis of a deliverable contract that Strategic Control companies have encountered most difficulty. In this sense, the objective-setting process is harder for Strategic Control companies than Strategic Planning companies, who give clear priority to the 'broad way forward' aspect, or Financial Control companies, who emphasize the 'contract' dimension unequivocally.

Monitoring Results

All the Strategic Control companies have monthly and quarterly reporting systems to track actual results versus plan. There is therefore extensive reporting of results versus the budget or operating plan; indeed, some of the businesses complain that the frequency and detail of reported information are far greater than central management can in fact use. It is notable that ICI's move to fewer, more aggregate objectives has been linked with a reduced amount of detailed reporting, and that the divisions have welcomed this wholeheartedly.

The monthly and quarterly reporting is usually a matter of written reports rather than face-to-face meetings. Responsible corporate management will refer to monthly reports in their periodic contacts with divisional and business managers, and will take up exceptional deviations from plans as and when they occur. But there are no regular, formal review sessions between the annual planning exercises, and there is some sense at the business level that the regular reports are greeted in the main by a resounding silence.

Monitoring of results achieved against longer-term plans and capital appropriation requests is generally much less well developed. Reference to previous years' plans may be made when new objectives are set, and ICI have a selective post audit of capital projects. But there is not the fullness, the frequency or the formality in monitoring performance against longer-term objectives that is found for annual plans.

In Strategic Control companies, therefore, the information system exists to permit monitoring of actual performance against plan to take place, but it is used on a management by exception basis. Discussions between corporate management and business management of results against plan are rare ocurrences, generally to be avoided. We shall see that this is in sharp contrast to the Financial Control companies where regular reviews of actual results versus plan are an important part of the management process.

Action and Incentives

A distinguishing feature of the Strategic Control companies is that management perceives that control objectives are now tightly enforced. In ICI, Imperial and Vickers this may be partly a reaction to a previous management regime in which objectives were clearly not tightly enforced. As one ICI division chairman put it: 'In the past, if you came in halfway through the year and said you would be £5 million down, the response would be: "That's too bad". And if in the event you were £15 million down, the response would again be: "That's too bad". Now all that has changed, and targets really matter.' The belief that objectives matter, and that their achievement will translate into personal consequences for the responsible manager, is common to all five Strategic Control companies. Richard Lapthorne, Courtaulds' finance director, summed it up well: 'If a man misses his budget two years in a row', he said, 'we'd conclude that he doesn't know enough about the business to run it.'

The enforcement of objectives has both a stick and a carrot aspect. Evidence of the stick can be found in the rate of management turnover in senior positions. Over half the managers in the top 300 positions in Vickers have been changed in the past 5 years; in Imperial, three out of four division heads changed after Geoffrey Kent took over; and in all these companies it is perceived[4] that failure to achieve targets will be severely penalized. The carrot is represented by career advancement, and by the increasingly popular incentive compensation schemes and stock options. Table 5.4 lays out the nature of the compensation schemes in these companies. Managers at Imperial, Plessey and Vickers can increase their compensation very substantially through the bonus element. 'Tight' control therefore is an important part of the Strategic Control approach.

Due to the difficulty of defining long-term strategic control objectives, the 'tight' control process tends to stress control against budgeted financial results. Lacking precise 'strategic' targets, the control contract focuses on short-term profit and cash flow figures. Therefore, although all five companies are committed to review processes for long-term strategy, the objectives that count most in the control process are in fact budgeted

Table 5.4 Strategic Control companies: incentive compensation schemes

	Incentive bonus	Basis	Average level (%)	Maximum level (%)	Stock options
Courtaulds	Yes	Judgement	— Varies —		Yes
ICI	Yes	Judgement	< 10	—	Yes
Imperial	Yes	Mainly actual vs budget RoCE	33	—	Yes
Plessey	Yes	Actual vs budget RcCE	30–40	—	Yes
Vickers	Yes	Actual vs budget RoCE	25	60	Yes

[a] Percentage of base salary.

financial results for the coming year. As one manager in Imperial put it: 'Despite strategic planning and management by strategy, the company behaves as if the budget is the key thing.' This is reinforced by the emphasis on budgeted return on capital targets in the incentive compensation systems. Where the bonus is mainly geared to achievement of budgeted RoCE, this tends to become the most powerful motivator. We were told of managers who, for example, faced a mid-year choice between cutting stocks and marketing expenditures to achieve annual profit targets, and pushing ahead with an agreed market penetration strategy to the detriment of their budgets. In these circumstances, with the potential to earn a 50 per cent bonus on base salary, it calls for a high degree of self sacrifice to put strategy before the budget. This problem is recognized by most of the Strategic Control companies, and attempts are being made to introduce more flexibility into bonus formulae. Plessey, for example, are moving away from an exclusive reliance on RoCE and including a variety of more qualitative targets as well. But qualitative targets also mean that managers are more reliant on the subjective judgements of their superiors, and are less clearly motivated towards objectively measured profit goals.[5] This can lead to more corporate politics and dissatisfactions than a clear budget emphasis.

Admittedly in the Strategic Control companies the budget is set in the light of the strategy, and long-term strategy can be a valid excuse for non-achievement of budgeted objectives. At ICI division chairmen are expected to take whatever action is necessary to achieve their budgeted profit and cash flow targets, but only *provided* this does not jeopardize their long-term strategy. In the event that they feel compelled to take action that could alter their agreed strategy plans they are formally required to refer the matter back to the centre for decision.

This provides some balance to the power of shorter-term financial objectives. But it also opens the door to an array of less valid excuses and special pleading, where 'strategy' and 'long-term potential' can be invoked year after year to avoid hard decisions in problem areas. In one Strategic Control company we were told of a business that was still, after 10 years of losses, asking for one further chance to revise its strategy and embark upon a route to long-term improvement.

In some Strategic Control companies it is argued that stock options provide a medium- and longer-term performance incentive. While in principle valid, it has also been pointed out to us that the tendency for the stock market to react strongly to half-yearly earnings figures re-establishes the impact of next year's profits as a central determinant of the value of stock options.

Control for the Strategic Control companies attempts then both to be tightly enforced (as in Financial Control companies) and to balance long-term strategic objectives and short-term financial objectives (as in Strategic Planning companies). While theoretically attractive, this approach to control encounters practical problems of implementation. The difficulty of identifying and measuring strategic goals can mean that the strategic element of control is either crowded out by tight financial controls or becomes the basis for excuses that undermine the tightness of the whole control process. Balancing strategic and financial control has not been easy for these companies.

Summary of Strategic Control Characteristics

The common denominators between the companies whose style we have termed Strategic Control are therefore as follows:

- Devolution of responsibility for strategy development to divisional and business level.
- Strong divisional management level which handles coordination between businesses in each division, but little corporate attempt to coordinate across divisions or achieve synergies.
- Extensive formal and informal plan review processes to raise the quality of business thinking.
- General avoidance by the centre of strategic themes, thrusts or specific suggestions for businesses.
- Central allocation of resources to support agreed strategy, and setting of priorities between projects.
- Capital projects and new business entries generally proposed by businesses, with few major corporate initiatives except on closures and divestments.
- Objectives set in terms of long- and short-term goals and strategic and financial targets.
- Detailed reporting of performance for each profit centre to the corporate management.
- Tight control, in terms of incentives and sanctions, for actual performance versus planned objectives.

Although all the Strategic Control companies adhered to these main principles, the precise way in which each operates is of course different. For example, the details of the review process are different, and the willingness, on occasion, to make specific strategy suggestions to businesses varies. Also, the level of detail and breadth of coverage of control objectives, and the ways in which incentives and sanctions are applied, are not uniform. Equally, there may be differences of emphasis in the corporate–business relationship between the centre and different parts of each company. These differences reflect different personalities and different strategic priorities in each business. Nevertheless, we have been much more impressed by the similarities between the corporate styles of these five companies, and by the uniformity of the philosophy and approach as it is applied to different businesses in each company. It is based upon these similarities that we have felt justified in identifying Strategic Control as a distinctive style of corporate management.

Results

We will now review the results that have been achieved by the five Strategic Control companies. Appendix 1, which gives background information on the companies, provides support and detail for many of the points that we make. As with the Strategic Planning companies, we will be concerned with financial results; the building and maintenance of long-term competitive advantage; and satisfaction within the companies on the quality of the dialogue between the centre and the businesses on strategy issues. We shall find that the Strategic Control style has led to major achievements, but that it has also been accompanied by certain problems and dissatisfactions. This balance of advantage and disadvantage is characteristic of each of the styles of corporate management that we have identified.

Courtaulds

The greatest achievement at Courtaulds has been the turnaround in performance of the fibres and fabrics businesses, from returns on capital of 0 per cent and –2 per cent in 1981 to 24 per cent and 17 per cent in 1985. The combined effect of tighter control and heavy redundancies and closures has been a considerable reduction in the cost base of these businesses, which has enabled them to take full benefit of improved demand conditions in the past couple of years.

A second success concerns the improvement in general management capability and strategic thinking at the business unit level. This has been a continuing preoccupation of Chris Hogg, and a major purpose both in pushing strategic responsibility down to business unit level and in concentrating corporate effort on quality control for business unit strategy thinking. Although the company remains aware of the need for further progress in this area, much has been achieved.

On the debit side, it can be argued that the centre has done less to help business units build long-term competitive strength than to rationalize their costs bases. The emphasis on financial control targets has sometimes seemed to be at odds with the call for better strategic thinking, and managers of growth businesses such as Carbon Fibres have perceived a conflict between business building objectives and control targets. It is also accepted that the management style has not pushed for the achievement of potential synergies between divisions. A final concern is that the company has launched no major new growth initiative in recent years. There is some feeling that a closer involvement of the centre in strategy development for the businesses might have led to the identification of more opportunities, and/or to a greater willingness to move aggressively on such ideas as have emerged.

Despite these drawbacks, the view is that the centre adds value at Courtaulds. Business management finds Chris Hoggs's questioning perceptive and helpful, and they generally agree that the company's strategic decision-making process has improved greatly in the past 5 years. The establishment of the new groupings for Textiles and for Chemical and Industrial are seen as moves to bring the centre closer to business strategy development and to improve the coordination of divisional overlaps. This may help to re-balance the tension between long-term strategic business building and short-term financial control.

ICI

The overall assessment of Sir John Harvey-Jones's version of Strategic Control at ICI must also be positive. Again the company has achieved a turnaround in financial performance, with tighter control yielding major cost reductions within the divisions, and a cyclical upturn in the world chemical business in 1984 and 1985 boosting margins further. Investment and growth has also been concentrated on the more profitable divisions, such as Pharmaceuticals, which has raised the average return for the portfolio as a whole. Within the company, the greater decentralization of responsibility to the divisions has had a liberating effect. This new freedom, spurred by Harvey-Jones's repeated calls for greater entrepreneurialism, has led to faster, bolder, more flexible strategic decisions.

In spite of this, some problems have been more intractable, and although large improvements have been made in Fibres, Organics and Petrochemicals, these divisions still fail to make a satisfactory return. It is recognized that these commodity industries have faced extreme difficulties, and that given the major asset base, full recovery of performance would have been very hard to accomplish. Nevertheless, if these divisions had been independent companies, without support and cash flow from elsewhere in ICI, the need to survive might have dictated even more radical change. For these divisions, corporate willingness to think strategically and long term may have prevented financial controls from biting as sharply as was needed to maximize short-term performance. These divisions have now been combined with the other bulk chemical interests in a single organizational grouping, ICI Chemicals and Polymers Group, which is intended to be financially self-sufficient.

A second area in which progress has been comparatively slow is in the shift to higher added value specialty products and international markets. The decision to move in this direction was taken over a decade ago.[6] And although there has been some acceleration since Harvey-Jones became chairman, there has still been no fundamental restructuring of the portfolio along these lines. As in Courtaulds, the centre's relatively detached role in strategy development may have inhibited the emergence of more substantial thrusts. The recent corporate initiatives in electronics, advanced materials and specialty chemicals, and the Beatrice, Glidden and Stauffer acquisitions, are intended to increase the ICI push into these areas, and to augment divisional moves, without departing from the Strategic Control style. As such, they are directionally helpful. But to achieve real change in the balance of the portfolio, the centre may need to be more closely involved in the formulation of the strategies required – a style that is incompatible with the Strategic Control approach.

However, a measure of the success of the strategic decision-making process in ICI is the positive attitude to it at divisional level. The Harvey-Jones style encouraged debate, new ideas, openness; it frowned on bureaucracy and formality. Admittedly, given the diversity and size of ICI, the centre is seldom in a position to be closely knowledgeable about divisional affairs, and this can lead to difficulties in its relationships with the businesses. But with ICI's Strategic Control style, the centre's contribution now lies more in creating a favourable atmosphere and context for divisional strategic management. This makes less demand for detailed central knowledge about the businesses in the portfolio, and, subject to the reservations about rapid changes and bold moves, has worked well. It will be interesting to observe the further evolution of ICI's style under Denys Henderson.

Imperial Group

As at ICI and Courtaulds, Geoffrey Kent's chairmanship at Imperial Group was marked by a return to higher levels of profitability from a low point in the company's fortunes. Again, the control emphasis saw cost reductions and margin improvements in most businesses. The disposal programme was, however, much more active. The poultry, the eggs and the paper businesses and, finally, Howard Johnson, were all sold, on the grounds that they could not be made adequately profitable and did not fit with the company's long-term strategic thinking.

The strategic planning system introduced early in Kent's tenure was generally felt to provide a better information base for strategy development, a clearer rationale for resource allocation decisions, and a better forum for communication between the centre and the divisions than under the previous *laissez-faire*, Holding Company approach.

In the mid 1980s, however, some discontents emerged. The strategic planning process began to seem repetitive and bureaucratic, with too much emphasis on formal submissions and too little informal debate of issues. Furthermore, the level of corporate questioning, initially seen as valuable, did not keep pace with developing sophistication in the businesses, so that the quality control role became less effective. On the control side, financial objectives were seen to dominate discussions, and the concern with shorter-term profit targets was paramount. The company recognized the need for some modification to the strategic decision-making process, and work was under way to refine the approach at the time when the UB–Hanson Trust battle began.

The combined effect of the Strategic Control approach was therefore cautious, incremental progress. The resolution of the HoJo problem took time, and no major new avenues for growth were supported by the centre until the proposed UB merger. Although Imperial management argued the strategic rationale of this merger strongly, some City comment suggested that it stemmed from a mutual need for defence, as much as from a clear view of a way forward. In the event, Imperial has now lost its independence, and become part of Hanson Trust, one of our Financial Control companies. This will entail some changes in style for Imperial.

Plessey

Plessey's Strategic Control style dates back to the adoption of the Plessey Objectives Strategy and Tactics (POST) planning system in the late 1970s. The POST system was welcomed. It created a more disciplined approach to planning, and was intended to shift responsibility on to the businesses and divisions and away from the centre. Furthermore, clearer control objectives and sharper financial disciplines served to reduce costs and push up profitability. In addition, the underperforming Garrard consumer electronics business and other smaller businesses were divested. Results also benefited from the assumption by British Telecom of responsibility for the R&D costs associated with System X, allowing profits from the older generation of public switches to come through increasingly to the bottom line. After the introduction of POST, up to 1985 when Plessey, along with several other electronics companies, encountered the recession in the industry, the company was highly profitable.

Yet despite the strong profit performance, there is evidence of underlying competitive problems persisting throughout this period. Plessey's UK share of turnover, in an increasingly global competitive environment, actually rose from 47 per cent in 1978 to 71 per cent in 1986. The company acquired Stromberg Carlson in the United States. But the telecommunications business remained a small and relatively weak player in world terms. Real growth in sales, net of inflation, was low. Significant changes in divisional strategies were not forthcoming, with the exception of Components, which adopted a more speciality focus. The recession in the world electronics industry in 1985 brought these problems into much more prominence. Profits dipped, and Plessey faced an unwelcome bid from GEC.

It can be claimed that the Strategic Control style adopted by Plessey was not ideally suited to coping with these problems. Decentralization did not make it easy to develop an integrated corporate view of the businesses in which Plessey was competing; or for the centre to devise imaginative, aggressive strategies to deal with the company's difficult competitive position. At the business level, a strong corporate emphasis on financial control targets did not encourage bold long-term moves; it may even have led to some sacrifice of competitive position. Moreover, central concern with the underlying long-term strategy of some businesses was comparatively easily rebuffed by those business managements who could demonstrate a strong recent profit record, who were more closely knowledgeable about the details of their business, and who did not wish to make fundamental changes. The particular circumstances of Plessey, and the nature of Strategic Control as operated by them, appear to have led to a situation in which the company has not yet embarked upon the strategic changes needed. Recent amendments to the strategic planning process are intended to allow more time to debate the underlying strategic issues in each business, and to determine the right long-term directions. Furthermore, there have been several senior management changes, including the appointment of a new chief executive, Sir James Blyth. Plessey's approach to strategy in future will no doubt reflect these changes.

Vickers

The pattern of improved margins, cost-cutting and divestment of low-performing businesses is also found in Vickers. The recovery in profitability is more recent than in the other companies. Vickers had to wait until 1984 and 1985 to reap the benefits of earlier cost reductions, a recovery in demand for Rolls–Royce motor cars and the disposal of the Diesel Engine division, the South African interests, and a large part of the Australian business. Growth has also been concentrated on the more profitable Marine Engineering, Defence and Lithographic Printing Plate divisions. In these divisions, there have been investments in new production and marketing facilities as well as selective acquisitions (e.g. the Marine Engineering division acquired Sofec to enhance their position in the United States and to extend their product line, and the Defence division acquired the Royal Ordnance Factories tank business at Leeds). The Strategic Control approach has enabled David Plastow to be more selective in his allocation of resources, to press for improved margins through tighter controls, and to begin to rationalize a previously very disparate and diverse portfolio. In addition, as at Courtaulds and Imperial, the strategic planning process has yielded benefits in terms of an improved information base, higher quality strategy thinking and analysis, and a clearer forum for formal debate and determination of strategic directions. There is a feeling throughout the company that the quality of the strategic decision-making process has greatly improved since David Plastow became chief executive.

But there are also shortcomings. Although there has been rationalization of the portfolio, the company remains very diverse, spread across ten essentially unrelated divisions. Businesses such as KTM Machine Tools and Packaging Machinery underperformed for several years, yet still remained part of the portfolio. New growth points are emerging in Healthcare and Instruments, and in Office Furniture, both of which have made recent acquisitions to strengthen their overseas competitive strategies. But the long-term shape and coherence of the portfolio remains unclear, with the intention to concentrate behind selected 'core' businesses so far only partially realized.

Within the company, there is ambiguity concerning the strategic role of the centre. It is clear that extensive efforts are expended on the strategic planning process, both by the centre and the business units. But business unit management still feel – probably inevitably given the spread of the portfolio – that the centre is distant from the details of their businesses, and is not well enough placed to criticize plans constructively or to make suggestions for new directions. The financial emphasis in the control system can also be seen as at odds with longer-term thinking, and the incentive compensation system creates pressures to sacrifice long-term position to the achievement of budgeted profitability where trade-offs have to be made during the year. This is a particular problem for new growth businesses such as Medelec in the Healthcare field.

Recognition of these problems has led to the introduction of more selectivity and flexibility into the strategic planning system, to trials in some businesses of variations on the RoCE incentive compensation system, and to efforts by the centre to gain a more detailed understanding of business unit strategies. It is hoped that further concentration of the portfolio will facilitate these developments, and that the new structure with two main board group heads with corporate rather than business responsibilities will be helpful. The ambiguities perceived in the balance between planning and control are not likely to disappear, however, and the quality of Vickers' strategic decision-making process will essentially turn on how well the company learns to live with them.

Summary

In summary, the Strategic Control style has yielded real benefits for its proponents in terms of improved financial performance; portfolio rational-ization; systematic, structured and analytically based planning processes; and business unit motivation and capability for strategic thinking. Tighter controls have pushed up margins and reduced costs in many businesses. Where persistent low profitability or lack of strategic portfolio fit has occurred, closure or divestment decisions have been taken. New, more rigorous approaches to strategy planning have raised the quality of business level strategy thinking, brought new information to bear on strategy issues and improved the communication between the centre, the divisions and the businesses. And the decentralization philosophy has been welcomed by more capable and aggressive business level managements. These are impressive achievements and the Strategic Control companies in our sample include some of the best managed and most successful companies in the UK.

Nevertheless, Strategic Control has drawbacks. The balance between long-term strategic thinking and short-term control is hard to maintain, particularly given the difficulty of defining clear strategic control variables. This can lead to short-term and financial targets taking precedence over long-term strategy. By devolving responsibility for strategy development, the centre can become distant from the issues in each business, and therefore less able to contribute to their thinking. This, in turn, can prevent really major strategic initiatives that require corporate sponsorship from being taken. As a result, the Strategic Control companies have concentrated more on incremental moves in developing their portfolios. Building largely on existing business initiatives, they have, for example, made acquisitions which extended into new countries (Stromberg Carlson – Plessey Telecoms; Conforto – Vickers Office Furniture); related products (Beatrice – ICI Advanced Materials; Sofec – Vickers Marine Engineering); or related upstream or downstream stages of added value (Teca – Vickers Healthcare). But these acquisitions have been relatively modest in scope, and have tended to emerge from business unit strategies, perhaps with corporate encouragement, rather than from essentially corporate initiatives. This is in keeping with the decentralization philosophy, although both ICI (Glidden) and Vickers (Airshields and the Royal Ordnance Factory, Leeds) have made some significant acquisition moves in 1986. A rather remote corporate management can also lead to the Strategic Control planning process degenerating into bureaucracy and routine, and to potential cross-divisional synergies being missed.

Strategic Control can work well in a variety of circumstances. It is more able to handle a widely diverse portfolio than Strategic Planning, since the centre is less closely involved with each business. And it is better placed than Financial Control to take account of the long time horizons that some businesses require. However, companies that choose Strategic Control need to be aware of the drawbacks associated with the style, and to manage in the light of them.

Style Changes

As with the Strategic Planning companies, the Strategic Control companies have undergone changes in style in the recent past. Table 5.5 shows the styles of these companies before they adopted Strategic Control, and the approximate dates of the changes. There appear to have been two primary purposes behind the changes.

● Desire to introduce control into companies where it had previously been weak, or where divisional barons had been so strong that the centre had

Table 5.5 Strategic Control companies: style changes

	Previous style	Approximate date of change
Courtaulds	Centralized	late 1970s–early 1980s
ICI[a]	Holding Company[a]	early 1980s
Imperial	Holding Company	early 1980s
Plessey	Centralized	mid–late 1970s
Vickers	Holding Company	late 1970s

[a] But see ch. 7, n. 1.

wielded little influence. This motivation applies particularly to those companies that were previously in the Holding Company category.

● Desire to force line management to think more strategically and to take more responsibility for strategy. The previously Centralized companies felt this to be especially important.

As with the Strategic Planning companies, none of these transitions was made rapidly or easily. Vested interests tended to oppose the imposition of tighter controls. The ability to think strategically was not rapidly acquired by business managers who had been used to taking instructions from their superiors. In all cases the changes followed after, or were coincident with, a period of evident performance problems. Often these performance problems were at least partly caused by new acquisitions that had increased the diversity of the company, but had failed to achieve the results anticipated at the time of the acquisition. And in all cases, except Plessey, the changes were pushed through by new chief executives, without whom the changes would have been much less likely to occur. Frequently, extensive senior management changes were also necessary to reinforce and support change.

Looking forward, we see some evidence that the Strategic Control companies are today moving in the direction of Strategic Planning. The belief in devolved responsibility remains, but in each company attempts are being made to avoid the problem of the distant centre. The nature of these attempts differs. In Courtaulds, it is through the creation of the two major business groupings; in ICI, through the sponsorship of selected initiatives; in Plessey, through modifications to the planning system to allow a better informed dialogue on strategy; and in Vickers, through reducing the diversity of the portfolio, bringing the centre into closer contact with the remaining businesses and pushing forward more aggressively on the acquisitions front. The common thread is some enhancement in corporate management's planning influence on strategy. At the same time – but less strongly – there is a greater acceptance that controls in some businesses may need to be more flexible to encourage growth and adaptation.

The movement towards Strategic Planning is a recognition of some of the drawbacks and ambiguities in the Strategic Control style. We believe that it is a natural development in companies that have followed the Strategic Control style for some years – as is the reverse move from Strategic Planning towards Strategic Control. In both cases the balance of advantages and disadvantages associated with the styles means that a stable long-term equilibrium is less likely than a continuing shift in emphasis between them.

Notes

1 The field work for this research was carried out mainly in 1984 and 1985, and our descriptions of the companies refer to this period of time, although we note

obvious changes since then. For example, we discuss Imperial as an independent company, rather than as part of Hanson Trust, and we refer to Sir John Harvey-Jones as chairman of ICI.

2 The executive committee consists of the chief executive (Sir David Plastow), two group heads, the finance director, the commercial director, and the planning director.

3 The exception here is Plessey, which initiates the planning process by proposing certain objectives for each business from the centre, with the expectation that businesses will then devise plans to achieve the objectives set. During 1985, Vickers also began to move in this direction.

4 Perceptions of divisional management are more important than actual events in creating motivation to perform. In both Courtaulds and ICI it is generally perceived that control is now much tighter than it was, although relatively few people have in fact lost their jobs as a result of failure to perform.

5 Sir David Plastow believes that the importance of having a clearly understood and objectively measurable basis for incentive bonuses is so great that subjective strategic measures do more harm than good.

6 The history of ICI's slow progress towards these objectives is fully documented in Andrew Pettigrew's book, *The Awakening Giant* (Basil Blackwell, 1985).

6

Financial Control Companies

In Financial Control companies, the centre sees its main tasks as sanctioning expenditure, agreeing targets, monitoring performance against the targets and taking action to reorganize management teams that are performing poorly. The main differences between Financial Control and Strategic Control are:

- Financial Control companies have no formal planning systems; Strategic Control companies have elaborate planning systems.
- Financial Control companies are concerned mainly with the financial results and they control only against annual targets; Strategic Control companies try to measure strategic achievement and take a longer-term view of performance against targets.
- Financial Control companies apply strict short-term (2–4 year) payback criteria to investment decisions; Strategic Control companies are less rigid about avoiding long payback investments.

The Financial Control companies from our sample are BTR, Ferranti,[1] GEC, Hanson Trust and Tarmac. We will describe the management approach of these companies as before under the headings of planning influence and control influence.

Planning Influence

Like Strategic Control companies, Financial Control companies exert little influence on the formulation of strategies. They try to simplify their organization structure; they focus their review process on short-term performance; they sanction strategic direction rather than suggest it; and they tend to ignore interdependencies.

Organization Structure

The guiding theme of the structure of these companies is simplicity and accountability. They go to some length to create stand-alone business units that are run by managing directors with clear lines of responsibility. In this sense the structure is similar to that of Strategic Control companies. But Financial Control companies go further in decentralizing responsibility and setting up separate business units. Table 6.1 shows the divisional structure for the five companies.

Table 6.1　Financial Control companies: organization structure

	Number of divisions[a]	Overlaps between divisions[b]	Number of businesses[c]	Overlaps between businesses[b]
BTR	27	Low	150[d]	Low
Ferranti	5	Low	3	Medium
GEC	12	Low	170	Medium
Hanson Trust	9	Low	70	Low
Tarmac	6[e]	Low	6	—

[a] We use the term 'division' for the most aggregated organizational unit whose senior line executive is held profit-responsible for results.
[b] Judgemental assessment of degree of overlap in terms of common technologies, resources, markets and potential for synergies from coordination.
[c] Businesses that submit separate plans, budgets and reports to the centre.
[d] In total, BTR has almost 300 identified profit centres.
[e] In a recent reorganization Tarmac has reduced the number of divisions to 5.

BTR is probably the company in our sample with the largest number of profit centres to manage. The 300 or so profit centres are initially grouped into 150 subgroups. For example, the three hose and belting profit centres based at Farington, Lancashire report to a manager based in Farington and the seven Scandinavian mechanical handling companies report to a group manager based in Sweden. Above the subgroup level are group chief executives who may be responsible for one large business such as Tilcon (UK) or as many as 30 profit centres. The group chief executives in turn report to four regional chairmen – two for Europe, one for the Far East and one for North America. Supporting the regional chairmen are Sir Owen Green, chairman, John Cahill, the new chief executive, and Norman Ireland, the finance director.

As in the other Financial Control companies the philosophy is decentralization. BTR create general managers as low down in the organization as possible. In most cases, profit responsibility lies firmly with the profit centre managers. Subgroup, group and regional managers are all seen as extensions of the centre. They are agents of the centre playing the role of 'peripatetic chairmen' to the businesses, and the businesses submit information and reports directly to the centre with no filtering or editing at group level.

Subgroup managers and group chief executives have no staff of their own. 'They have a chauffeur and a secretary', explained Lionel Stammers, joint chief executive of the European Region. Corporate level staff functions other than accounting report to the regional chairmen. In the European Region, for example, there are legal, personnel, property, business systems, publicity, purchasing and financial control functions.

GEC is famous for its decentralized management structure. Each of the 170 or so unit managers is directly profit-responsible to the centre in Stanhope Gate, and can expect from time to time to get a telephone call from Lord Weinstock with questions on the previous month's figures. 'There is a solid line between Lord Weinstock and the units', explained Derek Roberts, joint deputy managing director (technical) of GEC.

Managers are expected to produce results for their units. Issues of coordination or integration with other units always take second place. If coordination is required, units may be combined. In 1981, the Office Systems Unit was set up with the intention of achieving coordination between the PABX, fax and computer activities. However, in 1984, in the face of poor results, the pressure for performance and accountability caused GEC to separate Office Systems into its original constituent parts. 'We were never able to identify the product', according to Malcolm Bates, deputy managing director. 'They kept telling us about this great opportunity in office systems and why we needed to put computers together with word processors and telephones. But we could never find the product. Our units are based on products. We then know what we are dealing with.' Unit managing directors report to a group managing director (group MD). 'The role played by the group MDs depends on the individuals concerned', explained John Lippitt, associate director. 'Most of them are located with the operating units and see their role as supporting the unit managers. They represent Stanhope Gate to the units and the units to Stanhope Gate. Most would feel closer to the units than to the centre.'

Staffing varies; some group MDs have only a secretary; others have a substantial staff, including finance, technical, legal and personnel departments. Some may be managing directors of a unit and will have responsibility for overseeing other units; others will be more remote and the managing directors of each unit will report to them.

There are 12 group MDs. The grouping of businesses is fluid. As a manager rises in stature in GEC, he is likely to be given responsibility for more and more businesses. Some of the groupings are of similar businesses, such as Marconi; others are more a result of circumstances or location.

The management of businesses around the world is also handled in a variety of ways. In the main, group MDs have responsibility for businesses located on the same continent; but not necessarily. A single unit reporting to a group MD may own a business operation in another country, and a product grouping may include businesses in different parts of the world. Stan Keyworth, for example, used to run Dorman Diesel in the UK, but he was also responsible for diesel businesses in France, Australia and Canada.

In summary, GEC has a patchwork organization structure. The units can be identified clearly and their responsibilities made explicit. The way in which the units fit into the hierarchy differs from group to group and it changes over time.

Hanson Trust's organization structure is simpler. Divisions are defined with clarity of accountability for profits. The businesses in the divisions report results directly to the centre and must negotiate budgets and capital expenditures with the centre, but their management line is to the division chief executive.

Hanson has two centres – one in New York with two group chairmen reporting to Sir Gordon White and one in London with three. Both these headquarters are very small, with about 20 executives in the UK and 12 in the United States. The group chairmen take responsibility for different divisions. Unlike the group MD in GEC, the Hanson group chairman's first loyalty is to the centre. He is part of corporate management; he is not profit-responsible; rather he acts as a particularly well informed non-executive director. His main concern is with management calibre and motivation, with senior appointments and with monitoring strategic developments in his divisions. The division chief executive, on the other hand, is not part of corporate management. He is the senior line executive for the businesses under his responsibility.

Ferranti's structure is similar to Hanson Trust's. Ferranti has five groups each responsible for ten or so businesses. The centre is small – less than 50 managers. There is a finance function that accounts for the bulk of the central staff, a personnel function containing a handful of people, John Pickin acting as technical coordinator across the group, a business development department (two people), a public relations and advertising department and other central coordination departments such as a patent office and transport office.

The philosophy is decentralization. 'You get far more out of people if they can see and understand a piece of the business and feel some ownership', explained one of Ferranti's group managing directors, who are referred to as 'the barons'. 'We do not overrule group managing directors. But we like to debate their plans with them and the three-year plan has to be approved by the board', explained Derek Alun-Jones, Ferranti's chief executive, as he described his philosophy of delegation with debate and controls. In turn, 'the barons' push the responsibility as far down as possible. In some, group management actively influence the strategies of the businesses. In others, the group headquarters is little more than a support activity monitoring progress and sanctioning expenditure. However, in all cases the group managing directors are profit-responsible line executives.

Ferranti's structure has one important difference from that of the other financial control companies – its Executive Committee. This committee is the main decision-making and monitoring body. It includes the group chief executives, Derek Alun-Jones, the finance director, the personnel manager and Lester George, an ex 'baron'. It meets once per week to review performance and take decisions. In the other Financial Control companies monitoring and decision-making is carried out directly between the centre and the division. Executive committees, as far as they exist, are not powerful decision-making committees, but are used as a discussion forum for joint policy issues.

Tarmac's organization structure is simpler still, reflecting its smaller size (sales of Tarmac £1.3bn, BTR £3.5bn, GEC £4.8bn). The company is divided into divisions reporting to a small headquarters in Ettingshall, Wolverhampton. The divisions are largely single businesses – Construction, Property, Housing, Quarrying – although each may comprise a number of profit centres. For example, the Housing division has 19 subsidiaries.

Tarmac places great emphasis on decentralization. 'We want division chief executives to feel that they have complete control over their businesses, that they are responsible for the costs of their inputs and the prices and volumes of their outputs', explained one Tarmac manager.

The centre of Tarmac performs two roles – an executive role and a support role. The executive role includes:

— reviewing and sanctioning budgets;
— monitoring performance against budget month by month;
— sanctioning capital expenditure proposals;
— managing the appointment and remuneration of the top people;
— controlling the development of strategy;
— managing the relationship with the financial community.

These activities are carried out by a four-man team – Sir Eric Pountain as chairman and chief executive and three group managing directors (group MDs). Each group MD takes a special interest in one or more of the divisions; but the formal lines of responsibility run directly from the division chief executives to the chairman.

The support role includes the provision of treasury, central accounting, tax, company secretarial work, press relations, planning, personnel and legal services to the businesses.

In summary, all five companies have highly decentralized structures in which the divisions or business units report directly to the centre, and group managers play a linking and surveillance role between the units and the centre.

All five have small headquarters. Tarmac's headquarters staff is under 100 and Hanson's is less than 50. BTR, Ferranti and GEC have similar-sized operations. BTR's headquarters is an inconspicuous building in a square near Vauxhall Bridge better known for its cricket pitch than its business achievements. The GEC headquarters at Stanhope Gate is renowned for its spartan, even austere, atmosphere. It signals clearly to the business units that extravagant expenditure on decorations or desks is not approved. This central cultural signal is picked up and amplified by the group level managers. While showing round the editor of *Business* magazine, who was doing a feature on GEC, the chief executive of

Marconi opened a door in the passage with flourish to reveal a darkened room. 'I bet we are the only £5bn company that turns the lights out in the executive loo', he said.

The five companies also have strong finance functions. Finance directors in the business units recognize their responsibility to central finance whether they have a formal dotted line relationship or not. Moreover, they play a more important role in decision–making than in Strategic Control or Strategic Planning companies. The financial orientation of the centre ensures that the finance functions in the businesses have a higher status than they otherwise would. 'The finance directors in the divisions know that they can always talk to me if they feel their managing director is about to do something silly', explained one group finance director. 'The numbers are important in this company', stated another manager, 'hence the status of accountants, controllers and finance directors is higher.'

Review Process

Strategic Planning and Strategic Control companies have elaborate formal processes for reviewing strategies and budgets. Financial Control companies have only one regular formal planning process – for reviewing and sanctioning the annual budget.[2] There is a philosophical as well as a practical reason for this. Jim Earle, a manager at Tarmac, expressed the philosophical reason: 'The danger is that managers have their eyes on the horizon when there are potholes in the road ahead', an appropriate comment from a company in the roadstone business. The assumption is that good managers will always be looking and planning ahead. In Financial Control companies, the centre provides the discipline to make sure they have got the next 12 months right.

A division managing director at BTR explained the practical reason, using as an example the 83–page strategic plan for a business that had just become his responsibility as a result of a major takeover. 'If each of our businesses submitted a document this size to our group executive, he would be swamped. It's not possible to take all of it in on one day. With 100 of these, half a year would be taken up.' He then referred to the 3-year plan for his other three businesses which comprised one page of text and three exhibits. Financial Control companies do not see *formal* strategic planning as a useful activity.

This operating style does not mean that business strategy takes a back seat. John Lippitt of GEC explained: 'I would not like you to think we ignore business strategy. We are constantly talking about our businesses and our products. There is a continuous discussion between management at all levels about whether we should bring out this new product or that, and whether we should develop it ourselves or license someone else's technology or buy from another manufacturer.' At which moment, as if to prove the point, the telephone rang and he was engaged in a 20-minute discussion about some important export contract. In Financial Control companies these discussions about strategy go on informally and continuously.

The sole purpose of the annual budget review is to agree what should be done over the next 12 months within the context of a continuous dialogue about the direction of the business. Indeed, the business managing directors generally appeared to be just as knowledgeable about the strategic issues in the businesses as those in Strategic Control or Strategic Planning companies. But they spend less time documenting these issues.

Financial Control companies also place considerable emphasis on ad hoc reviews. Hanson has a team of accountants that can be sent to a business at short notice when the explanation for a downturn in performance is unclear or unconvincing. GEC carry out similar reviews, sometimes initiated by a telephone call from Lord Weinstock. BTR are famous for carrying out price audits on their companies to test whether management have succeeded in putting prices up by the amount planned in the budget. The managers in the businesses are not offended when central management check up on their explanations. As one manager of a profit centre explained, 'It has happened this year. For the past 3 months we have not done what we said we would do. My material content has been high due to a change in product mix. My group MD has chosen to check up on this and asked the corporate finance people to come up and talk to my accountant. They confirmed the change in mix.'

In Ferranti, reviews are carried out through the line structure. An issue may be raised in an Executive Committee meeting and Derek Alun-Jones might say 'I would like to have another view on this one.' These reviews are then led by one of the small team of central managers. They use the finance people in the divisions for support, since there are no audit teams or financial analysts at the centre ready to go out on assignment.

Tarmac avoids this type of central review, for motivational and management development reasons. In its place they have a much more elaborate monitoring process. 'It is just when a management team are in trouble that you most want to interfere. Yet it is at this moment that it is most important to step back and let *them* sort it out', commented a Tarmac manager, to explain their preference for elaborate monitoring rather than ad hoc reviews.

The formal review process that results in the formulation of a budget for the next 12 months is the major event of the year in Financial Control companies, providing a rich source of anecdote and legend. We discuss these different budget processes in the section on agreeing objectives.

Broad Themes, Major Thrusts

The centre in Financial Control companies does not give guidance to business unit management in the form of broad themes or major thrusts. The centre believes that the business unit managers must be free to develop their own businesses, because they are closer to the market and the opportunities, and that the role of the centre is to sanction or reject the proposals put to them.

Tarmac's gradual expansion in North America is an interesting example of this philosophy. In a Strategic Planning company, the centre might tell the managers of the business units that the company as a whole wants to expand in the United States, and would actively seek opportunities and encourage business unit managers to do the same. The psychology in Tarmac is different. Central management recognize that the company needs to expand into the United States if it is to continue its growth, and are prepared to review proposals for acquisitions or expansion. For example, one of the group MDs spends half his time in the United States.

The centre does not encourage business unit management, however. Rather, it applies a restraining influence in the form of searching questions designed to find out whether management are ready to take on this extra complexity; what direct experience they have had in US markets; how successful they have been in acquiring and managing businesses at a distance. If all the signs are favourable, the centre will sanction the proposal.

One business unit manager in Tarmac explained:

> The home market is stable. Trying to gain market share would be counter-productive. I need to look abroad to grow the business. Because of personal contacts in the US I favour going there. Also I know the centre are receptive to moves into the US. I have floated the idea with my division chief executive and the group managing director. The response has been to go cautiously. The division needs to be more firmly grounded before the centre is likely to support this kind of move.

The philosophy in GEC is similar. Lord Weinstock sees his role as acting as a constraint on business management rather than as encouraging them to be bold. As Derek Roberts explained, 'Weinstock would say that if you come to him with a project and he says to you "No, don't go ahead with that one", and you go away and never raise the subject again, then your project can't have been very important. If he is initially unenthusiastic, he will weed out many of the badly thought out projects or half developed dreams.'

The lack of active support from the centre can cause problems in these companies. It makes business unit managers more cautious. While in Strategic Planning companies decisions can get bogged down in endless reviews and discussion, in Financial Control companies decisions are often delayed until the mood is right. This means they can be postponed repeatedly. A number of managers told us of projects that would have gone ahead faster if the centre had not been so cautious. In defence of the style, the centre recognizes this and argues that 'poorly thought out projects should be reconsidered, postponed or never presented in the first place.' Interestingly, the greatest level of unease with the system occurs at GEC where the centre imposes no formal controls on capital expenditure. In fairness, we did not talk to any manager at GEC who was able to identify a project currently being suppressed because of the cautiousness of the centre. But Derek Roberts believes that the weaker managers can fail to invest out of fear of exposing themselves to failure, a point corroborated by a variety of ex-GEC people to whom we talked. It appears that it is the centre's failure to approve decisions – capital requests or budgets – that can scare off managers. In an uncertain world they need the psychological support of an approving centre to boost their courage.

Specific Suggestions

Central management in Financial Control companies do, however, make suggestions on specific issues. In budget review meetings, in monthly or quarterly monitoring meetings, when capital requests are being considered, and informally on the telephone or in discussion, business level management receive specific advice of all kinds from central management. It may be about operating issues: 'The quality of photographs in our product literature needs improving', or 'Why don't you use our printing company for your printing?' It may be about management: 'You need a higher quality accountant.' Or it may be about strategy: 'You should do something about that business. Why don't you close it if you can't sell it?' Central and group managements in Financial Control companies are not, as the caricatures might suggest, 'distant bankers'. They follow financial performance closely and are quick to make suggestions if it does not match the plan. 'We peer at the business through the numbers', said John Lippitt of GEC. 'We are quick to give advice when we think the manager needs it', said a group chief executive at BTR.

We asked central and business managers why these suggestions did not amount to central influence on strategy, i.e., high planning influence. The reply of Graeme Odgers at Tarmac was typical: 'It doesn't matter how much advice I give a manager, because it's his reputation that is at stake. Unless he is convinced that a certain course of action will be successful, he won't do it. It is his budget, his targets and his head that is on the block.' A BTR profit centre manager commented: 'It comes back to me in the end. There is no point in my agreeing to a suggestion of Clive's [the group MD] if it will cause me to miss my budget or reduce my ability to move profits ahead.'

Another reason why the volume of suggestions does not add up to high central influence on strategy is the attitude of central management. They do not want to be in a position where they are telling subsidiary managers what to do. One group level manager illustrated this vividly: 'If you take our philosophy to the extreme, it means that you should never tell a managing director what to do. If you feel you have to *tell* him, you know it is time to replace him.'

Management of Interdependencies

Financial Control companies largely ignore interdependencies between businesses. They try to design the business units so that there are no interdependencies. Where there are overlaps, the centre does not manage the coordination between the businesses. It may arbitrate when necessary, but most intercompany transactions are carried out at arm's length.

In Hanson cross-division issues emerge only rarely. In Tarmac there are few overlaps between the Construction, Quarrying, Housing and Building businesses. Where there is a need for coordination, as in bitumen, sales are made at market rates and there are no central policies about managing the overlapping strategies.

In Ferranti the centre fosters fertilization across the group but draws back from interfering. The business development department is increasingly becoming involved in cross-group initiatives. There is a Defence Sales & Marketing Committee which meets every month to review all major up-coming contracts to decide which division, even which business unit, should take the lead. For the past few years, the centre has sponsored a management conference for the top 300–400 managers. This has been in part an opportunity for some management education and in part a chance for managers to discuss the business. At a recent conference the working groups recommended more cross-department and cross-group cooperation and proposed the creation of a Communications Committee to manage Ferranti's offering of communications products.

Within groups the position varies. In some groups, such as Computer Systems, coordination between the businesses is important. 'One of my main tasks is to get them [division MDs] to work together. They would prefer to go back to the days of free bountying', explained a group manager. In others, such as Instrumentation, the seven businesses are treated as completely independent companies.

The trend at Ferranti is towards more coordination between businesses. 'A matrix is now forming', explained one manager. Interestingly, greater coordination is not causing problems with the philosophy of decentralization because it is being pushed from the bottom up. 'The centre has not told the barons to cooperate. The centre has encouraged them to discover the need to cooperate for themselves. This has strengthened the centre's position. They are now doing jobs that the divisions want them to do', commented one division baron.

Ferranti's reaction to increases in the linkages between businesses is classic Financial Control behaviour. In other types of companies the centre might be setting up committees, appointing additional central staff and remonstrating with the businesses that are slow in recognizing the opportunities. In Ferranti, the outward appearance is the reverse. The centre maintains a head of steam for cooperation by dragging its feet and reacting slowly to bottom-up initiatives. Privately, our impression was that the centre wanted to encourage the trend, but, in public, the centre takes care that the initiative is seen to be a bottom-up pressure.

Formally, GEC takes a similar view towards overlap issues – each unit must take sole responsibility for its performance. But some attempt is made to manage linked businesses through the groups. For example, the group manager in charge of the Marconi businesses holds a monthly meeting with his managing directors to discuss common issues. In addition, a UK board has been formed consisting of the senior group managers in the UK. So far this board is no more than a talking shop; it has no important powers. It is however, a signal that greater coordination may be needed.

GEC recently decided to invest in a plant that will produce very large scale integrated (VLSI) chips, to service GEC's other businesses. Traditionally this would be a difficult decision to make. Malcolm Bates, the deputy managing director, expressed his discomfort with the project because all sales will be internal, and thus the payback and return on investment calculations will depend on transfer pricing policies for which there are no comparable market rates. It will be difficult to measure performance and even more difficult to define accountability – a problem that GEC likes to avoid. However, the plant is going to be built; a signal perhaps that GEC may be softening their strict Financial Control style.

BTR, like GEC, are active in managing some overlaps between businesses. Because the markets for some of their products are declining, they have found it necessary to merge profit centres to achieve overhead and efficiency savings. In the rubber hose and belting industry BTR have a number of profit centres in the UK and in Europe. Recently they have used a retired employee to analyse the position and recommend how they can achieve further rationalization to make best use of the available equipment.

In comparison, BTR appear to spend more time managing overlaps. This may, however, be due to the fact that they have disaggregated their businesses more than other companies causing more overlap issues to be exposed.

It is not surprising that Financial Control companies miss opportunities for synergy between businesses or that they avoid businesses where coordination and cooperation is essential. As a result they have few global businesses requiring manufacturing, research and marketing in a number of countries simultaneously. The cell structure cannot respond to the management complexity these businesses demand. The style appears to be more suited to simple, basic businesses or niche positions.

Resource Allocation

We will discuss two aspects of resource allocation: the capital approval process and the process for making major acquisition, divestment or closure decisions. The capital approval process in Financial Control companies has three distinct features. First, the payback criterion used for assessing projects is short – less than 4 years, frequently only 2. We asked one BTR manager why they used a 3–year payback criterion: 'Well, we tend to look for a 2–year payback. Three years is stretching it a bit. But 3 years has become the philosophy.' Second, the philosophy is that all 'good' projects will be funded. Each project is treated on its own merits, rather than set within the context of some overall strategic plan, and the centre accepts responsibility for raising sufficient finance to support all projects with the required payback. There is no sense of competition between projects for scarce capital resources. Third, the process is taken very seriously. It is used to establish the commitment of the managers proposing the investment. It is seen as an important aspect of the management system and is used to keep tight control. Moreover, the approval authority of division managing directors is much lower than in Strategic Control or Strategic Planning companies (table 6.2). These three features do not mean that capital requests are frequently turned down or sent back for revision. Most formal applications are approved without substantial discussion. Business managers quickly learn what proposals are likely to be acceptable and attempt to ensure that major issues have been addressed beforehand in informal discussion.

Table 6.2   Financial Control companies: limit of divisional authority for capital expenditures

	£'000	As % of net assets of company
BTR	~ 30[a]	< 0.01
Ferranti	25	0.02
GEC	—[b]	—
Hanson Trust	0.5	< 0.01
Tarmac	~ 50[a]	0.01

[a] Varies by division.
[b] GEC do not have any official approval levels for capital expenditures.

Hanson Trust's capital approval controls are well known. Every capital expenditure above £500 in the UK and $1,000 in the United States must be submitted to the centre for authorization. Furthermore, capital appropriations are not finally approved until they have received the chairman's blessing. The procedure clearly emphasizes the importance Hanson attaches to the reinvestment of shareholders' money and the need to justify expenditure with clear return on investment and profit commitments.

The approval process is not highly formalized, however. The business manager decides on the amount of supporting detail to be attached to the basic financial figures. The centre does not want highly specific information on technology or market forecasts. Its main concern is to establish that the manager in question believes he has a good opportunity to earn a return on the money he wants to invest.

Anthony Alexander, a group chairman at Hanson, explained: 'The accountants act as a counter or challenge to the enthusiasm of local management. The process of gaining their approval for a project ensures that projects will provide an adequate return to shareholders. Although local management tend to win, having to meet the challenge of the accountants generates very strong commitment.'

In Tarmac, approval levels are substantially higher than Hanson's and differ between divisions. Above a certain level, capital investments must be approved by the centre. The centre's criteria are clear. They want to know who the sponsors are and what their credibility is. They ask whether the proposal fits the current business and supports the direction the business is going in. They seek assurance that the return on investment will enhance the profitability ratios. And they look at the level of commitment of the sponsoring management team.

The formal approval process is not analytical, nor is it intended to provide for wide discussion. The analysis and discussion will have already taken place informally. The approval process is almost a ritual for generating commitment: 'The system depends on Sir Eric looking the man in the eye and saying "Can you make that work", and the manager replying "Yes".'

In GEC the process is also designed to generate commitment. Lord Weinstock's naturally probing, occasionally cynical style ensures that managers propose only investments they fully support. The difference at GEC is that no formal approval is required from the centre or given by it. Certain types of investments, for example in buildings, do need approval. But there is no figure, such as £100,000, above which capital requests must be approved by the centre. One GEC manager told us: 'When I arrived, I started looking for the rule book. I wanted to make some capital expenditure that was different from the proposal in the budget. I wanted to know what the procedure was. People told me "There is none. If you think it is the right thing to do, then go ahead and do it".'

Many managers like to inform the centre of their investment plans by submitting a capital request in the hope of gaining the centre's support. However, Lord Weinstock does not like to 'give approval'. He reserves judgement until he sees the results. He is happy to give an opinion, make suggestions and ask questions; but he believes that managers should do what they think is right and be prepared to be judged on the results.

The approval processes at BTR and Ferranti are similar to those at Tarmac. The difference lies in the authority given to each level in the hierarchy. At BTR a profit centre manager will have approval authority up to a certain level (say £5,000), subgroup managers at a higher level (say £15,000) and so on. At Ferranti, the approval levels are similarly structured although the amounts are different. Group managing directors can approve up to £25,000, the Executive Committee up to £100,000 and after that the proposal must go to the board.

The other major resource allocation process concerns the design of the portfolio. The initiative on decisions affecting the design of the portfolio – acquisitions and divestments – comes mainly from the centre, although it differs between companies. Hanson and BTR's acquisition activities are famous. There are certain principles of portfolio composition that guide acquisition (and divestment) policy in these companies. Hanson Trust have stated publicly that they favour basic industries with mature demand. They avoid businesses with long investment cycles, rapid technical change and high capital intensity. They prefer strong market positions in national or local businesses. BTR's main interests lie in markets where they can build specialty positions; they dislike commodity products. Directed mainly from the centre, both companies have made huge acquisitions, such as Thomas Tilling and Dunlop by BTR and British EverReady, London Brick, SCM and Imperial by Hanson. Acquisitions are also initiated lower down in the structure, but they are few and have much less impact.

At Hanson the immediate post-acquisition phase is critical. A complete freeze is placed on all capital expenditure until Hanson Trust management feel they have got to grips with the new company. During the early months a Hanson Trust group chairman will take responsibility for major decisions on which businesses in the new company to keep and which to divest, and on management organization and staffing; and for installing the Hanson reporting and control system. The philosophy, however, is to retain the corporate identity of the acquired company and to make maximum use of existing management in the company. Thus Berec was actually renamed British EverReady, the name under which the company had historically traded; and, although all the board members and a sizeable fraction of middle management departed, many of the remaining middle managers were promoted. 'We frequently find that detailed improvement plans already exist in a company', claimed Tony Alexander, one of Hanson's corporate acquisition team, 'but they have got enmeshed in a web of vested interests. Lacking past involvements, we can break through the inertia and recreate the will to make decisions.'

Identification with Hanson Trust comes from bringing managers into the lucrative Hanson stock option scheme, and providing generous incentive bonus opportunities. As results begin to come through, identification with Hanson is further enhanced by feeling part of a winning team. After a few months of hands-on transitional management, during which many of the 'nasty' decisions have been made, the group chairman withdraws to his normal surveillance role, leaving the running of the businesses to the management team he has appointed. This procedure, combined with clearer objectives and sharper financial controls, has dramatically improved the performance of a number of Hanson acquisitions.

In Ferranti the philosophy of decentralization also influences the way decisions are made about the shape of the portfolio. The stimulus can come from the divisions (e.g. gate arrays), from the centre (e.g. cellular radio) or from outside (e.g. the joint venture with GTE). Before any major action is taken, however, the new activity must be supported by one of the barons. In the case of the PABX joint venture with GTE, the Computer Systems Group was already fully committed with projects. The joint venture would, therefore, have been unlikely to go ahead if it had not been enthusiastically embraced by the Instrumentation Group.

The centre's role in these initiatives is that of catalyst and facilitator. The centre will not cross the line between sell and tell, although Derek Alun-

Jones is apparently increasing the amount of advice he gives to the groups. 'He thinks we should be doing more business in the States. The pressure is there. He also said that we should be considering local acquisitions. He is constantly pushing me to expand. But it's my decision', explained one group managing director.

GEC prefers not to initiate acquisitions from the centre. Central managers expect proposals to come from unit managers or group level executives. These proposals may result in the creation of a new group, as with the acquisition of Avery, the weighing machine company. But the sponsorship does not normally come from the centre.

Tarmac also follows this policy.

> The centre's role is to sanction and monitor. The sponsorship for initiatives must come from the divisions. We do not make centrally determined initiatives. We do have siren voices that say: 'Why don't you make a major acquisition?' We don't see that as necessary. Moreover, it would dilute our management philosophy and could reduce the centre's effectiveness in monitoring and sanctioning.

The type of acquisitions made by BTR and Hanson are also different from those made by Tarmac and GEC. BTR and Hanson make major acquisitions of businesses that they expect to be able to manage better. They may have few links with the existing portfolio. The important issue is whether the business will respond to the Financial Control style of management. Both these companies now have such a broad range of businesses in their portfolio that there is likely to be some linkage between their existing businesses and acquisition candidates. But the main reason for the acquisition is manageability rather than industrial logic.

GEC and Tarmac focus more on acquisitions that have some industrial logic. GEC's acquisitions of Avery and AB Dick were both made with the expectation of bringing some GEC skills and technology to support the company. Tarmac's quarrying and roadstone acquisitions, such as Hoveringham, were made to strengthen their existing Quarry Products division and have been fully integrated with the existing management structure. Tarmac management use their sanctioning role to control the development of the portfolio, and they encourage division chief executives to focus their attention on contiguous business areas. 'I do not like the concept that because things are difficult in areas you know, you should try something new in areas you don't know. There are always things you can do to improve; you build from the bottom up; you grow in controlled steps', stated one group managing director.

But in all the Financial Control companies, there is scepticism about 'strategic' acquisitions that cannot be justified on short-term payback criteria, but which are proposed to achieve strategic goals. The same demanding financial criteria are applied to investment in acquisitions as to organic capital expenditure proposals.

Fewer differences exist between Financial Control companies on divestment and closure. All four companies are willing to act speedily to exit from the businesses that are not performing or do not easily fit with the Financial Control style. Cornhill Insurance (BTR), Plascom (Tarmac) and Courage and Glidden (Hanson) were sold, in part because they did not fit easily with the Financial Control style. The tyre business of BTR, office systems in GEC and British EverReady's operations in Europe were closed, or disposed of, because of poor performance.

Control Influence

Financial Control companies focus on control, defining simple, clear objectives and controlling against them. Failure to perform brings immediate danger to the responsible management team; while success is rewarded with money, status and additional responsibility. Here we will examine the way in which they agree objectives, monitor results and apply incentives.

Agreeing Objectives

The Financial Control companies set similar objectives for their businesses: business management must meet their agreed budget figures for the year and improve performance year on year. The critical occasion, therefore, is the annual budget review. The companies use different processes, but all are designed to the same end: to set for the next year a stretching standard of performance that business managers are committed to achieve.

At Hanson Trust business management prepare the budgets and post them to the centre. Up to this point there is little discussion with the centre. The budget is then reviewed in turn by a corporate controller at the centre, by the finance director, by the group chairman responsible for the business, and by Lord Hanson himself. The corporate management group discuss the budget before final approval. There is no formal sequence of meetings. The issues raised are dealt with briefly or extensively. On occasion a phone call will be sufficient; at other times, the issues will be debated at length.

Two kinds of pressure are put on business managers at the annual review: to submit a budget they know they can achieve; and at the same time, to aim for results that are, if possible, better than the previous year's. The centre does not tell the businesses what their budget should be, but tries to 'energize' the ambitions of the business management team.

At Ferranti the budget process is preceded by a 3-year business plan (discussed in more detail in the section on Financial Programming). The medium-term plan enables the Finance Director to refine and adjust the objectives for the annual budget. 'I send out target profit and cash flow objectives for each business. I develop these from looking at the 3-year plans and talking to Derek [Alun-Jones] about the overall balance of the business. It usually involves knocking off a few million from the cash requirements and adding a few million to the profit figures', said Charles Scott, Ferranti's finance director.

The annual budgeting process is designed to stretch the targets for divisions and groups. First the centre provides suggested financial targets for each group. Each business then produces a budget based on what it thinks it can achieve. The group managing director will review the budgets against the objectives he has been given and identify weaknesses. Where a business expects to perform substantially below group standards, the budget is only likely to be passed if the 3-year plan looks right.

After the group managing director has completed his review, Derek Alun-Jones and the finance director will examine the budgets. They would normally spend a whole day at each group. At this stage some budgets may be discussed at such length that further revisions are necessary. Also, Derek Alun-Jones may stretch the budgets along some dimension important to the overall picture. It would usually be cash flow or profit.

Finally, the budgets are pulled together into a total Ferranti budget and the whole package is presented to a joint meeting of the board and the Executive Committee. At this stage the outside directors take up the role of challenger and Derek Alun-Jones plays a linking role. The result of this last stage in the process may be further stretching of the budgets of one or two departments as well as an enhanced commitment to the plan. 'The iterative nature of our planning process is important. We can't finally agree budgets until we have been back and forth a few times. It can be frustrating but it means we are all committed to the plan', explained Derek Alun-Jones.

The importance of the outside directors in Ferranti is an unusual feature. In most companies the role of the outside directors appears to be minimal; they are never spontaneously mentioned as an important part of the process. But in Ferranti, they have a critical role. Since Ferranti is the smallest company in the sample, the outsiders may find it easier to understand the business. But their role in the process is not based on special business knowledge; they apply another round of objective financial criticism. 'They probably get together before the meeting and divide the work load up. But they always seem to have done their home-work and focus in on the few weak spots', explained a group managing director.

In BTR the budget is called a 'profit plan': 'We call it a profit plan not a budget because it's about making money not spending money.' The process starts with the group chief executives issuing performance expectations to the managing directors of the profit centres. 'We make an assessment of where the business is going in process terms (i.e. costs), in product terms (i.e. sales) and in acquisition terms. We then set specific growth and profit targets. The purpose is to prevent the business from coming in with a profit plan that is widely out', explained Clive Stearnes, a group chief executive.

BTR's focus is to stretch the business managers. Once the centre is comfortable that the manager is going to submit a budget in line with expectations, there is little informal discussion. The important event is the review meeting attended by the group chief executive, the regional chairman and, possibly, Sir Owen Green and the finance director. At this meeting the managing director of the profit centre, his subgroup manager, their finance director and possibly one other manager will present the plan – two pages of commentary, a summary sheet of ratios and seven or eight supporting pages.

The questioning and challenge is very thorough. Cost ratios, pricing and margins are all discussed in detail. It is not unusual for the questioning to result in a revision of one of the ratios and an adjustment (usually upwards) to the profit forecast. 'As a generalization, we end up by giving a bit more [profit]. We may have forecast a margin decline from 10 per cent to 9 per cent because of a change in mix. In the discussion they may squeeze us back up to 9.5 per cent. They have refined the system of reporting so that it is very difficult to hide anything', stated one business manager. At the end of the meeting the profit plan is agreed and becomes the target for the year. It takes Lionel Stammers one month to agree profit plans for each of the 85 profit centres in his half of the European Region.

Tarmac places emphasis on stretch – getting managers to commit themselves to a budget that will make great demands on them. Graeme Odgers explained:

> The budgetary process is critical, more so than in most other companies. We want to establish for the year ahead what the actual performance will be of each division, broken down into sub-elements where necessary. We do not *impose* standards on divisions from the centre. We ask the divisions to *put themselves* on the 'high wire' – something that, when achieved, will make everyone feel highly satisfied with their efforts.

The centre is close enough to the businesses to know when the budget does not stretch management. When this happens, the centre rejects the budget and asks the managers to go back and try again. Each year a third of the budgets may be rejected at the first review. It can be a tense time. Division managers may be afraid to promise more profit; but they are also afraid of failing to rise to the centre's challenge.

In Tarmac the chairman, the three group managing directors, the division chief executive and all his senior management team are present at the budget review discussions. The purpose is to achieve team commitment to the targets at both divisional and central levels.

At GEC the centre and the management team of each unit meet to discuss the budget, but the meeting has a different purpose from that in Tarmac. The GEC meeting is used to challenge and probe rather than to give approval. The atmosphere is informal; Lord Weinstock may wander in or out. Any member of the central management team can ask questions of any member of the business management team. The meeting has no formal ending. It may be interrupted by lunch, or it may peter out as central managers are called away. As with capital investments, Lord Weinstock likes to reserve judgement. His philosophy is that managers should always be striving to do better and that his role is to find out if they are doing as well as they can. Then, if they appear to be doing so, he urges them to do better still. A budget is never rejected, although Lord Weinstock or deputy managing director Malcolm Bates may say that he considers it inadequate. It is then for the unit management team to try to perform substantially better than proposed in the budget. Only 5 per cent of units produce a new budget as a result of the review.

Although this process is similar to the process used by Strategic Planning and Strategic Control companies, Financial Control companies devote much more effort to probing the figures, and 'stretching' the targets, and to obtaining the commitment of business managers to these targets. More-over, the process is characterized by a seriousness that stems from the recognition that the centre may not accept failure. The budget-setting process is a time when careers are at stake.

Monitoring Results

Financial Control companies regard it as essential to catch variances from budget before they have gone too far. To this end they monitor results on a monthly and quarterly basis. In all five of our companies the business units submit monthly results directly to the centre on standard forms.

BTR's system is a good example. Four days after the end of each period the profit centres produce a 'flash report' which consists of a few important numbers such as sales and orders. After 11 working days, companies are expected to produce a full profit statement and balance sheet. Together with some brief prose and a system for highlighting peak events, this pack is sent to the centre, the regional level and group level managers. If the reports show that something is going wrong, the centre asks for the reasons why, and business management are expected to answer convincingly. We asked Malcolm Bates of GEC how many years a manager could fail to meet his budget before expecting to lose his job. His response was telling and only partly tongue-in-cheek: 'How many years? You mean how many months. He might last for six months or he might not.'

At BTR, Hanson and GEC the financial controllers at the centre review the monthly results and then pass them to the line management with comments. At GEC, Lord Weinstock or Malcolm Bates may telephone a unit manager or his group manager directly to ask about his figures. GEC's group managers play a similar role *vis-à-vis* unit managers. As a result, the monitoring system operates on an exceptions basis. There are few formal meetings and almost no regular review meetings.

One note from Lord Weinstock to the unit managing directors emphasized the importance of this direct contact. It explained, in blunt language, that Lord Weinstock found himself talking too frequently to telephone operators and secretaries. He pointed out that managers should be answering their telephones in person. He hoped he would have less trouble getting through to the person he wanted in future.

At Hanson and BTR the group managers act as non-executive chairmen and review the results for the month at the regular board meetings for each company. These meetings focus closely on variances from plan, the causes for the variances and the actions needed to change the position. On major items, the financial controllers in the centre are likely to have been in touch with the local finance function prior to the meeting. This gives local management some advance notice of the main issues of concern.

Ferranti's monitoring process is unusual because it involves managers in different groups. The Executive Committee is the formal review body. It meets monthly and the main item on the agenda is the performance of each group during the previous period. 'It's all a process of keeping each other on our toes. If Derek [Alun-Jones] doesn't kick me every now and again I am likely to relax. It's the same with my people. The system is carefully designed so that once per month the wheel turns round, picks you up, gives you a good going over, and drops you down again', explained one group chief executive referring to the monthly Executive Committee meetings.

These meetings are masterfully handled by Derek Alun-Jones. Inevitably, the barons will not normally 'initiate discussion on an issue in someone else's area'. So the main burden of probing falls on Alun-Jones and Lester George: 'They have no compunction about embarrassing a manager and asking awkward questions.' However, it is not a one-way discussion. Alun-Jones will bring in the other group managing directors by asking them what they think. The probing is firm, dedicated to uncovering the true facts and ensuring that a sound course of action will be taken. 'After one occasion, when Derek really gave me a grilling, he came up afterwards and explained that he had put me on the spot to make sure that I could see the weakness in my position', recalled a group chief executive.

The monitoring process at Tarmac is formal, involving close contact between the centre and the divisions. The chairman and the group managing directors hold a monthly meeting with the full management team of each division to review results. They focus on the previous month's performance and on the issues it has raised. The meetings are seen by the centre as important and valuable. According to one of the group managing directors, they have four aims:

1 To acquaint senior management with what is happening in each division. They like to be totally immersed in the business issues.
2 To evaluate the quality of the chief executive of the division and his management team.
3 To provide an opportunity for the centre to influence decision-making. It's a bottom-up approach. But if the centre says that something looks interesting, the division will certainly give it some attention.
4 To put pressure where necessary to bring current performance into line with expectations.

The division managers also find the meetings useful. They see them as a form of feedback on their performance rather than as problem-solving sessions. They are highly sensitive to the atmosphere. 'Sometimes we are laughing and joking and other times it is very serious. The atmosphere depends on how much poking around Sir Eric [Pountain] does. It is the atmosphere he establishes that is important, rather than any specific statements he makes', commented one division chief executive.

The workload for central management is high. The meetings can absorb 2 weeks, including preparation, in every month. But they are the key to Tarmac's system. They are used to keep the pressure on management to meet the promised budget figures. 'A division chief executive can only revise his budget downwards if he goes through some personal trauma. We can't stand the confessional. If management confesses that they have got it wrong, they are just transferring the problem from them to us. We resist changes in budget very strongly.'

The insistence that business management meet the agreed budget is much greater in Financial Control companies than in Strategic Control or Strategic Planning companies. The budget is viewed as a contract (or in Tarmac's language 'a promise') between the centre and the business. The monitoring process is used to maintain the pressure for performance. 'If they don't deliver they should feel very bad. They should feel that they have failed themselves and that life is awful. On the other hand, if they succeed they will feel like winners. They will be basking', commented one senior manager.

Central management's close surveillance of results enables them to ensure that no business goes too far astray before remedial action is taken. It also gives central management an understanding of the reasons for variances from budget. Where the business is stable, this knowledge enables the centre to judge next year's budget without the elaborate planning processes used in Strategic Planning or Strategic Control companies.

The centre faces a problem when the business is unstable. Inevitably, businesses miss their budgets and managers do not always lose their jobs as a result. 'Part of the process is to allow a management team to go over the cliff and catch them before they hit the bottom', explained the group chief executive of Tarmac's Housing division. If the manager is good, he will realize that the business is in trouble and learn from the experience. If not, he will be replaced. But when the business environment is unpredictable, the centre may not be able to see the edge of the cliff or catch the manager before he hits the bottom. As a result, Financial Control companies appear to avoid unstable businesses, especially those with fierce competition. At a discussion meeting we asked managers from Hanson Trust and BTR how they reacted to Japanese competition. They agreed that 'those are good businesses to avoid.'

Action and Incentives

The Financial Control companies believe firmly in the 'stick' as a motivation tool. Their incentive systems – the financial carrot – may not differ substantially from those used by Strategic Planning and Strategic Control companies. But they are quicker to replace managers, fiercer in applying pressure through the monitoring process, and more effective at recognizing and acclaiming good performance. They believe that management changes are necessary to raise the quality of managers. They feel that it is not possible to judge a manager's ability until he is given the opportunity to demonstrate it, and that it is important to move him on quickly if he does not rise to the occasion.

In Tarmac, three division chief executives have changed jobs in the past 4 years. At GEC, it is not uncommon for unit managers to be encouraged to move on. 'In any year there are 20 managers who leave the budget reviews shaking in their shoes', said Malcolm Bates. Hanson regularly replaces senior members of the companies it acquires and, in one of BTR's group, four of the 16 managing directors have been replaced for performance reasons in the past 3 years.

Failure is not tolerated in Financial Control companies. As one business manager put it, 'If you succeed, you are rewarded. If you don't, you are out.' Because the performance criteria are clear, both sides know whether or not they have been met. Surprisingly, division management are not demoralized by the threat of what might happen if they fail. Instead they try harder, knowing that their achievement will be clearly recognized if they succeed. A manager at BTR, referring to the tight corporate control process and the examination of performance ratios, observed that: 'They exude something that makes you feel encouraged even though what they're doing to you is mightily unpleasant.'

Hanson operates a bonus scheme for all senior division managers based on the individual division's performance against RoCE and profit growth targets. In theory, a manager could double his base salary; in practice, the bonus is more likely to be between 25 and 40 per cent of salary (table 6.3).

Table 6.3 Financial Control companies: incentive compensation schemes

	Incentive bonus	Basis	Average level[a] (%)	Maximum level (%)	Stock options
BTR	No	—	—	—	Yes
Ferranti	Yes	Actual vs budget	< 7	12.5	Yes
GEC	No	—	—	—	N/A
Hanson Trust	Yes	Actual vs budget	—[b]	—	Yes
Tarmac	Yes	Group results	~ 25	—	Yes

N/A Not available.
[a] Percentage of base salary.
[b] Size of bonus can vary widely, even up to 100 per cent of salary in exceptional circumstances, although it is more normally between 25 and 40 per cent.

At Tarmac the bonus system is related to the performance of Tarmac as a whole and includes senior managers. The average payout is less than at Hanson. The main incentive at Tarmac is to be at the top of the achievement ladder: 'We want our managers to feel like winners. We help them set objectives that they will be proud of achieving. It's like Manchester United. They won't accept anything less than the top three places. We want our managers to feel like that.' The target-setting and monitoring process is designed to help managers achieve this feeling of satisfaction.

The motivation system at BTR is similar to that at Tarmac. Financial incentives are limited to a stock option programme that has proved highly profitable. But the real motivation is to be part of the BTR success and to be able to perform better than the average BTR company.

At Ferranti there is a bonus scheme for senior managers with a maximum payout of 12.5 per cent of salary, although it is more likely to be in the range 5–7 per cent. The bonus is linked to budget targets and Derek Alun-Jones can vary the target depending on the priority for the year. One year it might be based mainly on return on capital, another on profit and another on cash flow. Ferranti also have a stock option plan for the top 200 managers.

GEC's system has few structured incentives. Management do not receive large bonuses and praise from the centre is rare. 'A lack of criticism is considered sufficient praise', said Malcolm Bates. 'GEC consider that the manager's job is to apply all his effort to improve his business. Success is to be expected. Anything less is not acceptable.'

Summary of Financial Control Characteristics

The common denominators between the companies we have termed Financial Control are, therefore, as follows:

- Delegation of responsibility for strategy development to business unit and even profit centre level.
- Group level managers that provide a transparent flow of information between the businesses and the centre.
- A focus on the budget process as the most important planning process.
- Avoidance of initiatives from the centre in the form of themes or thrusts, yet liberal use of suggestions from the centre where appropriate.
- Clear screening of investment projects and the use of short-term payback criteria to eliminate weak projects.
- A philosophy that the centre will fund all 'good' projects.
- Major use of acquisitions, initiated by the centre and by divisions, as the engine for growth.
- Insistence that the budget is a contract between the centre and the businesses and that annual financial performance is the critical measure of achievement.

● Frequent monitoring and review of performance against budget.
● Strong pressure immediately applied to businesses with performance problems, and management changes readily made in the face of continued problems.

In the previous section we have emphasized these common elements in order to clarify the Financial Control style and contrast it with the other styles of management. But we have also identified differences between the companies. For example:

1 GEC's and Ferranti's group level managers are positioned differently from those in the other companies. They feel closer to the divisions than to the centre and spend more energy representing the divisions to the centre than vice versa.
2 GEC and Tarmac focus more on contiguous acquisitions that have industrial logic. Hanson and BTR have become conglomerates looking for acquisition candidates in any industry that will respond to the Financial Control style. Ferranti have made little use of acquisitions.
3 Tarmac's and Ferranti's monitoring processes are unusual. Tarmac's process is elaborate and time-consuming and does not operate on an exceptions basis. Ferranti's process is similar, but it is carried out in open session with all division managers present. As a result it is less time-consuming, but runs the risk of becoming political.

These differences are fascinating and may well reward further study. But taken as a whole, the similarities are many and the differences few.

In describing the Financial Control style we are not, therefore, saying that all the Financial Control companies have identical management processes. Rather, we are saying that along certain key dimensions they are similar and that, as a group, they are different from Strategic Control or Strategic Planning companies.

Results

We have assessed the results of the Financial Control style in the same way as for the Strategic Planning and Strategic Control styles. We looked at the nature of corporate and business unit strategies, the level of management satisfaction with the system and the financial performance. Taking the five companies together, the main features are that they have (with two exceptions) a limited, mainly financial role for corporate level strategy; they pursue business strategies that are cautious, often aimed at higher margin niches; they generate high levels of motivation and satisfaction in their managements; and they produce excellent financial results. Their main weakness is a failure to grow organically.

Hanson Trust

Hanson Trust's corporate strategy is evident from the acquisitions they have made. As Lord Hanson himself stated, 'We aim to invest in good basic businesses, producing essential products for which there is a clear continuing demand. We avoid areas of very high technology. We do not want to be involved in businesses which are highly capital intensive and where decision-making has to be centralized. We want to be concerned with businesses where our 'free form' management approach is appropriate.' Companies such as SCM (typewriters), Imperial (cigarettes), EverReady (batteries) and London Brick (bricks) fit this mould. Hanson has been quick to sell off parts of these acquisitions that do not fit.

But the corporate strategy involves more than acquiring businesses in the right industries. It also involves finding businesses that are undervalued because of poor management or poor relations with the financial community. The two most recent acquisitions, SCM and Imperial, demonstrate this philosophy best. With SCM, Hanson has sold off about 70 per cent of the businesses in the original company, and in the process recouped the total acquisition cost of $1bn. The remaining businesses with annual profits of $160 million have in effect been acquired for nothing. The Imperial acquisition is more recent, but the same policy is being pursued. Hanson has sold the brewing interests (Courage) to Elders IXL and Golden Wonder crisps to Dalgety. In addition, the Imperial headquarters was almost completely eliminated. Some 250 of the 300 or so headquarters staff were issued with redundancy notices within 3 weeks of the takeover.

The corporate strategy is, therefore, to acquire undervalued businesses in basic industries; to apply Hanson's decentralized management approach to these businesses; and to sell businesses that do not fit the management approach or that are worth more to someone else than they are to Hanson. This last point is a particular feature of Hanson's strategy. As one senior manager commented: 'All our businesses are for sale, all of the time. If we think we can get more for them than they are worth to us, we will sell.'

At the business unit level, there is no formula for a winning strategy. Each business makes its own way forward, guided only by return on capital and profit objectives. All business units search for and eliminate underutilized assets and loss-making operations, and there is normally a strong focus on improving basic production costs and efficiencies. Most newly acquired businesses, therefore, go through a phase of retrenchment and efficiency improvement which may last for 3–5 years. Once the base business has been protected, different strategies are developed for different situations.

In EverReady the strategy is to contain the advance of Duracell without disrupting the price levels in the UK. The focus is on advertising and cost reduction rather than aggressive warface. In Butterly Bricks, one of Hanson's original businesses, the emphasis has been on growth to exploit the special advantages of Butterly's products.

Hanson Trust in particular, along with GEC, has been criticized for a management system that causes the units to milk their businesses. It is true that the emphasis in Hanson has been on return on capital and cash flow rather than market share growth, but we have not found evidence of obvious milking strategies in support of these objectives.

Within Hanson, as in the other Financial Control companies, there are few critics of the management approach. Satisfaction, motivation and energy levels are high, even for the nasty jobs like cost cutting and rationalization. There are managers (now no longer with Hanson) who believe that the system adds little to the businesses. But there are many others, even including some who were made redundant from Imperial for example, who argue that the changes brought in by Hanson were long overdue.

Hanson's financial performance cannot be faulted. Although return on sales and return on capital have been below that of the average of our sample during the period 1981–5, return on equity at 17 per cent has been higher than all companies except Plessey (appendix 1). Hanson is also top of the list in share price growth and earnings per share growth. The one blot on Hanson's performance record is organic growth. Between 1981 and 1985, Hanson averaged an annual decline of 9 per cent in its ongoing fixed asset base, offset by an annual increase in assets of 66 per cent from acquisitions net of divestments. It is this that has caused many observers to accuse Hanson of asset stripping.

BTR

BTR's overall results are very similar to those of Hanson. Corporate strategy is focused on acquisitions of mature businesses with weak management teams. Business unit strategies are frequently cautious, focusing on high margin business. Management satisfaction is high and the financial performance has been almost as good as Hanson's.

There are, however, some important differences. BTR does not have a 'for sale' sign on its businesses in the same way that Hanson does. There have been few divestments and those that have been made have occurred only after BTR decided that the business would not respond well to the BTR management approach. Cornhill Insurance, bought with Thomas Tilling, was sold after 3 years in the BTR portfolio and only after management had decided that it was not their sort of business. In the same way, BTR's book publishing interests were sold to Octopus after the management style had been tested and BTR realized that Octopus would be likely to do a better job. Interestingly, BTR sold the business in exchange for shares and have retained a large shareholding in Octopus.

Another difference between the results of BTR and Hanson is caused by BTR's focus on return on sales. Lionel Stammers pointed out that BTR prefers niche businesses rather than volume manufacturing and particularly businesses that involve customer problem-solving. In the belting and hose businesses in Farrington, BTR had gradually withdrawn from the major volume business and focused more attention on interesting niches such as steel cord belting and high pressure water hoses. The emphasis on high return on sales (10 per cent) probably pushes BTR's business units into more niche strategies than Hanson's.

In BTR more attention is devoted to monitoring, and managers at the bottom appear to relish the chance of sitting down with their bosses to review the annual budget or quarterly performance. 'Corporate management are very clever. They are always able to ask questions that pinpoint important issues or throw light on some problem', said Brian Lees, a unit managing director. This respect for senior management creates high levels of satisfaction lower down.

Like Hanson, BTR's financial performance has been excellent (appendix 1). At 15 per cent, BTR has the highest return on sales performance, and excellent return on equity and capital figures. Share price and earnings per share performance has been only slightly below that of Hanson. However, like Hanson, BTR has not achieved much organic growth measured by fixed asset increases. Ongoing fixed assets have declined by 3 per cent per year, offset by net acquisition growth of 51 per cent per year.

Tarmac

Tarmac's corporate level strategy has not included acquisitions. They have encouraged acquisitions at the division level, but they have not initiated any from the centre. Even the divestment of Plascom, the oil subsidiary, was initiated at division level. The centre was involved and encouraged the move, but the initiative came from the division.

Strategies at the division level have varied. The Quarry Products division has grown mainly by acquiring quarrying assets and integrating them under the existing management team. The profits of the Construction division have grown by focusing on high margin contracts and cutting out marginal business. Since 1980, sales of the Construction division had fallen by more than 25 per cent after adjusting for inflation. The Housing division has achieved remarkable growth by organic expansion, driven by better management skills and better products. In 4 years they have moved from number three in the industry to the number one position, ahead of Wimpey and Barratt. The variety of strategies at Tarmac may be no different from that in Hanson or BTR, but it demonstrates that Financial Control is not a style that forces managers into one kind of strategy.

The difference between Tarmac and Hanson or BTR is in organic growth. Growth in Tarmac's ongoing fixed assets was in the top third of the sample, averaging an 11 per cent per annum increase, only slightly less than the 14 per cent per annum increase due to acquisitions (appendix 1). On other financial performance measures, Tarmac has done well, though not quite as well as Hanson and BTR.

Ferranti

Like Tarmac, Ferranti has not made major acquisitions from the centre. In fact, Ferranti's growth has been almost all organic. Because Ferranti's base markets, defence and electronics, have been growing fast, the role of the centre has been focused more on trying to contain the growth and ensure that capital is available for the best projects, rather than on making acquisitions to drive growth forward. Ferranti's catch phrase, 'Selling Technology', is the essence of their corporate strategy.

In the businesses, the strategies fit the mould of financial control companies. Cautious, small-sized investments have been made in a variety of areas to spread the risk and avoid becoming overcommitted. Ferranti has not made bold moves in electronics in the same way as STC. It has, as a result, avoided any major setbacks. It provided the technology for Sir Clive Sinclair's personal computer, but decided not to dive into the market. It had numerous opportunities to get into micro-computers, and declined most of them. Now it is providing a manufacturing base for an IBM clone – the Advance – in a move which is more a toe-in-the-water than a definite decision to 'get into micros'.

Even in gate arrays, where Ferranti invested in a technology that gave it a 3 to 5-year lead, the strategy was cautious. As the market exploded, Ferranti chose to focus on a defendable niche, rather than grab a major share of the mass market.

Ferranti's financial performance has been good. Its profitability ratios are in the top half of the sample, and its growth has been higher than inflation (appendix 1). However, on earnings per share growth and share price growth, it is in the bottom half of the sample. This may be due in part to the recession in electronics in 1985, and on both these measures it has outperformed GEC, Plessey and STC, the other competitors in defence electronics.

GEC

GEC's results are somewhat different from those of the other Financial Control companies. Like the others it has little corporate level strategy; but, unlike them, it has built a large cash mountain. Acquisitions have been made – Avery's, Picker International, Yarrow Shipbuilders – and the centre has been involved in some bold initiatives concerning British Aerospace, Westland Helicopter and its recent bid for Plessey. However, the main initiatives have come from the level below the centre, and in total these initiatives have not been sufficient to eat into the cash reserve held at the centre.

Within GEC the business units follow a complete range of strategies. Marconi is boldly expanding its position in defence electronics; Hotpoint is focusing on holding on to a highly profitable share of the UK appliance market; Avery has revamped its product range and is now regaining lost market share in weighing machines; and businesses such as Ruston Gas Turbines have gradually built a world leadership position in a niche market.

The financial performance of GEC has not matched that of the other

Financial Control companies (appendix 1). It has delivered excellent profitability ratios – return on sales, return on equity and return on capital – but a poor growth performance. Share price growth, earnings per share growth and sales growth have barely matched inflation, and on each measure it is among the bottom four performers in the sample.

In GEC the level of satisfaction is generally slightly lower. Strong managers appear to be satisfied; many are forging ahead with their businesses and welcome the tough but fair style. But a few managers are less satisfied and we talked to some ex-GEC managers who criticized sharply the severity of the GEC system and the constraining influence of Lord Weinstock's style. At the centre, we detected a recognition of this criticism and some movement away from the strict Financial Control style.

Summary

The Financial Control companies have important similarities in their results: little corporate strategy; cautious business unit strategies; high levels of management motivation; good financial performance; lower than average levels of organic growth. There are differences between the companies, but overall the results are more similar than they are different, and they are sufficiently different from those of Strategic Planning and Strategic Control companies to conclude that there is a link between style and results.

Financial Control companies have been widely criticized for milking their businesses, for asset stripping, and for failing to expand. This criticism is not altogether justified. GEC saved the British electrical industry by buying and rationalising AEI and English Electric. Since Tarmac embarked upon the Financial Control style in 1979, its stock market value has increased from £100 million to £1.3b and the Housing division, for example, has gained market share from Wimpey and Barratt. Ferranti has developed a major position in one of the fastest growing areas of electronics, gate arrays. Hanson has achieved growth from Butterly Bricks and may have succeeded in changing British EverReady's strategy just in time to save it from collapse under the attack of Duracell. Moreover, many of the businesses of Financial Control companies are in static or declining markets: turbines, bricks, rubber and quarrying cannot be expected to produce explosive growth. Even so, some subsidiaries, such as GEC's Ruston Gas Turbines, have produced excellent performance and grabbed worldwide market leadership.

On the other hand, the Financial Control style does favour more cautious consolidation strategies aimed at high profitability ratios and minimizing the use of shareholders' money. In some cases managers are tempted to milk the business and Financial Control companies have no wholly satisfactory means of ensuring this does not happen. We asked Graeme Odgers of Tarmac what would happen to a manager who takes an excessively short-term view. His reply was guarded: 'We would not discourage a management team from maximizing profits.'

Malcolm Bates of GEC gave a more specific response to the same question: 'You get to know those who are adventurous, those who are cautious, those who will try to play games with the system. We have means of finding out if someone is trying to milk the business.'

Finally, the financial performance of these companies is very good. Over the 5 years from 1980 to 1985, pre-tax return on capital has averaged 22 per cent; return on sales has averaged more than 12 per cent; real growth rates in sales, earnings per share and dividends have been around 100 per cent over the period; and stock price after adjusting for inflation has risen by more than 200 per cent. These results continue a trend of excellent financial performances that go back 15 and more years.

It must be noted that the high growth rate in sales and stock price has been heavily influenced by successful acquisition policies. Partly because of the businesses these companies are in and partly because of the management style, internal growth has been less important than acquisitions. BTR, GEC, Hanson and Tarmac have made and continue to make major acquisitions that have contributed to their earnings per share growth (see appendix 1). The most important recent moves include Hanson's £2.3bn acquisition of the Imperial Group, GEC's £1.2bn bid for Plessey and BTR's £1.2bn bid for Pilkington.

It is these ever-bigger acquisitions that cause critics to question the sustainability of performance in the Financial Control companies. They argue that the Financial Control companies are mostly locked into low growth or declining businesses and that they need to make larger and larger acquisitions every year to produce satisfactory earnings growth. At some point the acquisitive needs of these businesses will exceed the availability of suitable companies for sale and the earnings growth record will be shattered.

We do not disagree with this analysis. We recognize that the earnings growth of BTR and Hanson, for example, is not sustainable for the long term. 'Someone calculated that if we went on growing at the current rate, we would be larger than the UK economy by the year 2003', pointed out Lionel Stammers of BTR. However, we do not believe this fact discredits the Financial Control style. We recognize that the style, like the other two major styles, has a number of advantages as well as disadvantages. In chapter 12 we demonstrate that, under certain circumstances, the Financial Control style is likely to be the best choice.

Financial Programming

Two of the Financial Control companies, BTR and Ferranti, are more involved in the strategies of their businesses than the other three companies. This greater central involvement is displayed in the fact that both these companies have formal 3-year planning processes. Moreover, the centre is less sensitive about giving suggestions to the managers running the businesses. In other words, in these two companies the centre has more involvement in business level decisions, but without reducing the tight financial controls. We have called this style Financial Programming. We view it as a version, a subset, of the Financial Control style rather than as a separate style in its own right.

The formal 3-year planning processes of BTR and Ferranti are not strategic planning systems in the traditional sense, because they do not focus on the strategy of the businesses. The format varies. In BTR, the 3-year plan is a page of text and three or four exhibits showing the trends in financial ratios and the planned capital expenditure. In Ferranti, the 3-year financial numbers are sent separately to the finance director, and the plan itself is five or six pages of text and exhibits, with each business choosing its own format.

The purpose of the plans is the same, however. They are designed to highlight financial performance issues a year or two in advance of the annual budget cycle, and to estimate the medium-term capital needs of the business. The value lies mainly in the financial forecasting. By asking the businesses to estimate their cash needs and expected profit outcomes, the group finance function can steer managers away from a course of action that could lead to a major cash or profit problem. It is an early warning system that helps the centre plan its financial posture.

Inevitably it is also an opportunity for unit managers and central managers to talk strategy. But the purpose does not appear to be mainly strategic; rather it is used to pinpoint problem areas early and, in Ferranti, it is part of the process of assessing managers and allocating resources.

BTR and Ferranti produce a 3-year plan every year. Interestingly, the philosophies are different. At Ferranti the 3-year plan is seen as a forerunner of the annual plan. The 3-year plan gives subsidiary managers and head office time to make adjustments to their thinking before the annual plan is developed. In this sense it is more like the system in a Strategic Control company. In BTR, the philosophy is reversed: the 3-year plan is viewed as coming after the annual plan. As one manager put it; 'The philosophy is, first, "what are you going to do next year?" Then, "now you know what you are going to do next year, what are your plans for the two years after that?".'

The outcome is the same, however. Corporate managers and subsidiary managers have a forum for discussing the future of the business. At BTR the emphasis is on profit growth. 'It draws out the need for finding a new balance or the need to change posture', explained Lionel Stammers of BTR. 'The value is that it pushes managers into carrying out gap analysis based on the gap between what they can achieve on a steady state basis and what they ought to be aspiring to achieve', commented a BTR group chief executive. The dialogue this generates can lead to changes in strategy. In one BTR subsidiary the manager was predicting good but static earnings. 'He [the group chief executive] kept asking me what I was going to do to make profits grow. The pressure he put on forced me to devote time to that business which resulted in us moving it to another location and substantially reducing overheads', explained the manager.

At Ferranti the attention is more likely to be aimed at cash flow. Ferranti are frequently faced with demands for cash that exceed central resources. The 3-year plan provides early warning of the size of the problem. It is also helpful in resolving the allocations that are finally made. 'If a business has been forecasting a need for cash for a year or two and it has been performing annually in line with its 3-year projections, we are much more inclined to support the request. We like to know that it is part of a longer-term plan rather than a whim of management', stated one manager.

The 3-year plan is, therefore, used by BTR and Ferranti to help with the target stretching and resource allocation processes. It leads inevitably to greater involvement from the centre. But it does not appear to result in slackening of the tight financial controls.

Another aspect of the style of BTR and Ferranti is that, on some issues, they will tell profit centre managers what to do. This cuts across the philosophy of decentralization but it does not seem to disturb it. Whereas the other Financial Control companies avoid giving instructions, central managers at BTR and Ferranti are prepared to take the lead on certain issues.

Group level managers 'have a very active involvement with the businesses. They don't expect the MD [of the business] to be a magician. If they think you need help, they will come and give you advice and on occasions give you instructions', stated one business manager. 'On occasions BTR will say "do this". For example they may say "stick your prices up" even if we are strongly resisting. However, it is rare for them to get to the dictate stage,[1] commented another manager. In BTR and Ferranti we identified examples where group level or central managers had overruled business managers on a pricing decision, the rationalization of two businesses, the appointment of a chief accountant for the business, and the choice of export agent. Although these interferences from the centre are more frequent than in the other Financial Control companies, they do not appear to reduce the feeling of authority and responsibility of the managers of businesses. They are seen as exceptions to the basic Financial Control system rather than as the heavy hand of the centre.

A further example of the Financial Programming style reflected in BTR's management system is that the headquarters has a greater degree of operating involvement with many businesses, particularly those that are part of the original four divisions – Hoses, Conveyor Belting, Rubber Extrusion and Aero Products. BTR has a number of operating 'disciplines'. There is a central buying function for major items such as rubber and the prices charged out to the businesses can frequently be higher than the open market price. All the properties of BTR companies are owned by the central property company and are leased to the businesses on 6-month contracts. BTR head office takes over any account that is more than 6 months overdue and collects the money directly. There is a central insurance policy on some bad debts. These disciplines are in the main good housekeeping, but they influence the plans and strategies in the businesses. 'It upsets some of our customers. We have a lot of guerilla warfare with them and some won't deal with us as a result. It is probably the right way to handle them, but, without the discipline, we would not be that tough with them', commented one manager. Another explained that the property arrangements allowed for much more flexible thinking: 'You normally assume you are tied to your building and the overheads they generate. But, with a 6-month lease, you can consider all sorts of alternatives you might otherwise reject out of hand.'

In summary, Ferranti and BTR are examples of an additional style – Financial Programming. The centre has more desire to be involved in reviewing the medium-term prospects for its businesses, and more willingness to interfere in decisions than is typical for Financial Control companies. However, these tendencies are set within a style whose dominant features remain those of Financial Control.

Style Changes

There have been fewer style changes amongst the Financial Control companies than in the Strategic Planning and Strategic Control groups. Three companies, BTR, GEC and Hanson Trust, have been operating a Financial Control style since before 1970; Ferranti changed to Financial Control in the early 1970s and Tarmac adopted Financial Control in the late 1970s. These changes are summarized in Table 6.4.

Table 6.4 Financial Control companies: style changes

	Previous styles	Approximate date of change
BTR	Financial control since before 1970	—
Ferranti	Holding Company	1974–5
GEC	Financial Control since before 1970	—
Hanson Trust	Financial Control since before 1970	—
Tarmac	Strategic Planning	1979/80

BTR, GEC and Hanson's style reflect long-established beliefs about business and management on the part of their chief executives and senior managers. They have had constant styles for 20 or more years in line with the stability of their leaderships.

Ferranti's style changed when the company was rescued by the National Enterprise Board. In 1974 the NEB appointed Derek Alun-Jones as chief executive. His primary goals were to pay off the debt, establish a financial track record and free the company from government ownership. As a result, the focus in the early days on financial ratios, cash flow and short-term financial performance was inevitable. Yet the simplicity and effectiveness of the style has caused it to be retained. One manager commented, 'The barons became just as excited about making profits as they had previously been about elegant engineering advances.'

Tarmac's style changed for slightly different reasons. In the 1970s Tarmac had diversified geographically and into new industries. A cash squeeze in 1979 and the appointment of Sir Eric Pountain signalled the moment to change from a Strategic Planning to a Financial Control style. The fact that Tarmac has settled into a Financial Control style is partly to do with the cash needs in the early 1980s, but it is probably more a result of the personal philosophy of Sir Eric Pountain, supported by the then finance director, Graeme Odgers, who came from GEC.

The long period of time during which the majority of these companies have pursued Financial Control has allowed them to refine the style and to adjust their portfolios of businesses to suit the style. Part of their success relates to the sophistication of their versions of Financial Control, to the widespread understanding of the style within the companies, and to the match they have achieved between the characteristics of their businesses and the Financial Control style.

In BTR, Hanson Trust and Tarmac there are no planned changes of style in prospect. Unless results suddenly deteriorate rapidly, or unless there is extensive change in senior corporate management, we would anticipate continuation of the Financial Control style for the foreseeable future. In GEC and Ferranti a change to Strategic Control may occur. There are pressures in the defence and electronics industries for longer-term, more coordinated investment decisions and strategies, and we have noted, in GEC, some moves away from strict Financial Control. Nevertheless, the success that these companies have enjoyed under the Financial Control style, and the commitment of their senior managers to it, mean that radical changes in style are unlikely without a major reversal in results or new appointments at the top.

The comparative stability of the Financial Control style is interesting. The style has clarity and internal consistency, and has delivered the goods for its leading proponents. They see no reason to change it, and where frictions exist they are more inclined to adjust their portfolios or their management teams than to modify their style. As we shall explain in chapter 13, which discusses how different companies build their portfolios to match their styles, this approach depends on Financial Control companies being able to avoid head-on competition in businesses requiring longer-term investments. Major changes in style are only likely if they are unable to continue with this policy.

Notes

1 Ferranti is one of the few companies we found difficult to classify. Its management systems appear to be a mixture of the Financial Control, Financial Programming and Strategic Control styles, as we have defined them. On balance we have characterized Ferranti as a company with tight financial controls because of the perceptions of group level management. We recognize that Derek Alun-Jones perceives the style as closer to Strategic Control and we detect that the style is moving towards Strategic Control. Lower level managers however are still focused on the financial dimension, believing that meeting budget is a more important goal than strategic targets. We suspect the Ferranti managers are still influenced by the cash crisis in 1974 and the tight controls that were imposed in the latter half of the 1970s.
2 Financial Control companies also have capital appropriation systems that are described in the resource allocation section. Although not part of a regular planning cycle, these systems are an important part of the influence process. Ferranti and BTR also have a 3-year planning process described below in the section on Financial Programming.

7

Holding and Centralized Companies

Holding and Centralized companies represent extremes of corporate detachment and involvement in strategy decisions. We will discuss each of these styles only briefly, since both have significant drawbacks and appear to be in decline amongst leading companies. Indeed none of our participant companies today falls into these categories, though some have had recent experience of them. Our discussion is therefore intended simply to sketch the nature of these styles and to identify some common problems that arise with them.

Holding Companies

The Holding Company approach minimizes the centre's strategic role. Corporate management intervene little to influence strategy at business unit level, and allow each business or division to develop and pursue its own strategy. The centre is passive in the resource allocation process, and there is little sense of corporate strategic direction behind resource allocation decisions. Businesses tend to reinvest their own funds, and where there are bids for investment that exceed the businesses' own cash flows, the choice of proposals to fund becomes a political one.

There may be budgeting and planning processes, but control of actual achievement against plans is loose and business units regard the planning processes as empty paper exercises that add little to their thinking.

The shortcomings of this style are evident. Since the centre is essentially passive, it adds little to business unit management, except overhead. Individual parts of the group would lose nothing of value if they were to be floated off separately, and often perceive this as a desirable – if unattainable – outcome.

Our work has concentrated on successful, state-of-the-art companies, and our sample therefore contains no firms that are now run on a Holding Company basis. However, four of them (BOC, ICI,[1] Imperial and Vickers) have shifted within the past few years from styles with Holding Company elements to other styles. Their accounts of the problems that arise under a Holding Company regime are salutary, and worth recording.

- No focus in resource allocation. All these companies, with the exception of ICI, had gone through extensive and rather haphazard diversification programmes during the 1960s and 1970s. They had failed to concentrate resources on the growth of selected businesses in which the companies saw their long-term future.
- Diversifications and new business entries that often reflected political bargaining among senior managers rather than strategic logic. It would be invidious to cite examples, but a number were provided to us privately.
- Inability to turn around, or dispose of, non-performing businesses due to loose controls. The portfolios of the companies came to be weighted down with certain persistently unprofitable businesses. A major task of both Geoffrey Kent at Imperial and David Plastow at Vickers was to dispose of some of these.
- Individual senior managers acting as 'barons', protecting their own patches from any corporate interference and tacitly supporting each other in preserving their autonomy. We have noted the importance that Sir John Harvey-Jones at ICI attached to making executive board members feel that their loyalty and concern was for ICI as a whole, rather than for the particular divisions within their remits.
- No attempt to manage interdependencies between divisions to add value or create synergy.

In these circumstances, corporate strategy and results are no more than the sum of individual business strategies and results.

Our sample does not provide sufficient breadth of evidence to prove that Holding Company firms perform less well than companies with other styles, although there is plenty of anecdotal data that points in that direction. However, a questionnaire survey by Charles Hill[2] of the top 500 UK firms suggests that Holding Companies do in fact perform less well, in both their level of profitability and in their growth rate of earnings. According to Hill's work, moreover, in excess of 30 per cent of UK companies still fall into the Holding Company category. The apparent popularity of this type of corporate style therefore makes its shortcomings important to understand.

Centralized Companies

In terms of corporate style, companies adopting a Centralized style are at the opposite extreme to Holding Companies. Here corporate managers play a very active role, themselves determining strategy for each business and allocating resources in support of these strategies. Because there is no separation of responsibility for proposing strategy and controlling results, control of strategic achievements is more difficult. Since the centre devises the strategy, business management can be held responsible only for making operating decisions that conform with the strategy. Thus, the centre is faced with the awkward and in some respects infeasible task of controlling itself strategically. Anything other than a flexible strategic control style is therefore difficult (see the section on Strategic Programming, pp. 79–80).

The Centralized approach does have certain strengths. The businesses and the relationships between them can be managed and optimized within a coherent overall corporate strategy. The chief executive and corporate management can take a broad view of what the individual business strategies will add up to, and can assess whether they will amount to a balanced and tenable strategy for the company as a whole. In a less diverse portfolio, with extensive overlaps between businesses, the Centralized approach can allow a powerful chief executive with a depth of personal experience in the businesses to drive the whole company forward in a coordinated and focused fashion. Centralized management works best and is most common in functionally organized and vertically integrated companies, with high degrees of overlap between business units.[3]

However, full Centralization also has important drawbacks, most of which relate to the emasculation of responsibility it implies at the business level. Again, none of our participant companies is today Centralized in approach, although several (BP, Courtaulds, Plessey, UB) have moved away from this style in recent years.

Reasons given for rejecting Centralization include:

- Removal of responsibility from the front line management who are closest to the business, and consequent reduction in strategic thinking and motivation at business level. During Lord Kearton's regime at Courtaulds, in the 1960s and 1970s, the major decisions were taken at the centre, and the company was run as an integrated and interlocking whole. Whatever benefits this style may have brought in optimizing the company's competitive position in the textile business as a whole, they are now seen by those who lived through this era as more than offset by the reduction of responsibility among the general managers in the group. Because the centre took the strategy decisions, business unit managers did not themselves feel so responsible, they were less committed to the implementation of strategy, and they became less skilled in thinking strategically. This explains why – as noted in chapter 2 – Chris Hogg felt that strategic thinking in the company was weak when he took over as chief executive in 1980. There is therefore a danger that too much central influence on strategy development will inhibit strategic thinking and will result in less 'ownership' of the strategy on the part of those who must put it into practice.
- Difficulty of developing general management experience, capability and judgement down the line. Problems of succession frequently occur with highly powerful chief executives. UB have been concerned for some years with creating the next generation of management to come after Sir Hector Laing. And in Plessey, one senior manager observed that the period after Sir Allan Clark's death had been one of some confusion: 'There were all the makings of a strategy, but he had never told us what to do with them.'

- Excessive burden of understanding and decision-taking at the centre. In its move in 1980 to 'business streaming' (i.e. the establishment of separate, profit-responsible divisions) BP recognized that an effective, speedy response to oil shocks and swings in demand was less likely to be forthcoming from a powerful, but overloaded, corporate level than from division management. The centre can never have as much detailed knowledge of individual businesses as their local management, and too much centralization leads inevitably to 'span of comprehension' problems in multibusiness firms.
- Failure to create and encourage multiple views of strategy, and consequently increased risk of tunnel vision and inflexible strategy plans.

These are serious weaknesses,[4] particularly as companies grow and become more diverse.[5] In very large organizations, centralized decisions are liable to be wrong decisions, and business unit management tend to lose profit orientation and market responsiveness. Participant companies, such as BP, have therefore expressed a willingness to forego some of the theoretical benefits of coordinated central strategy, preferring instead to create a clearer sense of personal commitment, responsibility and accountability at the business unit level. For these reasons, we do not believe that Centralized management is an appropriate style for the sorts of large companies that have formed the subject of this research.

Notes

1 During the 1970s much of the decision-making authority in ICI rested with main board directors, each of whom were responsible for particular parts of the company. There was comparatively little collective, corporate influence over the decisions that each director took in his parts of the company. There were in this sense elements of the Holding Company style. Viewed from the divisional perspective, however, it appeared that the centre, as represented by the individual main board directors, retained extensive powers and functions – leading to criticisms of the company's style as Centralized. The strong baronial power of the individual main board directors is the key to understanding this apparent paradox.

2 See Charles W. L. Hill, 'Internal organisation and enterprise performance: some UK evidence', *Managerial and Decision Economics* 1986. Hill specifically tried to establish the incidence of Williamson's types of divisionalized firms in the UK (see n. 3 to chapter 2), and to measure their performance.

3 See Derek F. Channon, *The Strategy and Structure of British Enterprise* (Division of Research, Harvard Business School, 1973) and Richard P. Rumelt, *Strategy, Structure and Economic Performance* (Harvard University Press, 1974). Both books explore the relationships between diversification and organization structures. We return to this topic in chapters 12 and 13.

4 Probably due to the problems of Centralized management, it is interesting that Hill's study indicates that only 1.5 per cent of large UK companies remain Centralized in approach.

5 Academic studies have shown a clear association between increased diversity in companies' portfolios and increased decentralization. This is one of the fundamental points made by Alfred Chandler in *Strategy and Structure* (MIT Press, 1962).

8

The Styles Compared

The three most popular management styles are Strategic Planning, Strategic Control and Financial Control. All the companies in our sample were able to identify with one of these styles as a more or less accurate description of their approach. Of course, an individual company may not conform to all aspects of a particular style, any more than individual people can be conveniently categorized as, say, 'introvert' or 'extrovert'. Companies, for better or worse, normally include elements from different styles. Most are predominantly of one style, but even they have different styles in some divisions of the company, or for specific aspects of the management process.

Our purpose in this chapter, however, is to assess the key differences of principle between the styles, rather than to describe actual organizations. The discussion is based on our research findings with the 16 companies, but it represents an attempt to distil out and summarize only the salient features of the styles we have encountered. This will allow us to state and compare the underlying philosophies behind each style.

As we compare each aspect of the styles, it is important to stress that many style differences relate less to formal structures and systems than to ways in which they are operated. Budgetary processes, capital approval systems and information flows may look similar. The important differences lie in the attitudes and intentions of top management and, therefore, in the way in which formal systems are used. Our comparisons between the styles attempt to catch the cultural differences between companies as well as the more obvious differences in formal systems and processes.

Organization Structure and the Coordination of Overlaps

Financial Control companies push strategy down to the level of their profit centres. To make sure this decentralization works, they limit corporate interventions and coordination between businesses.

Strategic Control companies have a similar intention, but are more prepared to accept a divisional role in coordinating between businesses, and a corporate role in checking that opportunities have not been missed.

Strategic Planning makes each profit centre responsible for its own strategies, but encourages advice, comment and proposals from elsewhere in the organization. Managers in these companies accept that coordinated, integrated strategies may be needed in some business areas, and that divisional and corporate management have a role to play there. The centre not only reacts to business proposals, but also takes the initiative in putting forward ideas and coordinating strategies between businesses.

Table 8.1 sums up how organization structures and roles vary with the degree of commitment to decentralization.

Table 8.1 Organization structure and the coordination of overlaps

Strategic Planning	Strategic Control	Financial Control
Independent profit centres		
Profit centres propose strategy	Profit centres are the primary source of strategy	Profit centres set strategy
Multiple perspectives on strategy from other levels and units. Centre proposes strategies and reacts to proposals from below	Some coordination of strategies at divisional level, but centre mainly reacts to strategies proposed	Little or no coordination. Centre wholly reactive
Integrated strategies developed where needed. Centre co-ordinates between businesses	Prefer to avoid overlaps between businesses and divisions	Actively discourage overlaps between businesses

The Planning Process

The basic purpose of the planning process differs between styles (see table 8.2). Strategic Planning review processes provide a two-way dialogue between the centre and the business units on the best way forward. They are designed to allow corporate management to be an effective partner in this dialogue. The planning process is therefore extensive and time-consuming, particularly for businesses that the centre regards as being strategically important. The management views agreement on a long-term strategy as fundamental; shorter term, more detailed plans are intended to follow from the strategy once it is agreed.

The formal planning processes in Strategic Control companies are very similar, if somewhat less selective. However, their purpose is more to audit the quality of business-level thinking than to advocate a particular corporate view.

Table 8.2 Planning process

Strategic Planning	Strategic Control	Financial Control
Extensive formal planning and budgeting process		Budgeting only
Budget intended to be detailed first year of strategy plan		Budget is an end in itself
Often selective focus on main issues	Comprehensive, annual reviews with each business	Reviews of annual budgets only
Planning used both to audit the quality of thinking in the businesses and to bring together ideas from the centre and elsewhere (multiple perspectives)	Planning used to audit the quality of thinking in the businesses	Budget reviews provide the opportunity for a wider discussion of strategy
——————————— Informal processes are also vital ———————————		

In Financial Control companies there are no formal, long-term strategy plans. The annual budget is emphasized as an end in itself, although the budgetary process provides an occasion for wider discussions of capital investment and long-term prospects.

In all three styles informal contacts provide an essential oil to keep the wheels of the formal process turning.

Themes, Thrusts and Suggestions

Strategic Planning is much more willing than other styles to be proactive in proposing strategic themes and thrusts, and in making specific suggestions to businesses. Both Strategic Control and Financial Control avoid taking the lead in strategy development, preferring to leave this responsibility clearly with lower level management. If corporate management in Financial Control companies makes suggestions, there is a general understanding that the businesses retain the final decision and may ignore the centre if they choose. (See table 8.3.)

Resource Allocation and Portfolio Design

Strategic Planning companies allocate resources to building competitive advantage in selected business areas. The centre is actively involved, and sponsors major initiatives that are expected to achieve advantage. Capital investments, acquisitions and divestments are reviewed and ranked against this background.

Table 8.3 Themes, thrusts and suggestions

Strategic Planning	Strategic Control	Financial Control
Centre proposes themes and thrusts to direct business unit strategies	Centre avoids themes and thrusts	
Centre makes suggestions based on knowledge of the business	Centre cautious with suggestions	Centre may offer suggestions, but business has the final decision

Strategic Control companies also use resource allocation to support long-term strategies for building competitive advantage, but the centre is less directly involved in sponsoring strategies; more of the initiative comes from the businesses. The corporate level uses portfolio planning techniques to set priorities in resource allocation and to identify disposal candidates.

For existing businesses, the Financial Control companies are more concerned with individual project appraisal than with underlying strategies. Provided the centre is convinced that business management is competent, committed to the project and to earning a satisfactory return from it, it will provide funds. In acquisitions (or disposals), however, corporate management may take the lead. The criterion that guides the search is whether the acquisition candidate can be expected to respond to the Financial Control management style and show improved financial results as a result. 'Manageability' is therefore more important than 'strategic fit'. (see table 8.4.)

Objective-setting

Strategic Planning companies expect objectives to emerge from the strategy debate. The businesses put forward objectives that are consistent with their proposed strategies, and the centre agrees their acceptability. Objectives cover long-term goals such as establishing a leading position in the US market, short-term strategic milestones – for example, achieving a 5 per cent share of the US market by the end of next year – and budget targets, which include detailed goals for growth in sales, assets and profits. Strategic milestones and long-term goals tend to be less precise and measurable with less objectivity than financial budget targets.

The objective-setting process is similar in Strategic Control companies, except that more emphasis is given to defining short-term standards of performance as a basis for control.

Financial Control objectives focus on the annual budget, which is regarded not only as a forecast of performance but also as a contract on which the business promises to deliver. The centre expects the business to

Table 8.4 Resource allocation and portfolio design

Strategic Planning	Strategic Control	Financial Control
Strategic criteria important. Individual projects are reviewed as part of a strategic plan		Financial payback is an important criterion. Projects are taken one at a time on their individual merits
Centre active in ranking priorities between projects		All 'good' projects accepted
Portfolio shape follows from the strategies	Portfolio planning techniques used to assess portfolio fit and balance	Financial results and 'manageability' are more important than strategic fit in building the portfolio
Centre sponsors initiatives to grow existing businesses and to enter new businesses	Most portfolio building initiatives come from division and business levels. Centre gives encouragement	Centre and businesses are active in seeking acquisitions in new manageable businesses. Centre discourages diversification at the business level

propose budget objectives, but will press the business to stretch its objectives until they represent 'high wire' performance. It is also expected that, year-on-year, there will be improvements in performance, either growth in profits and/or higher return on capital. (See table 8.5.)

Table 8.5 Objective-setting

Strategic Planning	Strategic Control	Financial Control
Objectives give precision to the strategic plan	Objectives arise from strategy plans, but are also used to set short-term performance standards	Annual budget is a 'contract'. 'Improvements' are expected each year
Businesses propose targets; centre reviews for acceptability		Centre 'stretches' target
Objectives include long-term goals, short-term strategic milestones and budget targets. Budget is essentially first year of strategy		Financial objectives dominate

The Styles Compared

Performance Monitoring

All styles have detailed information systems to monitor performance against plan. Financial Control companies, however, provide fuller and more frequent feedback to business management. This may entail regular face-to-face meetings, or more ad hoc comments. It also involves discussion of actions that should be taken. In Strategic Control and Strategic Planning companies, management by exception means that the centre only comments on actual performance versus plan where major deviations have occured. (See table 8.6.)

Table 8.6   Performance monitoring

Strategic Planning	Strategic Control	Financial Control
——————— Detailed monitoring of results against plans ———————		
Centre seldom comments on performance versus plan, except with major deviations		Centre comments frequently and directly on performance versus plans and insists on action plans to correct variances

Sanctions and Incentives

Financial Control companies create very strong psychological, career and compensation incentives to meet short-term budget targets. There is clear personal accountability for results, and a belief that these can be objectively measured in financial profitability terms. Meeting demanding targets is itself a psychological reward, reinforced by frequent public feedback from the centre. Performance against targets is also rewarded in career progress and cash (salary, bonus or both), while failure to deliver leads to rapid management change.

Strategic Control companies also aim to create strong incentives and sanctions, but they find it more difficult to define strategic targets objectively and precisely than financial objectives. These companies therefore may have to make complex trade-offs between strategy and profitability, and between the short term and the long term. This complicates the control process, and can lead to ambiguities.

In Strategic Planning companies, 'strategic progress' can be a valid reason for failing to achieve short-term objectives; and poor performance results, in the first instance, in a search for new strategies rather than a change of management. The involvement of the centre in setting strategy can also reduce people's sense of personal accountability. In summary, Strategic Planning companies are more flexible in the way they exercise control. (See table 8.7.)

Table 8.7 Sanctions and incentives

Strategic Planning	Strategic Control	Financial Control
Broad strategic progress and precise targets both matter; short-term objectives are inter-preted flexibly	Strong incentives are provided to meet agreed targets, but some ambiguity exists in trade-offs between strategic and financial targets	Very strong pressure is applied to meet short-term budget targets
Unit managers are accountable for strategic progress and financial performance; but the accountability is complicated by the centre's involvement in setting strategy and by subjective measures of performance	Unit managers are accountable for strategic progress and financial performance; but accountability is complicated by subjec-tive measures of performance	Unit managers are accountable for financial perform-ance. Targets are clear.
Reaction to poor results can be slow. Units are allowed time to search for new strategy	Reaction to poor results is fast; but excuses are often accepted for strategic reasons	Reaction to poor results is quick. Little time is allowed for finding new strategies

These different characteristics stem from different perceptions of the sorts of planning and control influence that are productive. What then about the results they produce?

Results of Major Styles

The kind of business strategy, corporate strategy, financial results and management satisfaction typically achieved under each style varies considerably. We will take each of these aspects in turn.

Business Strategies

Individual businesses within Strategic Planning companies are encouraged to push for maximum competitive advantage. In 'core' businesses, which form the basis of the corporate portfolio, bold initiatives to build competitive advantage over the long-term are supported by the centre.

In Strategic Control companies, business strategies aim to balance the desire to reinforce competitive advantage with the need to satisfy financial objectives. Successful businesses are encouraged to grow. Though there is acceptance of the need for long-term investments, growth strategies are more often incremental than radical.

Financial Control companies concentrate on stretching for maximum financial performance. Individual businesses seek high margins, often in more protected speciality niches of a market, or through cost reduction programmes. They are unwilling to sacrifice margins, or to risk long payback investments in the defence of competitive advantage. But they are concerned to find opportunities for continuing profit growth over time. (See table 8.8.)

Table 8.8 Business strategies

Strategic Planning	Strategic Control	Financial Control
Pursue major initiatives in 'core' business areas	Develop successful areas incrementally	Seek high margins, speciality niches, and opportunities for profit growth
Build competitive advantage	Reinforce competitive advantage	Defend competitive advantage, consistent with high margins
Support long-term developments	Accept long-term investments	Avoid long payback investments
↓	↓	↓
Push for maximum competitive advantage	*Balance* competitive position with financial ambitions	*Stretch* for maximum financial performance

Corporate Strategy

The portfolios of Strategic Planning companies are built around a few (two to three) core business areas consisting of businesses with linked strategies, often competing in a global arena. The core areas are supported with bold investments and major acquisitions, in an attempt to create positions of competitive strength. Growth comes in the first instance from extending the operations of the core businesses into new geographical areas or new product markets. But if growth opportunities in the core businesses are limited, corporate management will seek to identify and enter potential new core business areas. Businesses that do not fit within the core areas, and are troublesome, will be divested.

Strategic Control companies aim to identify strategically sound businesses, around which they rationalize their portfolios and seek balanced growth. This means supporting the expansion plans put forward by a variety of successful divisions and businesses, but divesting poorly performing businesses with weak competitive positions. However, aggressive building of a small number of selected core areas is less common. Companies with this style consider a wide range of potential acquisitions in new businesses with attractive strategic potential, but bring relatively few acquisition plans to fruition.

The corporate portfolios of Financial Control companies are based around businesses that respond well to the Financial Control style and are in this sense 'manageable'. These companies grow through supporting the expansion plans of successful manageable businesses, and in particular through acquiring new manageable businesses. The acquisitions are intended to spread risk across industries and countries, and to provide profitable growth opportunities by buying assets that are undervalued and can be made to perform better through the imposition of Financial Control disciplines. Financial Control companies divest poorly performing businesses which cannot be turned around speedily, or which do not fit the preferred style. (See table 8.9.)

Table 8.9 Corporate strategy

Strategic Planning	Strategic Control	Financial Control
Build core businesses with bold investments and related acquisitions	Support expansion plans of successful divisions and businesses	Support expansion plans of successful and 'manageable' businesses
Expand internationally and seek new growth areas in core businesses; enter new core businesses if existing opportunities are not seen as adequate	Consider acquisitions in new businesses with attractive strategic potential	Spread risk across industries and countries, and acquire 'manageable' businesses that are undervalued
Shed troublesome non-core businesses	Rationalize or divest poor performers with weak competitive positions	Rationalize or divest poor performers, or businesses that don't fit
↓	↓	↓
Build linked international *core* business areas	*Rationalize* portfolio and seek *balanced* growth in strategically sound businesses	*Acquire manageable* portfolio of businesses with high profit potential

Financial Results

A review of the financial performance of our companies in the period
1981–5 is given in appendix 1. Table 8.10 sets out the main points that
emerge.

Table 8.10   Financial results

Strategic Planning	Strategic Control	Financial Control
Fast sales growth	Limited sales growth	Acquisition-based sales growth
High profitability in core businesses with competitive advantage; lower profitability in non-core and development businesses	Improving profitability-ratios	High profitability; turn-arounds in acquired companies
Some share price growth	Share price recovery	Rapid share price growth
but	*but*	*but*
Some setbacks and slower reaction to poor performers	Fewer major initiatives	Less organic business building

Strategic Planning companies have tended to be consistently profitable,
with high return on sales, return on equity and return on capital. On
average the performance has been above that of the Financial Times
Industrial Average, significantly above that of Strategic Control companies,
but below that of Financial Control companies. Within the portfolio,
Strategic Planning companies normally have excellent profitability ratios
for their established businesses and less good performance from new
'development' areas or 'non-core' businesses. One of the features of these
companies is their willingness to support subsidiaries that produce poor
performance over long periods.

The sales growth of Strategic Planning companies has been above
average and tends to come from organic asset expansion rather than from
acquisitions. These companies have the highest organic growth rates. In
contrast, earnings per share growth has been less satisfactory. This is due
mainly to the major setbacks encountered by companies such as Lex,
Cadbury and STC. As a result, Strategic Planning companies have the
lowest stock price growth.

On average, over the period Strategic Control companies have been
just above the industrial average in all three profitability ratios. But they

have seen a dramatic improvement during the period. Return on equity, for example, rose by 200 per cent. By 1985, Strategic Control companies were as profitable as Strategic Planning companies. This improvement has caused a big rise in share price, although not to the degree seen in Financial Control companies.

Sales have grown only at the rate of inflation. Yet behind these numbers is an organic growth in assets higher than in Financial Control companies. The reason for the discrepancy is that the growth has been masked by net divestments as these companies cleaned up their portfolios.

Financial Control companies have produced the best all-round financial performance. They substantially outperform the industrial averages. They have high profitability ratios and growth rates. Their main weakness is in organic growth, where fixed asset growth (4 per cent per year) has been less than inflation and less than half that of Strategic Planning companies (10 per cent per year).

As a category, Financial Control companies have bought assets rather than grown businesses. Asset growth by acquisition has been 28 per cent per year compared to 7 per cent for Strategic Planning companies and –2 per cent for Strategic Control companies.

Management Satisfaction

The strength of the Strategic Planning companies is that managers in the core businesses can identify with the company's strategic ambitions. Business unit managers value central advice, support and suggestions that are knowledgeable and well-founded. But they can be frustrated with corporate interference and lack of freedom to run their business units as they feel they should. This problem is sometimes compounded by bureaucracy in the review of strategies and by a lack of clarity in the performance targets, against which they are assessed.

Managers in Strategic Control companies typically welcome the autonomy and responsibility they receive. At its best, the centre provides a thoughtful and constructive review of their plans, with few constraints on their freedom of action. This enhances their motivation to perform. But managers may also feel that the centre is too distant from the businesses to be helpful, and that review procedures are unnecessarily bureaucratic. More fundamentally, managers can be left confused by the ambiguous priorities between strategic and financial goals.

Motivation and commitment are frequently high in Financial Control companies. Managers feel that they own their strategies, and the clear financial standards and strong monitoring systems reinforce their desire to succeed. This can lead to a 'winners' psychology, in which successful managers grow in confidence in the knowledge that they have met demanding standards. There is, however, frustration amongst managers who want to follow long-term, coordinated strategies in their businesses. These individuals seldom remain in a Financial Control environment for long. (See table 8.11.)

Table 8.11 Management satisfaction

Strategic Planning	Strategic Control	Financial Control
Identify with the company's ambitions for its core businesses	Welcome the greater autonomy and clearer responsibility for performance	Highly committed due to feelings of owner-ship and a 'winners' psychology
Value knowledgeable inputs by the centre	Value thoughtful reviews of strategic plans by the centre	Value clear standards and incentives set by the centre
but	*but*	*but*
Some frustration with lack of autonomy, bureaucracy and un-clear performance targets	Concern about 'distant' centre, bureaucratic procedures and un-clear and ambiguous goals	Some frustration in businesses that need more long-term, co-ordinated strategies

It is evident that these differences in results are closely linked to the different approaches to planning and control influence we have described. What is striking, however, is that no style emergences as clearly superior. Each style achieves good results in certain dimensions of performance, but is comparatively weaker in others. No style seems to achieve uniformly strong performance on all the relevant measures. This clearly presents a conundrum to the corporate chief executive who is concerned to identify the style that is most likely to be successful for his company. In the next three chapters, we will explore further the factors that create this conundrum.

9

Balancing Tensions

As we have seen, different companies give different answers to the question of how large diversified corporations should be managed, and adopt different strategic management styles. None of these styles achieves conclusively better results than the others; all have their advantages and their disadvantages. In this chapter we will look at the reasons why there is no one right or ideal style. We will find that all styles must cope with basic conflicts or tensions that exist in the role of central management. These inherent tensions force choices and trade-offs which are responsible for the strengths and weaknesses of each style. These tensions are best illustrated by comparing the two extreme styles, Financial Control and Strategic Planning.

The Financial Control enthusiast would see the role of the centre in terms such as these: *Establish an organization structure with separate responsibilities; allow freedom to lower level managers to devise and implement strategiess unfettered by corporate planning bureaucracies; and build tight controls at the centre to monitor performance and provide real motivation to perform.* This prescription contains many of the basic tenets of good management. Yet, on closer inspection, each proposition turns out to be debatable. BOC and BP believe in overlapping responsibilities; Lex see real value in a cooperative effort between the centre and the businesses in formulating strategy; ICI and Vickers assert that a strategic planning process is needed to probe the thinking of business management and to underpin long-term resource allocation decisions; and UB consider that, when the going gets tough, controls should become more friendly rather than more fierce.

The Strategic Planning enthusiast would therefore see the role of the centre in quite different terms: *Adopt a fluid structure that encourages a variety of views to be expressed; set up a planning process that will allow strong leadership by the centre and encourage cooperation between units; and avoid inflexible objectives that will constrain managers from seeking creative long-term strategies.*

Both viewpoints are attractive. Clear responsibilities are highly desirable; so is broad debate. Autonomy at the business unit level leads to a greater sense of responsibility; but strong leadership produces purpose and direction. Tight controls give managers more motivation to perform; flexible controls support efforts to meet long-term objectives. It's heads on one side of the coin, tails on the other, and both are capable of coming out winners.

The tensions exist because the benefits of each style are polar opposites. You can't have both simultaneously, and so a choice has to be made. If you are committed to a profit centre focus that gives clear responsibilities, you cannot at the same time set up a matrix organization designed to bring people together over major decisions. If you believe that strategy should be developed by the general manager closest to the business, you cannot impose strong leadership from a centre far removed from the business. In the same way, tight controls cannot be combined with a flexible response to results achieved. Full adherence to the Financial Control aim means that the Strategic Planning aim has to be rejected.

If a balance is struck it can only be through some degree of compromise. Graeme Odgers, of Tarmac, described the task of the centre in terms of balance:

> Our approach is designed to achieve a balance between encouraging entrepreneurial activity, high energy levels and a drive for growth with very tight central controls and monitoring. In some sense these two objectives are in conflict. But we believe we have a good balance. By getting individual management teams to set their own standards and develop their own plans for growth, we can help them feel like winners. Our central control and monitoring ensures that they meet their own standards.

It is the management of these kinds of tensions that is the task of the centre; and it is the choices the centre makes that create the different strategic management styles. In this chapter we will examine the five fundamental tensions that we encountered. These are:

1 Clear responsibilities versus multiple perspectives.
2 Detailed planning versus entrepreneurial decisions.
3 Strong leadership versus business autonomy.
4 Long-term strategic versus short-term financial objectives.
5 Tight controls versus the flexible pursuit of long-term objectives.

Each style represents a different balance of emphasis between these tensions. Understanding these tensions, and the trade-offs they imply, is crucial to understanding the balance of advantage and disadvantage in each style.

Clear Responsibilities versus Multiple Perspectives

Both Strategic Control and Financial Control companies believe in clearly defined, separate profit centres as the basic organizational unit. Graeme Odgers again:

In Tarmac, we have a highly decentralized type of operation. We [the centre] are not going to be able to make detailed operational decisions, so these need to be done at the operating level. Only if the business units have got a high degree of autonomy are you going to get the commitment to perform. If you pull the responsibility away from the operating unit, you lose control rather than gain it. We want the mechanism for driving creativity and performance.

Motivation, accountability and the need to be close to the detail of a business all argue for decentralized, separate profit centres.

This point of view is reinforced by the experiences of BP, a Strategic Planning company. Once the oil business was broken up into the separate business streams (Exploration and Production, Downstream Oil, Gas), it became easier to see where profits were and were not being made, and to make the decisions necessary to restore the business to financial health. As BP chairman Sir Peter Walters commented, 'Under the old integrated structure, it would have been difficult to isolate those parts of the business that were not performing and take the necessary action with them.' Breaking a business up into discrete profit centres provides information that can be disguised by more aggregated reporting.

Those who favour independent profit centres generally argue that the boundaries round them should be drawn in such a way as to allow the profit centre manager maximum independence and discretion over the decisions that have the greatest impact on competitive advantage in his business. In this way responsibility for performance is made coincident with responsibility for strategy.[1]

The independent profit centre view, however, is less easy to implement where there are unavoidable overlaps between business units. For example, in Vickers' marine engineering interests a variety of separately manufactured products are sold to a common customer base. Here there are important sources of competitive advantage at both individual product group and common customer levels. Exclusive strategic responsibility at either level is liable to be sub-optimal. A separation between business unit level (i.e. the individual product groups) and divisional level (i.e. the aggregate of all product groups) goes some way to resolving the problem, but introduces an extra layer of management and additional communication and reporting needs. The clarity of separate profit centres is somewhat compromised.

A more intractable problem is posed by businesses which need both global coordination and integration of strategy, and a strong local presence and organizational focus in individual countries and regions. Here, we have seen companies such as BOC, BP and Cadbury Schweppes moving towards matrix organization structures, which balance global product responsibility with local geographical responsibility. But this structure is much more complex than the pure profit centre approach, and moves away from individual responsibility and accountability. It builds in the real need to share responsibility and consider different interests in arriving at strategic decisions, but it complicates the management task.

Perhaps the most difficult organizational problems are posed by businesses whose affairs are normally separate but can overlap importantly (and unpredictably) from time to time. In ICI, we were told of a technology developed by the Plant Protection division for spraying crops that happened to be potentially important to the Pharmaceuticals division in drug delivery systems. This opportunity was not perceived for some time due to the absence of any direct organizational linkage between the Plant Protection R&D laboratories and the commercial function in Pharmaceuticals. When, largely by chance, the opportunity did come to light there were further delays – involving interventions by corporate staff and other divisions, scepticism about the technology's real value for Pharmaceuticals, and various attempts to define suitable ad hoc working groups. This is the sort of problem that all profit centre structures can encounter at times, since, by drawing any fixed organizational boundaries, there is always the possibility of issues arising that require difficult coordination across those boundaries.

As a partial defence against the danger of missing important strategic issues that require combining the perspectives of more than one organizational unit, some Strategic Planning companies consciously try to build multiple perspectives into the strategic decision-making process. The organization structure is set up to allow, and encourage, cooperation and coordination between different parts of the company, and to draw out different views on major issues from throughout the organization. 'Many of the decisions that we are making can have very long-term impact on our businesses', observed Peter Walters of BP. 'It is necessary for us at the corporate level to have input into these decisions and to get a multitude of views.'

A fluid, multiple-perspective organization does have advantages in getting a range of views considered; but it also has drawbacks. For example, the decision-making process is apt to be slower and less entrepreneurial. There is also some danger that the general manager who feels a range of onlookers is breathing down his neck may become protective, and this may reduce the openness of debate. Furthermore, the motivation and accountability, so often found in independent profit centres, may be undermined. In chapter 4 we alluded to these problems.

There is therefore a tension between the desirability of separate profit centre responsibility and the need for a variety of viewpoints and for cooperation across the organization. An emphasis on individual profit centres means foregoing some of the benefits of the cooperative, multiple-perspective oganization, and vice versa. There is no way of combining the two to achieve the full benefits of autonomy, independence and accountability, while at the same time encouraging coordination, cooperation and mutual support. The tension is, to this extent, unavoidable, and choices of emphasis must be made.

Something *can* however be done to loosen the tension – in two ways. First, organizational units should be defined as far as possible to encompass the key leverage decisions in competitive advantage. Second, divisional groupings should be adopted that draw together overlapping businesses, thereby reducing the need for coordination across divisional boundaries. An atmosphere of mutual respect and commitment to a common cause (see chapter 15) can also mitigate problems that arise with more complex overlapping structures.

In practice most organizations strike some sort of compromise between extreme profit centre separation and the reverse. But the different styles that we have identified can be seen as choosing different emphases between these extremes.

Detailed Planning Processes versus Entrepreneurial Decisions

In chapters 4 and 5 we explained why the centre, in Strategic Planning and Strategic Control companies, established demanding and thorough review processes for business plans. In brief, these companies see such reviews as providing central management with the opportunity to establish minimum standards in terms of information and analysis to support strategy proposals. They also believe it enables them to ask questions about the issues being tackled at the business level, to contribute a second, broader view as to how they might be resolved, and to understand the long-term prospects for each business.

This practice can help to counter the natural tendency for business level management to become locked into obsolete strategies. Corporate managers in almost every Strategic Planning and Strategic Control company complained that business management was neither sufficiently aware of, nor sensitive to, developments in its external competitive environment – in technology, in market demand, in competitors' strategies. They all saw a role for themselves in sharpening these perceptions. Thus, an effective review process allows the centre to challenge entrenched strategy patterns, to bring out and test assumptions behind strategies, and to stimulate the search for better alternatives.

A thorough review process 'legitimizes' the decisions eventually taken. In David Plastow's words: 'The formal system provides legitimacy and a rationale for decisions that get taken, both in terms of facts and figures and in terms of providing a forum for debate and agreeing those facts and figures.' Painful choices, such as the closure of the Schweppes Italian operation, were justified more readily because it could be seen that every effort had been made to explore and analyse all the options, and that all interested parties had had an adequate opportunity to put forward their views. 'Due process' of this sort is a side benefit of a formal and thorough planning system.

However, formal reviews inevitably impose a restrictive structure on the discussion of strategy. Specific formats, timetables and setpiece meetings may not always breed the sort of innovative thinking and flexible responses that are ideally required. A number of companies felt this problem sharply.

Any sort of strategic planning process can be death to creativity. The problem is that most large, orderly businesses are not a very good growing ground for it anyway.
(Planning director, Strategic Control company.)

Any one-year cycle provides insufficient time and resource to achieve the difficult task of putting in place a believable strategy model. To do this requires going off-line from the regular planning cycle.
(Chief executive, Strategic Planning company.)

We were trapped by too rigorous a framework.
(Planning director, Strategic Control company.)

An even more fundamental question is posed by some companies: what can the centre conceivably add through formal planning to a competent and sophisticated business management, except overheads? Business management will normally be much closer to the detail of the business. Planning reviews by the centre run the danger of simplifying issues too much, and hence of missing the vital nuances that should guide eventual choices.

The planning system worked well at a time when there was considerable operating slack to be taken up. It is less good at opening up new questions and handling ambiguous issues. It helps to improve the performance of businesses that are clearly inadequate, but is much less satisfactory for attempts to crack the more difficult questions of fine tuning strategies in businesses whose performance is not disastrous.
(Planning director, Strategic Control company.)

Formal planning reviews can easily be counterproductive if they have to be conducted at a level that simplifies choices and suppresses relevant detail.

If management seizes the opportunities for discussing strategic issues afforded by the budget and capital appropriation systems, and maintains regular informal contact between the centre and the business, there may be little that formal strategic planning reviews can add. That is why the Financial Control companies have dispensed with these processes, taking the view that lower level management should have 'freedom to devise appropriate strategies unfettered by corporate planning bureaucracies'.

The Financial Control view is that there is more to be gained by encouraging business managers to act entrepreneurially, to maximize profit opportunities as they see them, than by tying them down with strategic planning formats and processes. They tend not to emphasize formal, long-term planning systems, even if they thereby reduce opportunities for the centre to influence the strategic thinking of the businesses.

Of course, not all strategic planning systems are beset with the worst excesses of bureaucracy, rigidity and oversimplification. Effective strategic planning systems can add value. They are able to:

— focus attention on key issues;
— surface implicit assumptions behind strategy proposals;
— bring together relevant information, analysis and views on proposals;
— provide sufficient time, both in formal meetings and in more informal contacts, to explore the major strategy options fully;
— create a forum for arriving at decisions and gaining support and conviction for them in the organization.

If the company does use formal strategy planning systems, they must provide an effective challenge to strategic thinking in the business units. Thus, the centre must be willing to cross the threshold of effort necessary to make this sort of contribution. An across-the-board annual cycle that spreads effort thinly across all businesses is unlikely to achieve this, unless the basic disciplines of strategic thinking have previously been absent in the businesses. There also needs to be a short-circuit procedure for reaching rapid decisions off-line from the formal planning system. Effectiveness is in part a matter of the design of the strategic planning process, but is much more a matter of how it is operated. These issues are explored more fully in appendix 2.

But, however good the planning process, basic tensions remain; between devoting time and effort to checking and reviewing business units' strategy thinking and allowing them the maximum scope to operate independently and entrepreneurially; between spending enough time in structured reviews of plans to provide a genuine challenge to them and supporting creative thinking by eliminating rigorous frameworks; between belief in the value of the challenge provided by corporate management and belief in the importance of asking those closest to the detail to make the decisions. These are tensions that lie behind the different attitudes to planning reviews that are found in each strategic management style.

Strong Leadership versus Business Autonomy

In chapter 4 we described a number of reasons why corporate managements believe that strong central leadership in strategy is desirable. These included the broader perspective and experience brought by corporate management (BP), the management of overlaps and 'synergy' between businesses and divisions (STC), the provision of strategic themes that build on, and reinforce, corporate strengths (Lex), putting forward new ideas and suggestions to enrich business unit thinking (UB), and the establishment of priorities and clear decisions on the most contentious and difficult strategic decisions (BOC). The advantages of corporate participation and leadership in strategy development are, of course, stressed more strongly by Strategic Planning than Strategic Control or Financial Control companies.

The Control-orientated companies are both more sceptical about the benefits of corporate leadership and more aware of its drawbacks. The primary cause of scepticism relates, again, to corporate management's comparative lack of detailed knowledge of the businesses.

In one of our larger participant companies we were told of an initiative to enter a new, but related, business that corporate management had decided was desirable for one of its divisions. After corporate research into the opportunity, and discussion of its implications, the division chairman had been informed that it was now up to him to enter the new business. In the words of the corporate chief executive, this 'enlarged the thinking of the division, and pushed them towards an opportunity they were overlooking'. The same events were described very differently by the divisional chairman: 'A curious procedure. If they had known more about the business, they would certainly not have asked us to go ahead, at least not in this way.' More pointedly, another view from the divisional level was: 'They come up with daft ideas that we then have to lose.'

Divisional and business criticism of corporate management's role in strategy most frequently comes back to lack of real knowledge about the business unit's affairs. The root of the problems seems often to lie in a disparity between the centre's view of its competence to propose strategy and the business's view of the value it adds. One comment: 'The chairman sees himself as a strategist – especially concerning collaboration and acquisitions. He tends to throw out ideas. His understanding of the business may be rather weak, however, so some ideas can appear strange.' The centre needs to make a realistic appraisal of its strategic capabilities.

Doubts about the value of corporate interventions and leadership are compounded by concern that decentralization and business autonomy will be disrupted, with all the worrying consequences that entails. Strategic Control and Financial Control companies recognize these problems and hold that good business unit general managers value their independence and autonomy highly. The sense of freedom to run their own show as they think fit brings out the best in them, and ensures that they are constantly seeking new opportunities and ways of responding to the competition and the market. The more the strategic initiative is pulled back to the centre, the more this will be resented by competent general managers.

The chairman of a Vickers division, describing his attitude to freedom and responsibility argued:

> In giving freedom, it's a bit nerve-wracking at times because you feel you're not in control, not in charge. But the result is that they take more initiative and they perform better. And they feel responsible for their actions, whereas if you at the centre always ask questions, always try and monitor things very, very carefully you get a reaction that they're not really responsible for the decisions, that you're really controlling things and so if it goes wrong, it's as much your fault as it is theirs.

Conversely, a business unit manager in a Strategic Planning company, who felt that he had suffered from too much central interference with the detail of his business, claimed that cooperative approaches to strategy were hard to make work: 'The secret is not to have to spend too much time defending your own policies and implementation decisions from corporate intervention.' Inverting Baldwin's words, it is responsibility without power that has been the complaint of the business unit manager throughout the ages.

The development of future generations of general management can also be damaged by too much central strategic leadership. As we have discussed, the danger in centralized companies is that there will not be sufficient opportunities for lower levels to take early responsibility for strategy. Ultimately, any company's ability to create and retain competent general managers in the business units will be impaired if the centre intervenes too much in strategic decision-making. This can become a problem in Strategic Planning companies. We have also shown that business units can respond to the possibility of active central intervention by becoming less open and more protective in their dealings with corporate management. These efforts to preserve their freedom of action do nothing to enhance the quality of the strategic decision-making process.

Close involvement in strategy-making can also inhibit corporate objectivity in reviewing business unit strategic thinking and exercising quality control. Once the centre has become caught up in the strategy development process, it is less easy for it to stand back dispassionately and criticize its results. The failure in BOC's central group to perceive the 'amber lights' around the carbon investment illustrates this point well (see chapter 4, p. 72.)

The powerful claims that central leadership adds value can therefore be balanced with equally strong opposing arguments. As long as there are opportunities, as there always will be, to improve the strategies proposed by business unit management, there is an important role for central leadership. At the same time, as long as the centre itself is fallible, and as long as there is value in devolving responsibility to separate business units, there will be countervailing forces. This is the classic centralization–decentralization tension.

Although none of our chosen companies has been able to avoid this tension, it *can* be loosened. When central inputs are advisory, rather than directive, the value of a second view can be preserved with less impact on business autonomy. The quite detailed suggestions from the centre at BTR are taken in a constructive spirit by business managers, since they know that in the last resort the decisions will be left to them. Conversely, in another company, a business manager who felt strongly the frustrations of central interference commented thus on his chief executive: 'If you ask for advice, you'll get an instruction.'

A self-denying ordinance is in order here for corporate management, since its questions, let alone its advice, cannot avoid carrying substantial weight, given the power of the boss in the corporate hierarchy. As one senior planner rather naively put it: 'It's surprising how, if the chief executive simply asks a question, next time you come back it's led to all sorts of changes.' There is relatively little danger that advice from the CEO will not be listened to and taken seriously.

Similarly, the more constraining a corporate theme, the more resented it will be. In Cadbury's the core businesses see few problems with the corporate theme of concentrating on the major confectionery and drinks brands and expanding internationally. This accords well with their own sense of where the company's strengths lie, and allows considerable latitude for strategy development within it. The non-core businesses found the theme much less acceptable, since it conflicted with the directions in which they would have wanted to move forward.

The best themes for development do no more than make explicit a consistent and productive strategic direction that has begun to emerge from the strategies of each business unit. 'Service excellence' may be a mission that can drive all of Lex's businesses, but only because most of these businesses had already moved towards the high service end of their respective markets. The value of the theme then lies in making this direction explicit, and reinforcing it in future strategic moves. A theme that runs counter to existing strategies in many businesses is likely to fail.

Finally, it is vital that corporate inputs should be seen as based on sufficient knowledge and insight to add value. Although in some sense obvious, this does militate against off-the-cuff expressions of intuitive prejudice – not unknown among our participant companies. It tends to favour leaders who have a demonstrable track record and depth of personal experience in a business (Peter Walters in oil, Hector Laing in biscuits), and advice grounded on in-depth study of the business and its relationships with other parts of the company (the ISRs at BOC, STC's review of IT strategy).

Our research suggests, however, that there is no way for strong central leadership to avoid entirely the drawbacks we have identified, since it must to some extent inhibit business autonomy. Different styles of strategic management make different judgements about how much value leadership by the centre adds, and about how serious are the problems that it brings.

Long-term Strategic Objectives versus Short-term Financial Objectives

The belief in the desirability of long-term strategic objectives follows from the conviction – undoubtedly justified in at least some businesses – that following through a strategy to a successful conclusion can take several years, and that purely financial measures of success may not reveal the factors that make for competitive advantage. It would, for example, be absurd to try to set objectives and controls for ICI's pharmaceutical business purely in terms of the next year's reported profits. The belief that long-term strategic objectives and thinking must complement short-term financial measures of performance united all the Strategic Control and Strategic Planning companies.

Long-term strategic measures of control have, however, proved difficult to implement. In terms of motivation, a target that is set 5 or more years ahead does not have the sharp reality of a more immediate goal. Feedback so far into the future cannot provide anything like the incentive that comes from feedback next month or next year; targets based on long-term forecasts are inevitably vaguer than next year's budget figures. The perceived importance of progress towards the long term therefore tends to be viewed very much within the context of shorter-term achievements. As an example, BP's minerals business has embarked on a strategy of building for the very long term future – time scales of over 20 years are not uncommon in this business. In the meantime, its reported results have suffered. Whatever view is taken of progress towards the 20-year goal, a series of red figures now inevitably creates strains within the business, and between the business and the corporate level: 'It is not good for us to see ourselves as constantly losing money and being discussed as a problem.' Some shorter-term achievements and successes are needed to create mutual confidence and the feeling that progress is being made, which is one reason why BP Minerals is now planning increased emphasis on finding ways of boosting shorter-term results.

Furthermore, because of the uncertainties of the long term, revisions to a 5-year objective may well have to be made before control can be applied. Taken to extremes, this can mean that the day of reckoning never comes, and that a continuous series of revised objectives, always looking a little further into the future, postpones long-term control indefinitely. Tight control against long-term objectives is difficult, if not impossible, to achieve. Thus the tendency in some of the businesses of the Strategic Planning companies is for low profitability to be extended for longer and longer periods.

Financial Control companies argue even more strongly against long-term objectives. They insist that excessive concern with the distant future takes the eye off important potholes in the road immediately ahead, and that getting the short term right is the best way to get the long term right. This credo is reinforced by career moves that result in few business unit managers holding one job long enough to have to live with the pay-off to their long-term plans. One Hanson Trust director summed it up: 'The trouble with long time spans is that it is very hard to hold people accountable. If you have most of your attention on decisions that will pay off in 5 years' time, at that point someone else is running the business.'

Strategic Planning and Strategic Control companies have therefore sought strategic control variables that would provide shorter-term measures of progress towards long-term strategic goals. Such strategic milestones are intended to focus directly on measures of competitive advantage – for example, product developments, service levels, market shares – and to provide a balance with financial targets. But even though such measures are desirable, all our companies experienced great difficulty in establishing credible non-financial, strategic control variables.

I think the system needs to clearly identify key benchmarks within the strategic plan so that these can be built into the management information system and progress against them can be monitored. But this is seldom well done and many companies don't bother to do it at all. There is often confusion that the financial out-turn of the plan is itself a sufficient benchmark to justify if the strategy is working or not. As we all know, this is a totally inadequate measure.

(Managing director, Confectionery, Cadbury Schweppes.)

The difficulty in establishing strategic milestones, which we described in chapters 4 and 5, relates partly to the problems encountered in identifying the key factors that contribute to competitive advantage in a business; partly to problems of finding objective and measurable variables to indicate progress; and partly to the inability to be precise about how to trade off progress against different strategic variables and between strategic and financial variables.

Trevor Chinn of Lex had this to say on the subject:

> One of the problems we face is how you measure market share in businesses where the figures are not produced for you. In the motor industry it is well documented. In other industries the figures are not available and it can be very expensive to produce them. And then you're faced with problems like how do you measure quality. We believe that quality and service are the keys to our businesses. But we are finding it very difficult to measure against these stategic goals, especially when they are not susceptible to quantifiable measurement.

If strategic goals cannot be measured precisely and objectively, we have to rely on a degree of subjectivity, and this complicates the control process. Financial results at least appear[2] to provide a firm yardstick of performance; strategic goals are often cast in broader, more judgemental terms. A model of how progress against strategic variables feeds through to financial performance, and over what time period, might enable companies to establish agreed trade-offs between potentially conflicting strategic and financial goals. But such a model very seldom exists, even in rudimentary form. So companies end up in endless debate about how much slippage in financial achievement is acceptable to preserve the strategy, and vice versa. As a result, it is hard to disentangle legitimate deviations from budget from excuses that should not be tolerated.

In short, the introduction of many different, potentially conflicting, hard-to-measure strategic objectives makes control more complex and effective implementation more difficult to achieve.

All these points support the preference of the Financial Control companies for a much clearer focus on financial results for the immediate future. Because financial targets are more tangible and more objective, the control process is simpler and more internally consistent. Business units can be given more freedom, since the centre does not have to wait long to know whether results are on track; and managers can afford to act and speak more independently, since their performance will be judged against objective financial criteria. The subjective opinions of the centre concerning their management skills count for less. All of this is highly desirable.

There can, however, be situations where short-term financial measures allow a business to follow the wrong road. For example, there have been criticisms of Hanson for selling Berec's admittedly unprofitable European operations, together with patents and technical know-how, to Duracell, its major competitor. Given the competitive situation in this business, it is by no means clear that this was a 'strategic' error. But it can be argued that the focus on short-term profits did make it harder for Hanson to take any other course than that which it adopted. In businesses where there are trade-offs between short-term profits and longer-term security, this can cause problems.

Different companies therefore give different emphasis to strategic and financial measures of performance, and the choice of emphasis is a basic decision for corporate management. The choice is not so much *either* strategic *or* financial measures, but whether to combine strategic and financial measures or concentrate on the financial measures. To some extent the choice should reflect the circumstances and context of the business unit in question – a topic discussed further in chapter 12. But it also illustrates the way different companies look at the time horizons appropriate for building competitive advantage. There is a fundamental difference here between Strategic Planning and Strategic Control companies, on the one hand, and Financial Control companies on the other.

Attempts to balance strategic and financial measures of performance worked best in companies where central management had sufficient knowledge of the businesses to form a view on when exceptions to the control process were warranted. In Financial Control companies, corporate managements that were close to the business units were able to decide when (as exceptions to the rule) adhering too strictly to financial control would be damaging. In Strategic Control and Strategic Planning companies, closeness to the business meant that they could avoid naive application of broad strategic controls, and sift out blatant 'excuses' from valid strategy trade-offs. ICI feels it helps to start the review process with relatively little detailed information, but then to be prepared to go through a series of progressively more detailed iterations on more contentious issues.

It is Strategic Control companies who are the most concerned to preserve a balance between strategic and financial goals. One way for these companies to strike the balance appears to be to treat short-term financial objectives as minimum standards, as constraints that have to be met, while maintaining strategic goals as the real objective to strive for in the long term. This clarifies the role of different sorts of objectives. However, difficult trade-offs remain concerning the level at which to set minimum financial standards, and what is the right response when the achievement of even minimum standards appears to threaten strategic progress.

At a more mundane level, a number of corporate managements also stressed the importance of avoiding too rapid a rotation of managers. If a manager knows he will have to live with the results of his decisions, he will be less inclined consciously to sacrifice the long term – whatever the current incentives in the control system.

Finally, particular controls can be superseded by a broader sense of commitment to a common aim. We explore this possibility further in chapter 15.

Tight Controls versus Flexible Strategies

Tight controls entail the establishment of powerful incentives that align the personal goals of managers with corporate goals. By defining good performance, holding individuals responsible for its achievement, and then rewarding them in financial, career or psychological terms, corporate management make objectives much more personally binding for business management. The theory is that not all business managers spontaneously push themselves as hard as they could. They therefore set themselves goals that are insufficiently demanding and are tolerant with themselves if they fail to achieve them. By pressing business units to set themselves best practice standards of performance ('high wire' goals, 'finger tip reach'), and by motivating them to go all out to achieve them, the centre raises the sights of the whole organization.

Although tight controls place more pressure on business unit management, those who survive come through 'feeling like winners'. The knowledge that tough targets have been set, and have been seen to be achieved, is itself a strong motivating factor. In chapter 6 we quoted the Tarmac group managing director who said:

> If business unit management don't deliver they should feel very bad. They should feel that they have failed themselves, failed us and that life is awful. On the other hand, if they succeed they will feel like winners. They are basking. And they are rewarded.

It is worth noting that he then added: 'Although the reward is mainly in the mind.'

Rigorous control processes do appear to create high levels of personal commitment to the achievement of agreed targets. It is for this reason that both Financial Control and Strategic Control companies stress their value. But they can also have less desirable consequences – attitudes that are risk averse, inflexibility in management thinking, conflict with planning influence, and emphasis on motivation through control.

1 *Avoidance of Risk*   In large companies, really biting sanctions for non-performance can be provided more easily than corresponding rewards for success. One executive in a Strategic Planning company even argued that corporate incentives and controls never rewarded innovation adequately. As he put it: 'If things go well, most senior and middle managers get a 10 per cent rise. If things go badly, they get fired.' This asymmetry can be redressed somewhat through incentive compensation schemes, stock options, fast track promotions and so forth. But the risk–return balance remains very different from that confronting the individual enterpreneur, particularly where there are severe penalties for failure.

The point was reinforced by a divisional director in a Strategic Control company, who argued:

> Tight control was and is needed. But it does mean that managers tend to cut costs and meet budget before thinking about building sales, and it does discourage risk-taking. Managers get kicked hard if they go for risky innovation and fail. The tendency is for more risky investment to drop out of the plan as it gets turned into the budget.

If, therefore, meeting agreed targets is seen as very important, proposals with a more uncertain or risky outcome may be suppressed. It is interesting that a number of corporate managements who extolled the value of tight control and stretching standards also complained about the lack of new growth options for investment coming forward to them, and about the tendency to reinforce strength, rather than create new businesses for the future.

2 *Loss of Flexibility*   When clearly measurable performance criteria are set in advance, management thinking may become less responsive to opportunities and threats as they arise. Innovation and creativity in strategic thinking are diluted: at the extreme, control becomes a straitjacket rather than a motivation to perform.

These problems are particularly acute for growing businesses. A Courtaulds manager who had been responsible for building one of the very few businesses in the UK with a leading worldwide competitive position, IP Marine, explained how corporate control processes can hamper long-term investment and introduce constraints on thinking; how stretching financial objectives can eliminate the slack that is necessary to invest as needed to meet the best competition irrespective of next year's budget impact; and how regular monitoring of progress against defined goals can restrict the constant adaptation that is frequently needed in the early stages of building a business. The secret of IP Marine's success during the 1970s, he noted, had been a large contingency reserve against possible future liability claims. This, together with corporate acceptance that rigid and precise targets for performance were inappropriate, gave freedom and flexibility to the business unit management to do what they knew to be right for the business. This is the antithesis of 'tight control'.

3 *Conflict with Planning Influence*   The control process can work against planning influence. If the goal becomes achievement of the control objectives, rather than of underlying competitive strength, it is more difficult to challenge the premises of the strategy. For Financial Control companies, who believe in leaving the strategy to the business manager, this drawback is less material. But for Strategic Control companies, it can cause serious difficulties. We were told in one Strategic Control company that the centre had become convinced that a particular business needed to change its strategy if it was to be viable in the long term. However, there

was enormous difficulty in persuading the manager concerned to consider a change, because he had so far been more than meeting his control objectives.

4 Emphasis on Motivation through Control Motivation through control discourages motivation through mutual confidence and commitment to a common cause. The underlying assumption is that managers cannot be trusted to do the best job of which they are capable without close monitoring and powerful personal incentives. One of the problems stemming from tight control is that the definition of specific control objectives can then lead to 'game playing' to achieve these objectives, no matter what the cost.

> Currently plans are unrealistic. The game is to put in a plan which fits the guideline objectives proposed for the business. If you do this, you get an easy ride at the reviews. The idea is that the first year of the plan then becomes the budget. In practice the art is to come back with a budget that is more conservative – you argue that things have changed since plan time.
>
>   (Business manager, Strategic Control company.)

So companies must make choices about how and to what extent they enforce control targets. Strategic Planning companies such as UB and Cadbury's regard strategic progress as the paramount objective. They accept that the changeability of today's business environment can cause slippage against specific targets. As one senior manager put it: 'Good strategy is the masterful administration of the unforeseen.' Control orientated companies, in contrast, believe that it is up to business management to find ways of accommodating to the changes in the environment without deviating from their objectives. Tensions thus exist between two prime considerations: establishing broad strategic advantage and adherence to the specific control objectives. The balance struck between these considerations carries implications for strategic flexibility, control motivation and risk aversion.

There are ways of loosening these tensions – for example, by establishing controls only against broad performance aggregates, and allowing flexibility as to how these objectives are met at a more detailed level. Chris Hogg of Courtaulds, whose watchword is 'control to get things done, not to stop them being done', has tended to concentrate on broad cash flow targets. He gives divisional and business managers freedom to meet these targets either by increasing profits or by reducing investment, and to apply them uniformly or selectively within their areas of responsibility. And although ICI under Harvey-Jones increased the emphasis on meeting control objectives, these are now stated in less detail than in the past, so allowing decentralized divisional management more room for manoeuvre.

But, when corporate management do set broad objectives, the control they are able to exercise is diluted. They are less able to check that best

practice standards are being applied in all phases of a business, and have to
be confident that business management do not misuse their freedom within
the broad objectives.

BTR, which believes strongly in the value of detailed control against an
extensive series of ratios, would feel that it had lost much of its ability to
intervene productively, if it concentrated only on broad performance
aggregates. Even within Courtaulds it is accepted that some divisions have
failed to make good use of the latitude and potential for flexibility and
selectivity created by the broad targets. These trade-offs, however, simply
reflect the underlying tensions between control and flexibility, which can
be lessened but not eliminated by the use of broad objectives.

To reinforce innovations, the establishment of a powerful 'upside' can
balance the 'downside' of failure, though rewards for high fliers too far out
of line with rewards for other managers can be organizationally disruptive.
A tolerance of 'useful' failures is in theory also desirable, though in
practice Control companies find it difficult to reconcile this with the
principle of tight control objectives. Harvey-Jones's repeated public
pronouncements on the importance of entrepreneurial initiative as a
counter to the tightened control process represents another device for
balancing control tensions that has had some success.

All the Financial Control companies build in an expectation of profit
growth to go with their strict budgetary procedures, thus creating an
expansionist pressure to counter any risk aversion that the Financial
Control process may produce. At Tarmac one of the managing directors
went further. He argued that the control system instils a psychology of
winning that, if anything, leads business managers to be over-ambitious:

> It's like Manchester United. They want to be top of the first division and they
> won't accept anything less than the first three places. We want our
> management teams to feel like that. Pure logic would argue that a
> management team would set a low budget because life will be easy.
> However, when they do put in a low budget we make them feel that they
> have let the side down. We make them feel that they are not ambitious to be
> part of the first team. On the whole, we have more problems in the other
> direction. The management have so much belief in themselves that they want
> to go in too deep. They may fall into the trap of thinking that they can do
> anything.

So Tarmac sees the restraining influence of the Financial Control corporate
approach as a positive benefit.

In the Strategic Control companies the whole strategic planning process
is intended to provide a long-term, strategic context for budgets as a
counterweight to the conservatism of control. ICI's insistence that
strategies should not be sacrificed to the achievement of budgets without
corporate approval is a case in point. But we have already commented in
chapter 5 on how easy it is for financial objectives to dominate strategic
considerations as a basis for control.

The preservation of a balance between tight control and flexibility, innovation and risk-taking, is therefore not easy for large organizations. The centre cannot at one and the same time effectively *both* insist on defined performance standards *and* encourage creative and adaptive business-building activities in high risk and uncertain environments (see the discussion of Strategic Programming in chapter 4). The tensions between control and flexibility can be lessened, but not eliminated; and the different styles embody different attitudes concerning how the balance should be struck.

Summary

The tensions in the role of corporate management concern organization structure, planning process, central leadership, objective-setting and tightness of control. In each of these areas, choices and trade-offs must be made, and express essential differences in management philosophy. The different strategic management styles that we have encountered in our research stem from different attitudes to the tensions we have identified. Table 9.1 summarizes these differences.

The tensions can be mitigated by sensitive corporate management processes. Some of the suggestions we have made are:

Tensions in:	Mitigated by:
Organization structure	● Businesses defined to encompass key points of competitive leverage ('SBUs') ● Businesses that need coordination structured into divisional groupings ● Mutual respect and common cause
Planning process	● Well-designed process (see appendix 2)
Central leadership	● Advice, not instructions ● Broad, unconstraining themes ● Understanding the businesses
Objectives	● Understanding the businesses ● Slow rotation of managers ● Common cause ● Short-term constraints, long-term objectives
Nature of control	● Broad goals ● Manage upside/downside assymetry ● Growth expectation ● Well designed strategic planning process

Table 9.1 Styles and tensions

	Strategic Planning	Strategic Control	Financial Control
Organization structure	Multiple perspectives	Separate responsibilities	Separate responsibilities
Planning process	Thorough review	Thorough review	Entrepreneurial response
Central leadership	Strong leadership	Division autonomy	Business autonomy
Objectives	Strategic and financial	Strategic and financial	Financial
Nature of control	Flexible	Tight	Tight

But the tensions cannot be eliminated by any of these means. All styles are liable to encounter the disadvantages that balance their attractions. It is for this reason that no one style emerges as the 'right way' to manage.

At base, the different styles and management philosophies stress different images of the successful corporation. Financial Control assumes that the organization is composed of strong individualists, highly motivated by personal goals, and that corporate management provides the context and incentives for them to drive themselves to ever-greater achievements. It also assumes a business environment where straightforward pursuit of profit can safely be made the dominant goal. Strategic Planning assumes that managers succeed by working cooperatively together to devise new, bold and creative strategies to build long-term advantage in a complex and uncertain world; and that corporate management should be contributing to, and catalysing, this creative and cooperative process. Strategic Control shares Financial Control's view of managers as goal-orientated individualists, but prefers Strategic Planning's account of business as concerned with long-term competitive advantage in an uncertain and complex environment.

Each of these images contains elements of truth, since in reality managers are both individualistically goal-orientated and cooperatively creative; and business is both about building advantage for the long term and making profit now. But by the same token, each image and each style also contains elements of falsity.

Therefore, whatever style is adopted, there is much to be said for remaining aware of its intrinsic drawbacks, as well as its advantages; and for remembering the strong points of other styles. Many of the managers with whom we talked seemed to feel it necessary to argue for their way of doing things to the exclusion of all alternatives. Our research suggests that the tensions inherent in the corporate management role are likely to be held in balance best by those who are most conscious of the choices they are making, and who are most willing to recognize the virtues of the styles they have rejected.

We will give the final word on this topic to Chris Hogg. Commenting on organization structures and styles he observed: 'An organization is like a pendulum. It swings from too much centralization to too much decentralization; and comes to rest only when the mainspring is dead.' We should expect to see a continuing evolution in the styles of successful companies as they attempt to balance the intrinsic tensions in the role of corporate management.

Notes

1 Dick Vancil (*Decentralization*, Harvard Business School, 1979) addresses the question of how far profit centres should be independent of each other, and how far they should employ shared resources. He concludes that the more functional authority profit centre managers have over their own separate resources, the more autonomy they perceive themselves to have in running their businesses.
2 The 'objectivity' of profit figures can of course be questioned. Creative accounting provides some latitude to reinterpret financial results. However, provided that accounting conventions are generally agreed, the financial numbers are normally accorded a reasonably objective status.

10

Avoiding Pitfalls

We argued in chapter 9 that no style will be free from drawbacks. Each style has inherent tensions that cannot be avoided, and which explain many of the problems encountered. However, by no means all of the problems we found stemmed from these tensions. We met stories of outrageously poor decisions, of seemingly blind bosses, or bureaucracy and meddling, and of many more ways in which companies fail to work effectively. From these stories, we have developed a list of 12 common pitfalls – problems that frequently distort the strategic decision-making process, but which we believe can be avoided with good management practice.

None of the companies suffered from all the pitfalls – they would find it hard to make any sensible decisions if they did; but all of them have, at some time and in some divisions, suffered from one or more of them.

1 'Habits of Mind'

In chapter 2 we referred to the tendency for managers to fall into habits of mind, i.e. to adopt tunnel vision with respect to their strategies. This is a widespread problem, and intervention by the centre is frequently aimed at breaking patterns of strategy that have not been adequately thought through or tested.

But it is also important for corporate managers themselves to defend against their own habits of mind. We spoke with the managing director of a business in a Strategic Control company who believes that the centre systematically undervalues the importance of sales and marketing: 'They visit the factories regularly, but almost never the sales offices,' he said, as an example of the corporate attitude. And in most companies the centre develops similar blindspots or enthusiasms that prevent its influence from being as objective as it could be. Who is it, in these cases, that guards the guardians?

The most effective way of dealing with the 'habits of mind' pitfall is to introduce fresh views and opinions continuously. The use of outside consultants, secondment of managers to training courses that challenge conventional thinking, special project responsibilities that cut across established organization structures, a willingness to recruit new blood at senior levels from outside the company; through these means the tendency to 'group think'[1] can be held in check, and habits of mind at business unit or corporate levels can be prevented from dominating strategy.

2   'Barons'

Corporate strategy is about allocating resources and making decisions for the benefit of the company as a whole, rather than to further the interests of particular groups, divisions or businesses. But managers have a natural tendency to fight their corners, to argue for growth and priority for their own areas of responsibility. Division or group heads sometimes see the size of their empires as a reflection of their status. They frequently seek maximum autonomy, demanding the right to develop their domains free from corporate constraints. We found that these 'baronial' instincts, in which senior group executives fight to build up their own territories with little regard for the corporate interest, are all too common .

Problems that arise with the barons include biased sponsorship of initiatives, censorship of information flowing to the corporate level, and rivalry between divisions or groups based on the personalities and power of their leaders. Decisions get taken on political grounds rather than on the merits of the case. 'They were motivated not to criticize the proposals being put up by their colleagues for fear of receiving criticism themselves. Or alternatively to criticize strongly in response to criticism they themselves had received. All this led to "equable" decisions which would not upset the political balance', was the comment in one Strategic Control company

To avoid baronial problems a number of companies, including BP, BTR, Hanson Trust, ICI, Tarmac and Vickers, now make a clear distinction between main board corporate roles and divisional line management. Executive members of the main board ('the executive team' as ICI calls it) may have responsibility for overseeing and liaising with divisions or groups of divisions. But board members (or group executives, as they are often called) typically have no, or very few, personal staff, and do not filter or process the plans or the results of their businesses in communicating them to the centre. They are a channel of communication between the centre and the businesses, and, in diverse companies, can be closer to the businesses than is possible for the chief executive. But they are not held personally profit-responsible for results. They are corporate players, with a wider view, not line managers.

The divisional heads are the line managers. They have profit-responsibility and must account directly to the CEO. As such, they devote all their energies to their areas of the business. They are not expected at the same time to adopt a broader corporate perspective on issues within or beyond their divisions. They are therefore not members of the main board.

Sir Peter Walters summed up the distinction as follows: 'I have six managing directors in the corporate offices who are my men. They are corporate managers [group executives]. Their role is to get the corporate message out and spread the corporate ethos. They are no longer barons. And the men running the divisions are no longer on the board.'

The drawback of this arrangement is that it complicates reporting relationships. The divisional line manager now reports to the CEO (or the board), but through the main board group executive. The group executive does not have personal decision authority, but the division manager is expected to tick things off with him ahead of corporate reviews. At its best, this procedure can lubricate communications and make for better-informed corporate decisions. But sometimes it leads to confusion and lack of clarity about how decisions are taken. Establishing new reporting relationships and a *modus vivendi* between division managers, group executives, the CEO and the board can take some time. But the pay-off in terms of a more rational and less political corporate decision process is regarded as well worth the effort by those companies that have made the transition.

3 'Interference'

At its worst, corporate influence over business unit strategies can be seen as little more than counter-productive interference. Many reasons, often specific to particular situations, lead to this reaction to corporate interventions. There are, however, three more general problems that we encountered with some frequency. They arise where interventions are seen as arbitrary and unpredictable, indiscriminate and across-the-board, or based on insufficient homework about the business in question.

Arbitrary and Unpredictable Interventions Nothing is more likely to undermine the quality of the corporate–business dialogue than corporate interventions that are seen as arbitrary or unpredictable: a sudden instruction to pursue a new market in contravention of previously agreed strategy; allocations of resource that appear to owe far more to the personal force and will of the proponents than to any assessment of strategic business priorities; detailed suggestions on factory layout divorced from any real understanding of the production process; and, perhaps most commonly, a unilateral and unexpected increase in budget objectives that takes no account of the consequences for the underlying competitive strategy of the business. By ignoring both the criteria and the processes that are normally applied to planning and control, these types of intervention undermine the credibility of the dialogue about strategy between the centre and the businesses. Senior corporate managers generally recognize how disruptive such interventions can be, but their ability to avoid them varies. Sufficient self-discipline to avoid this particular pitfall is a feature of those companies whose strategic decision-making processes are best accepted.

Indiscriminate and Across-the-board Instructions Arbitrary interventions often take the form of indiscriminate or across-the-board intructions: 'All businesses should aim to grow by 10 per cent' or 'All business should seek a 10 per cent cut in overheads'. The seemingly magic 10 per cent is frequently associated with these sorts of instructions, irrespective of their specific contents.

Across-the-board directives may have a superficial appeal on the grounds of 'fairness'. The following extract from an interview with a corporate financial controller illustrates the nature of the situation:

Controller   We have just had a decision from the centre that the coming budgeted profitability is not acceptable and capital and discretionary spends must be cut back by some 20 per cent. Corporate management argued for 2 days over how the cuts should be allocated but they failed to agree. I got the job of deciding.
Interviewer Did you try to be selective in who was cut hardest?
Controller   No, I'm not going to get involved in the politics of it. I figured out an across-the-board allocation that could be defended on the basis of equity.

Quite apart from the apparently arbitrary and unpredictable nature of the proposed cuts, the long-term damage they inflict on different businesses is liable to vary extensively. Across-the-board cuts are really an admission that corporate management does not know the businesses well enough to attune their instructions more sensitively to the circumstances of each one.

Uninformed Interventions   Particular problems arise where corporate management are seen by the divisional and business level as uninformed. 'We have to educate them in the basics of the business as well as going through the numbers and the proposal. We have been over the same ground again and again about the characteristics of the industry. All this reflects a lack of understanding of the business at the corporate level', complained a divisional chief executive, discussing debates with the centre about capital projects.

In chapter 9, on tensions, we have argued that a lack of detailed knowledge about individual businesses is inevitable for corporate management. On the other hand, we believe that there is no excuse for central management failing to do their homework thoroughly when required. Different styles call for different levels of knowledge about the business units, and the diversity of the portfolio needs to be matched by the style adopted (see chapter 13). But, for any style, there is a requirement for some minimum level of investment of time by corporate management in understanding the businesses.

To avoid this pitfall, there must be a free flow of information about each business to the centre, and the centre must devote as much time as is needed to assimilate and discuss this information. Companies with styles as different as Tarmac (Financial Control), Courtaulds (Strategic Control) and BOC (Strategic Planning) all place a premium on spending time learning enough about a business to be able to contribute effectively to its strategy, whether through planning or control.

4 'Exercise in Cleverness'

A common pitfall in planning and control processes is to fall into an adversarial mode, in which corporate and business levels try to score points off each other. This can rapidly degenerate into what one corporate planning director called an 'exercise in cleverness', with destructive criticism and nit-picking over disputed details taking precedence over the search for strategies that will succeed for the company. 'Too often we get a 30-page document the night before. We have a culture that it's safer to do everything at the last moment. This gives reviewers less time to formulate awkward questions', said one division manager. Reviews for the businesses in his division were not notably constructive.

This phenomenon seems most prevalent in companies where the centre does not feel confident about its grasp of the businesses and perceives that it lacks credibility with business unit management. In companies where the views of the centre are well respected, either because of track record or personal experience, or because of the background work they have done, an adversarial atmosphere is less likely to be found. A 'no surprises' agenda (see chapter 4, p. 53) also helps to ensure that the debate is constructive, not an ambush for the unwary.

5 'Bureaucracy'

We have referred several times to the danger that planning and control processes will degenerate into 'bureaucracy'. This pitfall is illustrated by the comments of a divisional chief planner:

> The process has tended to develop into a discussion of 5-year forecasts rather than of underlying issues. A great package of things arrives at corporate from time to time during the year. It is very standard and formal with little contact in between. This means that there is never enough time to get past the pat answers that have been prepared.

These concerns are reinforced by a senior corporate manager in a Strategic Control company who argued:

> Not everything can be written down, so that the uncertainties that are left in the formulation of strategies lead to differences in interpretation. Unfortunately the reliance on the formal system means that these are not reconciled by good direct informal communication.

In other words, the centre gets involved in divisional strategic thinking late in the process, infrequently and mainly through formal contacts. Not surprisingly this adds little value, and the planning 'exercise' simply becomes a repetitive annual event: 'Planning time was like a monsoon – a once a year event. We used to draw straws for who got to work it up.'

Control can be equally ineffective, with frequent detailed reporting but no follow up: 'Vast piles of bumph: what they do with it all, I've no idea', was one comment. A not uncommon complaint was that a good deal of time was taken up in complying with detailed corporate reporting requirements, but that there was almost no feedback from the centre in response. 'The reports are greeted with a resounding silence', said one divisional managing director.

Bureaucracy is at its worst in organizations with many different review levels. In one Strategic Control company there were no fewer than five general management levels between the business unit and the CEO. 'A whole series of rakings over at different levels, but all of them too shallow', was the view from one of the businesses. A structure of Business (major sources of competitive advantage). Division (important overlap issues across businesses). Centre (corporate review and control) can be defended, but any further levels should be avoided. This should mean that reviews that do take place are substantial.

Bureaucracy can be reduced if planning and control processes are flexible and selective, and focus on key issues instead of simply generating quantities of unused paperwork. They should provide both formal and informal opportunities for the centre to make useful contributions to business unit strategy and to influence the outcome of decisions. Appendix 2 discusses these points further. Personal feedback on control reports, though time-consuming, also pays dividends. A particular strength of the BTR and Tarmac systems is the provision for face-to-face monthly review meetings for discussion of results versus plan. This both reinforces the importance of control targets and provides an opportunity for the centre to discuss important issues as they arise and to contribute to their resolution.

6 'Non-core'

A number of companies, particularly those with the Strategic Planning style, have defined core businesses, which will represent the major components of their portfolios for the future. This is seen to provide benefits in communicating corporate priorities for resource allocation, and in creating a corporate identity. However, it causes difficulties for remaining non-core businesses.

These problems were brought out forcibly by the managing director of a non-core business in one of the Strategic Planning companies.

> They were not particularly interested in the strategy of the division. Some were interested in selling it; others were more inclined to hold on provided it performed adequately. The decision to stay in some of the lowest profit parts of the division was emotive; the company felt committed to them because they'd invested so heavily in the seventies, and because they didn't want to face the costs of getting out. What knowledge at the centre there was of the

business tended to be based on past personal experience of people who had worked in the area, often several years earlier at a time when circumstances were quite different. The central contribution to strategy has been mainly negative as a result of all this. One never knew from day to day when someone was going to come in and want to try to sell part of the business.

This is no atmosphere in which to plan and execute strategy.

Non-core businesses are less well understood by corporate management. As a matter of principle, they are unlikely to receive support for aggressive strategies. Yet corporate 'commitments' may prevent radical surgery. So strategic weakness is perpetuated indefinitely.

Several corporate managements argue for holding on to non-core businesses as long as they remain profitable. Yet this decision prevents a sale when a favourable price could be expected, and ensures that withdrawal will occur only when the business's weaknesses are becoming evident for all to see. Our belief is that once a business has been identified as non-core, an early exit decision benefits both the business and the corporate parent.

7 'Hockey Sticks'

All too often, long-term plans make projections that fail to materialize and, more importantly, were never likely to. 'Hockey stick' plans (a brief dip followed by a prolonged, substantial but improbable improvement) were referred to in almost all the Strategic Planning and Strategic Control companies. Over-optimistic projections reduce the value (and the credibility) of both planning and control.

Lack of realism is closely linked to the control process. If over-optimistic forecasts are rewarded, they will be made. A division chief executive in a Strategic Control company commented: 'We knew that our projections were unrealistic at the time we made them. But anything else would have been unacceptable to the chairman.' Furthermore, if failure to deliver against long-term targets is not penalized, people will be more inclined to make optimistic forecasts. Control against long-term objectives is not easy, but it is remarkable how few Strategic Planning and Strategic Control companies have any kind of formal control against long-range targets at all. This encourages the 'hockey stick' syndrome.

8 'Lip Service'

The competent business manager does not take long to discover the control objectives that really count in his company. If promotion and financial rewards accrue to managers who turn in high reported profits, strategic goals soon become a matter for lip service only. 'In this company the strategy is only accepted until the time of the next budget', claimed one business general manager somewhat bitterly. And those Strategic Control companies that call for extensive strategic plans, but gear bonuses exclusively to achievement of budgeted profitability, must accept that business managers will act accordingly. Equally, if the strategy matters more than the short-term targets, as in some Strategic Planning companies, the control process will be undermined.

The power of perceived rewards is illustrated through the poor acquisition record of one company. 'What's rewarded is doing a deal, not preventing it', we were told. Less emphasis on the results achieved by the acquisition than on bringing off the deal had led to some injudicious acquisitions, with not enough caution and prior research on potential candidates. Thinking through the impact of incentives and controls on strategies and actions is vital.

A conflict between strategy and controls can and should be avoided. The task is much easier for Financial Control companies, since they are not concerned with trade-offs between strategy and financial results or between the long and the short term. Yet all companies can attempt to see that bonuses do reflect targets they believe are important, and that promotion and prestige accrue to managers whose behaviour is in accordance with agreed plans. Though apparently elementary, this consistency by no means always exists.

9 'Control Games'

Control systems are intended to motivate managers to achieve corporate goals. But where control objectives become ends in themselves, there is a danger that gamesmanship to meet defined targets will actually impair the long-term health of the business. Controls can then 'come back and bite you'.

Stories of prices raised to meet profit budgets at whatever cost to market position, of necessary investment projects deferred to dress up short-term results, and of the pursuit of parochial interests are all too common. 'I was under so much pressure to increase my RoS that we ditched a systems development project that I know was important for our strategy', said one business manager in a Strategic Control company. 'Now I've told my finance director to hide some cash in reserves so that I can do the things I want and still keep them happy.' 'We move product about internationally, but, because we're autonomous, if we think we can screw money out of some other nation we do so. That's part of the game', said another profit centre manager, illustrating the way in which an excessive drive to maximize the results from individual units can damage the total business.

Whatever the sophistication of information systems, business management can usually use its superior local knowledge to conceal or distort results, and it may be some years before the consequences show up in control information.

But consistency over time and coherence across the whole range of controls can prevent the exercise of control degenerating too far into such game playing. This, together with openness of communication and cooperation in a common aim (see chapter 15), can avoid the paradox of the indirect consequences of controls working against the overall objectives that the controls are designed to secure.

10 'Moving the Goalposts'

> We had all agreed the strategy and the objectives, and we were pushing ahead on that basis. Half-way through the year, the CEO told us that things had changed. We had to cut back on research and overhead spending and forget the original targets. Running a business is impossible when the goalposts keep being moved like that.

This complaint, echoed in several of the Strategic Control and Strategic Planning companies, identifies the particular problem of shifting objectives. If those in charge of a business feel that the centre is liable to change its mind about what it wants them to achieve, confusion and demotivation result.

Pressure of external events, such as a corporate cash flow crisis, may of course dictate a change in objectives in midstream. This is uncomfortable, but understandable. What needs to be avoided are unprompted, capricious changes in corporate policy or preferences, to which those down the line are then expected to conform. The way to avoid this pitfall is through a constancy and consistency in corporate objectives that will resist temptations to change direction without careful prior consultation with the businesses concerned.

11 'Yes, Chairman'

In one company we were told of an extensive series of studies and outside consulting assignments that had been undertaken to arrive at conclusions that already enjoyed wide support within the organization. Their purpose had not been to generate fresh ideas but to provide a means of communication with the chief executive. This roundabout approach was necessary because the indicated strategy conflicted with the previously stated convictions of the chief executive, and because people were unwilling, as individuals, simply to disagree with him. The effective controls in the company were evidently perceived to penalize dissent from his policies.

In another company we met a division chairman shortly before he was due to see the chief executive to discuss the company's planning and control processes. Our meeting had revealed a number of cogent criticisms of these processes, and at the end we asked whether he would now be passing on these criticisms to his chief executive. The response was: 'Oh no. That's not what he would want to hear.' If openness and the expression of a variety of views matter in strategic decision-making, a 'Yes, chairman' atmosphere of this sort is very damaging.

It can be argued that efforts to please the boss are inevitable in any hierarchy, and that this pitfall cannot really be avoided. However, there is a clear distinction between the sycophantic, 'Yes, chairman' organization and the organization that encourages more robust debate. 'There is a view in this company that those who argue with the corporate view will not survive', we were told in one interview. The preferences of the CEO, and the sort of behaviour he is seen to reward, have much to do with the openness of debate.

12 'Strategy and Inaction'

A final pitfall concerns the failure of some planning and control processes to work at creating a consensus for action throughout the organization. The generation of ideas, the analysis of options, the establishment of controls may be exemplary. But the need to sell the strategy within the organization is overlooked, or left to take care of itself at lower levels. It was even asserted in one company that: 'In this company, it has never been our practice to make any formal communication of decisions we reach at the board. We expect the grapevine to pass the message on for us.' As a result, some fairly garbled messages were on occasion passed down the line, and good strategies were not always translated into action.

Nor can it be expected that a tightly argued memo will automatically be accepted and understood. 'Logic is not enough – the people element is very important and I lean heavily on experience in convincing people', claimed the corporate development director in one Strategic Planning company. 'It is important to pre-expose line managers, and give them time for their bath-time thinking.'

Communication and consensus building need to be an integral part of the strategic decision-making process, not left as an unmanaged after-thought. Companies that do use the planning process as a means of bringing people together, and as a vehicle for creating commitment to new strategies, gain enormously in the implementation phase. Within these companies, public presentations of proposed new strategies are used as an opportunity to show that the strategy has been carefully analysed and logically constructed. They also allow managers to air questions – an invaluable aid in building consensus.

Summary

Those, then, are the 12 pitfalls that damaged strategic decision-making most often in the companies we researched. We do not claim that corporate management does not recognize them; indeed the list could probably be extended by most chief executives with no difficulty. Nor do we believe that the pitfalls are easy to eliminate. If they were, it would be much harder to understand their prevalence. But we have tried to suggest ways in which the centre can avoid them, and we have based our suggestions on best practice in the participant companies. The points can be summarized thus:

Pitfall:	Avoided by:
1 'Habits of mind'	Fresh, outside views
2 'Barons'	Group executives with corporate role
3 'Interference'	Sensitive interventions, enough information and homework
4 'Exercise in cleverness'	Mutual respect, cooperative atmosphere
5 'Bureaucracy'	Few layers, focused planning system
6 'Non-core'	Exit
7 'Hockey sticks'	Rewards for performance, not plans
8 'Lip service'	Consistent strategy and controls
9 'Control games'	Consistent controls, openness, common aims
10 'Moving the goalposts'	Constancy in corporate objectives
11 'Yes, chairman'	Openness
12 'Strategy and inaction'	Building consensus

None of the pitfalls is peculiar to a particular style. However, the nature of each style makes it vulnerable to specific pitfalls. Thus Strategic Planning is particularly prone to 'interference', 'non-core' and 'hockey stick' problems; Strategic Control suffers most from 'interference', 'exercise in cleverness', 'bureaucracy' and 'lip service'; while Financial Control encounters 'exercise in cleverness' and 'control games' most frequently. 'Habits of mind', 'barons', 'Yes, chairman', 'moving the goalposts' and 'strategy and inaction' are common pitfalls under all styles.

But the avoidance of pitfalls, though important, is a negative objective for corporate management. In the next chapter we will therefore move on to consider how each style adds value, setting the discussion in the context of both the tensions and the pitfalls we have identified. Our aim will be to reach a better understanding of the balance of advantage and disadvantage that each style represents.

Note

1 The phenomenon of group think is explored in I. L. Janis, *Victims of Groupthink* (Houghton Mifflin, 1972) and in I. L. Janis and L. Mann, *Decision Making* (The Free Press, 1977).

11

Adding Value

We turn now to the key issue for central management under any style. Do the separate businesses gain from membership of the whole? Is the sum of the parts greater than the aggregate of the individual components? How and when does the centre add value under each style? Our test will be whether the individual business units perform better as part of the corporate portfolio than they would as independent entities. This is the harsh criterion that all central management groups should apply in rating their own effectiveness.

The added value issue also arises in comparing different companies. Often the question is not only whether a business would be better off as part of a group than as an independent company, but also whether the business would prosper more in one group rather than another. In acquisition battles, such as the fight between Hanson Trust and UB for control of Imperial, the option of continued independence may be ruled out early, and the outcome turns on judgements about which contender is likely to make the better parent organization. This means that the attractions of different companies with different styles have to be assessed. The assessment is based on asking which style, which parent company, adds the most value.

We shall find that the styles add value in different ways. None of them is inherently the best. Each has strengths and weaknesses, and can both add and subtract value. It is essential to understand this balance of advantage and disadvantage in assessing the merits of different styles.

All styles add *and* subtract value because of the tensions we described in chapter 9. Each style is positioned differently against these tensions. Predictably, therefore, the styles lead to different results and different advantages for the business units. But, by the same token, they also lead to different disadvantages. Each style highlights certain benefits and foregoes others. Figure 11.1 summarizes the choices made by each style and compares them to the capital market. Throughout this chapter we must remember that, whatever the style, the centre must add more value than could the capital markets alone if it is to justify its existence.

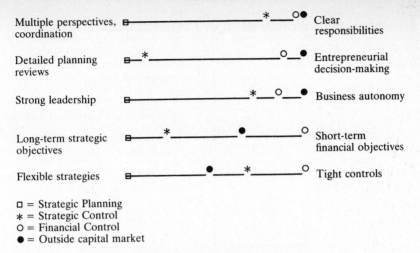

Multiple perspectives, coordination ←→ Clear responsibilities

Detailed planning reviews ←→ Entrepreneurial decision-making

Strong leadership ←→ Business autonomy

Long-term strategic objectives ←→ Short-term financial objectives

Flexible strategies ←→ Tight controls

□ = Strategic Planning
* = Strategic Control
○ = Financial Control
● = Outside capital market

Figure 11.1   The styles and the tensions.

Mechanisms for Adding Value

For the centre to add value, it must influence – and improve – the strategies of the business units in the group and/or the actions taken by managers. In chapter 3 we identified the main mechanisms through which the centre influences business unit strategy and actions. These are:

- Organization structure.
- Planning process.
- Central themes, thrusts and suggestions.
- Management of overlaps.
- Resource allocation.
- Objective-setting.
- Monitoring of progress.
- Central use of incentives and sanctions.

We will structure our discussion of each style around these mechanisms, assessing the added and subtracted value that the centre's efforts create.

It will be evident that each of the styles uses these mechanisms in different ways and to different degrees, and that these differences follow from each style's positioning in terms of the various tensions, as summarized in figure 11.1. For example, a company's processes for allocating resources and setting objectives will reflect the relative emphasis it places between long-term strategic goals and short-term financial goals. Similarly the nature of the organization structure will express the priority given to clear and separate business responsibilities as against coordination. The various mechanisms for influencing strategy correspond to the five tensions we have discussed as follows:

Mechanisms for influencing strategy	*Corresponding tensions*
Organization structure and management of overlaps	Multiple perspectives and co-ordination versus clear responsibilities
Planning process	Detailed planning reviews versus entrepreneurial decision-making
Central themes, thrusts and suggestions	Strong leadership versus business autonomy
Resource allocation and objective-setting	Long-term strategic versus short-term finanical objectives
Monitoring of progress, incentives and functions	Flexible strategies versus tight controls

For each mechanism there is an underlying tension, and it is these tensions that cause the different styles to add and subtract value in different ways.

We will therefore summarize the key features of each main style in terms of the mechanisms they employ for influencing strategy. We will show how these features can add value, but, paralleling the discussion in chapter 9, we will also bring out the tensions they involve and the more negative consequences they have. We will identify which of these negative consequences are intrinsic to the style, and which can be avoided. Finally, we will follow through some examples of how the styles typically handle the process of strategy change at the business unit level, and summarize the impact of each style.

Strategic Planning

Table 11.1 shows the key features of the Strategic Planning style. They have been expressed in terms that show how they relate to our discussion of tensions.

The *complex and overlapping organization structures* of these companies ensure that a variety of views on strategy will be expressed. They also allow the centre to inject its ideas into the formulation of strategy. So they bring

Table 11.1 Strategic Planning: key features

Organization structure and overlap management	– Multiple perspectives, matrix structures, strong staffs, coordination mechanisms
Planning process	– Extensive, strategic
Themes, thrusts and suggestions	– Strong central leadership
Resource allocation	– Part of long-term strategy
Objectives	– Longer-term, strategic
Monitoring and controls	– Flexible

the judgement and experience of a cross-section of senior managers into play to help define the best ways forward. This allows a wider discussion of issues and a more comprehensive search for new strategy options than would occur in an independent company. Coordinating committees and devices also allow strategies to be drawn together across a variety of businesses (or countries), to achieve benefits of synergy and integration that would not be available to separate companies. And strong staff groups at the centre allow economies of scope in the provision of central services.

The drawback of this structure is that business managers have less clear-cut individual responsibilities, less control over their own destinies. The emphasis on cooperation between businesses and across levels, and the need to coordinate strategies, means that they have less unilateral authority to take decisions for their businesses that they personally feel are right. The inevitable price of multiple viewpoints and synergy is some loss of autonomy. This, in turn, can reduce motivation, unless a sense of shared purpose compensates for the loss of individual responsibility.

The *extensive planning processes* of the Strategic Planning companies are an important means for getting different views aired. They are a test of business unit thinking, and can help to prevent businesses from falling into outdated or inappropriate strategy patterns. By challenging business managers' 'habits of mind', they perform a useful function that the independent company lacks. The questions posed by the central management in a Strategic Planning company should be much more informed, much more 'strategic' than is possible for the outside investors and bankers to whom the independent company reports. This is a prime value of the planning processes of the Strategic Planning company. They also constitute a vehicle for the exercise of central leadership in strategic decision-making, and a means by which the centre can learn more about the businesses. But extensive planning processes cannot avoid constraining business managers. As one line manager explained:

> The decision-making and planning process in our company is very pro-
> fessional. We are very open about discussing things. We chew over important
> decisions at great length. My boss will get involved and his boss will join in
> the thinking. It's all very constructive and I am sure we make a better
> decision as a result. But somehow after all the discussion, I don't feel it's my
> decision any more.

The need to communicate and justify plans to the centre inhibits freedom of action, slows down the decision process, and takes some ownership from lower levels of management. The independent company can be swifter and more entrepreneurial.

Furthermore, Strategic Planning processes are often cumbersome and confusing rather than probing and insightful. At their worst, they degenerate into rigid, bureaucratic exercises. The drawback of bureaucracy in planning may not be intrinsic to the Strategic Planning style, but it is an occupational hazard – a potential pitfall.

By providing *strong central leadership* through themes, thrusts and suggestions, the Strategic Planning companies are able to embark on bolder, more aggressive strategies than would otherwise emerge. Central sponsorship can enlarge the ambitions of business management, ensure that resources are available to support investments, and help to overcome risk aversion. We have given examples in each Strategic Planning company of the sorts of business building strategies that result, often looking towards the building of long-term advantage in major international businesses. It is doubtful whether these strategies would have been adopted by independent companies, without a supportive and well-resourced parent in the background to underwrite the effort. It is in this context that mission statements and broad policies can be valuable, by defining what will receive priority from the centre.

The downside of strong leadership is equally clear. Close involvement by the centre in strategy development inevitably reduces both the objectivity of the centre in reviewing strategy, and the sense of personal 'ownership' at the business level. This is the strong leadership–business autonomy tension.

Moreover, strong leadership can lead to a number of pitfalls. It can be seen as autocratic or ill-informed interference that overrules business level ideas; bold strategies can become risky and over-optimistic; sound opportunities in non-core businesses may be turned down because they do not fit with the grand design. These pitfalls are frequently associated with the Strategic Planning style, although the best exponents of the style are able to avoid them. In companies such as BP, strong leadership blends into a cooperative attempt to work together for a common aim, thereby generating a sense of shared purpose and commitment that goes far to offset the disadvantages we have listed.

Resource allocation and *objective-setting* in the Strategic Planning companies *are aimed at the long-term* development of the business. The centre acts as a sort of buffer to the capital market, protecting the business units from the need to satisfy the shorter-term performance criteria applied by the outside investor. This allows business managers to concentrate on building the core businesses, rather than trimming their sails with a view to meeting half-yearly earnings targets. It also means that they can make major acquisitions to support existing activities, or to build new ones, without an expectation that the pay-off to such moves will come immediately. Clear priority can be given to long-term objectives.

There are a number of businesses in the Strategic Planning companies that have benefited from this strategic, long-term resource allocation process. Without it, BOC would be a weaker force in the worldwide gases business; Lex would not have built up its electronic component distribution business; BP would not have achieved its successes in oil and gas exploration. But there are others which, it can be argued, might have reacted more quickly to adversity, or avoided risky and unpromising investments, if they *had* been exposed to the disciplines of the external capital market.

Several managers in Strategic Planning companies made us aware of the dangers of too much emphasis on strategy and the long term. 'The pressure on the long term took our eye off the short-term issues. They [corporate] and we undervalued the short-term profit impact of what we were doing', said one manager. 'Too much strategy and not enough graft', was the conclusion of another.

We have also pointed out the difficulty in defining clear, objective and measurable goals for monitoring long-term performance. This means that long-term performance measures open up the possibility of excuses. As Dick Giordano of BOC put it: 'This is probably one of the most difficult challenges. How do you have milestones that measure strategic progress without allowing excuse-making from business management?' But to point to these shortcomings is only to underline the tension that exists between giving priority to profits now or profits later, to short-term controls or long-term objectives. All Strategic Planning companies must accept some sacrifice in the clarity and enforceability of short-term objectives in order to allow for the allocation of resources to long-term aims.

Linked to this tension we noted that Strategic Planning companies are also prone to undue optimism about the future ('hockey sticks') or personal incentives that are not linked to strategies ('lip service'). Lacking both market disciplines and clear internal targets, the atmosphere can become too cosy. As one divisional manager put it: 'As part of the corporate entity, we have this shield and blanket around us to protect us.' This can mean that flexibility becomes tolerance, and tolerance becomes looseness. Motivation to perform is then lost. The fact that the Strategic Planning companies have been relatively inactive in divestments, closures and portfolio rationalizations, and that some have overextended themselves through rapid growth, is all evidence of this.

Furthermore, replacing the verdict of the stock market with subjective corporate assessments of strategic progress may not be an unmitigated gain. If second guessing what will impress the centre becomes the major goal, this can be even less conducive to strategic thinking than the short-term financial pressures of the City. It is in these circumstances that corporate 'politics' flourish, with decisions taken to reinforce personal positions in the hierarchy, rather than to improve the strategies of the business.

Finally, the *flexible control system* in the Strategic Planning companies adds value. By accepting that precise, short-term targets may have to be compromised in order to stay on track to build a business, it encourages a more tenacious pursuit of long-term goals. Furthermore, it is more tolerant of innovative strategies that carry with them the risk of failure, and of strategies that evolve continuously to meet the needs of rapidly changing markets. The centre in the Strategic Planning company is more sympathetic than the capital market to the manager who is struggling to create a major new business in a highly competitive and uncertain world.[1] As an example, we will discuss UB's achievements in the US 'cookie war' more fully on p. 214 below.

Flexible controls, however, can never provide clear and objective standards of performance. Hence it is harder for both the centre and the business manager to know whether results are 'on target'. An element of judgement enters into the assessment of performance, and increases the scope for discretion. The price of flexibility is ambiguous performance measures and a reduced sense of personal accountability.

Table 11.2 summarizes the key features and the added and subtracted value of the Strategic Planning style. We have divided the negative features of the style between those that are intrinsic, and those that represent characteristic pitfalls that can be avoided with skilful management. The negative features of the style can be minimized or avoided by:

Table 11.2   The Strategic Planning style

Key features	Added value	Intrinsic subtracted value	Common but avoidable pitfalls
Complex, co-ordinated structure	Wider discussion of issues Synergy Central services	Less individual responsibility and authority	Can reduce motivation
Extensive, strategic planning process	More thorough search for best strategies	Less freedom of action Slower decisions	Can be cumbersome, confusing, bureaucratic
Strong central leadership	Bolder strategies Shared purpose and commitment	Less 'ownership' by business Less objectivity by centre	Can become interference Can lead to risky and over-ambitious strategies
Long-term criteria	Building core businesses 'Buffer' to capital market	Slower reactions to adversity Less clear targets	Can lead to over-optimism, 'lip service'
Flexible controls	More tenacious pursuit of long-term goals More innovative, responsive strategies	Subjective assessments Less accountability	Can lead to politics

— sensitive, flexible and selective planning processes (see p. 169);
— avoiding autocratic leadership (see p. 171);
— well-informed central management (see p. 186);
— shared purpose and commitment (see p. 305);

— avoiding over-optimism (see p. 189);
— personal incentives aligned with strategy (see p. 190);
— strenuous efforts to identify, measure and act on strategic milestones (see p. 173).

But the style will always give less priority to individual accountability, responsibility and incentives, and to short-term measures of performance.

Financial Control

At the opposite extreme to Strategic Planning lies Financial Control. Table 11.3 summarizes the key features of this style.

Table 11.3   Financial Control: key features

Organization structure and overlap management	– Clearly separate, profit centre responsibilities
Planning process	– Budgets
Themes, thrusts and suggestions	– Business autonomy stressed
Resource allocation	– Project-based; short payback criteria
Objectives	– Shorter-term, financial
Monitoring and controls	– Very tight

The *organization structures* of the Financial Control companies stress *multiple, separate profit centres*, each with independent responsibilities. As far as possible, these structures replicate, for the profit centres, the circumstances of independent companies. The profit centres are set up to overlap as little as possible, and no attempt is made by the centre to coordinate between them. The profit centre manager is largely free to run his own show without interference from other parts of the company. 'We believe in the importance of the individual line manager in achieving success for his business and for the group as a whole. The management system has been devised to give maximum responsibility to the line management', said Martin Taylor of Hanson Trust. There are advantages in the simplicity and clarity of this structure. In particular it gives early general management responsibility, thereby developing the skills needed for the long-term success of the compnay.

But the structure is less ambitious than that of the Strategic Planning companies. It adds no value in comparison to the independent company situation; but at least it avoids the negatives which are also associated with the more complex structures of Strategic Planning companies.

The *planning process* in the Financial Control companies *concentrates on budgets*. The emphasis is on the short term, and on agreeing targets rather than on the means by which they are going to be achieved. As with Strategic Planning companies, the centre probes the plans of business managers, but the nature of the questioning is very different. For Financial Control companies the primary value arises from the pressure it creates for 'high wire' standards of profitability and growth in profits, not from probing underlying strategic logic. As Lionel Stammers of BTR put it: 'Many managers do not know what they can achieve until you ask them.' The Financial Control companies add value by asking for performance that is more demanding than that insisted on by stockholders or bankers; and they exert pressure for performance much more continuously. An independent company can produce unexciting results for long periods, in some cases for many years, before market pressure will cause a change in management. But in Financial Control companies controls are tight.

As a by-product of the budgeting process, managers may also have to think again about the validity of the strategies they are following. If they are unable to satisfy corporate requirements, they may be forced to consider changes of direction. But the centre will not typically question strategies directly, or expect to make much contribution to the definition of new and preferable strategy options. And the emphasis is on next year's results, 'the road ahead', not the long term. The focus on results not strategies leaves managers more free to make their own decisions, provided they turn in the required performance. Furthermore, the planning process can be simpler and therefore less prone to 'bureaucracy' than in Strategic Planning companies.

The major drawback of the planning process is that it cannot claim to add much value to the business manager in probing and thinking through his strategy options. Indeed the short-term results orientation may distract him from tackling long-term issues. If the stock market is felt to create an unduly short-term orientation, the Financial Control style serves to reinforce this bias. We noted, for example, that a number of the subsidiaries of Financial Control companies are losing market share. Their managers explained that they are retreating from less profitable sections of the market; and that market share is not a useful objective. As one BTR manager put it: 'We don't pride ourselves on market share. In fact, we don't like to refer to market share at all.' It is this focus on the short term that causes critics of Financial Control companies to claim that they are gradually harvesting their competitive positions. Taken to extremes the style can encourage managers to milk their businesses by cutting back too far on investment.

Although the centre may make occasional suggestions, *business autonomy* is preserved in the Financial Control companies by insisting that the final decision rests with business management, and by avoiding any broad, top-down corporate themes, missions or thrusts. This philosophy attempts to replicate the freedom of the independent company, and hence can obviously add little value when compared to it. If, however, constructive suggestions are made, but not imposed, the business manager may gain something which is denied to his fully independent counterpart. Nevertheless, it is clear that Financial Control does not attempt to add as much value in this respect as Strategic Planning; equally, however, it runs fewer risks of subtracting value.

The *resource allocation* process in the Financial Control companies adopts *objectives and criteria similar to the capital market*. There is no attempt to buffer the businesses from requirements for short-term profit. Rather, the Financial Control style sees itself as applying capital market criteria, but in a much more thoroughgoing and efficient manner. With detailed information on each business, and the ability to discriminate between them in resource allocation, the centre can ensure that funds flow only to those businesses whose proposals meet corporate criteria, and whose track records give confidence in their ability to deliver. The system reviews each investment on its merits, rather than as part of a long-term business strategy. It adds value by insisting that proposals will only be funded if they project high returns and fast paybacks, and if business managers appear committed to achieving their forecasts and have a track record of doing so in the past. By exposing all individual investments to this test, it goes much further than the capital markets in applying tough standards. The centre, however, does not pretend to have a detailed knowledge of each business's products and markets, or to be able to criticize, shape and add value to the strategies behind the investment proposals.

The centre is more directly active in acquisitions and divestments. The search is for acquisition candidates whose assets are underperforming. Value is added to these acquisitions by increasing their profitability through the application of Financial Control disciplines. Conversely, divestments are made of businesses that do not respond to these criteria.

The clear emphasis on *short-term* profit *objectives* in resource allocation and acquisitions simplifies the management task. But it can also result in missed opportunities. We were told of a number of opportunities that had been considered and rejected because of the risk or the length of payback of the investment. Although it is not clear that the opportunities rejected would have resulted in substantial profit growth, it is probable that many more of these opportunities would have been taken up by Strategic Planning (or even Strategic Control) companies. One example is the market for standard gate arrays. Both GEC and Ferranti had the opportunity to enter the fast-growing MOS-technology segment at the early stages. Both rejected the opportunity. Ferranti chose to stay with its proven bi-polar technology and GEC, after examining options, passed up the opportunity altogether. The bold strategies they rejected were pursued by LSI Logic which now has a leading position worldwide. The short-term focus does preclude longer-term, more speculative investments. The tension remains, and means that the Financial Control style will always create problems in businesses where long time scales are needed.

The main strength of the Financial Control style, however, is in the *tight controls* it imposes. Not only are budgets stretching; not only do investments demand short paybacks; but also the monitoring of results achieved and the feedback and follow through from the centre create strong incentives to deliever. The knowledge that there will be a speedy reaction to under- (or over-) achievement of monthly targets does create more motivation, more pressure for performance than is brought to bear on the managing director of an independent company. The simplicity of the criteria for judging performance also makes it easier for line managers to know where to focus their attention; and makes it perfectly clear who is doing a good job and succeeding, and who is not. Indeed, the knowledge that demanding standards have been set and can be seen to have been met is one of the prime motivating factors for successful managers in the Financial Control companies. In chapter 1 we quoted the BTR division head who was willing to forego £10,000 in salary in exchange for the psychological satisfaction of knowing he was going to be able to deliver on his budgeted objectives.

Those who do meet their objectives can be confident that they have earned the respect of the centre, and grow in self-confidence themselves. This has two benefits. It makes for a more open discussion of business issues with the centre, since the line manager can rely on his results rather than his words to impress the centre; and it creates a 'winners' psychology amongst business managers, which makes them feel more capable of overcoming obstacles and pushing on to further peaks of performance.

But the tight control process also has its downside. It can stifle creativity, snuff out experimentation and eliminate the entrepreneurial 'skunk works' activities. There is less flexibility to respond to opportunities. The point was made by a Hanson Trust group chairman in this way:

> Our business chief executives tend to be quite conservative in assessing the payback of potential investments. In order to preserve credibility with Hanson Trust, they will typically only promise what they are certain they can deliver. The chief executive knows he will be hung on it, and is therefore cautious rather than over-ambitious.

At its worst, tight control can mean that everything is sacrificed to meeting specified control objectives at whatever cost to the underlying health of the business. The 'Control games' pitfall can lead to the system becoming a straitjacket, not a source of added value.

Table 11.4 summarizes the key features and the added and subtracted value of the Financial Control style, again distinguishing between intrinsic problems and avoidable pitfalls. The negative features of the style can be minimized by:

— targets that require year-on-year *growth* in profits (see p 179);
— leaving business managers in post long enough that they have to live with the consequences of the strategies they adopt (see p. 175);
— informed central managers who will offer constructive advice and suggestions but without imposing their views (see p. 303);
— willingness to question and override control objectives if it is clear that they will damage the health of the business (see p. 175);

Table 11.4 The Financial Control style

Key feature	Added value	Intrinsic subtracted value	Common but avoidable pitfalls
Separate profit centres	Simplifies task Early general management responsibility	No coordination, synergy	
Budgetary planning	Higher standards Challenges strategies that won't deliver Avoids 'potholes'	Distracts from strategic issues	Can encourage milking the business
Business autonomy	Advice, not instructions	No cooperation, no 'help' for businesses	
Short-term criteria	Clearer criteria 'Efficient' internal capital market	Missed opportunities 'Control games'	
Tight controls	Faster reaction More motivation Winners' psychology	Less flexibility and creativity	Can become a straitjacket

— winners' psychology to provide energy to maintain growth momentum (see p. 179);
— acceptance that, in some businesses, the Financial Control style may be inappropriate (see p. 233).

But the style cannot avoid problems in businesses where long-term, coordinated strategies are needed, and cannot claim to provide much constructive help to business managers in the search for optimum strategies.

Strategic Control

Table 11.5 shows the key features of the Strategic Control style, again expressed in terms that relate to our discussion of tensions. Strategic Control is a blend of the features found in Strategic Planning and Financial Control.

By *structuring* themselves *around individual profit centre businesses that are grouped into divisions*, Strategic Control companies claim to achieve the motivational benefits of decentralization, while allowing important business overlaps to be managed at the divisional level. There is some added value from divisional coordination, but a minimum of interference with the independence of the business managers.

Table 11.5   Strategic Control: key features

Organization structure and overlap management	– Decentralized profit centres; some divisional coordination
Planning process	– Extensive, strategic
Themes, thrusts and suggestions	– Avoided; business autonomy stressed
Resource allocation	– Part of long-term strategy
Objectives	– Longer-term, strategic and shorter-term, financial
Monitoring and controls	– Tight

This view may justify the divisional structure. But, even if the divisional level is able to achieve synergies between businesses that would not be achieved independently, it is less clear how the corporate level adds value, structurally, to the divisions. Put simply, what would the divisions lose if they were set up as independent companies? As in Financial Control companies, the decentralized structure leaves little room for the centre to orchestrate the several businesses in the portfolio.

Strategic Control companies would argue that they make a prime contribution to divisional thinking via the quality controls in the *strategic review process*. The disciplines provide a continuing challenge that sharpens the thinking in the divisions and businesses. By its probing, the centre raises minimum standards of thinking and analysis, and prevents 'habits of mind' from forming. The intention is similar to that of the Strategic Planning companies, although Strategic Control companies limit themselves to a questioning role, and do not propose their own views from the centre.

Although we have found some evidence to support these contentions, our research suggests that, in reality, the challenge to divisional thinking is not always helpful. Extensive planning processes run into the same problem of acting as a constraint that we described for the Strategic Planning companies. Moreover the 'bueaucracy' pitfall is even more likely in Strategic Control companies, whose centres are that much more distant from the businesses. The comment in chapter 10 about planning being a 'whole series of rakings over, all of them too shallow', came from a Strategic Control company. This means either that the centre may fail to be well enough informed to raise useful questions; or that any benefits may be more than offset by the time-consuming and costly processes that they involve. 'Net' added value is not always delivered by corporate planning processes. Only if these processes are sensitively designed and administered, and if the businesses in the portfolio are likely to respond to a second view, can value be added by the centre.

Strategic Control companies generally *avoid* major *suggestions and initiatives*, and are not active in coordinating between divisions or businesses. The emphasis on *business autonomy* is well caught in the Vickers' quote (see p. 170), which argues that line managers will only feel responsible if given full autonomy. Otherwise: 'if it goes wrong, it's as much your fault as theirs'.

Strategic Control companies recognize that direction from the centre can subtract value. They stress the responsibility and independence of the business manager. However, this means that they are unlikely to add value by steering the development of strategy. Where ad hoc interventions do take place, our research would indicate that value was subtracted at least as often as it was added.

It is in *a resource allocation process that balances long- and short-term goals* that many Strategic Control companies add the most value. The centre provides access to a pool of resources, which can be made available for investment in long-term, large or risky projects. These projects might be turned down by outside investors, who have little knowledge of the business and who are often short-term or fashion driven in their attitudes, focusing more on past results than future prospects, and failing to assess technically complex or strategically innovative ideas. As Sir John Clark of Plessey argued: 'City pressures make life difficult if you're trying to balance short-term profit pressure and the requirements of the business in terms of competitive advantage.' Many of the business and divisional managements also see real value in this access to funding.

> Probably the greatest benefit of being part of ICI is that they were willing to fund us through 17 years of losses in getting the business going.
> (Chairman, ICI Pharmaceuticals.)

> We were able to take a major step forward in investment in new production capacity that would have been beyond us as an independent company.
> (Chief executive, Howson Algraphy division, Vickers.)

The downside of the long-term investment attitude is, of course, the same as in the Strategic Planning companies: a danger of undervaluing the importance of next year's profits. But the Strategic Control companies attempt to defend against this problem by balancing long-term objectives with short-term profit pressures. The ability of companies such as Courtaulds, ICI and Vickers to cut back drastically in some areas of their portfolios, while preserving growth momentum elsewhere, is evidence of their ability to make trade-offs of this sort. Indeed major corporate resource allocation decisions in the Strategic Control companies have concentrated at least as much on portfolio rationalization and profitability improvement as on long-term investment.

In practice, however, there are numerous difficulties in achieving the right balance of objectives. Assessing more speculative, longer-term investments is hard. If the centre lacks close familiarity with the business, it may be forced to rely on the credibility of the sponsoring management team, together with formal financial evaluations – much the same criteria as used by the outside investor. Where long-term projects *are* backed by the centre, the reason may be personal commitments to a business rather than clear-sighted strategic thinking. We encountered several examples of long term and continued support for a business by the centre that cost the company far more than a hard-nosed and early closure would have done.

Reliance on corporate funds for investment can also be a source of problems, since capital scarcity can cut out investments that might have been funded by the outside market. During the years of financial crisis, Vickers was unable to finance good proposals that were coming forward, and Courtaulds was short of funds for investments, even in growth areas. During this period, Courtaulds applied across-the-board cash targets to all its businesses regardless of previous success or failure. Now the company has set up its major business groups with capital structures to resemble as closely as possible the conditions of the publicity quoted parent company. It believes that the groups should be better placed to identify the consequences of their investment plans to their own balance sheets and take proper action in a more differentiated fashion to control the financing consequences of their business performance. This is a long way from viewing the value of corporate management mainly in terms of its ability to allocate resources.

Lastly, although portfolio rationalization has improved profitability ratios for the Strategic Control companies, it is less clear that divisions of these companies would have moved any less speedily to take corrective measures had they been independently set up. Strategic Control companies may move more decisively on rationalization and exit decisions than Strategic Planning or Holding companies, but the discipline of the outside capital markets would in some cases have been more pressing than that provided by corporate management.

The resource allocation process in the Strategic Control companies therefore attempts to combine the 'buffer' function of the Strategic Planning companies and the 'efficiency' function of the Financial Control companies. In some respects this achieves the best of both worlds; but in others it encounters the disadvantages that come from the lack of a clear commitment to either. This follows from the basic tension between short- and long-term goals. Furthermore, uninformed long-term investments, naive portfolio pruning and partisan preference for particular businesses are all potential – if avoidable – pitfalls for Strategic Control.

It is therefore only if the centre is genuinely better informed, closer to the businesses, and as objective as the outside investor that value is likely to be added.

Detailed monitoring and reporting allow the centre to pinpoint shortcomings more precisely; and incentives and *tight strategic and financial controls* create personal motivation in a much less blunt fashion than the outside capital market, where takeovers or palace revolutions are effectively the only sanctions against non-performing management. Provided, therefore, that the control objectives are conducive to the prosperity of the business, Strategic Control adds value.

Our research suggests, however, that the definition of strategic control objectives is fraught with difficulty. First, the objectives that Strategic Control companies establish do not always embody the strategies they have agreed. Financial controls can crowd out strategic objectives, thereby damaging the long-term interests of the business. Or vague strategic goals can become an excuse for non-performance. This means that the control process becomes bogged down in arguments over trade-offs, and the intention to create tight control languishes. Second, as in Financial Control, tight controls can subtract value, through causing inflexibility and risk aversion in strategies.

There is an intrinsic conflict between encouraging long-term, creative, strategic thinking, and imposing tight, short-term controls. Two quotes from divisional managing directors in Strategic Control companies are relevant. The first illustrates the tension between strategy and control: 'The centre is pressing us to grow. But it is unwilling to accept the negative impact on profitability this may entail.' The second illustrates the uneasy balance between strategic and financial control, and the difficulty of being poised between them: 'I asked the chief executive when I was appointed whether the company was a financial conglomerate or an industrial company. After 4 years the question still seems relevant, and the answer is always: "Ask me again in 6 months' time".' This remark found echoes in almost all the Strategic Control companies.

Making the controls supportive of flexible and innovative strategies is not easy. It can even be that the stock market, whose control process is less precise and rigorous, allows more latitude for business building than strategic controls that are poorly defined and insensitively applied.

Table 11.6 summarizes the key features and the added and subtracted value of the Strategic Control style. The negative features of the style can be minimized by:

— flexible planning processes (see appendix 2);
— willingness by the centre to spend the time necessary to get close to business unit strategies, to be knowledgeable about their competitive environments, and to discuss issues thoroughly (see p. 302);
— avoiding over-optimism (see p. 189);
— personal incentives aligned with strategy (see p. 190);
— strenuous efforts to identify, measure and act on strategic milestones (see p. 173);

But the style will always encounter difficulties in setting priorities between different sorts of objectives, and in encouraging business initiatives, while at the same time providing a check on strategic thinking from the centre.

Summary

We therefore find that each style has certain advantages and disadvantages. The nature of these – and the balance between them – is determined by

Table 11.6 The Strategic Control style

Key feature	Added value	Intrinsic subtracted value	Common but avoidable pitfalls
Decentralized profit centres: divisional co-ordination	Little by centre	No central coordination	
Extensive, strategic, planning process	Raises minimum standards of thinking and analysis Challenges habits of mind	Constraining	Can be bureaucratic; add cost, but little value
Business autonomy			Gratuitous suggestions
Long- and short-term criteria	Acceptance of longer-term investments Balanced objectives	Ambiguous objectives	Tolerance for low performers Capital rationing Uninformed investments and divestments
Tight controls	More motivation to perform	Risk aversion Subjective balancing of objectives	'Politics' 'Lip service'

the trade-offs that the style makes in terms of the tensions described in chapter 9. These trade-offs follow from and are part of the key features of the style. To appreciate the consequences of adopting a style it is therefore necessary to understand the links between its key features, its positioning in terms of the main tensions and the ways in which it can add and subtract value. We have also identified the classic avoidable pitfalls associated with each style, and suggested ways of managing around them.

In addition to breaking out the separate features and ways of adding value for each style, it is also useful to follow through each style's overall impact on businesses. We have claimed that the centre can only add value by changing the strategies and actions of business managers, and we will therefore conclude by examining some examples of how the different styles contribute to the management of change.

Managing Change

Changes in strategy tend to be messy sequences of events with no clear beginning or ending. Various writers have offered conceptualizations of the change process, and figure 11.2 shows the major steps that have been distinguished by some of the leading thinkers in this field. There are differences between these models, described more fully in appendix 3, but there is a broad measure of agreement on the essential phases.

There is an initial phase during which the key task is to *unfreeze* managers from the strategy that they have previously been following. The tendency for strategies to fall into fixed patterns that are resistant to change means that this unfreezing step is frequently painful and difficult. Attachment to old ways of doing things, and personal interests wrapped up with the status quo, militate against change. There is often a tendency to defer recognizing the need for a new strategy as long as possible. Without unfreezing from the old strategy, there is little chance of new ideas being accepted and taking root.

To achieve unfreezing, the manager must recognize some shortcomings in his present strategy. A failure to meet planned objectives that cannot be explained away, questions concerning the validity of the strategy that are hard to answer, new views from outside his immediate circle, all can play a part in unfreezing. What should not be underestimated is the level of effort needed to bring about unfreezing. We need to ask whether and how the centre contributes to the process.

The second phase in the change process involves *search* for better strategies to replace the old approach. It is here that planning plays a role; laying out and testing assumptions about the market and the competition, identifying opportunities and threats, developing a full range of alternative strategies. This may occur as part of a structured, formal process, or in a more informal manner. The search phase can be protected and thorough, or it can be much more concentrated and abbreviated. It can involve a wide cross-section of managers, or only the man in charge. It can be based on extensive information and analysis, or it can be more intuitive, resulting from experimentation and insight rather than planning. Whatever the search process, it will be a waste of time unless the unfreezing step is accomplished before the search is complete.

The final step is *consolidation* around a new strategy. This involves choice of a new way forward and building consensus and support for implementing it. It is in this phase that the rationale for the new strategy needs to be widely communicated and discussed; that pockets of opposition need to be won over, neutralized or replaced; that new structures, systems, controls and incentives need to be developed to support the strategy. The logic behind the strategy may be important in gaining legitimacy, but it is not itself enough to create personal commitment and motivation throughout the organization. The centre's contribution to the consolidation phase also needs to be drawn out.

To assess the centre's influence on each step in the strategy change

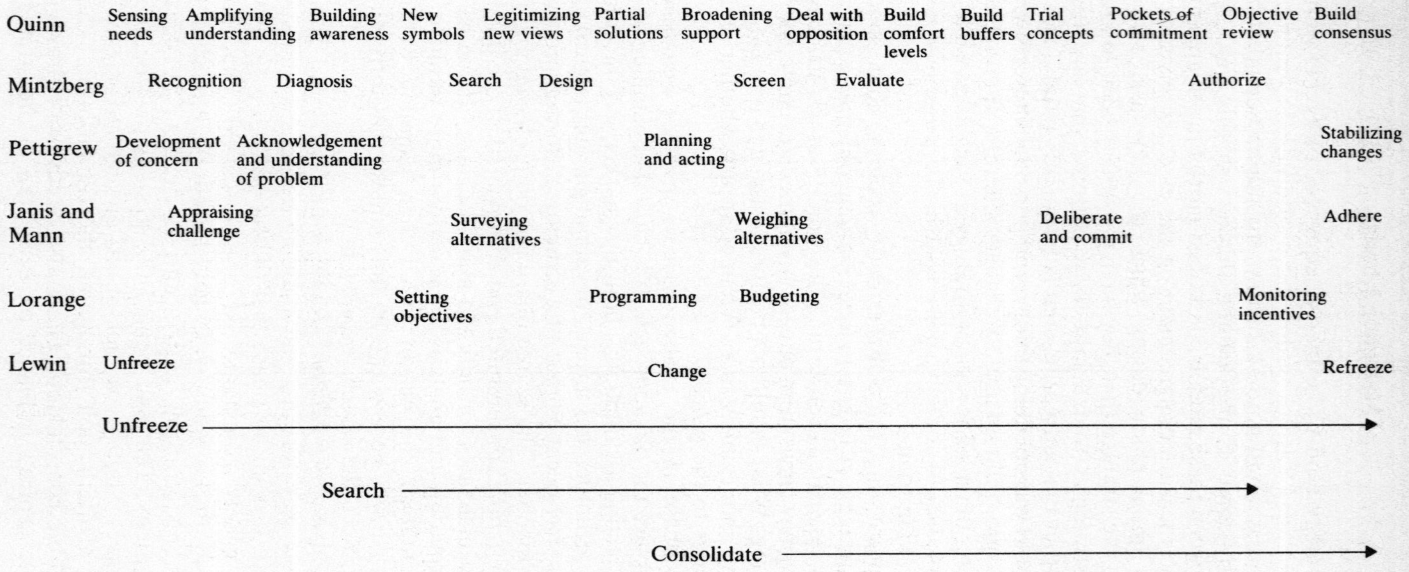

Quinn	Sensing needs	Amplifying understanding	Building awareness	New symbols	Legitimizing new views	Partial solutions	Broadening support	Deal with opposition	Build comfort levels	Build buffers	Trial concepts	Pockets of commitment	Objective review	Build consensus
Mintzberg	Recognition		Diagnosis	Search	Design		Screen		Evaluate				Authorize	Stabilizing changes
Pettigrew	Development of concern	Acknowledgement and understanding of problem			Planning and acting									
Janis and Mann	Appraising challenge				Surveying alternatives		Weighing alternatives				Deliberate and commit			Adhere
Lorange				Setting objectives		Programming	Budgeting						Monitoring incentives	
Lewin	Unfreeze					Change								Refreeze

Unfreeze ⟶ Search ⟶ Consolidate ⟶

Figure 11.2 Strategic process phases.

process we will review five examples of changes that have occurred under each style.

1   BOC: Cryoplants

In BOC's gases business, the plant engineering and building (cryoplants) activity is organizationally separate from the rest of the gases business. During the late 1970s and early 1980s this activity was organized as two separate units, one based in the UK and the other in the United States. Both were profit centres, with some third party business; but both saw their primary role as serving in-house demand for plant. Neither had achieved adequate levels of profitability in recent years, although this was generally blamed on the difficulties of being mainly in-house suppliers. A variety of investigations, studies and projects were carried out within the businesses and by the gases division during the 1970s, with the objective of finding ways to improve cost effectiveness, technical capability and profitability. However, few changes in strategy resulted.

In 1982 an ISR (Intensive Strategy Review) was undertaken, with participation from corporate staff, the gases division and outside consultants. Dick Giordano personally chaired the steering committee for the ISR. The ISR lasted for about 6 months and accomplished two main purposes. First, it established conclusively that the cryoplant activities should conceive of their role as leading edge suppliers of plant to the world market, rather than as an in-house resource. This led to important conclusions about organization, functional competences, resourcing and objectives. Secondly, it created a fuller data base concerning world markets and competitors, as a background for strategy changes. Despite strenuous arguments and disagreements along the way, the ISR ended with general agreement on the changes that needed to be made. In the period since 1983 gradual progress has been made in implementing the new strategy.

This process reflects the Strategic Planning approach to strategy change. Unfreezing was not easy, but some success was finally achieved through focusing a great deal of very senior attention on the business in the ISR. The ISR also encouraged expression of a variety of views concerning the right mission for the business, and allowed these views to be thrashed out. Finally it brought a quantity of data to bear on the market and on the division's past record in it. All these factors contributed to a growing perception of the need for change.

The ISR was also a good vehicle for the search process. It created a forum and a data base for the exploration of all possible conceptions of the business, and for the evaluation of alternative strategy options. Again, there were opportunities for a range of views from outside the business to be expressed. The ISR was terminated only after substantial agreement had been reached on the preferred future strategy.

Lastly, the ISR established strategic and financial objectives for the business. But it made less contribution to the consolidation step behind these new strategies and objectives.

2   *UB: The 'Cookie War'*

United Biscuits (UB) owns Keebler, one of three major US cookie manufacturers. In 1983 Procter & Gamble (P&G) entered this market by launching a new product, the 'soft cookie'. The new cookie was based on a different technology developed by P&G. Test market results in Kansas City showed that the new product could take as much as 30 per cent of the market in only a few months. The existing manufacturers, therefore, faced a unique crisis, which caused all of their stategies to be unfrozen. A reaction to P&G's new product was obviously needed. The question was not 'should we react?' but 'how should we react?'.

The three competitors chose basically different courses of action. One decided to concentrate on a swift response. It brought out a product rapidly to compete with P&G. This prevented some share erosion, but the product proved inferior to P&G's. The second company attempted to get to the market with an identical product to P&G's. Though successful, this caused patent suits from P&G and did not succeed in rolling back the P&G advance.

The UB approach was more ambitious. Keebler had been performing successfully for several years, gaining market share and turning in good profits. Sir Hector Laing was therefore quick to support the local management, who wanted to use this period of instability to gain still more market share. They agreed to aim for an improved soft cookie – one that would be seen to be superior to P&G's product, and which would allow them to capitalize on the industry turmoil.

After some months of development, a new product was launched. When it was seen to be a winner, Keebler decided to use it to expand in the West Coast where the company's other cookies were poorly represented. By the 1984 Annual Report, Sir Hector was able to announce record volume growth of 21 per cent in Keebler, in a cookie market that grew 12 per cent. Keebler's product was well received and had succeeded in gaining market share. But the cost had been substantial: trading profit was down 23 per cent and return on capital had more than halved due to the high capital cost of new plants.

UB's style (Strategic Planning) had helped the business unit (Keebler) to search for a good strategy, by giving management time and resources. It had also supported managers in their implementation programme. At Keebler the managers did not have to worry about their poor short-term financial performance. They knew the centre would back them, and this gave added determination to follow through.

In the event, the cookie market stopped growing and the soft cookie's popularity declined. So, although Keebler's strategy worked and market share was gained, the prize at the end was less attractive than had been expected. Profits in 1985 were also poor. But by 1986 the market began to settle down to a new equilibrium.

3 Courtaulds: Use of Consultants

In the early 1980s Courtaulds made extensive use of consultants to help managers in the business units change their strategies. In most cases the consultants were hired by the division or business unit. But this was made easier by an approving centre.

In some cases, the consultants were part of a major study to re-evaluate the business, as, for example, in the reassessment of the oriented polypropylene (OPP) strategy of the films subsidiary, BCL. BCL is one of the leading suppliers of cellophane film. But during the seventies and early eighties, cellophane came under increasing challenge in the market place from OPP. The issue therefore concerned the degree to which BCL should invest in OPP. In 1981 concern developed that BCL was not adopting a sufficiently aggressive stance on OPP. The suspicion was that the business was trying too hard to protect its main cellophane business, and under-playing the new opportunity in OPP. This was understandable in terms of immediate profit impact, but potentially dangerous for the long-term health of the business. BCL decided that an outside consulting study should be undertaken. In the event the consultants confirmed the need to invest more heavily in OPP, and helped to put together a substantial investment proposal, which Courtaulds subsequently accepted.

In other cases, the consultant's involvement was less intense. In the hosiery business and in Wolsey, a single consultant from McKinsey was used part-time to help local managers rethink their options.

The purpose of using outsiders was to upgrade the thinking of managers and to improve the data they were using. The primary value of the studies was to unfreeze managers from a historic strategy and give them the data and the logic framework needed to develop a new strategy. The consultants helped with the unfreezing and search phases of change, leaving the consolidation phase to the line managers. The centre's role in these interventions was facilitative. It provides a context in which managers were encouraged to use outsiders to improve their thinking, and ensured that their findings were taken into account in subsequent decisions.

4 Hanson Trust: Berec/EverReady

Hanson Trust acquired Berec in December 1981, at a time when the company's fortunes had been declining for several years. The Berec strategy had been to build a global brand in standard zinc carbon batteries, producing from large, centralized sites. The company had downplayed the threat from Duracell's new long-life alkali batteries. As a result, the company was losing money heavily in trying to penetrate new overseas and export markets, and was beginning to see its share of the profitable home market eroded by Duracell.

The new Hanson Trust approach involved much more rigorous financial and cost control targets. These resulted in divestment of several overseas subsidiaries, withdrawal from many export markets, reduction in R&D

budgets and severe cost-cutting exercises. On the other hand, proposals from the business to make a serious entry against Duracell in the long-life market segment and to increase UK advertising very substantially were accepted, due to their high expected returns. The business responded well to these changes, and has become highly profitable, though smaller.

Margins are up on the base business at home. The EverReady product range has been rationalized, with the introduction of a competitive long-life product. The erosion from Duracell continues, but more slowly. Outside the UK, losses have been stemmed. Global brand ambitions have had to be abandoned, but local market strengths in countries such as South Africa have been reinforced. Overall, competition from Duracell and others will remain intense, but there is at least a profitable base from which to respond.

The advent of Hanson in this situation clearly produced rapid unfreezing. Quick decisions on disposals were taken by the Hanson Trust central management team, a number of senior Berec managers departed, and the remaining managers were left in no doubt that the name of the game had changed. Unless the business's strategy could be changed in ways that would dramatically improve results, no one's future was secure.

In the search for new strategies to meet the Hanson targets, the onus was placed firmly on the business managers. Hanson's contribution was simply to make clear that failure to find such strategies would be unacceptable. This was well illustrated by a conversation we had with Ron Fulford, the man installed by Hanson to drive the process. We asked Fulford if he knew how Berec could achieve the profit improvements and cost reductions required before the changes began. His reply was: 'Oh yes. That was easy. I just made it clear to everyone that if they didn't hit the targets, they'd be gone.'

The emphasis is therefore on providing very strong incentives to support the new targets (and thereby helping with the consolidation phase), but not on helping business managers to think through the detail of the options they have.

5　Tarmac: Housing

Tarmac's Housing division is another example of the power of the Financial Control style to unfreeze managers and consolidate them around a new strategy.

Tarmac has a target of annual 'growth with profitability'. The Housing division had achieved this regularly since it had been acquired in the mid 1970s. Eric Pountain had run the division until 1979, when Ron King took over after Pountain became chief executive of Tarmac.

In mid 1980 problems began to emerge. Profits had not grown over the first 6 months of the year and debt levels were escalating. Part-exchange houses were proving difficult to sell and the market for second-time buyers, on which the Housing division was mainly focused, had declined. At the time, however, these problems were seen as temporary. There were no alarm bells ringing and there was no obvious reason to change strategy.

In December 1980 the Housing division failed to meet its promised budget figures, and the centre removed Ron King as chief executive of the division. For 6 months the division was run by Sir Eric Pountain himself from the centre. He then appointed Sam Pickstock, who had been deputy managing director of the division. Pickstock's first move was to re-establish a decentralized management philosophy. He brought two successful managers into the centre to help him, and then decentralized as much as possible to the regional subsidiary companies. In other ways he kept the same strategy. By the autumn of 1981 the pressure to change strategy was greater. 'Barratt was the market leader. He was telling the world about the importance of first-time buyers. When his results came out, I was under pressure', explained Sam Pickstock.

This pressure from the centre for better performance forced Pickstock to consider alternatives: 'I woke up one morning, and realized what we should do.' His formula was to move two-thirds of sales to first-time buyers, and demand that each subsidiary should grow by 100 houses per year.

The Financial Control style had acted to unfreeze the managment of the Housing division quickly, not only by removing the previous chief executive but also by continuing to demand better performance. However, the search phase was limited. There were no long market reports or competitor analyses or planning meetings. The task was left largely to Sam Pickstock whose 'inspiration' came under severe time pressure.

Once the new strategy had been decided, the Financial Control style was helpful in consolidating the management team around the new plans. 'It would have taken me three times as long to make the changes if the pressure had been more relaxed', explained Pickstock.

Interestingly, it was not support from the centre that caused the management team to respond quickly. In fact, Pickstock felt throughout 1982 that the centre was out of sympathy with his strategy. He felt that the centre was watching Barratt and arguing that the Housing division should consider a centralized structure and a marketing approach that matched. However, because of Tarmac's strict Financial Control style, the centre's views were not imposed; instead the centre maintained pressure on performance. It was this hands-off but tight control style that helped Pickstock make changes.

Summary

From our previous discussion of added value under each style and from these examples, we are able to summarize the contribution of the centre to the strategic change process (table 11.7).

Strategic Planning and Strategic Control both have mechanisms for unfreezing, although, in practice, this phase does not always receive the attention it deserves under these styles. Financial Control is powerful at unfreezing, but only when financial performance standards are not being met.

Strategic Planning is the most effective style in the search phase,

Table 11.7   Contributions to strategic change

Phase	Strategic Planning	Strategic Control	Financial Control
Unfreeze	Through probing, questioning and direct involvement	Through probing and questioning; and through tighter control	Through higher standards and tighter controls
Search	Through wide and extensive debate, and leadership from the centre	Through encouraging businesses to think again	Limited
Consolidate	Through consensus on the best strategic directions	Through control process	Through business accountability, incentives and sanctions
	but	*but*	*but*
	Signals for unfreezing may be too weak. Motivation for action may be low due to lack of 'ownership' in the business units	Ambiguous objectives may be less effective in unfreezing and creating motivation for action. Detached centre may result in a failure to consider bold strategies	Time in the search phase may be too short to produce creative strategies. Fierce controls may rule out risky options

providing assistance to business managers in identifying new strategy alternatives and allowing time for testing and experimentation. Strategic Control also provides encouragement to business management in the search phase, but gives less direct help. Financial Control's search role is much more limited, which can lead to a failure to expose the full range of options. In the consolidation phase, the control processes of Strategic Control and, particularly, Financial Control are powerful. They motivate managers to follow through on agreed changes. Strategic Control can, however, suffer from ambiguity in its control objectives, causing managers to be uncertain about priorities. Strategic Planning does not stress tight controls, and creates less incentive to act; but it attempts to replace the stick and carrot of tight control with a shared consensus on the best way forward.

Conclusions

This chapter is central to our thesis. It explains the nature of the value created by the centre: it shows how the centre can help business units and why multibusiness companies can outperform single-business companies. This, in a sense, is the end of the journey we started in chapter 2.

We conclude that each of the three main styles can add value. The individual business unit can gain advantages from membership of the corporate whole which are not available to the independent company reporting directly to the capital markets.

The advantages, however, tend to be balanced by corresponding disadvantages. Though some of these disadvantages can be avoided, or at least minimized, each style inevitably subtracts value as well as adding it. The task of managers at the centre is to ensure that their net contribution is positive. This requires sensitive management of the tensions and pitfalls that we have identified.

It is important to remember that value is created largely through the strategies of the business unit managers. The centre cannot execute strategy. Central managers cannot make products or money: this has to be done in the business units. Value is therefore added by the centre only if it changes the thoughts and actions of unit managers, hence our focus throughout the previous chapters on the word 'influence'. The centre adds value by influencing unit managers; by giving unit managers a philosophy and, in some cases, a broad strategy within which to work.

The centre's influence goes beyond persuasion because the centre has the power of appointment. Part of the value the centre adds comes from its ability to select the right managers, and to remove managers who have lost their way. The objective is to find and develop managers with the right mind set, managers who will respond to the particular influence style chosen by the centre; and to 'unfreeze' or remove managers who have become locked into a wrong way of thinking.

The management styles are, therefore, about how to get the best performance from people. When creating budgeting systems, planning systems, management committees and so on, the centre must be constantly aware of the people who are going to use these systems. How will they react? What signal will the system give them? Will the message be clear? What motivations will the managers need to have to get the best out of the system? How can these motivations be created? As we have seen, each style makes different assumptions about the answers to these questions.

The conclusion of our analysis is that at least three different management styles are effective and there is no 'right way' to manage a portfolio of businesses. We have seen how each style has different strengths and weaknesses, different advantages and disadvantages, and in the next two chapters we explore how these can be matched to the nature of the business environment and the organization's resources in order to produce better overall performance.

Note

1 Venture capital firms, however, are set up to provide funds for these sorts of businesses.

12

Matching the Style and the Business

In chapter 11 we argued that different styles add value in different ways, and, by implication, are more or less suited to different business circumstances. In this chapter we will identify more precisely the factors that determine how well a company's style matches the circumstances in which it is competing.

The idea that management styles are influenced by the characteristics of a company's business mix is intuitively appealing to senior managers. 'We have power to shape our portfolios. But once you have fixed your portfolio the (management) options are not that great', claimed Dick Giordano of BOC. Despite the differences between the Strategic Planning and Financial Control style this sentiment was echoed by Martin Taylor of Hanson Trust, who observed, 'The style of management derives from the sorts of businesses you are in.'

Other senior managers, however, pointed equally strongly to the need for a match between internal factors (such as the personality and preferences of the CEO) and the company's management style. 'There are many things that are pressure points on the choice [of management style]. The information systems are hugely different in different companies and the styles of the CEO's are different', said Trevor Chinn of Lex Service Group. Any account of the match between management style and business circumstances will need to take account of both internal and external factors.

This chapter will focus on the relationship between the centre and an individual business unit. What factors determine the appropriateness of different styles for managing a given business unit or division? Should the style be dependent on the type of business that the unit is in? Or on the financial and human resources available to the company? Or on a mixture of both?

In the following chapter we will go on to discuss the way in which a company manages its whole portfolio. Should a company manage all its business units in the same style? Should it have multiple styles, managing one group of businesses one way and another group differently? Should style changes be encouraged? How should it grow the portfolio? What sort of businesses should be acquired?

Determinants of Management Style: the Centre and the Business Unit

It is evident from our sample that companies with different management styles tend to be different in other important respects as well. The differences between Strategic Planning and Financial Control companies are most obvious. For example, STC has a portfolio of businesses linked together by the needs of the telecommunications and office systems markets whereas BTR has a broad range of completely diverse businesses, such as tennis rackets, rubber belting and aero-engine parts. Cadbury's soft drinks and confectionery businesses are in mainly growing markets whereas 12 of Hanson's 15 main businesses are in declining industries. UB has a visionary leader who likes to guide the strategies of his subsidiaries and support poor performing businesses if he believes the strategy is right. GEC, on the other hand, has a leader who prefers to 'peer at the businesses through the numbers' and who subjects poor performing subsidiaries to a fierce challenge from the centre.

The problem we faced was to identify which of these differences most affect the choice of strategic management style. The work of previous researchers and the academic literature on strategic management gave us some help. In the 1950s, two observant and sensitive academics, Tom Burns and G. M. Stalker,[1] carried out pioneering studies of 20 companies in Scotland. They were studying organizations as communities of people. They wanted to know how these people behaved and what influenced their behaviour. They found that companies in stable business conditions behaved differently (had different management systems and processes) from companies in businesses facing a high degree of uncertainty. They described the two extremes of management behaviour as 'mechanistic' (suitable for stable environments) and 'organic' (suitable for fast-changing environments). Burns and Stalker were pioneers in the now extensively travelled field of contingency theory. This theory states that the optimum organization structure and management processes are contingent on the nature of the business environment.[2]

While contingency theorists have been looking at the types of management processes that fit with aspects of their business environment, Professor Igor Ansoff has been examining the conditions under which different decision-making styles are most appropriate. Ansoff's work is especially important since he is widely regarded as the father of the term 'strategic management' through his article 'The concept of strategic management' (1972) and his book *Strategic Management* (1979).[3]

In a more recent book, *Implanting Strategic Management*, published in 1984, he proposes a link between decision-making behaviour and the 'environmental imperatives'.[4] He concludes, very much in the contingency theory tradition, that the nature of the business, and in particular the strategic challenge facing management, should be the determining factor in the choice of decision-making behaviour. He points out that, under some circumstances, a company needs to operate highly sophisticated decision-making processes, whereas under other circumstances it is more cost effective for the company to rely on 'ad hoc' decision-making.

The work of these previous researchers helped us focus on some aspects of the nature of the business that are important in determing the best strategic management style. However, to date, no consensus has been reached on which aspects of the nature of the business are most important. Moreover, the models developed by other researchers do not fully explain the differences we observed. For example, managers we interviewed identified a number of factors they considered to be important that were not adequately reflected in the models of previous researchers:

1 The financial condition of the company was mentioned in a number of interviews. The cash problem facing Ferranti was important in affecting the style of management chosen by Derek Alun-Jones when he took over in the mid 1970s. The cash squeeze in Tarmac in 1979 also had an effect on the way Sir Eric Pountain decided to run the company. The financial problems faced by STC apparently caused major changes in that company's management style.
2 Many of our interviews focused on the personality of the chief executive. 'An interesting issue is whether this management style would work as well with another chief executive. I don't know how far it depends on his individual qualities. Would we be able to make it work in the same way with another man at the helm?' pondered one group managing director.
3 The size and riskiness of investment decisions was another factor identified in our interviews. As Sir Peter Walters of BP explained, 'Many of the decisions that we are making are of national importance and can have a very long-term impact on our businesses. It is necessary for us at corporate level to have input into these decisions and to get a multitude of views. It is appropriate to have a more ponderous decision-making process.'

We therefore set about developing a simple model that would be consistent with our research data and help management to think about the problem of matching their strategic management style to a particular division or business unit.

Figure 12.1 summarizes the model we have developed. It illustrates our belief that the strategic management style adopted by the centre with regard to a business unit should be shaped by the nature of the unit's business and the resources available in the corporation as a whole.

Our model describes the strategic management styles that fit or fail to fit in different circumstances. It has been developed by thinking through the characteristics of the different styles. By reviewing the advantages and disadvantages of each and considering the different results each causes, we

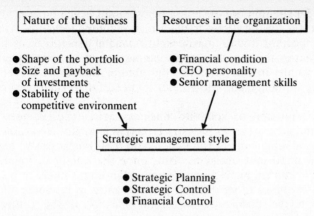

Figure 12.1 Model for development of a strategic management style. The centre's style should match the nature of the business and the resources in the organization.

have reached conclusions about the circumstances that should make the style more or less appropriate.

We believe that the model is consistent with much of the evidence from our research and that it provides a logical and intuitively appealing account of the factors that should be considered when selecting a style. We recognize that our data do not provide proof that the relationships exist. However, at this stage we are proposing the model as an aid to management. The best test of its validity will be the model's usefulness in helping senior management think through style choices.

In the remainder of this chapter we describe the factors in the model and present some of the evidence behind our conclusions.

The Nature of the Business

We believe that the centre's style should depend on the nature of the business: i.e. the centre's style with regard to a particular unit should match the nature of the unit's business environment. The factors in the environment that matter most are: the shape of the portfolio that the unit is part of; the size and payback time of the major investment decisions needed in the business; and the stability of the competitive environment in which the unit operates.

Shape of Portfolio

The strategic management style that the centre adopts for a given business unit should relate to the portfolio the unit is in. The relationships we are proposing are:

- The larger the number of separate businesses in the portfolio, the more difficult it is for the centre to use a high planning influence style and the more important it is to impose tight financial controls.
- The greater the number and complexity of the linkages between business units in the portfolio, the greater the centre's need for high planning influence and the greater its need for flexible controls.

While the number of separate business areas (i.e. sectors that are unconnected in strategic or industry terms) in a portfolio remains at two or three, central management can understand their businesses well enough to help make important decisions. But, once the number expands beyond about three, central management's understanding is likely to be stretched too far. It becomes more difficult for the centre to influence the strategy decisions in the businesses successfully. And, if the centre fails to understand the conditions of the individual businesses, strong central influence can be dangerous.

The centre needs, therefore, to rely increasingly on control influence, by imposing tight strategic or financial controls. With less contribution to the planning process, the centre will exercise influence by agreeing objectives and controlling tightly against them. Strategic and financial objectives can be used where the number of businesses in the portfolio are below 50 or so. Once the number of businesses rises to 50 or 100, the centre should rely increasingly on simple financial controls. With over 50 businesses it becomes hard for the centre to have the understanding necessary to set strategic objectives.

The second relationship concerns the linkages between businesses. Businesses may be linked because they serve common customers, buy products from each other, have a common production technology, or share an essential marketing or product development skill. Where strategies are linked, it is necessary for the managing director of one unit to coordinate with other units before he can decide how to proceed. If these linkages are important, higher levels of management (often the centre) need to be involved to ensure that the managing directors are coordinating in a way that is best for the whole company. This planning influence does not necessarily mean that the centre takes all the decisions. But it does mean that the centre designs the decision-making process, deciding who should be involved in the decision and authorizing the agreements made. As the linkages increase in number and importance, the centre's influence in planning increases.

Another feature of the linkages between businesses is their influence on the control process. If business units are dependent on each other in developing strategy, they are probably also dependent on each other in achieving results. The performance of one unit will depend on how well others have performed and one unit may need to 'take the heat' to support efforts in another unit. Under these circumstances it becomes hard to impose tight controls. There are too many possible excuses. Therefore, as the linkages increase it becomes more appropriate for the centre to use flexible controls.

Our research has illustrated these relationships at work. Tarmac, for example, moved away from high planning influence as the diversity of the business increased. In the 1960s and early 1970s, Tarmac grew into a major quarrying and construction group through strong central leadership. The business was broken up into separate divisions, but many of the major initiatives were still sponsored from the centre. In the 1970s a number of further diversifications were made into international construction markets. These initiatives were not successful, and led to a performance crisis and a loss of confidence in the central management team. This resulted in the CEO stepping down. Division management felt that the centre had had too much influence in detailed strategic decisions.

Table 12.1 summarizes our data on the number of businesses and the amount of linkage between businesses. BTR, GEC and Hanson are the companies with the largest portfolios and the least linkages between divisions. All have adopted tight financial controls. The portfolios of the Strategic Planning companies, which show the highest levels of linkages between businesses, tend to be grouped into two or three core business areas in which the centre is closely involved.

Table 12.1 Linkages between businesses

| | | Linkages | |
| | Number of businesses | Between divisions | Between businesses |
Companies			
Strategic Planning			
BOC	37	Low–Med	High
BP	11	Med	High
Cadbury Schweppes	45	Low–Med	High
Lex	9	Low	Med–High
STC	20–25	Med–High	High
UB	13	Med	Med
Strategic Control			
Courtaulds	30–40	Low–Med	Med
ICI	50–60	Low	High
Imperial	20–25	Low	Med
Plessey	20–25	Med	High
Vickers	25–30	Low	Med
Financial Control			
BTR	150	Low	Low–Med
Ferranti	43	Low	Med
GEC	170	Low	Med
Hanson Trust	70	Low	Med
Tarmac	6	Low	

Data are taken from tables 4.1, 5.1 and 6.1.

In summary, therefore, we believe that the choice of style adopted by the centre for managing a business unit should be a function of the shape of the portfolio: if the portfolio is large and diverse, the centre is likely to be most effective if it limits its involvement to control influence; if the business units and divisions have important linkages and overlaps, the centre will need to be involved in helping to make decisions through high planning influence.

Size and Payback of Investments

The nature of the major investment decisions in a business should have an influence on the management style chosen. The relationships we are proposing are:

— the larger the size of discrete investments, the more involved the centre should be in planning;
— the longer the payback for investments, the greater the need for flexible controls.

Where investment decisions are large relative to the size of the total company, as they can be for an oil rig purchase, a major plant renewal, or an important new product range development, top management have a responsibility to be involved in the decision. Where the decision may be placing the future of the organization at stake, top management should be involved in shaping the risks being taken. Therefore, in a business where major discrete investments are periodically needed to remain competitive, central management should adopt a high planning influence style.

Where decisions have long payback periods, central management will find tight controls ineffective. If the wisdom of a decision is not going to be evident for 5 years, there is little value in close monitoring of performance in the interim period. Take advertising, for example. The effect of advertising on a brand can build up over 5 years or more and take as long to erode. If the budget is halved this year the effect in financial terms may not show through for the next five years. Tight financial controls are inadequate for checking the quality of this type of decision. By the time the controls have pointed out the error, it may be too late to take corrective action.

Strategic controls may be more useful as a means of measuring the impact of long payback investments. But the practical problem is to find objective strategic measures that can be controlled against tightly. It seems, therefore, that the more long payback investments there are in the business, the more appropriate is a flexible control style.

Our research has provided us with many examples to support the relationships between style and type of investment decision. Of the Strategic Planning companies, BP, BOC and STC are all involved in large discrete investments with long payback periods; and Cadbury and UB are involved in businesses where the long-term defence of their brands is key to their strategies.

Conversely, Financial Control companies seem to have less involvement in large investments with long paybacks. Some actively avoid such investments: 'BTR has consciously moved away from investments in projects that require major outlays or long payback periods', stated a group chief executive. One of the features of the Financial Control group is the focus on 2-, 3-, or 4-year payback criteria in their capital approval system.

Finally, some quotes from our interviews will serve to underline the importance of these relationships in the eyes of managers.

> In businesses with very long-term financial payoffs we have to control through strategy. We learn from last year's strategic decisions and control next year's strategy and actions. We are really controlling against last year's actions. For example, if a manager says that he is going to buy so much property in Indonesia, we can measure whether he has done it. The thing we can't measure is whether it was a good commercial decision. We won't know that for five years.
>
> (Sir Peter Walters, BP.)

> If you have a concentration of businesses which present big chip bets for capital expenditure and R&D and the life cycle of these is 4 or 5 years, I cannot see how you can justify your pay unless you are deeply involved in decision-making.
>
> (Dick Giordano, BOC.)

> If you work on a decentralized system you need to control the scale of work. In the last 6 years we have grown from £85 million to £1.2 billion market capitalization. The largest individual investment was an acquisition of a company in the US for $80 million. Not all that great compared to a £1.2 billion capitalization.
>
> (Graeme Odgers, Tarmac.)

> In semiconductors, it will cost you £300 million in R&D and plant to decide to develop a major new chip. Those are the numbers we have to deal with. It's a completely different kind of decision when the numbers get that big.
>
> Sir Kenneth Corfield, STC.)

In summary, the nature of the important investment decisions will affect the relationship between the centre and the business unit: where the decisions are large, the centre should usually be involved in making the decision, i.e. it should use a high planning influence style; where the investment decisions have long payback periods, the centre will find it hard to impose tight controls, making a flexible control style more appropriate.

Stability of the Competitive Environment

The third element that characterizes the nature of the business is its competitive environment. The battle for market share moves back and forth between three types of competitive environment. We call these 'open', 'fierce' and 'stable' battles:

Open
● High level of market uncertainty.
● Competitors not fighting head on.
● Key factors for success unclear.
● New companies entering market.
● Ultimate winners unclear.

Fierce
● High level of competitive uncertainty.
● Competitors meet head on.
● Dramatic change in fortunes for some companies.
● Key success factors becoming clear.
● Small and large companies dropping out.
● Winners emerging.

Stable
● More predictable business situation.
● Competitors positions stable.
● Key factors for success clear.
● New entrants have little impact.

Different strategic management styles appear to be appropriate to different types of battle.

In *open battles*, such as UB's fast foods business in the UK, competitors are not fighting head on. Either because the market is growing fast enough or because companies have highly differentiated approaches, the battle for market share has not really started. New companies are still entering the market; new opportunities are still developing; and, most importantly, the factors that will sort out winners from losers are not yet clear.

The most important management task in open battles is to test the business concept and build competitive advantage. The worst outcome, one that happens all too frequently, is where the company grows large in a friendly market environment, but lacks any competitive advantage. When the battle becomes fierce, the weaknesses are exposed and the company may be forced out of business.

In open battles, tight controls are unlikely to suit the strategic challenges facing the business. Tight financial controls are unlikely to | improve strategic decisions. Since the battle has not yet fully developed, high margins are easy to find. But focusing on high margins may be the wrong strategy. It may attract additional competitors, providing an umbrella under which they can become established, or it may push the business into a dead-end niche that currently looks attractive but has no long-term defence against larger companies.

Tight strategic controls are potentially more useful, but they are particularly hard to set in open battles. The critical factors that will determine competitive advantage – technology, cost position, product range, distribution, service, etc. – are unclear. Enforcing tight controls against strategic measures may, therefore, reduce the flexibility of local management and limit their ability to compete.

In summary, a flexible control style (Strategic Planning or Strategic Venturing) is likely to be best suited to open competitive battles.

In *fierce battles*, such as Cadbury's international soft drinks business, the companies in the industry are meeting with each other head on. These competitive clashes may be brought on by factors such as volatility in the demand for the product, aggression of one or more competitors, or technologically driven substitution in the market place. In these circumstances, as in open battles, there is a high level of uncertainty about the future evolution of the business. But, in contrast to open battles, the uncertainty is often associated with depressed industry profit levels. This is a result of the intensification of competition. Possibly for the first time, the strengths and weaknesses of the competition are exposed. Margins may fall dramatically as companies reduce prices to compete. For weaker companies the fierce battle can cause a dramatic change in fortunes. As a result both small and large companies may drop out of the market. It is during a fierce battle that the critical factors determining competitive advantage are fully exposed and the winners and losers are identifiable.

In fierce battles, the most important task of management is to decide quickly whether the business has a competitive advantage that can be defended. If it does not, it may be best to sell the business to a company that does have an advantage. The worst outcome is to fight it out and lose. If the business does have a sustainable advantage, management should be alert to opportunities. Fierce battles can frequently provide particular opportunities to gain market share or strengthen competitive advantage.

In a fierce battle, all three management styles may be appropriate. The style should depend on the strategy management want to pursue. If management plan to fight it out and win, the centre will need to apply flexible controls to the business unit. Results will be unpredictable during a fierce battle and the premium will be on the company that can move fastest when opportunities present themselves or new ways of gaining competitive advantage become evident. Tight strategic or financial controls are likely to constrain decision-making and limit options.

If management decide to remain in the battle but takes a cautious approach, then a tight strategic control style is likely to be best. By monitoring the strategic measures of performance, management can assess how the battle is proceeding. If their advantage appears to be eroding, they can pull out or sell. If margins or the market improve, they can become more aggressive. It is necessary for management to use strategic controls to assess the state of the battle because financial controls may be misleading. Margins across the whole market are likely to be low and financial controls will not measure the relative strategic positions of the competitors.

If management decide to withdraw from the business unless profits can be maintained, or to seek a more profitable niche into which to retrench, a tight financial control style is likely to be best. Management may be concerned that the fierce battle will continue for many years or that their company has little defensible competitive advantage. Tight financial controls will ensure that the decision about what to do with the business is not left to drift. Either local management succeed in identifying a niche in which they can earn good returns, or the centre will exit the business through sale or closure.

In summary, the type of controls that the centre imposes on a business unit in a fierce battle depend on the strategy being pursued: a 'win' strategy requires flexible controls, a 'hold' strategy requires tight strategic controls and a 'retrench' strategy requires tight financial controls.

This analysis of fierce battles points to the importance of identifying a fierce battle correctly and choosing explicitly the strategy to follow. Most companies will enter a fierce battle with an existing management style. Their choice of strategy is more likely to be influenced by their style than vice versa, resulting, in many cases, in unsuitable strategies or styles. The key that unlocks the problem is the judgement of the strength of the company's competitive advantage at the beginning of the battle.

In *stable battles*, such as Hanson's UK bricks market,[5] the winners in the industry are well established and competitors have high respect for each other. The technology, and the market are normally more predictable and mature. The competitive advantage of each player is well understood and unwritten agreements may exist between companies about the product or market areas that they should focus on. In stable battles the friction between competitors is less severe than in fierce battles. A market leader is likely to exist. Market share positions are more stable and new entrants to the business are rare. Even if there are temporary shifts in demand, input prices or the like, industry profit levels are maintained through implicit cooperation between the leading competitors.

In stable battles management should be focusing on maximizing their financial return. Additional market share is likely to be expensive to get and attempts to destabilize the market will be strongly resisted by competitors. The task is to focus on that part of the business where the company has a competitive advantage and to produce the highest possible margins.

In these circumstances, tight controls are essential. Tight financial controls help managers focus on maximizing margins. By setting stretching financial targets, the centre can ensure that business unit managers focus on the profitable parts of the business. The centre also places severe pressure on costs, which improves efficiency and reduces marginal development activities. To guard against the danger of sacrificing long-term competitive position by maximizing financial performance, financial controls can be complemented with strategic controls. We have therefore concluded that Strategic Control and Financial Control are appropriate styles for stable competitive battles. There is, however, some danger that strategic controls will not provide such clear motivation to maximize the profit potential of the business.

To summarize, we believe that the type of control influence adopted by the centre should be matched to the competitive environment of the business. In particular:

- In open battles, a flexible control style is likely to be most appropriate.
- In fierce battles, the control style should be matched to the strategy:
  — an ambitious 'win' strategy should be matched with flexible controls;
  — a 'wait and see' strategy should be matched with tight strategic controls;
  — a strategy of retrenchment should be matched with tight financial controls.
- In stable battles, a tight control style is likely to be most suitable.

We have not documented in detail the competitive environments of all the businesses in our research sample. Our conclusions concerning these relationships are therefore tentative. However, in companies where the central style fits most easily with the portfolio, we believe these relationships exist. And in situations where the style does not match the competitive environment of the business unit, we believe the mismatch is creating some problems.

The telecommunications business, for example, has recently become a fierce battle as a result of the privatization of British Telecom and the inclusion of overseas competition. Previously the business was shared between a few major companies in a stable relationship with their main customer. Now the Financial Control styles of GEC and Ferranti are less suited to the new environment, one of the reasons why both companies are moving towards the Strategic Control style.

This concept of the stability of the competitive battle seems, for us, to capture many of the elements that other researchers and other theorists have found relevant. For example, the types of competitive battle can be overlaid on the concept of the industry life cycle.[6] An open battle is likely to exist in the emerging and growing phases of the cycle. A fierce battle frequently occurs in the maturing or mature phases. And a stable battle is often the norm in the mature and declining phases.

Lord Hanson's statements that his style is best suited to basic, stable industries and Sir Owen Green's comments that BTR does very well out of mature businesses fit with our concept. In addition, the success of venture capital firms (a flexible control style) in nurturing emerging businesses supports our proposed relationships.

Yet the concept is different in important ways. We believe that the competitive battle can move back and forward between open, fierce and stable phases, rather as supermarket chains move in and out of price wars. If technology advances or the behaviour of a major customer changes, a battle may move from stable to open. If demand suddenly declines, the battle may change from stable to fierce. Morever, we envisage that certain industries can become locked into a long-term fierce battle, and hence our concept includes the 'stalemate' industry[7] in which companies cannot gain competitive advantage over each other and yet cannot afford to get out of the business.

The competitive battles concept can also be linked to uncertainty, and its effect on organization process (management style and systems). As we noted earlier, the contingency theorists led by Burns and Stalker identified uncertainty as a critical factor in affecting the way managers behave. Uncertainty is highest in open battles: the key factors for success are unclear, the competitors are unclear and the nature of customer needs are frequently unclear. A flexible control system is most likely to cope well with these levels of uncertainty.

In fierce battles the uncertainty is diminishing and will depend on the strategy management choose to pursue. A retrenchment strategy limits the amount of uncertainty; a win-at-all-costs strategy multiplies the uncertainty. Furthermore, in stable battles uncertainty is lowest, making it possible for management to impose a system of tight controls without reducing the business unit's ability to compete. Consequently, different control styles match with different levels of uncertainty in the company's environment. But our focus is more on the competitive reactions to and consequences of uncertainty than on the state of uncertainty itself. It is the effect of uncertainty on competition that is most relevant for purposes of strategic decision-making.

We have therefore developed the concept of competitive battle types because we believe it is easier for managers to understand and more relevant to them than the industry life cycle or the uncertainty concepts used by other researchers.

In summary, we believe the relationship between the centre and the business unit should be influenced by the competitive environment facing the business unit: in open battles the business unit must be free to respond as events unfold, implying that the centre should use a flexible control style; in fierce battles the style of the centre should depend on the strategy the business unit is following; and in stable battles the challenge is to maximize financial performance, implying that the centre should use one of the tight control styles.

There are, therefore, three main factors concerning the nature of the business environment which should influence the choice of style.

The style the centre adopts with an individual business unit should depend on the shape of the portfolio the unit is in, the size and payback of investments needed to compete in the business and the stability of the competitive environment. Matching a style to a business unit involves determining the appropriate type of control influence and a suitable level of planning influence. For most businesses there will be a choice of suitable styles although in many cases one of the three main styles will be preferable. In table 12.2 we summarize the relationships we have described in this section.

Table 12.2 Matching strategic management styles to the nature of the business

Nature of the business	Strategic Planning	Strategic Control	Financial Control
1 Shape of portfolio			
● Size			
— more than three sectors	−	+	+
— more than 50 businesses	−	?	+
● Linkages			
— many linkages	+	−	−
— few or no linkages	−	+	+
2 Investment			
● Size			
— few large investments	+	?	−
— many small investments	?	+	+
● Term			
— long payback	+	+	−
— short payback	?	+	+
3 Competitive environment			
● Open	+	−	−
● Fierce			
— win	+	−	−
— hold	?	+	?
— retrench	−	?	+
● Stable	−	+	+

+ nature of business matches style.
− nature of business does not match style.
? match with style unclear.

In some circumstances conflicts will exist. A business unit may be in a stable battle (i.e. tight controls), but have investment decisions that have long payback periods (i.e. flexible controls). Or a business unit may be part of a large diverse portfolio (i.e. low planning influence), but have major linkages and overlaps with some other units (i.e. high planning influence). It is not possible to provide any formula solutions to these conflicts. Frequently a Strategic Control style will prove to be an acceptable compromise. The alternative is to decide which of the factors is dominant and let it guide the choice of style.

Resources

Whereas the discussion so far relates mainly to factors external to the organization, the other part of our model – resources – consists of factors internal to the company. In our interviews, managers talked to us about culture, about history, about personalities and about resource constraints such as cash availability.

Our problem was to sort the important from the unimportant and to decide which was the chicken, and which the egg. We needed to distinguish between factors that were created by the style, such as risk aversion, and factors that influenced the choice of style, such as a financial crisis.

The solution came from looking at the major factors associated with a change in style. In chapters 4 to 6 we described the style changes that have occurred with each company. We identified three important driving factors internal to the company:

1 Changes in financial condition.
2 Changes in chief executive officer (CEO).
3 Changes in senior management.

We concluded that it was resources, in terms of money and the skills and personalities of senior managers at the centre and in the subsidiary, that were the most important internal factors in shaping management style.

Financial Condition

The financial condition of the organization as a whole is important. When cash is tight, financial controls are needed to rectify the situation.

The easiest way to improve performance or generate cash is to decentralize, apply demanding performance standards and close down loss-making units. When organizations are faced with financial difficulties they turn to the control dimension rather than the planning dimension to help them decide what to cut out or cut back. Moreover, it is hard to apply tight controls and at the same time maintain high planning influence. Subsidiary managers who are being asked to perform to demanding targets will want autonomy of action to achieve these targets. As a result, when faced with a financial crisis, companies normally move from Strategic Planning towards Strategic Control, or even Financial Control.

Tarmac and Courtaulds provide examples to support this relationship. Tarmac's cash crisis in 1979 caused a change from a Strategic Planning to a Financial Control style. The solutions to Tarmac's performance problems were straightforward: a combination of cutting out or cutting back poor performers, concentrating on the major strengths of the business and providing encouragement to parts of the business that offered potential for a quick turnaround in results. The tight financial controls imposed by the centre were a mechanism both for the centre and for division managers to reinforce those decisions. Although the problems had been created by losses in Nigeria, the Middle East and Germany, as well as a cash squeeze in housing, the tight controls were applied universally across all Tarmac's businesses. Courtaulds' performance crisis in the late 1970s caused a change in style, from Centralized to Strategic Control. Chris Hogg imposed cash targets across all the businesses in the face of a severe and prolonged industry downturn.

However, there are some exceptions. In 1984 and 1985 UB was under cash pressure as it fought the cookie war in America. Although this caused additional performance pressure on the other divisions it did not result in a major change in style. The problem was solved by a rights issue and by raising margins in the UK biscuits and snacks businesses. As a result, UB's predominantly Strategic Planning style has been maintained at the centre. But for most companies a cash squeeze has caused a tightening of controls from the centre.

The relationship does not appear to work in reverse. Abundant cash does not appear to cause companies to move towards the Strategic Planning style. BTR, GEC, Hanson and Tarmac all have sufficient cash resources and excellent profit performances; but none is planning to change styles. Abundant cash appears to be a necessary but not sufficient condition for a company to adopt the Strategic Planning style.

Personality of the CEO

The personality of the chief executive officer (CEO) of the whole organization is critical to the management style. If the CEO's personality and ambition do not fit the style, uncertainty and confusion can arise. The relationship we are proposing is simple. Managers have different personalities: some are more suited to a control style and some fit more easily with a planning style. The style should take account of these differences. The fact that so many changes in style were initiated by a new chief executive appointment is evidence of the power of this relationship.

We have observed very different personalities and ambitions in the CEOs of our sample companies. They each have strong philosophies about how businesses should be run. We do not believe that, for example, Sir Hector Laing could manage a business in the same way as Sir Christopher Hogg, that Sir Owen Green could emulate the style of Sir Peter Walters, or that Sir John Clark could manage like Lord Hanson. The following quotes illustrate the differences in philosophy of some of the CEOs we have spoken to.

Sir Hector Laing: 'The job of the chairman is to lay down a return on capital, the share of market and things like product quality. The operating company head then translates these into an operating strategy.' 'Financial control is a rod to beat our backs with, it must not be a God.' 'The be all and end all is staying in business and creating wealth for the country.'

'My nature is to stamp my style on the business.' 'I run the business from the nose and from the pants. I don't have any paper. I don't like to write things down and I use the telephone a lot.'

'I run the business very much as a team. It's grown up from a family business. Teamwork and the feeling of being part of the whole are important.' 'Business has to be fun. It's much too serious a business to take seriously. If things are going wrong, you identify with the management and help them out.'

Sir Peter Walters: 'My responsibility is for the broad philosophy of the business which must be communicated in simple messages and in the financial controls and objectives I set.' 'I do not get closely involved in the details of the strategies. Just sufficient to make sure that they are in line with the broad policies. My role is to ask pointed questions testing the soundness of the strategies.'

'It is important for me to be well-grounded in the oil business to carry the respect of the managers.' 'In the review, criticism must be balanced with encouragement. It is important not to be negative and to develop creativity in thinking.'

'Frequently you are measuring the accomplishment of strategic actions rather than results. It is the actions you are measuring and not the effect of that on performance because it is very difficult to tell the outcome when you have long-term strategic decisions.'

Dick Giordano: 'The centre must develop the fullest possible under-standing of the strategic options facing its businesses. This can only be done with infrequent but intensive reviews of the critical businesses. You have to focus your effort on a few.'

'The chief executive should be the principal source of initiative in strategy decisions. It is rare for an individual running a business to be willing to propose real alternative strategies in his business.'

'The biggest challenge is to get objectivity into the process. The greatest mistake I made was as a result of one manager who was in love with his business and got me to fall in love with it too.'

'My role is to push out a few messages that can be simply communicated. For example, "let's do more in Japan" or "we should be forecasting where our technology is going". These messages can have a dramatic effect on the whole atmosphere in which decisions are made.'

'One of the most difficult challenges is to have milestones that measure performance but do not allow excuse-making from the management team.'

Trevor Chinn: 'Strategy is about change. There are not many strategic issues that occur in a steady state business. The centre has to be involved at the moment of change. We believe the local manager should play a major role in strategy. But the centre must have a role too.'

'One of the values the centre adds is rigour. But business has become so complex that you can't add rigour nowadays unless you understand the business.'

'Discussing and communicating strategy is critical. Our top seven people meet four times per year for two days, as do the top 25 managers in a separate session. "Service excellence" is now being debated by all management. It may take five or more years to communicate and implement but that is the nature of strategy.'

'Measuring strategic performance is hard. How do you measure service quality or excellence? They are not easy to quantify.'

'We found by the end of the 1970s that in almost every business we were in that our winning competitors were only in that business. And so we realized that we had to be in few enough businesses in order that we could behave as if we were only in that business.'

'It's not easy to be diversified. I admire with wonder those who are in a large number of businesses and who manage it successfully.'

Sir Christopher Hogg: 'The corporate level acts as a detached but sympathetic and knowledgeable 100 percent shareholder.'

'The HQ is not only judging the content of strategic plans. We judge the process, how the plans were put together, the experience and track record of the man and the way he handles his people. Process control is important. People will accept criticism if you approach it sensibly rather than criticism of content *per se*.' 'At the centre our role is to enforce quality standards in strategic thinking and we have a role in helping to educate and develop managers. This is more important than substantial influence in specific strategic directions.'

'Controls are important. But they should not be threatening. It is important to avoid fear. It reduces a manager's effectiveness. Also, controls must not be bureaucratic. They must allow some freedom of movement in the businesses so that all managers can feel some sense of achievement.'

Sir David Plastow: 'The purpose of the planning process is to get facts out on the table and challenge the gut reactions of managers. My role is to establish and structure the process. Although occasionally I will dive into a key decision, for example on acquisitions.'

'I have been trying to create an open debating climate encouraging disagreements on strategy issues (or at least not discouraging them). Perceptive debate can do a lot to avoid prejudice.'

'The Group Planning function have an important role. I use them to put ferrets down holes. In some cases I nudge managers into using outsiders for more detailed reviews.'

Dominic Cadbury: 'Establishing objectives is an important first step in strategy. You need financial and market oriented objectives. They have helped us set priorities between different strategic proposals, helping us rationalize and focus on a smaller number of strong brands. Not all businesses meet all objectives. You need to apply them flexibly.'

'Control of strategy is an essential central activity. By asking questions I can steer operating management. It is the ability to ask the right questions that is the key.' 'Good questions help to raise the quality of strategy. It is a gradual learning process but it is better than changing the managers and bringing in a new team.'

'We are failing in our job if we do not understand the business. We [the centre] can bring skills and knowledge to all SBUs. We can knock down walls, the boundaries between businesses, to make sure management are co-operating.'

'When you are looking at core businesses the centre has a far more positive role to play. Chocolates and soft drinks I do attempt to get to know. I am trying to ensure that we are maximizing our opportunities for synergy. Making sure we are transferring skills, product knowledge and sharing assets.'

Lord Weinstock:[8] 'Every company has its own style of management. There is a distinction between "style" and "system" because systems can be changed at will, while style depends on the natural and developed characteristics of the managers.'

'The real succcess of our company depends on you (the individual managing directors of our product units). Our help (or lack of it) from HQ does not relieve you in the least of your responsibility for that part of the business which is in your charge. Our philosophy of personal responsibility makes it completely unnecessary for you to spend time at meetings of subsidiary boards or of standing committees.'

'The managing director of every operating unit is responsible to me.'

'The restraining influence of our style only works on inferior managers. A real man rings me up and says what he wants to do anyhow.'

'I don't treat managers like small boys. I don't need to approve their plans. They have to decide what to aim for and then show that they can do better than that. They can do whatever they are able to do. You can't persecute people because they perform badly against budget. But you can't tolerate bad managers. It is not a question of whose fault it is, but rather who is responsible, and that must be clear.'

'What people write down on paper does not control anything. Budgets are just signposts in a wilderness of uncertainty. You can't control everything through a budget, but you can control expenditure. You can say that overheads are too high for a given sales volume, or you can say that money is being wasted when not enough of it is being spent to achieve a desired result.'

'There is no such thing as good enough. Nothing is good enough. The question is how much better is acceptable. If there is room for improvement there should be more of it.'

Sir Owen Green: 'I personally believe in a low profile, particularly inside the organization. I believe it is important to play down the person and play up the company way – BTR's way.'

'We have a sort of federal system. We are more federalized than unitized. They can all speak their minds.'

'The view that you have to make investments with a vague view that you might get your money back in 10 years is a cop out. As we have gained experience, we have not found it necessary to take these long view investment decisions.'

'When I look at some of your strategically led companies, I can't help but think (and of course I am entirely unprejudiced!) that, if you look at their financial performance . . . well, I know what I would do as an investor.'

Sir Eric Pountain:[9] 'The group operates on a highly decentralized basis, giving to its divisions and individual profit centres maximum authority to operate autonomously within the confines of agreed budgets and specific capital expenditure approvals.'

'Divisions and profit centres are encouraged to set demanding objectives and the process of ratchetting up low budgets to more acceptable levels is a matter of persuasion and debate rather than direction. This commitment is seen as a personal compact between operating managers and the centre. Failure to perform to budget is taken seriously by both sides.'

'Return on investment is obviously of paramount importance in the short and long term, because the aim of new investment is to improve ratios not to dilute them. This approach means that investment tends to take the form of relatively small add-on projects rather than large acquisitions.'

'I believe that our monitoring procedures, the pooling of experiences and the sharing of commitment are the touchstone of our success and the foundation of our future growth.'

These direct references to the priorities and styles of some of the CEOs demonstrate the fundamental differences in personality and management philosophy that exist. And they illustrate the importance of ensuring that the CEO's philosophy matches with the desired management style.

Senior Management Skills

We have identified the importance of matching the CEO's personality with the strategic management style. We believe the same relationship exists between senior managers – managers at corporate HQ and division MDs – and the style. It is not necessary that all senior managers are clones; in fact one of the interesting aspects of all of our companies is the variety of 'characters' that exist in the centre and in the board rooms. But senior managers must have skills that are appropriate to the style.

Trevor Chinn of Lex made this point:

> In a successful company there is a very close fit between style, the management skills and the strategy. I would expect that there is a huge difference between the companies [in the sample]. We will have different information systems, different senior managers and different styles of chief executive. Therefore I can see that the corporate role is likely to be hugely different.

We can see the importance of senior management skills in some of our companies. Tarmac had a tradition of a strong finance function and budgeting skills at the centre and in the divisions before 1979. It was therefore easier for Sir Eric Pountain to introduce a Financial Control style to the business when he took over. The Building Products division of Tarmac, however, has specialized in buying small companies manufacturing for the building industry. These companies have few financial or budgeting strengths and it has proved difficult to apply the Financial Control style as effectively in that division.

In UB the finance function traditionally plays a less central role in controlling performance and sanctioning expenditure. As a result, the centre would find it hard to impose a Financial Control style on the businesses. UB has been built on strong leadership at the centre with the inevitable effect that there have been few opportunities for strong general managers to develop underneath. At one stage 30 per cent of senior management appointments were made from outside and the rising stars in UB – Bob Clarke, Frank Knight and Eric Nicoli – were trained in other companies: Cadbury, Colgate and Rowntree. This management trio are pushing now for a more controlled, more 'professional' approach to management. Over time, it may be that UB's style will evolve from Strategic Planning to Strategic Control.

In Courtaulds, Chris Hogg found it hard to change to a Strategic Control style in the late 1970s. Under Lord Kearton, the managers in Courtaulds had been trained in a period during which the centre gave the lead and took many of the critical decisions. Many of them lacked strategic thinking and strategic planning skills. Moreover, the central management team had not been accustomed to taking a back seat and letting subsidiary managing directors lead the way. It took a number of years, probably more than 5, for the change of style to be effectively implemented. During this period, Courtaulds made extensive use of consultants to bolster the efforts of division and business unit managers.

The importance of senior management skills is also demonstrated in the backgrounds of the senior managers. In BP, where knowledge of the oil business is essential to execute a Strategic Planning style, all of the eight executive directors have a long history of working in the oil industry. Contrast this with Hanson, where knowledge of acquisition strategies and financial controls is critical, and where six of the nine board directors have accounting backgrounds.

In summary, the style chosen to manage a particular business unit must reflect the skills of the senior managers concerned. The skills in turn will reflect the history and culture of the organization as well as its systems and the type of people in the company. If, for example, the business unit managing director has had little experience of developing strategies, it would be unwise for the centre to adopt a low planning influence style. On the other hand, if the central management team normally 'peer at the businesses through the numbers' and have no direct operating experience in a particular business unit, it would be inappropriate for them to adopt a high planning influence style.

Mismatches between style and skills can also occur on the control dimension. Central management should not try to implement tight financial controls if the company's accounting rules and financial disciplines are not developed and policed through a strong finance function. Conversely, tight financial controls are easier in companies that have highly developed financial accounting skills. In BTR, for example, business unit managing directors volunteered that the accounting package is so tight that they have 'nowhere to hide'. This is an excellent foundation stone for tight financial controls.

This chapter has described a model that central management can use to match their strategic management style to the needs of an individual business unit. The style should reflect, on the one hand, the nature of the unit's business in terms of its links with other units, the size and payback of its investments and the stability of its competitive environment. On the other hand, the style must fit the resources, human and financial, that are available at the centre and in the business unit. It must match the financial condition of the business, the personality of the CEO and the skills off senior managers.

How far are managers able to select and fine tune their management styles? In principle, BOC could be managed like GEC; Cadbury could have the same acquisition philosophy as Hanson Trust. However, in practice we have noted that changes in style are not easy to bring about, and occur infrequently. Indeed, we have suggested that the personalities and skills of the CEO and his senior team go far to determine the style that is actually adopted by a company – and, without changes in management, these change only slowly, if at all.

Those changes in style that do occur are normally a result of financial pressures. Such changes have often had a dramatic impact on performance, as witness the turnarounds achieved by Chris Hogg at Courtaulds and John Harvey-Jones at ICI. These changes in performance come, we believe, from a better match between the companies' styles and their business circumstances. We have concluded that it is the match between style and business circumstances that is most important. Ideally, the internal resource factors, the nature of the business circumstances and the style should all be matched. If the style has evolved in response to management preferences and no longer fits the needs of businesses, changes, however difficult, must be made. And at the forefront will be changes in senior managers and the have concluded that it is the match between style and business circumstances that is most important. Ideally, the internal resource factors, the nature of the business circumstances and the style should all be matched. If the style has evolved in response to management preferences and no longer fits the needs of businesses, changes, however difficult, must be made. And at the forefront will be changes in senior managers and the development of new skills.

Ideally a company should be able to grow without making style changes. Some of the most successful companies in the world have been those who have retained their management values and philosophy as they have grown. In the next chapter we examine this issue and suggest ways in which companies can set about building portfolios of businesses that will not need the trauma of style changes.

Notes

1 Tom Burns and D. M. Stalker, *The Management of Innovation* (Tavistock Publications, 1961).
2 There have been a variety of important contingency theory writers. These include Joan Woodward, who argued in *Industrial Organization: Theory and Practice* (Oxford University Press, 1965) that the technology used by a firm determined its appropriate organization structure; James Thompson, who provided a fascinating, but wholly theoretical, account of how organizations cope with uncertainty by structuring themselves to respond to different sorts of environments (*Organizations in Action*, McGraw-Hill, 1967); and Paul Lawrence and Jay Lorsch, whose *Organization and Environment* (Harvard Business School, 1967) is perhaps the most complete, research-based account of how organizations should manage themselves in different environments to achieve optimal economic performance.

   A good summary of these and other contingency theorists' views is provided by Raymond Miles and Charles Snow in chapter 14 of *Organization Strategy, Structure and Process* (McGraw-Hill, 1978).
3 H. Igor Ansoff, 'The concept of strategic management', *Journal of Business Policy*, Summer 1972; H. Igor Ansoff, *Strategic Management* (John Wiley, 1979).
4 H. Igor Ansoff, *Implanting Strategic Management* (Prentice-Hall, 1985).
5 Although the brick market is a stable battle between brick producers, developments in other building materials may make the battle between brick companies and producers of substitutes less stable.
6 A clear description of the industry life cycle and its uses in theory and in management decision-making is given in *Strategic Management* by Arnaldo Hax and Nicolas Majhuf (Prentice-Hall, 1984).
7 The best description and analysis of stalemate industries is given in The Boston Consulting Group's Commentary, *Stalemate; The Problem*, 1984.
8 The first three quotes are drawn from a memorandum Lord Weinstock wrote to the managers of English Electric in 1968 following the takeover by GEC.
9 Taken from the 1985 Annual Report.

13

Managing Diversity

We are in a range of different businesses. We regard this diversity as a source of strength. It spreads our risks and gives us the opportunity to switch resources from low growth, low return areas to fund expansion in opportunity areas. But we do pay a penalty in the complexity of the management task this creates. Whether our degree of diversity is manageable, I'm not sure.

This concern, voiced by the planning director of one of the Strategic Control companies, must strike an echo in the board rooms of many multibusiness companies. In this chapter we will examine different ways in which companies manage the problems of diversity.

Why do companies diversify? First, diversity is claimed to reduce risk. Lionel Stammers made this point when talking about BTR's objectives. 'We have some measurable objectives in terms of reducing risk. We have objectives to spread our risk across geographic areas and across business areas and we can measure against our achievement of that.' By having a broadly based business, companies believe they can produce a more stable financial performance. When one industry or economy is performing badly, it can be offset by other businesses in the portfolio that are producing good results. Stable performance is important to the financial markets. But it is also important for competitive reasons. A large company with a spread of businesses has more staying power and can resist competitive attacks more easily.

The second reason often given for diversifying is that it creates opportunities for growth. A presence in a range of industries gives the company more growth options and hence makes it possible to select only the best. Companies in mature industries, in particular, frequently invest in faster-growing areas as a means of maintaining a growth track and using up excess cash flow.

We have discussed the arguments for and against diversity in chapter 2 and the debate continues. However, whatever its theoretical benefits and problems, for managers at the corporate headquarters of most large companies, diversity is a fact of life. Not only are subsidiaries frequently spread across many industries and many countries, but they are also at different stages of maturity, with different growth rates and different patterns of financial performance. Understanding and controlling each of the businesses in a portfolio of this sort is a severe test of corporate management. In particular, it may not be easy to match the corporate style to the requirements of each business.

In the previous chapter we identified three key factors relating to the business environment that should influence management style. We argued that managers should choose a style for the centre that matched with these factors – the linkages between businesses, the size and payback of investments, and the nature of the competitive environment. In a diverse portfolio of businesses, these factors are likely to differ in different parts of the portfolio, implying that the centre should adopt a different style for different businesses. Hence, in a diversified company, the centre may need to adjust or fine tune its relationship with each subsidiary or group of businesses.

Courtaulds, for example, includes within its portfolio small, national clothing businesses, with short lead times, fragmented competitors and a need for careful financial control; and also an international marine paint business that requires global coordination across markets, state-of-the-art research into new coatings and a willingness to invest for long-term competitive advantage. These businesses require rather different handling by the centre, in order to match the nature of the business to the corporate management style.

Furthermore, as businesses change – encountering new competitors, breaking into new markets, employing new technologies – the centre's style may need to change to reflect the new environment.

As an example, STC grew up as a subsidiary of ITT, with most of its business in the supply of telecommunications equipment to the British government. This was a stable and comparatively protected competitive situation. ITT's emphasis on meeting budget was appropriate. In the early 1980s ITT reduced its shareholding to a minority interest, British Telecom was privatized, liberalizing its purchasing to include overseas suppliers, and the technologies and markets of telecommunications, data processing and computing began to converge rapidly. STC found itself in a different business environment. It began to create a new management style with greater emphasis on long-term planning to cope more effectively with the dramatic changes in the nature of its business circumstances.

Ideally, therefore, corporate management need to be flexible in the styles they adopt for different parts of the portfolio, and to fine tune those styles as businesses change. But is this feasible?

In our research we found that companies tend to employ a uniform style across most of their businesses. We found few examples of the central team adopting a different style with different parts of the portfolio. We also found that changes in style occur seldom. When they do come, they normally involve the trauma of changes in senior management and of the chief executive.

These two findings make sense. They reflect the importance of simplicity and consistency in effective organizations. With a single style across all businesses it is easier for the centre to communicate its priorities and intentions to managers in subsidiaries. It can also ensure that information systems, organization charts, incentive and career development systems are supportive of the underlying style. Whereas with flexible or changing styles, clarity of communication is harder, and subsidiary management can more easily be confused about the signals they are receiving. The power of a shared corporate culture has been made clear;[1] flexible or multiple styles are at odds with any such unifying values.

Organization theory, developed by the consultants McKinsey & Co., supports the idea that organizations will perform better if they focus on one management style. In the 1970s, McKinsey set up teams of consultants to develop and document current thinking about strategy on the one hand and organization on the other. Two members of the organization team were Robert Waterman and Tom Peters whose work has since produced *In Search of Excellence*.[2] One of their earlier contributions was the 7S Model (figure 13.1).

This model states that organizations can be managed (or rather organization change can be managed) only by recognizing the full array of factors that make up a working, functioning organization. Structure alone is not the key, nor even strategy and structure together. A broader range of

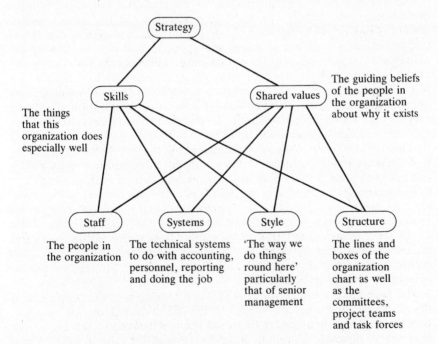

Figure 13.1 The 7S model (developed by McKinsey & Co).

factors is important. Robert Waterman classified these factors as the 7S elements of organization – strategy, structure, systems, staff, skills, style and shared values.

The best performing organizations are those where these seven elements support and reinforce each other. Where the values of the organization match the strategy, the systems reinforce and strengthen the structure and the style suits the people, the organization will be effective. Where parts of the organization don't fit – the skills don't fit the strategy, the style jars with the values and the people don't fit into the structure – effectiveness will be reduced. McKinsey consultants discovered the importance of fit by working with the model on client assignments. The successful organizations seemed to have fit: the ones with problems had mismatches.

In *In Search of Excellence* Tom Peters and Robert Waterman have expounded another organization theme – 'keep it simple'. They see organizations as highly complex interactions between people. They recognize that people have an ability to add layers of complexity and intrigue to most events. They have observed that effective organizations succeed because they 'keep it simple'. They don't try to do too many things at once. They don't try to manage against complex objectives. They avoid elaborate matrix structures. They limit the complexity of the information and reporting systems. They focus on a few core skills and, most important, they drive forward behind a few well-communicated values.

The concepts of 'fit' and 'keep it simple' are echoed in the works of other organization theorists.[3] The message, however, is the same: where possible, managers should build simple organizations with clear objectives and consistent values; the management system should help to simplify the manager's task without blocking out the natural uncertainty and complexity of the business.

The implication we draw from these concepts is that the management approach should be clear and consistent across the organization. It follows that the central organization should focus on one management style. The CEO should choose a style and build his organization and portfolio around it. The 'fit' and 'keep it simple' concepts imply that a central management team that try to adopt different styles with different business units will be less effective than a team able to focus on one style of management.

Even more fundamentally, we noted in our research that companies' styles almost always reflect the personality and views of their chief executives. The style is an embodiment of the beliefs and attitudes of the CEO. Since many of the CEOs in our sample have strong personalities and philosophies of management, as explained in the previous chapter, this makes it hard for them to operate different styles with different managers, or even to change style over time.

The problem is reinforced by the fact that managers at the centre and in the divisions build up an image of the CEO based on his 'normal' behaviour. They then appear to mould their behaviour to suit the image they have developed, rather than to respond to the CEO's actual behaviour. Derek Roberts talked about this problem at GEC. Lord

Weinstock can see the need to change some of the aspects of GEC's management style, but it is not easy, because unit managers are slow to respond to the different stimulae and signals he is giving. A sort of 'communication inertia' prevails in which new messages from the centre take a long time to become accepted and internalized down the line.

It is therefore difficult for most CEOs to adapt their style to the needs of different businesses in their portfolios. But not only is it hard for them to change the way they manage: it is also hard for divisional and business managers to understand the different styles their boss is using.

Diverse and changing businesses that require different styles are therefore hard to reconcile with the need to maintain simple organization structures and systems within a unified corporate culture. This means that building and managing a successful corporate portfolio encounters some intractable problems:

● How to handle a diversity of business types without running into unmanageable complexity.
● How to maintain simplicity without major problems of style mismatch.
● How far, and in what circumstances, diversity should be sought or avoided.

These issues are part of the ongoing management agenda in almost all the companies in our sample. Few seemed wholly comfortable with their current levels of diversity and few were able to give clear messages about how to resolve the issues.

However, from talking with managers and observing what the companies are actually doing we have been able to document three basically different philosophies for managing diversity. These broadly correspond to the three most popular management styles. They are:

● Core Businesses (Strategic Planning style).
● Diverse Businesses (Strategic Control style).
● Manageable Businesses (Financial Control style).

Table 13.1 shows the salient characteristics of these philosophies.

Core Businesses

In its 1984 Annual Report, Cadbury Schweppes stated its group objectives in these terms:

● The Group will concentrate on its principal business areas. . . . Our objective is to maximize the use of existing assets rather than to diversify into unrelated ares.
● In confectionery we at present hold a 5 per cent share of the world chocolate market and are ranked as the fifth largest company in it. We

Managing Diversity

Table 13.1 Philosophies for designing the portfolio

	Core Businesses	Manageable Businesses	Diverse Businesses
Strategic management style at the centre	Strategic Planning	Financial Control	Strategic Control
Type of businesses in the portfolio	Related businesses in two or three core industries	Diverse businesses in different industries but with the same competitive and business environment	Diverse businesses in a cross-section of industries
Method of building the portfolio	Build existing businesses and buy related businesses that help strengthen the core business areas	Back winners, drop losers, and buy underperforming businesses that will respond to the style	Channel funds to the most 'attractive' industries, and buy into new 'attractive' industries

intend to increase that share and to climb the league of international chocolate companies.

● In soft drinks, we are currently number three in the market outside the USA, but fifth in the world overall. Our aim is to become the world's leading non-cola carbonated soft drinks company.

During the year following this statement, Cadbury's divested itself of two major divisions, Beverages and Foods and Health and Hygiene, to concentrate more exclusively on the core areas of confectionery and soft drinks. Recently, it has acquired Canada Dry.

This is classic Core Businesses thinking. The company commits itself to a few industries (usually two or three), and sets out to win big in those industries. Growth is through organic development of the businesses in these industries, and through related acquisitions that help to strengthen and extend the core businesses.

A push into international markets is often a feature. More peripheral (non-core) businesses are starved of funds or divested. The organization structure of the typical Core Businesses portfolio is shown in figure 13.2. The CEO has strong central functional support, and the businesses operate in some form of product-geographic matrix, to ensure global coordination of strategy. Examples of companies from our research adopting the Core Businesses philosophy are Cadbury, BOC, Lex and STC. (See table 13.2.)

In a Core Businesses portfolio, the Strategic Planning style works best. Limited diversity means that the centre can be knowledgeable about each

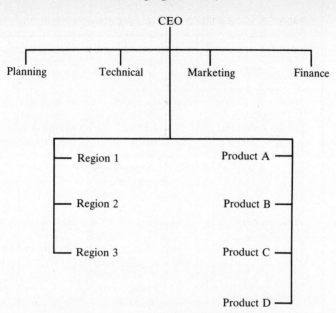

Figure 13.2 A Core Businesses organization structure.

of the core businesses, and can make constructive suggestions about their strategies. Furthermore, they can provide coordination between businesses where this is needed. At STC we were told: 'For our approach to succeed, the centre must understand the businesses well to be able to challenge the management companies on the quality of their proposals. Our limited size and diversity allows us to do this.'

The core businesses are selected, in part, because they offer opportunities for major growth, and hence strategies for the core businesses often involve big, bet-your-company decisions. To reach agreement on these decisions close corporate involvement and sponsorship is needed. The payoff to these decisions is sought in the long term, and it is accepted that there may be hiccups along the route. Lex would probably not have plunged so heavily into the wholly new business of electronic component distribution without strong corporate sponsorship; nor would they have weathered the storms in the business during 1985 and 1986 without continuing corporate support.

A Strategic Planning style – close central involvement in strategy development and flexible strategic controls – is therefore generally appropriate to the portfolio and to the ambitions associated with this philosophy. If applied consistently across the whole portfolio, it causes few serious problems of mismatch.

The strengths of the philosophy are, therefore, that it gives industry focus, making it easier for the centre to add value; it provides growth

Table 13.2 Examples of the Core Businesses philosophy

Company	Core businesses	Recent investments, acquisitions (1980–5)	Recent disposals, closures (1980–5)
BOC	Gases Healthcare Carbon Products	Japanese and S. American gases acquisitions Healthcare acquisitions Major investment in carbon graphite electrode business	Computer services division Welding interests Variety of smaller businesses
Cadbury Schweppes	Confectionery Soft Drinks	Joint company with Coca-Cola for UK soft drinks Various soft drinks acquisitions in US and Europe (e.g. Canada Dry) Investments to increase share of US and European confectionery	Beverages and Food division Health and Hygiene division
Lex	Vehicle Distribution Electronic Component Distribution	Nine electronic component distribution companies in UK, US and Europe	Transportation interests Hotel division
STC	Information Technology	IAL ICL (Computers) Major component investments	(Several since 1985)

opportunities within the core businesses; it can be managed with a single style, thereby permitting shared values and organization simplicity.

There are, however, weaknesses in the philosophy.

1 Lack of diversity across industries provides less spread of risks. The downturn in the electronics industry left both STC and Lex exposed. Moreover reliance on the core industries for growth creates problems when those industries mature, as companies in the tobacco and oil businesses have found. The traditional, well-understood core businesses no longer provide sufficient growth potential, and entry to major new sectors is liable to cause problems, precisely because they are new and therefore unfamiliar.

2 Changes in the business environment can make the Strategic Planning style less generally appropriate, leading eventually to the need for a difficult change in style. In the mid 1970s Courtaulds began to feel that the linkages between their textile businesses were less important than flexibility and responsiveness. This led them to move away from high central planning influence, towards more devolution. But it took a further 7–8 years before the move to a Strategic Control style was fully established.

3 Non-core businesses that remain within the portfolio tend to feel unloved and constrained in their strategies. These problems have already been discussed in the chapter on Pitfalls (see pages 188–9).

In summary, the Core Businesses philosophy is a viable approach to the problem of managing a large multibusiness portfolio. It achieves a match between the Strategic Planning style at the centre and the businesses in the portfolio by concentrating on a few sectors, each of which contain linked businesses with growth potential. But it can handle less diversity across industries, and encounters problems when the core businesses mature.

Manageable Businesses

Like Cadbury Schweppes, Hanson Trust spells out its objectives and philosophy in its Annual Report. In 1984, Lord Hanson, the chairman, stated his objectives ('determined 21 years ago') as:

> To invest in good quality basic businesses providing essential goods and services for the consumer and industry and to obtain an improving return for shareholders by maximizing earnings per share and dividend growth . . . Those in the operating companies have clear responsibility for running their businesses.

The notable points about this statement are that it is consistent with diversification into a wide range of industries, and that goals are essentially financial in nature. This is in sharp contrast to Cadbury's objectives.

In the period since this statement of objectives, Hanson has entered a range of new industries through their acquisitions of SCM in the United States and Imperial Group in the UK. These acquisitions have taken Hanson from 55th place in the Times 1000 largest British companies in 1983 to among the top ten in 1986.

Underlying the aggressive, acquisitive growth of Hanson, however, there is a strong sense of the types of industries ('basic businesses providing essential goods and services') that will respond best to Hanson's management style. Acquisitions in high tech, rapidly changing or capital intensive businesses are avoided, and any subsidiary that begins to show these characteristics is liable to be divested. We were told about a Hanson business that made turbochargers which had come up with an investment plan, indicating several years of negative cash flow to get established in a new and developing field of technology: 'This worried us a lot. We sold the business shortly afterwards.' The emphasis is therefore on selecting businesses for the portfolio which can be effectively managed using short-term financial controls. Hanson Trust is in this way a typical example of the Manageable Businesses philosophy. Other examples of this philosophy from our research are BTR and Tarmac (see table 13.3).

Table 13.3 Examples of the Manageable Businesses philosophy

Company	Style	Businesses
BTR	Financial Control	Construction, engineering, electrical distribution, valves, pipes, control systems, transportation, healthcare, sporting goods, ceramics, materials, laminates, agricultural equipment, cleaning devices, conveyor belting, polymeric fabrications, power transmission, automotive carpets, automotive components, radiators, reinforced plastics, safety equipment, paper machine clothing, publishing, dental supplies, hospital equipment, rehabilitation products, hosiery, furniture and insurance
Hanson Trust	Financial Control	Department stores, batteries, bricks, electrical and automotive, yarns and threads, engineering, machine tools, control systems, construction equipment services, fabrics, textile finishing machinery, soft furnishings, apparel, footwear, housewares, artificial flowers, meat processing, office and home furniture and furnishings, kitchen cabinets, vanities, fasteners, garden and industrial hand tools, wood mouldings, windows, building materials, lumber, energy equipment, engineering products and services, lighting fixtures fittings, tobacco, brewing, restaurants, retailing, hotels, catering, snacks, frozen foods, sauces
Tarmac	Financial Control	Stone, sand, gravel, concrete, asphalt, bricks, tiles, installation of building materials, construction, design management for building work, civil engineering, gas and oil engineering, house building, development of commercial and industrial property, oil and gas exploration, bitumen refining

The qualities that make businesses in different industries 'manageable' have been articulated by Hanson and BTR managers:

● We avoid areas of very high technology. We do not want to be involved in businesses which are highly capital intensive and where decision-making has to be centralized.

(Lord Hanson, Hanson Trust.)

● We are a fairly low risk organization. We avoid businesses that require major, risky outlays with long payback periods.

(Clive Stearnes, group chief executive, BTR.)

● We don't like mass production. We like niche situations that involve customer problem-solving.

(Lionel Stammers, joint chief executive, European Region, BTR.)

There may be extensive diversity in terms of industries, but there is homogeneity in the nature of the businesses and, hence, in the required style of management – the Financial Control style.[4] In practice, this means that the businesses should have few linkages with each other, should be in relatively stable competitive environments, and should not involve large or long-term investment decisions.

Growth is achieved mainly through acquisitions that add new, manageable businesses to the portfolio. Financial Control is less suitable for fast growth and unstable environments and does not encourage aggressive initiatives to achieve organic growth.

We sold Cornhill Insurance because the volatility and changes in the financial services sector made it less attractive to us than our more traditional mature businesses. Its wonderful how these mature businesses continue to grow for us.

(Sir Owen Green, chairman, BTR.)

Figure 13.3 is an organization chart for a typical Manageable Businesses company. The headquarters is slim, supported only by a strong finance function. Underneath, there are layers of general management, but prime profit responsibility is pushed right down to the lowest level. It is the high degree of decentralization of strategy and responsibility that allows the extensive diversity to be manageable. On the other hand, management throughout the company grows up with, and is trained in, the financial disciplines that are the hallmark of the approach.

This philosophy therefore achieves a strong culture based on the pursuit of short-term financial objectives despite a high degree of diversity across industries. It avoids mismatches between this style and its businesses by selecting the portfolio with 'fit' in mind. At Tarmac we were told that they had disinvested from their North Sea oil holding with some relief, since the size and timescale of exploration activities had been uncomfortable for

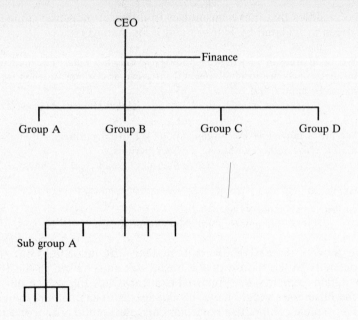

Figure 13.3 A Manageable Businesses organization structure.

them. And, at BTR, one central manager argued that one of the best decisions they made was to get out of tyres in the 1960s: 'To continue in tyre manufacture we needed to make a large capital investment. However, the business wasn't producing the sort of return we expected and we couldn't see the picture changing.' Portfolio selection and rationalization of this type greatly simplifies the management of diversity. As such, the philosophy has considerable strengths.

However, there are also weaknesses. The philosophy does not lead to much organic growth, and is liable to result in piling up excess cash from a whole range of profitable, mature, cash cows. Further acquisitions provide a partial solution, since they both create growth and use up the cash. But, when a company reaches the size of a Hanson or a BTR, finding new acquisition targets big enough to maintain the momentum of growth becomes difficult.

The Financial Control style is also vulnerable to aggressive competitors. When the going gets tough, management will typically retrench or divest. Selective tactical withdrawals may be fine, but a general willingness to retreat can be exploited by a well-resourced and ambitous opponent.

Lastly, the philosophy creates small, more specialist, 'niche' businesses rather than global players in big international businesses. From a corporate perspective, this may be no bad thing given the intensity of competition on the major international battlefields. But from a national perspective, there is a need for at least some companies who can compete successfully in international industries such as information technology, oil, automobiles and pharmaceuticals.

The Manageable Businesses philosophy is therefore an important option for central management.[5] It has produced some of the best performances from our sample of companies. However, it also has serious drawbacks. There are limits to acquisition based growth; it is vulnerable to aggressive competitors; and it does not lead to the building of large, global businesses with integrated strategies to achieve sustainable competitive advantage.

Diverse Businesses

In the Diverse Businesses philosophy, the emphasis is on diversity rather than focus. The centre seeks to build a portfolio that spreads risk across industries and geographic areas as well as ensuring the portfolio is balanced in terms of growth, profitability and cash flow. Resources are allocated to competitively strong businesses in attractive industries; and there is a willingness – even a desire – to extend the portfolio into a range of different markets, technologies and competitive situations.

Although confident and aggressive diversification of this kind was in vogue during the 1960s and early 1970s, the more recent fashion for 'sticking to the knitting' has meant that few, if any, of the companies in our research sample now wholeheartedly embrace the Diverse Businesses philosophy. The obvious problems in understanding and managing wide diversity have greatly reduced corporate enthusiasm for 'new legs' to the portfolio.

Nevertheless, there were a number of highly diverse companies in our sample, who seem to be developing a distinctive philosophy for managing their portfolios. This philosophy entails creating groups of businesses that have some logic either in industrial terms or in terms of manageability. Responsibility for strategy is delegated to the group level managers. Each group can then adopt its own, perhaps different, style for dealing with its portfolio. Figure 13.4 is a schematic representation of how such a company might be structured.

This sort of structure, with strong and largely independent groups or divisions, allows a portfolio with real diversity to be 'chunked' into more manageable pieces. The divisions can grow organically at their own rates – and new divisions can be added, by acquisition or subdivision, as appropriate.

Companies that appear to be adopting a philosophy of this sort include ICI, where each division has extensive freedom to manage itself as it sees fit, and Courtaulds, which has recently split the company into two groupings, Textiles and Chemical and Industrial, in the belief that each grouping needs a different type of management.

The central style in these companies tends to be Strategic Control. Only Strategic Control is likely to be flexible enough to accommodate different divisions, each with its own style. The old adage that it is hard to have a

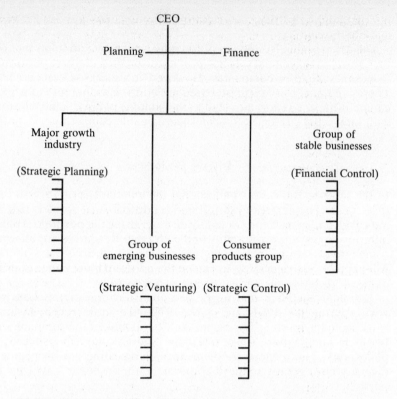

Figure 13.4 A Diverse Businesses organization structure.

longer time horizon than your boss suggests that a corporate style of Financial Control will preclude Strategic Planning or Strategic Control at the divisional level; while a corporate desire to adopt a Strategic Planning style forces divisional line managers to do likewise in order to be able to answer the questions asked by headquarters.

With Strategic Control, the centre is, in Chris Hogg of Courtauld's words, simply 'a sympathetic and knowledgeable 100 per cent share-holder', allowing the divisions to go their own way in terms of style. By structuring the divisions right, the centre can create homogeneous groupings of businesses, where few mismatches occur, and can adjust the composition of divisions over time, as businesses change.

The Diverse Businesses philosophy, then, appears to be a way of managing diversity with a single style, and without creating mismatches between business circumstances and central style. But there is a price to be paid. The centre must be willing (and able) to play a chameleon role, adopting a low profile relative to divisional management. This is not likely to be comfortable for a strong CEO, and also raises questions concerning the value added by the centre. If the centre is so low key, and the groups have so much autonomy, why would the groups not be better as independent companies without the corporate overhead?

But an even more difficult issue arises from the cultural complexity implied by different styles in each group. Is it really possible for different styles to flourish side by side, or will certain groups become second class citizens? One company that purports to adopt the Diverse Businesses philosophy told us:

> We adapt our style to the different companies in our portfolio. We use Strategic Planning where we are building businesses with a 5- to 10-year payback. Strategic Control is our normal style and an active strategic dialogue takes place between the group and the operating companies. And we use Financial Control for our 'dog' companies, when we are sorting out and preparing for disposal operations which do not fit our long-term requirements.

It is evident that the Financial Control divisions in these circumstances are a sort of 'sin bin' and face a very different situation from their counterparts in Hanson Trust or BTR. More generally, different styles, cultures and objectives in different divisions cause problems of communication and cooperation. The danger is that there will be jealousies, suspicions and less than 100 per cent commitment, rather than a tolerance for diversity.

Cultural complexity is also liable to create succession problems when the existing CEO retires. Candidates from the different divisions may have radically different approaches to management, and each may well find the low key central role incompatible with their styles. Moreover, if a new more positive central style emerges, it will be hard to preserve the divisional autonomy that characterizes the Diverse Businesses philosophy.

In summary, therefore, the Diverse Businesses philosophy has major attractions, since it has the potential of resolving the conflicts between organization simplicity, portfolio balance and change. In practice, however, the organization problems created by multiple styles are great, and there is some danger that the groups within the company would perform better as independent companies without the overhead burden and interference of central management.

The Diverse Businesses philosophy may, however, be the best immediate solution for many large multibusiness companies. Companies that have a presence in a number of industries and in businesses at different stages of development may be able to raise their performance by setting up groups that can be managed with different styles by strong group executives. If it proves possible to make the group structure work, the companies can continue to build their portfolios on this basis. If not, the companies can sell or float off some of the groups to enable management to focus on one of the other philosophies.

Review

Ideally, a company's approach to managing its portfolio will achieve:

— enough diversity across industries and geographic areas to spread the risks of sudden changes;
— enough balance in types of businesses to ensure an even profit and cash flow profile;
— a close match between the nature of the businesses in the portfolio and the strategic management style;
— organization and cultural simplicity;
— a means of generating growth and regeneration for future portfolio development.

Table 13.4 summarizes the ways in which each philosophy copes with the problems of managing and growing a diverse portfolio. Each represents an internally consistent, but different, approach to the task. Our research suggests that there are successful companies pursuing each approach, although the Diverse Businesses philosophy has few committed adherents.

Table 13.4   The philosophies compared

	Core Businesses	Manageable Businesses	Diverse Businesses
Diversity across industries	Low	Very high	High
Diversity across types of businesses	Fairly low	Low	High
Style at centre	Strategic Planning	Financial Control	Strategic Control
How mismatches avoided	Core businesses mainly responsive to Strategic Planning	Portfolio selection and retention of 'manageable' businesses	Structure into homogenous groups
Growth	Mainly organic	Mainly acquisition	Organic and acquisition
Drawbacks	Limited industry diversity Maturation of core businesses Non-core businesses	Limits to acquisition-based growth Vulnerable to aggressive competition Does not build long-term global businesses	Low key centre Limited central added value Cultural complexity

We have also found, however, that each philosophy has certain drawbacks. These drawbacks do not represent fatal flaws, but are best seen as contingent liabilities. They are problems which may be avoided for long periods of time, but which can come home to roost under certain circumstances.

Perhaps most surprisingly, we have found that in most companies the philosophy for managing diversity remains implicit. There may be an approach which approximates one of our philosophies, but it is not normally explicitly articulated and examined. In consequence, the ways in which the philosophy can be reinforced and strengthened are less clearly perceived, and the risks and drawbacks of the approach may not be adequately recognized. We are confident that improvements in performance can be achieved by companies that create a clearer focus on these issues, and make a more conscious choice of their portfolio building philosophy.

Notes

1 See Terence E. Deal and Alan A. Kennedy, *Corporate Cultures* (Addison-Wesley, 1982).
2 Thomas J. Peters and Robert H. Waterman Jr, *In Search of Excellence* (Harper and Row, 1982).
3 For example, Raymond E. Miles and Charles C. Snow, 'Fit, Failure and the Hall of Fame', *The California Management Review*, Spring 1984.
4 It can be argued that venture capital companies adopt the Manageable Businesses philosophy, but base it on the Strategic Venturing style. In chapter 14 we describe the Hewlett–Packard approach which seems to do just this.
5 In an article entitled 'The Dominant Logic: a new linkage between diversity and performance', *Strategic Management Journal*, Nov.-Dec. 1986, C. K. Prahalad and R. A. Bettis propose a somewhat similar concept to 'Manageability', calling it the 'Dominant Logic'. Our empirical work gives support to the theoretical hypotheses they propose.

14

International Benchmarks

We have presented our research results to many audiences. At these discussions managers have expressed two recurrent themes. First, they see Japanese companies as falling mainly into the Strategic Planning category, and they conclude that Japan is probably winning because of the ability of their managers to be effective at this style. Secondly, they argue that British managers are likely to be especially bad at managing away the tensions and potential disadvantages of the Strategic Planning and Strategic Control styles. They feel that the British culture, which worships status and hierarchy, praises the amateur and generates graduates whose long-term objectives are to become country gentlemen, is poorly placed to handle the subtleties of hierarchy management needed in the Strategic styles. They imply that we might expect to find solutions to some of our tensions by looking at companies from other cultures that are seen to be worldwide examples of excellence.

Japanese companies like Sony, NEC, Toyota and Komatsu are frequently described as having an almost inhuman ability to take the long-term strategic view, investing ahead of economic returns, developing new products before the old ones have become obsolete and aggressively working to gain market share. In the United States, IBM is cited as the ideal example of a Strategic Planning company. The question that is then raised is how do these companies overcome the negatives, the subtracted values, that are inherent in the Strategic Planning style. Interestingly, there is less common agreement about European exemplars. Siemens is mentioned by one, Philips by another; but each time tentatively. In Europe we seem to be less confident of our role models.

Our research looked only at British companies and focused, for practical reasons, on the relationship between head office and UK-based subsidiaries. We accept that our findings may therefore be mainly a statement about British management culture. For this reason we decided to carry out some limited desk research on a few non-UK companies which were widely acclaimed as well managed.

We looked for companies where articles, books or cases provided us with a reasonable understanding of the management systems, corporate strategy and type of people in the company.[1] This chapter, therefore, looks at four companies – IBM, GE and Hewlett–Packard in the United States and Matsushita in Japan. We have concluded, from the information available, that our framework, using planning influence and control influence to define central styles, is applicable outside the UK context. We also believe that companies like IBM, GE and Matsushita have not been able to avoid the tensions; they still suffer from the disadvantages that are inherent in each style. They appear, however, to be effective at dampening the effects of these disadvantages and at avoiding most of the management pitfalls. In other words, they have developed ways of reducing the negatives of their styles and getting the most out of the positives. In these companies it is cultural influence as much as management systems that brings forth the best from their styles.

IBM

IBM is a favourite role model for most managers. A Harvard Business School case book called *Implementing Strategy* by Professor Dick Vancil[2] provided us with a rich description of the management style and systems of IBM in 1979.

Frank Carey, IBM's chairman at the time, used the same words as Sir Peter Walters of BP to describe the decision-making philosophy: 'We aim for centralised policy making with decentralised operations.' The organization is structured to achieve the maximum decentralization possible, given a desire to reap all the benefits of synergy and integration. As one executive commented:

IBM is a very big organisation, distinctive in how tightly we link everything together. We want to integrate as much as possible and maintain control through centralised planning and tracking, but we also want to decentralise implementation and operating decisions. There are no major strategic decisions that are delegated.

IBM has a divisionalized structure (figure 14.1); but some of the divisions, such as the DP marketing group, are functional units rather than stand-alone businesses. In the US at least, IBM is really one business with research, marketing and manufacturing divisions reporting to the centre. As a result it is a complex matrix in which responsibilities overlap at many points.

In 1979, IBM had 42 production facilities in 15 countries. An executive explained:

Philosophically, everything that is sold overseas is built overseas. In practice, what happens is that when you start off with a new technology, you manufacture a component in one location to build up the learning curve. Then when you have mastered the process, you promulgate it. At mid-life,

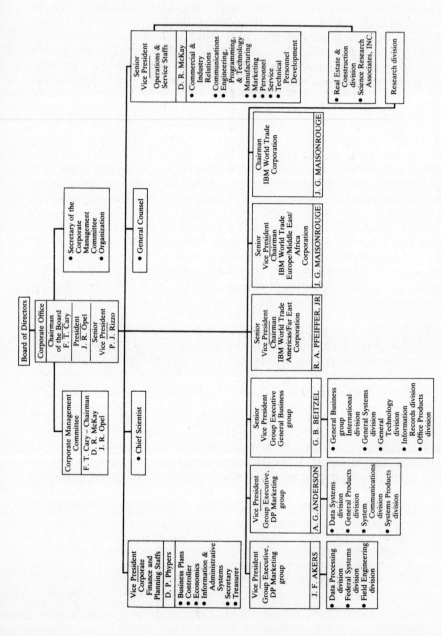

Figure 14.1 IBM corporate organization (from an original company document).

component manufacturing that is capital intensive and volume sensitive will be carried on both in the US and overseas as long as total demand is there. At the end of a product's life you may again sole source somewhere in the world to get scale economies.

For example, the General Products division made magnetic disk storage units that could be used in large processors sold by the Data Systems division. The processors could also be sold with printers made by the Systems Products division. In the US, a complete system would be sold by the Data Processing division and serviced by the Field Engineering division. Overseas, two non-US companies would be involved in selling and servicing the system. Integration across divisions is, therefore, critical to IBM's success.

Another feature of IBM's organization structure is the role of staff. The headquarters staff in IBM is large. There are more than a dozen major staff functions, varying from central treasury to units like real estate, that provide services to the divisions. The role of the staff function is to ensure 'functional excellence' in its sphere of influence. In practice this means that each staff function reviews the plans of each division and raises a flag if they feel uncomfortable. Marketing look at the profitability and positioning of the business plans; Engineering, Programming and Technology look at technical development programmes; and so on.

The process for reviewing plans in IBM is elaborate. The plans of each division are likely to affect the outcome in other divisions and are, therefore, open to the scrutiny of central staffs and divisional colleagues. William Eggleston, then president of the General Products division, explained:

> The staff in my division is very small; it's less than 10 per cent of our headcount, mainly financial and accounting with a small engineering staff that make tradeoffs between our three laboratories and two plants.

> The Group staff integrates the plans of the four divisions that make up the Product Group. The divisions are measured on the profit contribution they make; however, the Group staff price our products and make our forecasts and market estimates. They submit a Group plan and then allocate to us our pieces of the puzzle.

> The corporate staff do additional technical and business evaluations of the plans. The Group staff may disagree with the corporate staff over points of technology, competitiveness or financial outlook. Some corporate staffs, like manufacturing, are exceptionally strong. It is collegial, but not the kind that can be run over.

William Eggleston describes a picture of staffs talking to staffs and everyone having an opinion. It certainly fits our model of the way in which the centre exerts planning influence in a Strategic Planning company –

overlapping responsibilities, strong central staffs, multiple viewpoints on plans and elaborate review processes.

In addition, IBM has a system which we did not find in our UK sample of Strategic Planning companies and which may be unique – a system for handling disagreements. In IBM, they are called 'non-concurrences'. At any level any staff or line manager can 'raise a non-concurrence' if he believes the plan is inadequate or unrealistic. An operating unit would raise a non-concurrence because of a conflict or overlap with another operating area, whereas a staff department might raise a non-concurrence because of a technical disagreement. Most of these disagreements are resolved bilaterally. Dr Arthur Anderson, then vice-president in charge of the Data Processing product group, described the process:

> Where there is an issue of non-concurrence to something in a plan, the matter would be escalated through a chain of management from the local plant or laboratory to the division president. Assuming the disagreement continues, it would be escalated to me; and if it continued beyond that stage, it would become part of a presentation or a discussion by the Group to the Corporate Management Committee (CMC). An awful lot of things get settled before they go to the CMC. Neither side wants to lose and you have that exposure whenever you go to the CMC for a decision.

The CMC consists of the board chairman, Frank Cary, and the senior contact executives who make up the corporate office.

IBM's non-concurrence system appears to be the ultimate process to ensure that plans are thoroughly reviewed and that staff and managers take responsibility for the plans in other areas as well as their own. 'We have even taken issues to the CMC knowing we would almost certainly lose. We wanted to make top management more conscious|of all the aspects of the decision they were making. You want to be right, but sometimes there is value in making sure corporate management is aware there are alternative views', commented one staff executive.

By giving everyone the right to go to the top, some of the politics are taken out of the process. Managers are encouraged to respect each other's views and to listen to another manager's logic. If they don't, the issue could be taken to Frank Cary.

By looking at IBM's structure and planning processes, we have been able to position IBM as a company with high planning influence. It inevitably has the disadvantages of slow decision-making and a highly structured planning process. But IBM's culture and processes, like the non-concurrence system, work to reduce the impact of politics and the loss of 'ownership' that we observed in the UK companies.

It appears from looking at the planning dimension that IBM is a Strategic Planning company. But before we can make this judgement, we need to examine IBM's control processes. Performance targets are set as a result of three planning processes. First, there are 'program plans' based on individual decisions. These plans have a single objective and a timetable that fits the objective. Program plans can be started and completed at any time during the year. As one executive said

> Decisions are made all year around, night and day, not constrained by the annual planning cycle. People make a decision whenever it is time to make a decision. Program plans capture these decisions. Period planning in comparison [strategic plans and annual budgets] is a way to pull all of the decisions together to see if the aggregate meets the targets we are aiming at.

At the strategy level, IBM has 5-year strategic plans that are developed annually in the spring. The strategic plans are seen as an extension of the operating plan rather than the other way round. Unit managers agree an operating plan in October and, based on that 2-year budget, are then asked to consider how they will proceed in the following 3 years.

The operating plan is a 2-year rolling budget. 'The operating plan is the major management vehicle in IBM. It is the point at which all resources are approved – where you get your capital, your headcount, your expense dollars, your parts committed to you from other divisions', explained William Eggleston.

So IBM has three important target-setting processes – the program plans, the operating plans and the strategic plans. A line executive commented on the relative importance of the strategic and operating plans:

> I think the most scary thing about our process is that we're very serious about the strategic plan – to the point where we almost believe it. Most people would say that the strategic plan gets the back of the hand and the operating plan gets most of the attention. But the strategic plan does get a lot of the chairman's and the CMC's attention.

The three planning processes help IBM to take a balanced view of the short- and long-term issues facing the business. However, we have the impression that the long-term strategic objectives are seen as the most important. Paul Rizzo, then a member of the CMC, commented: 'We hold them to budgets. So it is very important. Very important. On the other hand, if there are things that the manager believes we have to do and he doesn't do them, and he uses budgets as an excuse, that's a worse offence than violating the budget.' In this statement we can see the tension between the short and the long term. Rizzo, however, comes down firmly on the side of the long term when there is a clash of priorities.

Moreover, although IBM have a thorough monitoring process that involves a monthly presentation to the CMC, the budget is not regarded as sacrosanct. The controls appear to be flexible. 'We review plans as required in the course of the year. The plan is a guide. It's not cast in concrete', commented one line manager.

Eggleston pointed out that making the budget was not his only priority: 'There is an ongoing measurement of how well you do in meeting your plans. If plans are changed people remember. But another major test of performance is whether you bring good products to the market in time, etc. It's not simply the numbers.'

Anderson commented on the tension that exists between short- and long-term objectives: 'It is very important to meet the plan or know why not. And when you know why not, it is very important to meet the plan. Short-term performance is very important, but IBM is an R&D company and that is so ingrained that there will always be discussions of long-range issues.'

Paul Rizzo expanded on this tension in describing the bonus system at IBM. Bonuses can range from 25 to 50 per cent of base salary, but are paid mainly against the performance of the company or group as a whole.

> We do not decide that people who didn't do as well as they said shouldn't get a bonus. In fact, my recollection is that some people have received some of their biggest rewards in periods when they didn't do as well as they said they would; but they did awfully well. We don't want to encourage people to put forward plans and objectives that are easy to attain. They must be difficult and people frequently miss. So we look at where people are coming from, where we were, how far we have come and how well we are doing compared to the market place and our competition.

These comments are very different from the philosophy of the Financial Control company, and our judgement is that they reflect a flexible control approach. We would need to discuss these issues in more detail with IBM managers to know whether IBM operates on 'flexible' controls or on a 'tight strategic' control approach.

Putting together our analysis of IBM's planning influence and our review of its control approach, we can categorize the company as either Strategic Planning or Strategic Programming. With current information, we would position IBM as a Strategic Planning company, and IBM's results would seem to support this.

IBM has pursued integrated strategies aimed at dominating world markets in most of its product areas. Growth has been mainly organic, although some important acquisitions have been made to strengthen particular business areas. Decision-making in IBM is certainly slow, as shown by IBM's ponderous response to competitive threats from, for example, companies producing clones of its mainframe CPU's and microcomputers. However, when the response comes the reaction has been effective and IBM's dominance of most markets has increased rather than declined.

The most notable achievement of IBM as a Strategic Planning company has been to avoid the major setbacks that have been a feature of our UK sample. Possibly the sophistication of IBM's planning process helps to avoid the major mistakes we have seen with other Strategic Planning companies.

Between the end of 1981 and the end of 1985, IBM's sales grew by 72 per cent and earnings per share by 90 per cent. Despite the maturing of the mainframe business, dramatic swings in the semiconductor industry and the emergence of a new microcomputer industry, IBM has continued to dominate the industry and earn a RoCE of over 30 per cent.

Since the mid 1970s, IBM has been faced with a core business – mainframes – where growth is slowing. Like the large oil companies, IBM has needed to diversify. However, unlike the oil industry, the computer industry has main fast-growing businesses that are loosely related to mainframe computers. It appears, therefore, that IBM will be able to diversify away from mainframes without changing its Core Businesses philosophy and without having to change its management style.

In a recent book on IBM,[3] David Mercer, an ex-employee and interestingly also an ex-employee of BTR, explains IBM's attempt to use 'Independent Business Units' as a means of diversifying beyond the mainframe computer business. From his explanation it appears that IBM tried to apply a strategic venturing style to these units like BP and UB have done.

He concludes that this attempt was largely unsuccessful with the exception of the personal computer division which has now been brought back into the main stream of IBM's core business. Our interpretation of his commentary is that IBM was able to stimulate growth and diversify into another related core business without changing its management style.

IBM's record is not without blemishes, and critics have argued that the company will not be able to respond to the latest changes in the industry. David Mercer in particular says that IBM is now facing probably its greatest challenge. This was underlined in 1986, when IBM reported a decline in earnings, and its major rival DEC produced a rise of 25%. However, for most, IBM is still an exemplar of good management. In the terms of our research, IBM appears to have made the best of the Strategic Planning style.

Three reasons for this stand out. First, IBM's portfolio of businesses appears to match well with the Strategic Planning style. IBM has stuck to a few core business areas, building its portfolio with a Core Businesses philosophy. Within these areas, the businesses are closely linked, sharing research, marketing, field service and other functions.

The important decisions in IBM are large, long-payback decisions that demand the attention of the centre and a long-term perspective. And the competitive environment is fierce and continually changing. All of these circumstances match well with a Strategic Planning style.

The second reason for IBM's success is its strong culture. Respect for the individual is legendary at IBM and is enshrined in the non-concurrence system. This encourages cooperation and responsibility, and so helps managers make better decisions. IBM's other two values, excellence and customer service, provide a common purpose and objective for managers, encouraging commitment and dedication to the cause.

Finally, IBM is led by a top management team who have grown up in the business. They have a deep understanding of the market place, the technology and the strategic issues. And they continue to keep abreast of developments. The non-concurrence system, the planning systems and the monthly reporting all help to keep the top team informed. As a result, they are able to steer the company forward with sensitivity and understanding.

By matching its style to its portfolio, by supporting the style with the cultural values of the company, and as a result of knowledgeable leadership, IBM appears to have a Strategic Planning style that works well and avoids some of the negatives we identified in chapter 11. However, certain tensions of corporate management are still evident. IBM has not eliminated the tension between short-term and long-term priorities. Nor has it been able to retain quick decision-making alongside its thorough planning process. But it does appear to have mitigated the reduction in ownership and responsibility that comes with central direction, overlapping structures and multiple viewpoints. We suspect that companies committed to a Strategic Planning style could learn a great deal by studying IBM's approach in more depth.

General Electric (GE)

GE can trace its origins back to 1878. Its original business was in electric lighting and electric motors. By the 1980s its businesses included lighting, appliances, aerospace, industrial services, nuclear power and financial services. Since 1984 GE has become even more diverse, acquiring RCA, a company strong in televisions and defence electronics, and Kidder Peabody, a Wall Street investment bank.

Since 1950 GE has been through a number of different organization structures and management philosophies.

> We came out of World War II a finely honed, centralized, functionally organised company. When we decentralised in the early fifties, we did so with a vengeance, almost to the point of acting like a holding company. Setting up the SBU's [Strategic Business Units] in 1970 was a recognition that we had gone too far, and that the strategic direction of the company should be made from the top to some extent. The sector executives in 1977 helped move the pendulum a little further in that direction.
>
> (GE executive.[4])

In terms of the management style matrix, we can see GE moving from a Centralized style in 1950 towards a Holding Company style in 1960. It then changed to Strategic Control in 1970s, and probably to Strategic Programming in 1977.

Since 1981 GE has had a new chairman and appears to have moved back to Strategic Control. However, GE is a company that is not easily categorized in our model. It is recognized as having one of the most sophisticated management systems in the world and, as a result, appears to straddle categories in our model. At least from the outside it appears to be able to gain benefits from both ends of some of the tensions we defined in chapter 9.

There is also some evidence that GE is adopting different styles from the centre for different businesses. For example, since 1981 Jack Welch has decentralized decision-making and energized group and division managers to feel 'ownership' for their businesses; yet he has also been highly influential in major thrusts, such as GE's well-publicized efforts to dominate the factory automation business. Based on these examples, Welch appears to be able to give central leadership in some areas and encourage autonomy in others.

Because of the fame of GE's management systems, they have been the subject of many Harvard Business School cases and articles.[5] To bring out the richness of GE's methods, we will start by discussing the management style as in 1980 and then discuss the changes made by Jack Welch.

GE in 1980

At this time GE was structured into departments (businesses), divisions, groups and sectors. Six sectors reported to the corporate office, and the hierarchy cascaded down from that point to 181 department general managers. Overlayed on this was a strategic planning structure that identified three strategic levels – corporate, sector and SBU. An SBU could be a department, division or group as shown in figure 14.2. There were 43 SBUs in total.

Reginald Jones, Jack Welch's predecessor, explained the reasons for the strategic planning hierarchy:

> [Before 1970] I was faced with looking at the so-called business plans for 200 departments. Well, you know, it was impossible. We then got it down to 40 to 50 strategic plans. Now those plans come in a document – a three ring binder. You don't read one of those in an evening and understand it. You can't just read the summary: they write so beautifully that you would sign up for everything. The resources requested were always double what we had. So that's when we said we are getting so cursory in our reviews that we've got to have help. That's when we went to sectors. I could sit down and go through six summaries in great depth.

In response to a question about whether he would go through the same evolution again, he replied:

> No, I would not do it over and I would not go to sectors initially. I would still want to see 43 SBU plans. It's amazing how people respond when they know you're interested and you criticise them constructively. You compliment them, and they walk out of there ten feet tall and convinced that, boy, they can do an even better job next year. And we have lost a little of that when we went to the six sectors.

In these comments Jones recognized the importance of the planning system as a vehicle for allocating resources and getting messages down from the

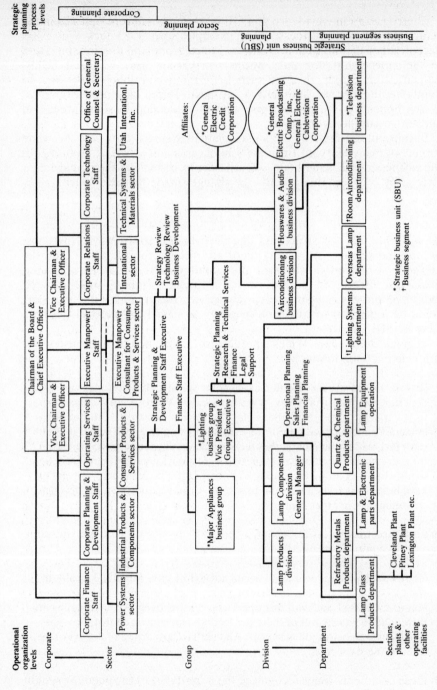

Figure 14.2 Partial representation of the organization structure of GE (from an original company document).

Strategic planning process levels

Corporate planning
Sector planning
Business segment planning
Strategic business unit (SBU)

Operational organization levels

Corporate

Chairman of the Board & Chief Executive Officer

Vice Chairman & Executive Officer
Vice Chairman & Executive Officer
Office of General Counsel & Secretary
Corporate Technology Staff
Corporate Relations Staff
Executive Manpower Staff
Operating Services Staff
Corporate Planning & Development Staff
Corporate Finance Staff

Executive Manpower Consultant for Consumer Products & Services sector
Strategic Planning & Development Staff Executive
Finance Staff Executive

Sector

Power Systems sector
Industrial Products & Components sector
Consumer Products & Services sector
International sector
Technical Systems & Materials sector
Utah International, Inc.

Strategy Review
Technology Review
Business Development

Affiliates:
*General Electric Credit Corporation
*General Electric Broadcasting Comp. Inc, General Electric Cablevision Corporation

Group

*Major Appliances business group
*Lighting business group Vice President & Group Executive

Strategic Planning
Research & Technical Services
Finance
Legal
Support

*Airconditioning business division
*Houswares & Audio business division

Division

Lamp Products division
Lamp Components division General Manager

Operational Planning
Sales Planning
Financial Planning

†Lighting Systems department
Overseas Lamp department
†Room Airconditioning department
*Television business department

Department

Lamp Glass Products department
Refractory Metals Products department
Quartz & Chemical Products department
Lamp & Electronic parts department
Lamp Equipment operation

Sections, plants & other operating facilities

Cleveland Plant
Pitney Plant
Lexington Plant etc.

* Strategic business unit (SBU)
† Business segment

top; but he could also see the tension between central leadership and motivation at lower levels.

By the late 1970s, GE was recognized as a leading exponent of strategy and planning. In August 1978, *Management Today* commented, 'Probably no single company has made such a contribution to the arts and wiles, the viewpoints and techniques of large, scale corporate management as GE. The technique uppermost in the minds of GE top management is planning – a preoccupation in which GE is an acknowledged master and innovator among corporate giants.'

The sophistication of the planning system was reinforced by the quality of staff support. Each level in the hierarchy had its own staff functions, depending on the services it was providing for lower levels. At the corporate level, there were six staff functions – finance, technology, production and operating services, corporate relations, planning and executive manpower. The function of these staffs was to 'add value' to the levels below and to help each level with the difficult capital allocation and manpower decisions.

There were also many boards and committees at the centre. The most important of these were the Corporate Executive Office, consisting of the chairman and two vice chairmen (full time members of the chairman's office), which took responsibility for running GE; the Corporate Policy Board, consisting of the chairman and key staff heads, which focused on specific planning issues; the Corporate Operations Board, consisting of the vice-chairmen and certain staff officers, which focused on capital spend decisions; and the Executive Board for each sector, consisting of the sector boss and his staff, aimed at helping the sector head review strategies, budgets and capital requests.

The planning hierarchy, the weight of corporate and sector level staffs and the layering of decision-making boards and committees all imply a high degree of planning influence for the centre. This was further reinforced by the way in which the strategic plans were initiated. The process started with the centre issuing corporate planning 'challenges' to the sectors and SBUs. The challenges identified topics that were relevant to most SBUs (e.g. productivity) and which the centre wished to receive special attention in the next cycle. Early in the year large meetings of managers were held to explain and discuss these challenges and to share background studies that had been done.

In GE, the centre appeared to make few direct thrusts or suggestions. The planning challenges were more like themes to follow than specific initiatives to be pursued. However, the combination of sector and corporate level activities certainly appear to have amounted to high planning influence.

GE's planning systems were supported by strong control systems. Profit responsibility was pushed down the organization beyond the SBU level to departments. Each department general manager was responsible for meeting his or her budgeted net income. The net income figure was calculated after interest and taxes and managers were also responsible for a return on investment figure.

The budget's overhead costs were divided between 'readiness to serve costs' (those essential for maintaining the existing capacity) and 'program expenses' (discretionary costs intended to increase future earnings). In this way the SBU and sector managers could manage the 'investment' in the future of the business and ensure that net income targets had not been achieved by 'eating our seed corn'. Although budget targets were taken very seriously, there was a recognition that the long-term position should not be threatened by short-term expedients.

This balancing of long-term objectives with short-term financial performance was also part of the manager's performance review. Each manager developed a set of financial and non-financial targets for the year – called a 'performance screen'. He then reviewed these with his superior, who would suggest revisions and changes, and agree relative weights for each measure.

A performance screen might include ten measures of performance, ranging from financial measures such as sales, net income, RoI, cash flow, to non-financial measures such as market share, relative cost position, progress of a programme or even a personal skill characteristic. These performance screens were formally reviewed at least once a year and fed into the performance evaluation system.

Incentives were organized into three pools for different levels of managers. Bonus monies were allocated to sector and SBU levels and the managers at these levels had broad discretion about how they should be awarded.

Throughout GE, managers recognized that the centre devoted great attention to the selection and development of managers and that a broad range of criteria were used to identify the best people. 'In an organization as diverse and as large as GE, you can never do the things you'd like to do by yourself. You always do them through people. So you'd better have the right people, and that means spending a lot of time in this area', commented Reginald Jones. And he went on to explain how GE uses new ventures to develop people: 'You're able to give a person a real management job at a relatively early age. It's a great developer of people.'

Without speaking to managers in SBUs and departments, it is difficult to know how 'tight' GE's control system was. Our impression is that it was neither loose nor rigid. There may have been a profusion of targets and objectives but, as far as possible, managers were expected to meet these objectives. At a minimum, they had to achieve their net income targets. We have, therefore, classified GE in 1980 as operating tight strategic controls.

We might summarize the position in 1980 as that of a Strategic Programming company, but with many of the problems and tensions that we have previously identified for that style. A review carried out in 1980/81 of the management systems was monitored by some students from the Harvard Business School. Some of their comments are instructive.

Concern was raised about the role of the International Sector as an integrator of strategies across sectors: 'While the need for dialogue, issue identification, and resolution is recognized, SBU managers in other sectors often charge that International does not possess the distinctive competence to understand specific product and market issues.'

Concern was also raised about the value of the staffs. The tensions surrounding this issue are best expressed in the following comments from managers:

- The corporate staffs often preclude the sectors from having to 'reinvent the wheel'. But they do not provide enough support on specific business needs.
- There is duplication between corporate and sector staffs.
- The company needs some means of coordinating projects that span two or more sectors.
- Why don't the sector heads review the plans of the corporate staffs? These are reviewed only by the CEO.
- How many corporate staff functions can there be and of what size, before the company can no longer claim to be decentralized?

The students also noted 'many executives feel that there are entirely too many boards'. 'There is a general feeling among GE executives that the issue of centralisation vs decentralisation is timely. They wonder how Jack Welch's management style will affect the delicate balance.'

In these comments we can see some of the tensions of the Strategic Programming style. How do staffs make a contribution? How should coordination be managed? What is the value of reviews by people who don't understand the product or market environment? When does planning become a stultifying bureaucracy? How much central planning can there be without damaging business level accountability?

GE in 1981

In 1981 Reginald Jones retired from GE after a 9-year reign as chief executive. The year he retired, he was voted the best CEO in America by 164 chief executives from the Fortune 500 list. He was far in the lead, getting more than 30 per cent of the votes. In the same poll, GE was ranked as the best managed company in America.

On 1 April Jack Welch took over. At 45 he was GE's youngest ever chairman. 'A maverick', 'a stutterer', 'a dynamo', all have been used to describe Welch. But he was obviously going to run GE with a different style and the emphasis would be on added energy.

Jack Welch talked about his view of GE to a Harvard Business School class in April 1981.

One of the things that's happened is with our planning system. It was dynamite when we first put it in. We had the best financial controls in the world in GE. We did not have an outstanding planning system. So we put one in. So you put thinking across good numbers; there's nothing like it. The first years were sensational. The thinking was fresh; the forms were little – the format got no points – it was idea-oriented.

Then we hired a head of planning, and he hired two vice presidents, and he hired a planner and the books got thicker and the printing got more sophisticated and the covers got harder and the drawings got better. The thinking kept going down. The meetings got larger. Nobody can say anything with 16 or 18 people there. You might as well come in with robes and incense.

Right away Welch started to make changes.

One of the things we have put in place is a way to achieve more candor, more constructive conflict. The objective is not sophistication – it's candor and it's conflict. So we've got to what we're going to call CEO meetings where the three of us [Welch plus his two vice chairmen] will have meetings with SBU managers, one on three, two on three, in a small room. We'll talk about real stuff, coats off, no ceremonies, and get at the issues.

During the first 6 months Welch spent almost half his time in small meetings with the 45 or so SBU managers talking about the business. This signalled a whole range of changes he has made in the past 5 years.

First, he led an attack on numbers. A policy that became known as destaffing, and won him the label of 'Neutron Jack' (a neutron bomb wipes out people but leaves buildings intact), resulted in a total workforce reduction of from 402,000 to 330,000. Much of the reduction came from reducing staff departments and layers of management, with Welch leading the way in attacking the corporate level head count. Welch also changed the planning system. He reduced the role of planning staffs; insisted on more face-to-face discussion between line managers; demanded a focus on issues not plans; and began to create a periodic (i.e. when necessary) planning system to replace the annual round. As Mike Carpenter, the head of planning, put it: 'We are trying to separate strategy and planning. Strategy is thinking through the basics of the business; planning is developing programs to support those strategies.'

In support of a more decentralized, more energized system, Welch encouraged more direct incentives. He rewarded people for major contributions. And special stock option awards were developed to build long-term identification with the company.

Finally, Welch began to drive the organization forward with an expanding set of slogans. In 1981, his slogan was 'Better than the best': all managers should aspire to it. He backed it up with action, insisting that all businesses that did not have a good chance of being number one or number two in their industry should be cut back or sold. By 1984 the slogans had been broadened into a management philosophy consisting of ten company values – better than the best, ownership, lean and agile, stewardship, entrepreneurship, excellence, quality, reality, candor, communications, invest in winners.

In essence, Welch seems to have moved GE from a Strategic Programming style back to a Strategic Control style. And yet, because of his personal dynamism and desire to get close to certain businesses, he appears to be managing with mixed styles. He has now grouped GE's businesses into three categories – core, high technology and services. The core businesses – such as lighting, appliances, turbines – are being treated as mature, stable businesses and the impression is that the centre applies tight controls with little interference (Strategic Control or Financial Control). The high technology businesses include some exciting growth prospects, such as factory automation. Here Welch has been personally involved in encouraging and developing the area (Strategic Planning).

The results of GE's style since 1981 have been impressive, and to a large extent follow the pattern of companies moving to a Strategic Control style – portfolio rationalization and slimming, leading to substantial ratio and profit improvement with flat sales. RoS has risen by almost two percentage points to 10.4 per cent and earnings have grown at a steady 10 per cent per year. This has also caused GE's stock to rise more than twice as fast as the S&P index. Meanwhile, sales remained flat, at around $28 billion.

There are two differences between the results of GE and those of the Strategic Control companies in our UK sample. The first concerns acquisitions. In 1986, GE acquired RCA with sales of $12 billion, and before that it had made a number of large buys including Employers Reinsurance Corp for $1.1 billion and Kidder Peabody for $600 million. While in the UK Strategic Control companies have looked hard at acquisition candidates, but completed few deals, GE has acted. In part this could be a result of timing. In 1984 GE had accumulated $5 billion in cash and the pressure on Welch to spend it was so great that he commented in the 1983 Annual Report: 'The question has been raised. What will we do with the money? The short answer is: It's not going to burn a hole in our pocket.'

The second difference has been GE's public and major setback in factory automation. The day after Welch was appointed chairman in 1981, GE kicked off its factory automation drive with the slogan: 'Automate, emigrate or evaporate'. GE committed $500 million to building a business expected to have sales of $5 billion by 1990. Major acquisitions were made (Calma $170 million and Intersil $235 million) and initial work was focused on GE's own factories. But by 1985 the project was still limping along after some years of big losses. This sort of major setback is more normally seen in Strategic Planning companies than Strategic Control companies.

The reaction of managers in GE has been largely favourable. They were proud of their company's management approach before Welch, but have supported most of the changes. 'During the first 2 years, I didn't see much change. But then we got a general manager who is right out of Welch's mould. Our business is now a different place – much more spirited, self-critical and energetic', commented one supporter.

For others, however, the conflicts of managing against multiple objectives with complex reward systems and a ten-value company philosophy caused problems. 'All the words sound great – enterpreneurship, ownership, risk-taking – but at my level it's making budget that still counts', explained a subsection manager. This comment is one we frequently heard in other Strategic Control companies.

As a final commentary on GE's style, it is interesting to consider how far the style matches GE's business environment and whether GE is following one of the three portfolio building philosophies we described in chapter 13.

GE's diversity, age and its more recent thrusts into new areas such as office automation have given it a portfolio that has every kind of business environment. In the core sector it has low tech, mature, basic businesses with stable competitors. In the high tech sector it has the opposite. Some of the businesses, most notably factory automation, are unstable and in high growth, high investment areas. Moreover, there is little connection between SBUs in different sectors of the portfolio.

Based on our analysis in chapters 12 and 13, we might conclude that GE is unmanageable except under a Diverse Businesses philosophy in which different parts of the portfolio are grouped under strong sector managers using different management styles. We do not have enough knowledge of GE to know whether this is the case. Currently it seems that Welch himself is able to offer some style variety. But his latest organization concept – core business, high technology, services – does not seem to be built round the principles of the Diverse Businesses philosophy.

There is no doubt that GE's long experience with strategy planning has led to a high degree of sophistication in its management process. Despite – or perhaps because of – this, the emphasis is now firmly on addressing the real business issues, rather than fine-tuning the planning system and the bureaucracy. But the best guarantee that the centre's contribution is helpful comes from the stress that Welch lays on high quality staff and in-depth understanding of the businesses. This is a company that is determined to avoid the pitfalls of superficiality in its strategy debates, despite the diversity of its portfolio.

Jack Welch also brings some unique qualities to GE – his energy and openness. These are attitudes that he is evidently trying to communicate throughout the organization. How far he will succeed remains unclear, but there appear to be signs that this new style is already leading to a better quality dialogue on important issues, and a greater commitment to action.

Matsushita

Like GE and IBM, Matsushita is an outstanding company on any scale. Founded in the 1920s by Konosuke Matsushita, the company had become a leader in the Japanese electrical appliance industry by 1930 and is now the largest electrical appliance company in the world. Led by Matsushita himself until around 1980, the company is as profitable as its major competitors – GE, Siemens, ITT, Philips and Hitachi – and is growing faster than all of them.

Historically Matsushita's energies have been directed at the consumer market. One of the strengths of the company is the unique direct distribution system it has in Japan. This has been the core of the business throughout its years of growth. Its latest success has been domination of the world video recorder market. Following Sony's introduction of the Betamax, Matsushita designed a better and cheaper range, and by the early 1980s was manufacturing two out of every three video recorders and selling them under the Panasonic and RCA labels.

Since 1980, however, the new leader of Matsushita – Toshihiko Yamashita – has started to focus the company on the office market place. He believes that the consumer electronics boom will peak around 1990, and is looking for the growth markets that will help Matsushita continue its amazing track record.

Fortunately, Matsushita is a company that has been extensively written up. Its management systems are described fully in the opening chapter of *The Art of Japanese Management* by Richard Pascale and Anthony Athos and in a case written by Professor R. Takahashi of Keio University.[6]

Central Management Style

Matsushita is, on the surface, a Financial Control company. The centre's relationship with the divisions and departments is similar to that in Tarmac, BTR and GEC. But Matsushita has some added ingredients that we have not observed in other Financial Control companies.

The company is decentralized. Each product and some functions, such as distribution, have been set up as business units ('departments' in Matsushita terminology). The general managers in charge of the departments are autonomous. They are expected to develop strategy and advance their businesses without assistance from the centre. All inter-company trading is carried out at arm's length – at the market rate. There are no centrally imposed transfer prices.

Departments are grouped into divisions of like products. The division managers have an important role in monitoring, encouraging and developing each department and the product range of the division. But, as in companies like BTR and GEC, the division layer is 'transparent' – the department general manager is responsible for performance directly to head office.

The central control process is focused on a 6-month operating budget. Whereas the Financial Control companies in the UK all use an annual budget cycle, Matsushita has a 6-monthly cycle. The budget is reviewed by the finance function and the division managers, and then goes to the president (previously Matsushita, now Yamashita) for approval. It is then handed back to the department as the 'Basic Management Programme' and becomes – in the company's own words – a 'promise between the president and the manager'.

The programme is monitored closely and variances frequently result in the formation of a task force, including controllers from the finance function, to get the department back on track. Failure to deliver on the 'promise' is viewed with great concern by both the department and the centre, and may result in the manager being assigned a different position 'where his talents are more suited to the task'.

In a sense, Matsushita's 6-month cycle gives a stronger short-term focus than the normal British cycle of 12 months. Directors in Britain complain about the short-term focus of capital markets that respond to 6-month earnings statements. But the response within Matsushita to variances against the 6-month programme of a department is much more acute and focused than the reactions of the capital markets. Mr Hino, director of finance, explained the system, using words similar to those we have heard from BTR or Tarmac: 'If a department's performance is good, we will give them a word of praise. If performance is bad, we offer understanding and advice. But we will not give them any special financial help. We expect their accounting to be merciless. We know there is a risk involved in leaving performance to the managers; but we view that risk as tuition for learning management.' The tightness of the control is evident in the phrase 'we will not give them any special financial help'. By this he means that the department is expected to solve the problem without help from the centre. Failure to solve the problem is likely to lead to a management change.

A further illustration of the merciless accounting is given in the case written by Professor Takahashi: 'When new departments are established, the company deliberately underestimates the department's need for working capital. Facing a shortage of operating funds, the new department must work hard to retain and accumulate its earnings.'

Almost all the basic elements of Matsushita's management system fit the Financial Control model – the company is divided into small autonomous units, the centre is careful not to interfere or overrule department managers, controls are based on a 6-monthly promise between the centre and the units, and failure to deliver the promise is treated severely.

Financial results have been excellent and, with a strong focus on profitability and a 'merciless' approach to poor performers, Matsushita is one of the most profitable manufacturing companies in Japan, with a return on sales of more than 7 per cent. Matsushita also builds strong loyalty and high levels of satisfaction among managers. There are critics of the management systems, but even they believe that overall the company is well managed.

To this point, Matsushita looks like a classic Financial Control company. But there are important differences. First, the centre does occasionally become involved in directing the company as a whole. Currently, as we noted already, Yamashita is leading a shift of emphasis away from consumer goods to office products. This is not normal for Financial Control companies. Second, Matsushita has achieved remarkable organic growth and departments within the company have attacked and won in many fierce, fast-growing and technically advanced markets, such as video recorders. Both the rapid organic growth and the bold strategies of the departments are unusual features. In fact, in chapters 6 and 12 we have argued that the Financial Control style is not likely to be suitable where business unit managers are trying to build positions in fast-moving, R&D led, highly competitive markets. Matsushita appears to have found a combination of values, systems and policies that go a long way to avoiding the disadvantages of the Financial Control style, without losing the benefits.[7] If IBM is an outstanding example of Strategic Planning, Matsushita seems to be an equally successful example of Financial Control.

The Matsushita Magic

Matsushita has five features of its management system that do not occur in other Financial Control companies. These are the features of the Matsushita system that help to reduce risk aversion and avoid the low levels of organic growth that are typically associated with tight financial controls.

1 Values   In 1932 Konosuke Matsushita became involved in a religious movement in Japan and came to recognize that employees would benefit from spiritual leadership. 'It comes clear to me', he said, 'that people need a way of linking their productive lives to society.' He set about developing a philosophy that articulated his own beliefs. 'A business should quickly stand on its own', said Matsushita, 'based on the service it provides society. Profits should not be a reflection of corporate greed, but a vote of confidence from society that what is offered by the firm is valued. When a business fails to make profits it should die – it is a waste of resources to society.'

The following extract gives 14 points of Konosuke Matsushita's business philosophy presented in Takahashi's case.[8]

> Chairman Matsushita taught his executives that the autonomous manage-ment method was still effective today; detriments could be complemented by managerial devices. Interpreting his ideology, all executives held firm belief that what was essential for the divisional organization system was everyone's way of thinking toward it, not a mere shape or pattern; unless top management, more than anyone else, displayed 'go-ahead' attitude, the system could not work; its success was up to top management whether it had a clear-cut policy or not.
>
> Ever since the foundation of the corporation, Mr Matsushita summoning all corporate members early every January, delivered a speech on his business philosophy and policy. In addition to it, whenever the corporation encountered newly developed situations, he expressed his basic attitude and direction to be taken by the members to cope with them.
>
> Listed below are some of his business philosophy that had supported the

divisional organization system, chosen from among those given at numerous occasions such as above. The item numbers have nothing to do with classification or the order of occurrence, but they are simply for convenience of the reader.

1 The purpose of an enterprise is to contribute to society by supplying goods of high quality at low prices in ample quantity.
   Happiness of man is built on mental stability and material affluence. To serve the foundation of happiness, through making man's life affluent with inexpensive and inexhaustible supply of life necessities like water inflow, is the duty of a manufacturer. The purpose of the enterprise is to materialize the duty and contribute consequently to society.

2 Profit comes in compensation for contribution to society.
   Profit is a yardstick with which to measure the degree of social contribution made by an enterprise. Thus, profit is a result rather than a goal. An enterprise in the red will make all cooperating people poor, and ultimately, the whole society poor. If the enterprise tries to earn a reasonable profit but fails to do so, the reason is because the degree of its social contribution is still insufficient.

3 Always direct your effort for 'mutual prosperity and existence'!
   You should always act with the notion in mind that you share your living, and you share prosperity with wholesalers, retailers and consumers as a manufacturer, with competitors as a business man, with the nation as a citizen, and with people abroad as an international man. The 'mutual prosperity and existence' is an idea based on the relationship of interdependence between enterprises. This ideal in business administration will first be realized under modest business activities where each man, paying respect to independence of his counterpart, engages in business dealings with an independent spirit, while always remembering that such dealings could not exist without mutual dependence, and that his prosperity and happiness are part of those for the whole society and people. Business dealings must be fair from beginning to end. You should never play meaningless bargaining tactics or tricks.

4 Fair competition makes progress.
   Serious effort under fair competition makes man and business more competent. We should sell those goods that are likely to grow under fair competition.

5 Meet what others expect of you!
   You should discern who expects what of us and try to meet his expectations. Never cling stubbornly to your stand only!

6 The responsibility of a manufacturer cannot be relieved until its product is disposed of by the end user.

7 Do not forget that you are a businessman!
   The true businessman will be sturdy, humble and modest.
   The true businessman always listens to what his client says.

8 Any business must be a success.
   Unsuccessful business employs a wrong management. You should not find

its causes in bad fortune, unfavourable surroundings, or wrong timing. Nourish in your mind a tough determination to be a winner!

No success will be forthcoming unless you succeed in letting the face opposite you turn to your side.

9 Always question yourself!

Carry out monthly accounting and check if there is any point to be improved! If you find it, lose no time to correct it. Never repeat the same mistake twice!

Ask yourself if you are doing the right work appropriate to total corporate strength!

10 Business appetite has no self-restraining mechanism.

Human appetite declines as the stomach is filled, but business appetite accompanies no such mechanism. When you notice you have gone too far, you must have courage to come back.

11 Continue business expansion within credit limit!

The scale of our business activities is to be determined by society which evaluates our contribution to it.

Business expansion should be made on a profitable basis within the limit, beyond which reasonable profit could not be secured.

12 Facility expansions mean a dividing point for business to rise or fall.

Facility expansions do not necessarily bring about cost reductions. It is you people that utilize facilities and raise profits.

13 The essence of management is to develop business, with parallel effort to foster men there.

You should treat your subordinates with confidence in job assignments, so that he can work on his own initiative to his fullest capability.

Let every corporate member have a sense of managerial commitment. The right assistance is to guide man and business to open their ways by their own hands.

Managerial stability must be secured by all means. However, you should not allow men to idle on it. What is important in stabilized management is to give difficult assignments to every individual member.

14 Human unity and harmony are indispensable for job achievement.

Always show clear objectives and perform business, unifying all members as a united whole!

The foundation for unity and harmony is sincerity.

A division manager explained the importance of this philosophy: 'Many Westerners tend to smirk at the higher purposes to which Japanese organizations avowedly dedicate themselves, and assume that these calls to higher values are just thinly disguised manipulation. But it becomes a belief system for thousands of people who work for that company – a human value beyond profit to which their productive lives are dedicated.'

Values such as 'continue business expansion within credit limit' and 'human unity and harmony are indispensible for job achievement' go a long way to easing some of the problems created by decentralization and by tight controls. Somehow, by a combination of the value system and the behaviour of central managers, the divisions and departments keep their eyes on the long term, while being pushed to deliver short-term performance.

The company has some systems that help to reinforce the need for cooperation, harmony and the greater good. For example, once a month department and division managers meet with the chairman (Matsushita or Yamashita) for an informal coffee morning. This provides managers with a chance to coordinate with others in the company. It is also an opportunity for the chairman to reinforce the values and ideals. Each morning before work, every employee recites the company values. 'It seems silly to Westerners', said one executive, 'but, it's like we are all a community.' Also three or four times per year each employee is expected to give a 10 minute talk to his work group on the firm's values and its relationship to society.

These systems make sure the values are imprinted on the company. But there are also systems to reinforce the importance of short-term performance. Division managers attend quarterly peer reviews, at which their performance is shared with the group. The managers are grouped into A, B, C and D classes. The A-rated managers give their presentations first and the Ds come last. No one is openly criticized, but each leaves determined not to be in the C or D class at the next presentation.

The observers of Matsushita agree that its value system is an essential ingredient to the success of the management approach. It makes it possible for managers to interpret the activities of the centre in the most favourable light. Criticisms from the centre can then be viewed as 'training'. The transfer of poor performers to more suitable jobs is seen as character-building for the individual and does not cause others to view it negatively.

It is the value system that makes managers feel comfortable with tight financial controls. And it is their belief in the values that causes them to maintain a long-term view. Despite the centre's insistence on meeting budget, one manager described the performance evaluation system as taking the long-term view.

> [They judge us] I'm sure, by our total abilities as men rather than our fragmented capabilities as managers. Even if our department's performance is very poor, we will not be fired. Rather we will be judged by the reliability of our policy and programs for the upcoming periods. Speaking for myself, I don't feel like I am being evaluated constantly, nor do I feel guilty for one year's bad performance. I am evaluated, I believe, on the long-term perceptions rather than short-term performance.

To an outsider, these words seem loaded with contradictions. But the contradictions are judged against a value system. By managing these values, Matsushita appears to have squared the circle; to have achieved a focus on short-term performance without sacrificing a long-term commitment.

2 People Development One of the central values is the importance of people. In the relationship between the centre and the departments, whether at a formal control meeting or an informal gathering, attention is always paid to the issue of how best to develop the managers involved. A pure task orientation is virtually non-existent. Every situation involves a task which is seen also as a training opportunity. Even when the centre is probing and challenging managers about some trouble spot, it is not seen as threatening. 'The curious twist to these interventions', says one Matsushita division manager, 'is that they never seem like inquisitions. You feel senior management is doing it to train you, to build your competence for the day when they will no longer be around.' A fundamental tenet of Matsushita is 'to develop extraordinary qualities in ordinary men'. This goal gives a human objective even in trouble-shooting sessions that might otherwise seem harsh and cold-blooded.

The emphasis given to people development resembles the approach of the highly successful Housing division in Tarmac. There, Sam Pickstock uses the phrase 'winning the battle for the hearts and minds'. He believes that it is more important to get managers to understand what needs doing than to fix the problem immediately. Once they understand, they will be able to avoid the problem next time.

In Matsushita, managers use a similar phrase. A product group manager talking about conflicts of opinion said 'we try to get the facts out on the table and let reason speak for itself. We build "acceptance time" into these discussions. By that I mean thinking about things. We press – but we always try to allow people to come around to a point of view in their own way.'

3 Centralized Functions Finance, personnel and training are all fully centralized. As a result, the centre contains 3,500 people (which compares with the 100 or so people at the centre of the other Financial Control companies).

In the finance function all controllers and accountants report directly to the centre. In practice, those in the divisions and departments have two bosses, reporting both to the centre and to their general manager. But their first loyalty is to the disciplines of Matsushita; they have a vital role in the control system.

The other two central functions, personnel and training, exist to create 'harmony' within the company. Mr Yasukawa, the personnel director, said 'The one word that best describes our personnel philosophy is "harmony". We are often told by our friends that Matsushita employees have no appeal outside the company. They say that we have no variety, that we are all alike. But I don't think so. To me we are quite varied.' In other words, the central role of these two functions is to help build and maintain the Matsushita culture.

People (what they believe and the way they think) are seen as *the* critical resource. As a result, no employee with qualifications beyond those of basic schooling is hired without central personnel screening. Every management promotion is also carefully reviewed by the centre. Moreover, all graduates go through an introduction training which involves 3 weeks of general education at the centre, 3 months working with retailers and 3 months working in a factory. The 3 weeks at the centre is devoted almost entirely to philosophy and to explaining the Matsushita values.

Another unusual aspect of the central personnel activity is job rotation. Each year 5 per cent of the employees rotate from one business unit to another. Equal numbers of managers, supervisors and shop floor employees are involved.

By controlling promotions, indoctrinating and vetting new recruits and moving people about, the personnel and training functions can keep the central values of Matsushita pure and can maintain its strong culture.

4 Control of Prices   Up until the 1970s chairman Matsushita himself controlled price levels. Product prices could not be changed without his approval. Since the 1970s this responsibility has been devolved to the division levels.

The importance of central decision-making on prices is unclear. It obviously must have a major influence. The most important influence is presumably to signal to the general manager of the department whether he should be going for growth or not. It would be fascinating to know on what criteria the centre choose one price from another and how the negotiation between the centre and the department is carried out.

In BTR there is substantial control of prices by the centre, with price audit teams available to check whether prices have been set at agreed levels. But in BTR the centre's influence is mainly aimed at raising prices to ensure good margins and to prevent price warfare with competitors. In Matsushita it seems that prices are frequently set below the market level. The centre's contribution is, therefore, a critical strategic input.

5 Financing Growth   The departments must submit 60 per cent of their profit to the centre, but they can retain 40 per cent for expansion and growth. In addition departments can borrow from the central 'bank'. The 60–40 split is not sacrosanct – some departments may be asked for more or less than 60 per cent – but it is a normal split.

The interesting aspect of this system is that it acknowledges that some of the profit and all depreciation belongs to the department. If the department think they can get a better return than the money market rates offered by the centre, they are free to invest as they please. This system is not operated in any of the British companies we researched, although in many there is an unwritten agreement that capital up to the level of depreciation charges can be reinvested.

Spending capital without reference to the centre is alien to the Financial Control style as practised in the UK, where vigorous approval processes are needed to justify expenditures. In Matsushita it appears that retained earnings can be spent freely. Managers believe this creates an added incentive to strive for high profitability, as well as helping to focus attention on growth. It also means that capital approval requests are limited to major proposals, where a business wants to reach beyond its own resources to expand. The central bank can then deal with these requests in much the same way that the capital markets would.

The five features of Matsushita's management approach – centralized functions, values, financing growth, people development and control of prices – are not without parallels. Aspects of them exist in Tarmac and BTR. But as a package they are unique, and as a package they seem to provide the basic Financial Control style with added benefits. In our framework, Matsushita would probably be rated as a Financial Programming company; but its management approach seems, on the surface, to be superior to that of the other Financial Programming companies.

Hewlett–Packard

IBM, GE and Matsushita are companies that seem to fit into our style classification. IBM appears to be a Strategic Planning company, GE a Strategic Control company with some history of Strategic Programming, and Matsushita a Financial Programming company. One style of which we have as yet had no example in this chapter is Strategic Venturing. Hewlett–Packard fills this gap.

Cases written by Roger Atherton from the University of Oklahoma provide the most easily accessible description of the Hewlett–Packard approach.[9] This material is to some extent out of date and it is much less informative than the cases on IBM, GE and Matsushita. Nevertheless, the essence of Hewlett–Packard's unusual management approach is adequately described. The organization is highly divisionalized. Each product division is set up as a self-standing unit (figure 14.3). The objective is to make the managers in charge of the unit feel like Bill Hewlett and David Packard did when they founded the company in 1958. The objective is to maximize individual initiative, innovation and flexibility, and to retain an entrepreneurial organization climate.

Each product division is part of a group of divisions and shares its sales force with that product grouping, so there are some overlaps between divisions. But group management are expected to prevent these overlaps from being restrictive or constraining. Reviews are held annually between the centre and the product divisions. These are big meetings with a broad cross-section of division, group and central managers involved. They run more like a conference than an annual review. The atmosphere is creative and supportive rather than probing and critical. The centre is not directive. The tradition of Hewlett and Packard was to be supportive rather than directive. This tradition has been carried on by John Young, who took over as chief executive officer in 1978. He has been labelled a consensus-style manager: he sees himself in the role of coach rather than traditional leader.

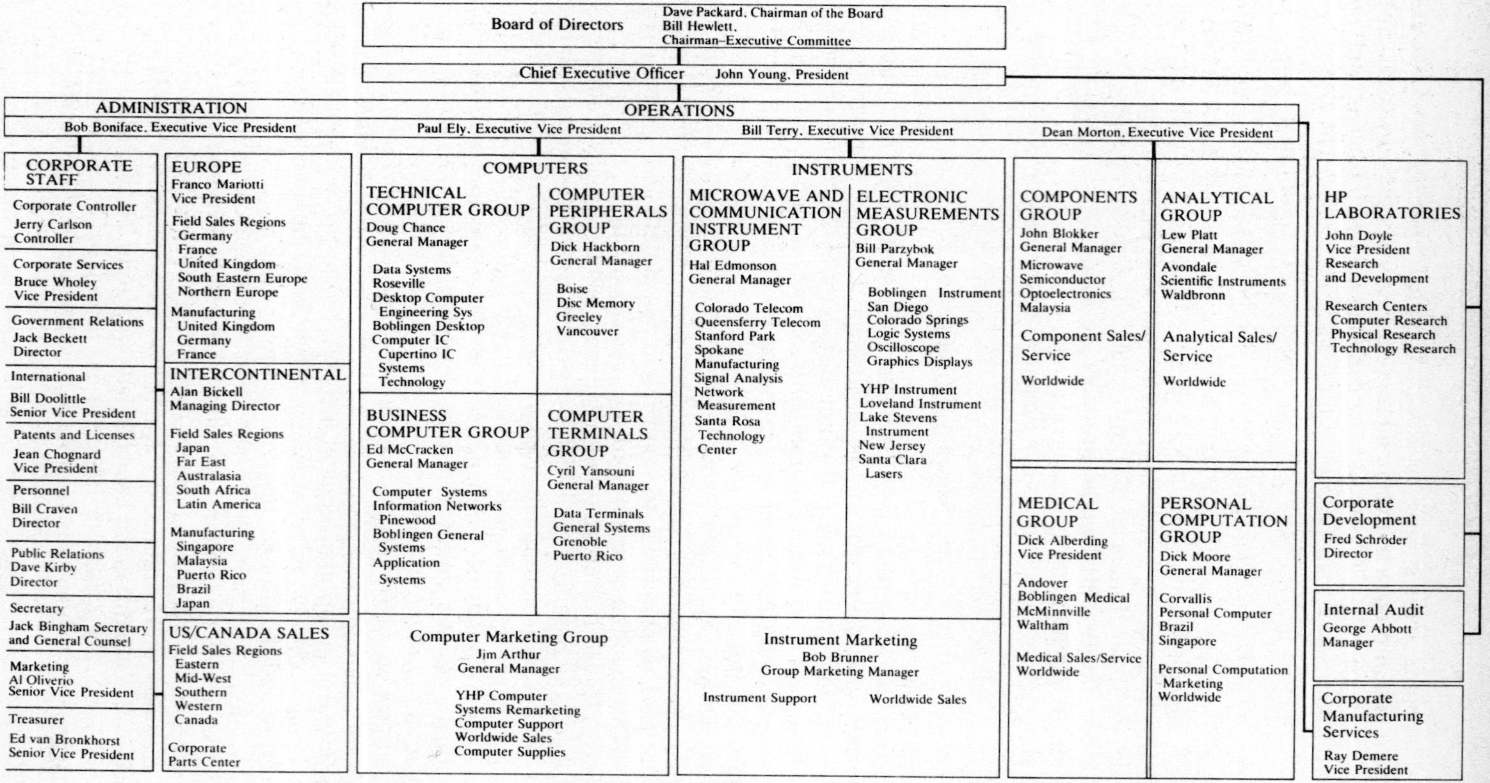

Board of Directors
Dave Packard, Chairman of the Board
Bill Hewlett, Chairman–Executive Committee

Chief Executive Officer — John Young, President

ADMINISTRATION
Bob Boniface, Executive Vice President

CORPORATE STAFF
Corporate Controller — Jerry Carlson, Controller
Corporate Services — Bruce Wholey, Vice President
Government Relations — Jack Beckett, Director
International — Bill Doolittle, Senior Vice President
Patents and Licenses — Jean Chognard, Vice President
Personnel — Bill Craven, Director
Public Relations — Dave Kirby, Director
Secretary — Jack Bingham, Secretary and General Counsel
Marketing — Al Oliverio, Senior Vice President
Treasurer — Ed van Bronkhorst, Senior Vice President

EUROPE
Franco Mariotti, Vice President
Field Sales Regions
- Germany
- France
- United Kingdom
- South Eastern Europe
- Northern Europe

Manufacturing
- United Kingdom
- Germany
- France

INTERCONTINENTAL
Alan Bickell, Managing Director
Field Sales Regions
- Japan
- Far East
- Australasia
- South Africa
- Latin America

Manufacturing
- Singapore
- Malaysia
- Puerto Rico
- Brazil
- Japan

US/CANADA SALES
Field Sales Regions
- Eastern
- Mid-West
- Southern
- Western
- Canada
- Corporate Parts Center

OPERATIONS

COMPUTERS
Paul Ely, Executive Vice President

TECHNICAL COMPUTER GROUP — Doug Chance, General Manager
Data Systems Roseville
Desktop Computer Engineering Desktop
Boblingen Desktop Computer IC Cupertino IC Systems Technology

BUSINESS COMPUTER GROUP — Ed McCracken, General Manager
Computer Systems Information Networks Pinewood
Boblingen General Systems
Application Systems

COMPUTER PERIPHERALS GROUP — Dick Hackborn, General Manager
Boise Disc Memory Greeley Vancouver

COMPUTER TERMINALS GROUP — Cyril Yansouni, General Manager
Data Terminals General Systems Puerto Rico

Computer Marketing Group — Jim Arthur, General Manager
YHP Computer Systems Remarketing Computer Support Worldwide Sales Computer Supplies

INSTRUMENTS
Bill Terry, Executive Vice President

MICROWAVE AND COMMUNICATION INSTRUMENT GROUP — Hal Edmonson, General Manager
Colorado Telecom Queensferry Telecom Stanford Park Spokane Manufacturing Signal Analysis Network Measurement Santa Rosa Technology Center

ELECTRONIC MEASUREMENTS GROUP — Bill Parzybok, General Manager
Boblingen Instrument San Diego Colorado Springs Logic Systems Oscilloscope Graphics Displays
YHP Instrument Loveland Instrument Lake Stevens Instrument New Jersey Santa Clara Lasers

Instrument Marketing — Bob Brunner, Group Marketing Manager
Instrument Support Worldwide Sales

Dean Morton, Executive Vice President

COMPONENTS GROUP — John Blokker, General Manager
Microwave Semiconductor Optoelectronics Malaysia
Component Sales/Service Worldwide

ANALYTICAL GROUP — Lew Platt, General Manager
Avondale Scientific Instruments Waldbronn
Analytical Sales/Service Worldwide

MEDICAL GROUP — Dick Alberding, Vice President
Andover Boblingen Medical McMinnville Waltham
Medical Sales/Service Worldwide

PERSONAL COMPUTATION GROUP — Dick Moore, General Manager
Corvallis Personal Computer Brazil Singapore
Personal Computation Marketing Worldwide

HP LABORATORIES
John Doyle, Vice President Research and Development
Research Centers Computer Research Physical Research Technology Research

Corporate Development
Fred Schroder, Director

Internal Audit
George Abbott, Manager

Corporate Manufacturing Services
Ray Demere, Vice President

Figure 14.3 Hewlett–Packard corporate organization, January 1982.

So, from this limited review, Hewlett–Packard appears to have a low planning influence style. What is interesting is that, at least up until 1981, this low planning influence was combined with a flexible control style.

Product divisions were thus controlled by long-term objectives and by commitment to the 'HP Way' rather than by setting annual targets and monitoring progress against them. Results were assessed against the management philosophy, the organization's long-term goals and the fundamentally technology-driven approach, rather than against particular performance objectives. The Hewlett–Packard system is one of MBO (management by objectives), but it is not the traditional system used for performance appraisal. In Hewlett–Packard MBO refers to the philosophy of using corporate objectives as a framework for coordinated decision-making and planning. MBO is not a target-setting system: it is a framework- or context-giving system.

The HP Way

BUSINESS PRACTICES
Pay As We Go – No Long-term Borrowing
- Helps to maintain a stable financial environment during depressed business times.
- Serves as an excellent self-regulating mechanisms for HP managers.

Market Expansion and Leadership Based on New Product Contributions
- Engineering excellence determines market recognition of new HP products.
- Novel new-product ideas and implementations serve as the basis for expansion of existing markets or diversification into new markets.

Customer Satisfaction Second to None
- Sell only what has been thoroughly designed, tested, and specified.
- Products must have lasting value, having high reliability (quality) and customers discover additional benefits while using them.
- Offer best after-sales service and support in the industry.

Honesty and Integrity In All Matters
- Dishonest dealings with vendors or customers (such as bribes and kickbacks) not tolerated.
- Open and honest communication with employees and stockholders alike. Conservative financial reporting.

PEOPLE PRACTICES
Belief In Our People
- Confidence in, and respect for, HP people as opposed to dependence on extensive rules, procedures, etc.
- Trust people to do their job right (individual freedom) without constant directives.

- Opportunity for meaningful participation (job dignity).
- Emphasis on working together and sharing rewards (teamwork and partnership).
- Share responsibilities; help each other; learn from each other; provide chance to make mistakes.
- Recognition based on contribution to results – sense of achievement and self-esteem.
- Profit sharing; stock purchase plan; retirement program, etc., aimed at employees and company sharing in each other's success.
- Company financial management emphasis on protecting employees' job security.

A Superior Working Environment

- Informality – open, honest communications; no artificial distinctions between employees (first-name basis); management by wandering around; and open-door communication policy.
- Develop and promote from within – lifetime training, education, career counseling to give employees maximum opportunities to grow and develop with the company.
- Decentralization – emphasis on keeping work groups as small as possible for maximum employee identification with our businesses and customers.
- Management-By-Objectives (MBO) – provides a sound basis for measuring performance of employees as well as managers; is objective, not political.

MANAGEMENT STYLE

Management By Wandering Around

- To have a well-managed operation, managers and supervisors must be aware of what happens in their areas – at several levels above and below their immediate level.
- Since people are our most important resource, managers have direct responsibility for employee training, performance and general well being. To do this, managers must move around to find out how people feel about their jobs – what they think will make their work more productive and meaningful.

Open Door Policy

- Managers and supervisors are expected to foster a work environment in which employees feel free and comfortable to seek individual counsel or express general concerns.
- Therefore, if employees feel such steps are necessary, they have the right to discuss their concerns with higher-level managers. Any effort through intimidation or other means to prevent an employee from going 'up the line' is absolutely contrary to company policy – and will be dealt with accordingly.
- Also, use of the Open Door policy must not in any way influence evaluations of employees or produce any other adverse consequences.
- Employees also have responsibilities – particularly in keeping their

discussions with upper-level managers to the point and focused on concerns of significance.

(*Measure*, Sept.-Oct., 1981, p. 14.)

In our research in the UK, we did not find any companies using the Strategic Venturing approach for the whole of their portfolio. Hewlett–Packard is, therefore, a particularly interesting example because it appears to combine low planning influence with flexible controls – the features of the Strategic Venturing style. The reason low planning influence and flexible controls have worked well for Hewlett–Packard appears to be a result of four factors

1 Common strategy. A fundamentally common strategy for most product divisions, i.e. to be the technology leader and to bring out novel products. It is interesting to note that, faced by the 1974/75 downturn, Hewlett–Packard raised prices by 10 per cent and increased R&D by 20 per cent at a time when other companies dropped prices to boost sales, and cut research spending to boost profits.

2 Unified culture. Clear communication of the corporate style and objectives (the HP Way), encourages managers to achieve the objectives in whatever way is best suited to their own area. One would normally call this phenomenon a clear and unified culture.

3 Empathy. Bill Hewlett and David Packard had empathy with and respect for the entrepreneurs in the product divisions. John Young has continued to focus on this symbol of the style. This empathy builds self-confidence as well as loyalty and commitment.

4 Management by walking about (MBWA). MBWA is the essence of the Hewlett–Packard culture. It encourages managers to enthuse their people. It encourages supportive behaviour. It is also a non-directive way of giving guidance and helping managers, and it is a way of monitoring and keeping some control on events without making people feel that they have to report at every step.

These features of the management approach seem to fit with the Strategic Venturing style. The common strategy reduces the need for lengthy discussions between the centre and the business units on which way the business should move forward. And the HP Way, senior management empathy and MBWA all encourage creativity, innovation and flexibility.

Hewlett–Packard's results have been much as one would expect from a company with a Strategic Venturing style. Explosive organic growth, bold new product strategies, and occasional setbacks when sales ran ahead of profits or major new products failed. Overall financial performance has been excellent and, like IBM, Hewlett–Packard has been acclaimed as one of America's 'excellent' companies. Interestingly, Hewlett–Packard has stumbled a little in the past 3 years. This does not seem to be a result of a normal setback coming out of excessive sales growth or failure of a major new product. The problem appears to be more deep rooted.

From the outside, it would appear that Hewlett–Packard is beginning to face a classic problem. Its success has come from having a close match between its management style and the nature of its businesses. It was operating in technologically fast-moving and fast-growing businesses where new product launches every year were necessary, and where sales growth might be 50 per cent per annum with volume growth possibly even higher. These are the 'open battles' we described in chapter 12. The Strategic Venturing style fits this environment well, and the results were excellent.

By the early 1980s, however, some of these businesses were becoming more stable, more steady, more predictable, more susceptible to 'professional' management approaches. Calculators, minicomputers and instruments are all markets that are maturing. John Young recognized this when he took over from Bill Hewlett and he began to make subtle changes in Hewlett–Packard's style. He put more emphasis on planning. He appealed to managers to become low-cost manufacturers and worked hard to improve the management of assets, particularly inventory and accounts receivable. He scotched the idea of research for research's sake. He cut out pet projects, and introduced a more commercial approach. He also focused on computers and semi-conductors. In total, he did not reduce the research budget, but he redirected it.

Together, these changes amounted to a major shift in focus. The attention switched to making existing activities more efficient and commercial, while refocusing the company into the office market. These changes in style moved Hewlett–Packard away from the Strategic Venturing style towards a Strategic Control style.

Possibly Hewlett–Packard is now caught in the middle. It has some established businesses that need a centre with a firm hand in either the planning or control dimension, but the management team are culturally attuned to a different philosophy. At the same time, it still has many opportunities to develop new enterpreneurial products in the same way that it has over the past two decades. The freewheeling, high-margin, better-technology approach that suits these new areas will not get the best out of the established businesses. Hewlett–Packard may now need two cultures and is likely to find it hard to run them together.

Summary

The management approaches of IBM, GE, Matsushita and Hewlett–Packard appear, based on public data, to fit our model. The framework we developed in UK companies does, therefore, seem to have applicability outside the British culture. But these exemplars of management practice certainly have a number of features and systems that we did not find in the UK companies. Items such as the value statements of IBM, Matsushita and Hewlett–Packard, the financial arrangements and centralized personnel function at Matsushita, the non-concurrence system at IBM, MBWA at Hewlett–Packard, and the long years of training in strategic planning at GE seem to work to the advantage of these companies.

However, they all suffer to a greater or lesser extent from the tensions we defined. IBM suffers from slow decision-making and group think, GE suffers from ambiguous objectives and a history of planning excesses and Hewlett–Packard has suffered from a lack of control. Matsushita is possibly an exception, though it is very hard to obtain a real understanding of Japanese management practices based only on published Western sources. Although these companies appear to be more sophisticated than some of the UK companies, the same underlying tensions exist.

Nevertheless, these companies have been more successful than many of their peers. From the perspective of the role of the centre four features stand out as likely causes of this success. First, they all enjoy strong competitive positions. Whether these follow from their management processes, or whether they guarantee that the outcomes from whichever management processes are adopted will seem successful, is unclear. In any case, the old adage that nothing succeeds like success does seem particularly apt for a company such as IBM. The vital importance of underlying competitive position seems to be the lesson from this observation.

Second, companies like Hewlett–Packard and IBM have clearly benefited from having a style that fits the nature of their business portfolios. When this fit begins to break down (Hewlett–Packard more recently, IBM in micros), either performance suffers or modifications to the style become necessary.

Third, the centre in each of these companies is perceived by subsidiary management as in tune with their businesses and the issues they face. It is not seen as remote or ill-informed. The centre is sympathetic and sufficiently knowledgeable to make useful contributions to business thinking. In some sense, these are 'activist' corporate centres – even in Hewlett–Packard – willing to get involved in constructive debate. But, at the same time, they are non-directive. Even in IBM the centre does not dictate decisions, and Matsushita and Hewlett–Packard stress the freedom given to their subsidiary managers. The tension between strong leadership and business autonomy remains; but it is eased by sympathetic, knowledgeable, but non-directive interventions by the centre.

Finally, and perhaps most importantly, there are a series of things concerned with corporate objectives and culture that seem to matter. Agreement on basic directions for the long-term development of the business, and on how to treat people within the firm, are perhaps the most essential common features of these companies. The agreement on direction allows managers to set their decisions within a broader context. For Matsushita this prevents Financial Control from becoming a short-term commitment; for Hewlett–Packard it prevents Strategic Venturing from degenerating into anarchy. The importance given to the recruitment, training and development of people both ensures that the team works well together and gives each member a sense that the company values his contribution and is intent on developing his potential to the full. A culture that is supportive, but not soft, towards individual managers seems to explain at least some of the loyalty and dedication that these companies receive from their staff.

Our limited research into these companies leaves many questions unanswered concerning how these features of their management processes became established and how they really work. We may have missed other important characteristics or misunderstood some issues; but we believe this analysis identifies some management processes that should be studied carefully by all diversified corporations.

Notes

1 In doing this research we reviewed the contents of books like T. Peters and R. Waterman Jr, *In Search of Excellence* (Harper and Row, 1982), and T. E. Deal and A. A. Kennedy, *Corporate Cultures* (Addison-Wesley, 1982) as well as major magazine articles on the companies. However, the most important and relevant source of information proved to be case studies written about the management systems of the companies.
2 Richard F. Vancil, 'Implementing strategy: the role of top management' (Harvard Business School, 1979).
3 David Mercer, *IBM: How the World's Most Successful Corporation is Managed* (Kogan Page, 1987).
4 R. F. Vancil, 'General Electric Company: background note on management systems 1981', Harvard Business School Case no. 181–111.
5 Aguilar, Hamermesh, Brainard, 'General Electric: 1984', Harvard Business School Case no. 9–385–315. 'General Electric: Jack Welch', Harvard Business School Case no. 5–182–024, transcript of video 9–882–004. 'General Electric: background note', Harvard Business School Case no. 5–182–023, transcript of video 9–882–003. 'General Electric: Jack Welch', Harvard Business School Case no. 5–183–102, transcript of video 9–882–054. R. F. Vancil, 'General Electric Company: 1981 Audit of Management Systems', Harvard Business School Case no. 181–112.
6 R. Pascale and A. Athos, *The Art of Japanese Management* (Penguin, 1982). K. Takahashi, 'Matsushita Electric Industrial Co.: Management Control Systems', Keio University. K. Takahashi, 'Matsushita Electric' (ed. by Bert Spector), Harvard Business School Case no. 9–481–146.
7 Gary Hamel and C. K. Prahalad have developed an interesting explanation for why Japanese companies appear to have tight short-term controls and yet can follow long-term ambitions. Traditionally this is achieved by the corporate level strategy which lays down medium-term ambitions. The Japanese do not seem to have corporate strategies. Rather they are committed to a 'strategic intent', a target that defines 'winning' for them, e.g. beat Caterpillar in the machinery business. Hamel and Prahalad argue that it is the combination of a 10-, 15-or 20-year strategic intent and a 1-or 2-year budget that enables Japanese companies to grow so successfully. Their article has been published as a Centre for Business Strategy, London Business School working paper (No. 14), *Unexplored Routes to Competitive Revitalization*, July 1986.
8 From Takahashi, 'Matsushita Electric'.
9 Roger M. Atherton, 'Hewlett–Packard: a 1975–1978 review' available from Lord Publishing, Dover, Mass. 02030. Roger M. Atherton, 'Hewlett–Packard, 1978–1981: the evolution of leadership', available from Lord Publishing, Dover, Mass. 02030.

15

Conclusions

We began this book with a series of questions concerning the role of the centre in strategic decision-making. As we pull our conclusions together, we need to return to these questions and summarize the answers that have emerged.

1 What Distinctively Different Management Styles are there and how should they be Classified?

We have identified eight different management styles. Three of these, Strategic Planning, Strategic Control and Financial Control, are the most popular amongst large UK companies today (figures 15.1 and 15.2).

The basis of our classification stems from the ways in which the centre influences business unit strategies. The two key dimensions on which we focused were the involvement of the centre in shaping the plans of business units ('planning influence') and the nature of the controls the centre exercises against results achieved ('control influence').

All of the companies in our research delegate the vast bulk of day-to-day decisions to business management; and all mix bottom-up and top-down influence on questions of strategy. The important issues, and the important distinctions between companies, concern how and where the centre exercises its influence. We have found that our classification both clarifies the options for the centre and describes the main differences in approach that companies take.

We view our classification as a first map of previously uncharted territory. No doubt the outlines on the map can be made clearer and more precise; the contours and the boundaries can be filled in more fully. But the main features have been established, and should make life easier for future navigators.

As is normal in research of this nature, we have raised more questions than we have answered. For example, we have only explored the three main styles in depth. It would be interesting to know more about the Strategic Venturing style as practised in parts of UB and BP, and in Hewlett—Packard. We would also like to determine whether the Strategic

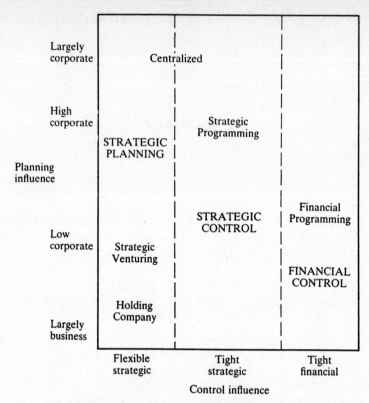

Figure 15.1 Strategic management styles.

Programming style is feasible. We noted that at least two of our companies have tried it and backed away. Apparently General Electric of America have followed a similar course. We would like to discover whether there are any companies that have operated this style successfully and consistently.

2 What kind of Results are achieved by the Different Styles? Are some more Successful than Others?

A major conclusion of the work is that different styles achieve different sorts of results, and that no one style is conclusively superior to all others.

Some styles are unsatisfactory. For example, the Holding Company style provides too little influence for the centre to have any significant impact on results; while the Centralized style takes too much power into the hands of the centre to draw out the best from business management. Neither achieves what Oliver Williamson[1] called an 'appropriate distance' for the centre. Similar, if less extreme problems appear to arise with the relatively detached Strategic Venturing style and the more hands-on Strategic Programming style.

The results achieved by the Strategic Planning, Strategic Control and Financial Control styles are different (see tables 8.8–8.11). It emerges that each style is biased in favour of certain sorts of strategies and results. Once the style is set, the effective strategy options begin to narrow down. Understanding what strategies fit most comfortably with each style is therefore essential in making strategy choices, and in assessing competitors' likely moves.

Strategic Planning companies build linked international businesses in core areas. The business units frequently follow bold strategies, stretching for the maximum advantage over competitors. Managers identify with the company's mission, but can become frustrated by a lack of autonomy. Sales growth, particularly organic growth, has been good, and profitability has been above industry averages. But some companies, such as STC, Cadbury's and Lex, have faced major setbacks when their bold strategies have run into trouble.

Strategic Control companies follow a more cautious corporate strategy. The centre frequently concentrates on rationalizing the portfolio and supporting balanced growth in the stronger business units. Managers enjoy the autonomy they have, and respond to the disciplines imposed by the centre. But they complain of ambiguous objectives, bureaucratic procedures and a 'distant' centre. These companies have produced excellent

Strategic Planning
BOC
BP*
Cadbury Schweppes
Lex**
STC**
UB*

    * Strategic Venturing
       for some businesses
** Strategic Programming
      attempted, but not
      sustained

Strategic Control
Courtaulds
ICI
Imperial
Plessey
Vickers

Financial Control
BTR***
Ferranti***
GEC
Hanson Trust
Tarmac

*** Trends towards
      Financial
      Programming

Figure 15.2 Company styles.

improvements in return on sales and return on capital, but they have been less successful at achieving growth.

Financial Control companies provide little or no direction from the centre to the business units. In some companies the centre is active in making acquisitions but, in others, it concentrates only on vetting proposals from below. Business units stretch to achieve the best financial returns and are prepared to sacrifice market share for high margins. Strategies are usually cautious, with few businesses following a global strategy or attacking major international competitors. Managers find the environment stimulating. They enjoy clear targets and the winner's glory when objectives are met. Problems can, however, arise if the short-term controls are seen as constraining. The financial results of these companies have been exceptional. They have produced higher profitability and higher profit growth than the other styles, but most of the growth has come from acquisitions. There are few examples of major growth coming from winning against important international competitors.

Each style therefore emphasizes different objectives, and achieves success in different dimensions. No style is superior in all dimensions, and there are highly successful companies operating under each main style. A single 'right' style does not exist, but different styles are more or less appropriate to the circumstances a company faces, a point to which we return below.

The conclusion that there is no one right style raises some questions about the scope of our research. Managers with whom we have discussed our work have speculated that this could be a result of carrying out the research in Britain. Supporters of the Strategic Planning style, for example, have suggested that UK managers may be less able to make it work well than their overseas competition. They have argued that US and Japanese managers may be able to handle the complexities of the style better, and that if we had done our research elsewhere we might have reached different conclusions. Similar points are made by proponents of the other styles.

Our scan of the published data on IBM, GE, Matsushita and Hewlett—Packard would suggest that these critics are partly right and partly wrong. These highly successful companies each adopt styles that can readily be fitted into our framework. But in some respects they achieve results that combine the best of different styles. Matsushita, for example, has grown organically with global product strategies, yet it has a Financial Control style. There are obviously important lessons to be learned from further research of this nature into non-British companies.

3 Why do Different Styles exist? Why have Successful Companies not been able to Converge on a single Right Style?

Different styles follow from different assumptions about the nature of the successful company. These lead to different emphases in terms of the five key choices or tensions that we have claimed always face corporate management: clear responsibilities vs cooperation, detailed planning vs quick response, strong leadership vs business autonomy, short-term vs long-term, and tight controls vs flexible strategies. Companies have not converged on one style because managers have different underlying assumptions about how to build a successful organization.

Strategic Planning companies stress the need for cooperation throughout the company to achieve certain key shared purposes; and for long-term strategies to achieve success in an unpredictable, rapidly changing and highly competitive world. The collaborative approach is needed both to define the best possible strategy, to modify it as circumstances unfold, and to achieve the motivation to see it through to completion. The long-term strategies are needed to insure that lasting competitive advantages are built up, whatever short-term problems may be encountered along the way.

Strategic Control companies also believe in long-term strategies, but place much more emphasis on the individual business manager in formulating and implementing these strategies. Personal responsibility and accountability are seen as the keys to informed thinking and clear-cut motivation. Cooperative approaches to strategy are dangerous because they confuse this sense of personal responsibility, and make for ineffectual compromises.

Financial Control companies share the Strategic Control assumptions concerning the importance of giving responsibility to individual managers; but they give more prominence to short-term financial performance in assessing strategies. Tight budgets are used to prevent managers from following unrealistic plans, and to focus on measurable criteria of success. By achieving tough performance standards, managers gain the confidence from which to seize opportunities quickly as they arise.

These are very different philosophies of how to develop a winning strategy; of how to motivate a management team; of how to succeed competitively (figure 15.3). The assumptions behind each style are different and incompatible, but each set of assumptions can be valid, in the right business circumstances and with the right management group. We expect to see continuing diversity in styles rather than convergence on a single preferred approach.

4 Do all the Management Styles Add Value to the Businesses being Managed, and if so How?

The question of added value is key to this book. The centre of a diversified company is, in a sense, an intermediary between the business unit and the capital markets. To exist, it must outperform the capital markets: its 'net' added value must be greater than its cost.

Each of the main styles does add value in distinctive ways. But, importantly, each style also tends to substract value. It is the balance of these effects that determines net added value. The nature of added and subtracted value under each style follows from the choices the style makes in terms of the five tensions.

		Competitive success comes from:	
		Long-term competitive advantage	Short-term results focus
Best approach to defining strategy and motivating management	Cooperative, collaborative, shared purposes	Strategic Planning	–
	Clear, individual responsibility and motivation	Strategic Control	Financial Control

Figure 15.3 Underlying assumptions of main styles.

Strategic Planning companies are at their best in helping businesses to embark on strategies to build long-term competitive advantage. They encourage a wider search for the best strategies, are willing to coordinate between businesses if needed, and provide a buffer against capital market pressures. All this leads to a more tenacious pursuit of shared long-term goals. But there can be problems, such as less clear accountability for results, tolerance of underperformance and slow decision-making. (See table 11.2.)

Financial Control companies are most powerful in drawing maximum performance out of established businesses. They give full autonomy to business managers, establish clear and stretching standards of performance, and act decisively to replace managers who are not delivering. Control processes are therefore more demandingly set and more efficiently applied than by the outside capital market. This creates a greater pressure for success, and an atmosphere that rewards those who do succeed. But it can inhibit innovation, risk-taking and long-term business building. (See table 11.4.)

Strategic Control companies aim for balance. They are willing to take a longer view than the capital markets; but they also set out to provide tight short-term controls to motivate managers. They allow considerable autonomy to divisional management; but they establish planning processes that ensure minimum standards of thinking and analysis are met. This balanced approach can add value in most situations, but it is less clear in its priorities. There is a danger that, rather than providing an optimum balance, it falls ambiguously between alternative options. (See table 11.6.)

The task for the centre under any style is to maximize its positive contribution and to minimize its negative effects. While some of the sources of subtracted value are inevitable, other pitfalls can be avoided (see table 10.1). It is the sensitivity with which the style is adopted, and the systems supporting the style, that determine the net impact.

Strategic Planning places a heavy burden on the capability and knowledge of the corporate management group. They must be sufficiently well informed about each of their businesses to be able to contribute to decisions; they must establish a cooperative approach to decisions, avoiding both autocratic imposition of their own views and endless debate without resolution; and they must maintain sharpness in the control process, without losing flexibility. Furthermore, they must be able to motivate business management to work together in pursuit of the core strategies. These requirements are most unlikely to be met in a company with a highly diverse portfolio. To attempt a Strategic Planning style in these circumstances is to invite disaster.

The simplicity, clarity and consistency of Financial Control make it an easier style to operate successfully, both for the centre and the business unit, than Strategic Planning or Strategic Control. A major requirement, however, is for highly capable business management. They are solely responsible for strategy, and they must be relied upon not to undermine the long-term health of the businesses in order to achieve their short-term targets. Although the centre can replace those that fall short on financial criteria, the success of these companies depends upon the ability of a high proportion of their business managers to find strategies that will allow them to meet demanding targets year after year. The centre encourage managers to rise to this challenge, and the psychology of winning provides the confidence to succeed. But the onus remains with the business managers. There is the potential for a virtuous circle in which success breeds confidence, which breeds new ideas for growth, which in turn succeed. But this virtuous circle can be broken. If success is in doubt, energy can go into attempting to batten down the hatches and dress up the figures in a destructive effort to meet targets at any cost. This sort of game playing with financial controls is when the underlying health of a business can be seriously damaged. Our sample contains only the most successful Financial Control companies who have generally been less prone to this vicious circle; but avoiding it is a major challenge for all Financial Control companies.

As with Financial Control, Strategic Control places a heavy load on the capability of decentralized business management. In addition, it calls for a greater level of understanding of the strategies of the businesses at the centre. Without this understanding, the planning process adds no real value, and the ability to identify strategic controls is lost. But the greatest challenge for both the centre and the business units in Strategic Control is to balance the tensions between strategic and financial controls. The success of the Strategic Control companies in our sample indicates that this can be done; but the problems that they have encountered show that the tension remains an essential feature of this style.

5   *When does each Style work Best? How should a Company's Style affect its Corporate Portfolio Building Strategy?*

Each style has different strong and weak points. As a result, the various styles are more suited to some situations than others.

In chapter 12 we identified the factors that managers should take into acccount when deciding which style the centre should adopt towards a particular business unit (see figure 12.1). Three factors concern the nature of the business – the degree of linkage between the business unit and other units in the portfolio, the size and payback of investment decisions needed to compete successfully, and the nature of the competitive environment facing the business unit. Three other factors are related to the resources in the organization – the personality of the CEO, the skills of senior managers in the centre and in the business units, and the financial health of the whole organization.

We concluded that Strategic Planning is most suitable for businesses that have close links with other units, where the decisions are large and have long payback periods, and where the competitive environment is unstable, either because the market place is wide open or because the companies are caught in a fierce battle.

The Financial Control style is likely to bring the best out of businesses where there are few linkages, where investments are small and the money can be recovered in 2 or 3 years, and where the competitors are not overly aggressive. Under these circumstances, the managers in charge of the business unit can focus on maximizing financial returns without worrying too much about loss of long-term competitiveness.

The Strategic Control style is likely to be best where neither of these two extreme sets of conditions exist, or where a business unit is in a fierce competitive battle but is uncertain whether to go all out for a win or to cut and run.

There is also a link between the company's resources and the type of management style it adopts. In general, the personality of the CEO, the senior management skills and the financial condition of the company should fit with the style. There is no point in trying to adopt a Financial Control style if the control function at the centre is weak and the business unit managers are not skilled at budgeting. And it is hard to adopt a Strategic Planning style with a business unit run by a bull-headed entrepreneur in a company facing a cash crisis.

The choice of style should, therefore, depend on the business and organizational circumstances. No style is best, but some styles will suit some situations better than others.

How then should a company set about building a portfolio of businesses? Should managers first choose a style, and then acquire businesses that fit the style and develop skills appropriate to the style? Or should managers begin by choosing a portfolio of attractive businesses, and then develop the appropriate skills and style to get the best out of the business units? Or should a company simply choose a chief executive, and build the style and portfolio around that chief executive's personality? There is obviously a need for fit, but the problem is where to start.

To provide some answers to this conundrum, we defined three strategies for building a portfolio – the Core Businesses strategy, the Manageable, Businesses strategy, and the Diverse Businesses strategy (see table 13.4).

In the Core Businesses strategy managers choose two or three business areas and grow their portfolio in those areas. Where the market is growing, the company can grow with it. When growth slows, the company must knock out competitors. The objective, therefore, has to be to dominate the chosen industries. With this strategy the centre adopts a Strategic Planning style.

In the Manageable Businesses strategy, the centre chooses a style, such as Financial Control, and builds a portfolio of businesses that respond to the style. The CEO's personality and the skills at the centre and in the businesses are an important determinant of the style.

In the Diverse Businesses strategy, the centre builds a portfolio by developing into attractive industries. Either through organic growth or through acquisition the company uses cash generated in mature business areas to grow into more attractive, higher growth markets. The centre encourages diversity as a means of spreading risk and increasing opportunity. Under this strategy, the centre adopts a Strategic Control style, with strong division CEOs being given freedom to adopt a style that best fits their parts of the portfolio.

Many interesting issues concerning the fit between management styles and business circumstances remain open – for example, on the issue of acquisitions we would expect to see a higher success rate for acquisitions where there is a style fit. Also we would like to document the progress of business units where the circumstances change, causing a style misfit. And we would like to study a company committed to the diverse businesses philosophy, since none of the companies in our sample were fully dedicated to this strategy for growing the portfolio.

6   Are there any Universal Right Ways of doing things?

By now, we would hope to have established that there are no easy answers, no simple rules, no standard recipes for corporate strategic management. It is a complex balancing process in which value can as easily be subtracted as added, and in which there are many pitfalls to avoid. Any prescriptions can therefore be quickly met with counter examples, and rules can only be applied in the most flexible manner, with the expectation of numerous exceptions. Nevertheless, we should not close without attempting to identify what common threads, if any, characterize those companies whose strategic decision-making processes seem to work best. We believe that there are certain underlying features of this sort, and, for want of a better term, we shall refer to them as 'ideals' for which corporate management should strive.

Matching   We have argued that all styles have intrinsic advantages and disadvantages, and that there is no one right style. This, however, does not mean that different styles are not better or worse suited to particular business circumstances. In certain situations the disciplines of Financial Control pay off handsomely and its drawbacks are of relatively little account. Hanson Trust has selected its portfolio with this in mind. In other cases, the support for cooperative, long-term strategies provided by Strategic Planning outweighs any problems that the style brings with it. The drawbacks in IBM's style appear to be more than compensated by its advantages, given interdependencies between the businesses in their portfolio. There is a need to seek a fit between the nature of the businesses in which a company operates, the resources it has at its disposal, and the strategic management style selected. Companies whose strategic decision-making processes are most successful achieve a match in all these dimensions.

   This question of fit has already been dealt with in chapter 12. We will therefore simply note here that matching the corporate management style to the company's circumstances is the first ideal to aim for.

Understanding the Businesses   Strategic decision-making works best where meetings between managers from corporate, divisional and business levels grapple with the real issues rather than skating over the surface. Decisions need to be based on facts and argument, rather than on gut feel and prejudice. This is not a question of the bulkiness of plans or the time horizon of forecasts. It concerns the depth of understanding of the business possessed by each level in the organization. Different managements, adopting different styles, may disagree on what the most important issues in a business are; but a willingness to dig deeply enough to get to grips with the key issues is characteristic of all the most successful companies in our sample.

   The requirements and emphasis are different under each style. A division chairman in Courtaulds described Chris Hogg's role in these terms: 'He does not try to guide the strategies of the businesses, but is willing to dig deeply into the proposals and to spend days going through their strategies to be sure he understands them and is willing to sign off on them.' This epitomizes the requirements of the Strategic Control style. It is no coincidence that, in Courtaulds, the Chairman's interventions are typically welcomed by business unit managers.

   A business stream manager in Cadbury Schweppes gave a somewhat different account of Dominic Cadbury's contribution:

   He will wish to hear about strategic changes that we propose, but is unlikely to question them or get into the detail of individual profit centres unless we are projecting results that fall short of overall plans. But in some businesses he will go further. He reviewed the segmentation data presented to him on the German business and suggested a new approach which emphasized a different pack size and a different approach to the trade. He used existing data to create a different insight into the appropriate strategy for the business.

This is the more proactive Strategic Planning style, but again there is the willingness to invest time and effort in understanding the business; and again there is recognition from the business level of the value of this sort of contribution.

The Financial Control style makes a different impact, but, at its best, also has the ability to dig into essential features of a business, and contribute to line management thinking. A quote from a BTR division head captures it well: 'Owen Green is primarily interested in return on sales and secondarily cash, rather than things such as market share. He believes that with high RoS this gives flexibility to deal with most business situations, and that high RoS will convert to strong cash flow and profitability on investment.' Corporate management conduct a close control of all the businesses in the group according to a standard ratio package. 'The ratios and forms are very illuminating. They showed me things I should have bloody well known: for example relationships between different elements of costs in the business, and how their movements compare to movements in price', commented a manager who had recently joined BTR with the Dunlop acquisition. There are monthly meetings to review performance, but 'the meetings are not a chore. The centre know what they're doing'. Finally, commenting on the contrast between Dunlop and BTR: 'Nobody has talked strategy at BTR, whereas at Dunlop you heard about it all the time'. In other words, the BTR style stresses profitability and cash flow, not long-term measures of competitive position and strategy. But the centre are well informed about the businesses and zero in rapidly on those issues that they believe affect performance. This can be much more useful to business management than ineffective strategic planning systems and ill-informed corporate advice.

Each style, therefore, has a different conception of the appropriate central influence on strategy; and of the nature of competitive advantage and how it should be built. But the common factor in each case is the willingness to devote enough effort to understanding the businesses to be able to exercise cogent corporate influence. This is a second ideal for corporate management.

Open Communication and Mutual Respect A third ideal of strategic decision-making is that corporate, divisional and business management should share information and views openly and have respect for each other's capabilities. As the planning director of one Strategic Planning company put it: 'For strategic management to succeed, there needs to be an openness of style, so that there will be free flowing of information and views at all levels in the organization, and not the typical hide and seek of ideas between businesses and the centre'.

At a technical level, modern information technology has made it easier for the centre to have direct access to divisional and business information.

But open information flow depends more on attitudes and people than on the technicalities of the information system. If information technology helps it is because, as Lionel Stammers of BTR said, 'IT makes it possible to cut out layers of management. We now have only one layer between the coal face and the centre'.

But the prime factor in creating open attitudes to information flow and expression of views is mutual respect between members of the management team. 'All managers tell lies. The question is not whether you are being told the truth or not. It is whether it is a big lie or a little lie', commented the chief executive of one of the companies in our sample. This attitude is in stark contrast to the culture of respect for the individual that exists at IBM. In a company where the man in charge does not trust his lieutenants it is hard to create an open atmosphere.

Mutual respect – and consequent self-confidence – is necessary to avoid the distortions that rise from perceived needs to impress each other in the strategic decision-making process. If the centre has (or is perceived to have) doubts about business unit management, then the strategic decision-making process is liable to be used by the centre to impose its views on 'incompetent' business managers; and by the business unit to convince the centre that they are really doing just what the centre wants. The result is either directive decision-making, or a highly political process in which second guessing what the centre wants to hear (and withholding any other information or views) is the paramount concern. If the business units have (or are perceived to have) doubts about the value added by the centre, this will often lead to the centre seeking to justify itself by finding holes in business unit strategies; and to the businesses avoiding any more than minimal contact with the centre. The result is adversarial confrontations, and territoriality and protectiveness by the business units.

In all these cases, the atmosphere surrounding the strategic decision-making process is not conducive to constructive discussion of strategy. Strategic planning becomes a facade for preserving personal interests rather than a genuine exploration of new ideas; and control meetings are more concerned with apportioning blame for failures than celebrating successes or working together to overcome difficulties.

Because there are clear criteria of 'good performance', it is in some ways easier to create an atmosphere of mutual respect in Financial Control companies than with other styles. We have already cited the way in which Tarmac instills a 'winners' psychology into its management team by establishing stretching objectives and challenging business unit management to succeed in reaching them. Everyone knows what the targets are, and that those who fail to deliver will not survive. By contrast, business unit managers who have survived, and who have consistently met their targets, are secure in the knowledge that they have demonstrably succeeded. And the freedom given to business unit managers to develop their own strategies makes it less likely that the centre will be seen as interfering, out-of-touch and authoritarian.

The management task in Strategic Control and Strategic Planning companies is more complex. Performance measures are softer and more subjective, and there is less ruthlessness in getting rid of non-performers. In consequence there is more uncertainty about personal performance and prospects. To counter this, it is necessary for the chief executive to go out of his way to create an atmosphere in which divergent views will be expressed, and new ideas tried; and in which line management do feel that they are or can become winners.

The importance of atmosphere, and its determinants, was brought out by an ICI division chairman, who conveyed his admiration for John Harvey-Jones in this way: 'He is willing to admit when he has made an error. He is more encouraging of new things. He is also tougher and more demanding on divisional management. A number of changes are matters of tone, symbol or signals, but they have nevertheless been important in changing the morale and atmosphere in the company.' ICI has become more successful partly because the climate in the company now expects success, and because management believe in their ability to achieve it. The same change in atmosphere was achieved by Jack Welch in GE.

In Strategic Control and Strategic Planning companies there is therefore a need to work at building mutual respect. Much depends on 'tone, symbol and signals', which can often be overlooked in processes that focus more on the content of decisions. But mutual respect also stems from central understanding of the businesses, as described above; and from attitudes to performance assessment that are tough enough to ensure that those who remain in charge of the major businesses do enjoy the confidence of the centre.

An atmosphere of open communication, then, is important in allowing different perceptions of strategy options to be put forward and argued out in a robust and constructive manner. Mutual respect, which provides the security for individual managers to speak their minds, is necessary to achieving it.

Energy and Common Purpose A last characteristic that the most successful companies shared was a common commitment from corporate, divisional and business management to work together to make the strategy succeed. There are two aspects to this ideal: energy to get things done, and a common aim to draw together efforts from different members of the organization.

In times of financial crisis, where the company is threatened, adversity creates both the focus and the impetus for action. Major changes were made with remarkably little dissent in BP, Courtaulds, ICI, Imperial and Vickers during the recession of the early 1980s. In each case cash flow and profit pressures concentrated the efforts of management at all levels behind turnaround strategies.

A common aim is harder for large diversified companies in times of prosperity. Peters and Waterman[2] have talked of the importance of shared values in holding together a company's strategy, organization and systems. And Bill Ouchi,[3] an American expert on Japanese management practices, has proposed the term 'clans' to describe organizations whose members are so motivated by shared goals that they can be relied upon to pursue these goals free from hierarchical control systems. Ouchi believes that the needs for delegated authority and flexible strategic responses mean that clans will be the most successful types of organization in the future.

But despite the appeal of these ideas, none of the companies in our research could be said to have achieved this degree of shared corporate purpose. Corporate ways of doing things and some consensus on underlying values typically exist; but a thoroughgoing commitment to corporate goals or themes is much rarer. Lex, with its 'service excellence' philosophy, is perhaps trying to move in this direction. But in the words of Trevor Chinn, 'It may be 5 to 10 years before it is fully communicated and accepted within the company.' More fundamentally, size and diversity make it hard to articulate any meaningful corporate goal that will knit together the efforts of the various businesses and divisions, and provide the energy for action.

Perhaps surprisingly, the Financial Control companies come closest to a sense of common purpose. But the goal is not some tangible strategic aim. Rather, it is simply 'winning', where winning means meeting financial targets. The psychological force of these targets, however, should not be underestimated: 'They want to be top of the first division . . . The management have so much belief in themselves that they want to go in too deep. They may fall into the trap of thinking that they can do anything.' This is powerful motivation, and the best Financial Control companies prosper because there is such high energy for achievement in them. Frequent face-to-face meetings and feedback on performance are important in generating this motivation. Although some Strategic Control and Strategic Planning companies are also driven by a shared quest for performance, it is generally a less strong theme in these companies.

Where energy and commitment are found, they often relate more to business level objectives, agreed with corporate management, than to corporate goals that unite the whole organization. Individual businesses can and do generate goals ('to become the leading supplier of marine paint in the world', 'to get the better of Proctor & Gamble in the cookie war') that capture the energy of their management teams. Corporate management's role is to support these goals with appropriate controls, and to reinforce the urgency to attain them.

Interestingly, Hewlett–Packard, IBM, Matsushita and more recently GE have all developed and documented their corporate values. Matsushita probably devotes more attention than the others to communicating its values within the organization. But anyone familiar with Hewlett–Packard or IBM would recognize the importance their managers attach to the companies' basic goals and value systems. It seems that formal documentation and, more importantly, communication of these values, has enhanced managers' feelings of common purpose and commitment in these companies.

But the pure process of formulating a value statement or a strategy does not guarantee that the objectives proposed will become a shared aim for all members of a management team. There is a need to provide leadership to create enthusiasm for new directions; this is a particular strength of CEOs such as Sir Hector Laing, whose personal charisma is recognized throughout UB. There is also a need to provide time and opportunities to explore the personal and business implications of new strategies, and air doubts that exist. The feeling that line management have been fully consulted, and that their views and interests have been taken into account, is essential to creating the energy for change.

The need to work at creating a common purpose was best brought out by a division manager in Hanson Trust who described how he communicated his strategy thinking to his team and built consensus around it. He stressed the role of twice-yearly conferences, at which he brought together the top 100 managers in the division:

> We send out an agenda saying what we're going to talk about, and also asking managers to prepare presentations on particular issues. They all then get their management teams to help to put the presentations together. So when it comes, they know generally what the content will be and they're involved in one of the presentations. In a sense we tell them what we are going to tell them, then we tell them, then we tell them what we've told them by issuing notes of the presentations. So it's reinforce, reinforce, reinforce. It's not really a decision-making meeting. It's basically 90 per cent communication. It winds up commitment and understanding and teamwork. What happens is that everybody in effect has an input into the strategy and therefore they're all committed to it. But at the same time they don't feel that they're sitting there working it out. They just are sufficiently informed to feel part of it. There's this kind of communal thing as much as anything else. Once we've done that our implementation you can almost take for granted.

Those organizations that cannot 'take implementation for granted' may have something to learn from this approach. A constitutional forum to question emerging strategies, to put forward different points of view and to satisfy lower levels that senior management have thought things through thoroughly is important in generating commitment to strategic objectives.

The ideals we have described – matching style to business circumstances, understanding the businesses, open communication and mutual respect, and energy and common purpose – concern attitudes, atmosphere and people rather than the design of formal systems and processes. As one disillusioned planning director stated: 'It's not that the system isn't there. It's that the people that are there to do it and the attitudes that they have are wrong.'

As such, our ideals may seem soft, difficult to pin down. However, we believe that they express the true common denominators of successful strategic decision-making. Corporate managements that attain these ideals will succeed, whatever style they adopt. Companies such as IBM and Matsushita appear to have achieved these ideals and some in our sample are close. The challenge for many companies, however, is to start on the road.

Notes

1 See chapter 2, p. 20.
2 See Thomas J. Peters and Robert H. Waterman Jr, *In Search of Excellence* (Harper and Row, 1982).
3 See William Ouchi, *Theory Z* (Addison-Wesley, 1981) and the *The M-Form Society* (Addison-Wesley, 1984). Ouchi's thesis is that 'clans', whose members share values and goals, prevent the pursuit of personal strategies at the expense of organizational goals. They reduce the control tension between valid strategic trade-offs and unfounded excuses, since the sharing of clan goals means that all members of the clan can be relied upon to bend their best efforts to the common goals; invalid and illegitimate excuses will not arise. How this desirable state of affairs can be brought about is, however, rather less clear.

Appendix 1   Company Backgrounds and Summary Statistics

This appendix provides a brief description of the companies in the sample and a summary of the financial performance of each. For a measure of profitability we have used return on sales (RoS), return on equity (RoE) and return on capital employed (RoCE). For a measure of growth we have used real growth in share price, earnings per share (EPS) and sales. To break out organic and acquisition-based growth, we have looked at growth in fixed assets, the only measure on which there is publicly available information concerning organic and acquisition-based growth. The statistics

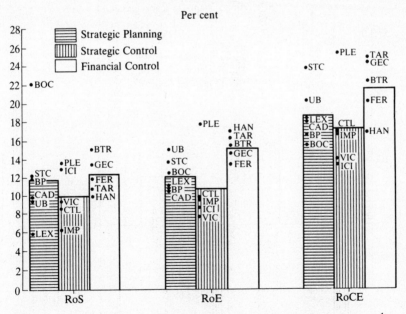

Figure A1.1   Four-year profitability averages, 1981–5 (from Datastream[1]).

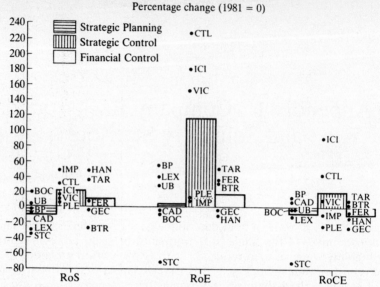

Figure A1.2 Change in profitability ratios, 1981–5 (from Datastream[1]).

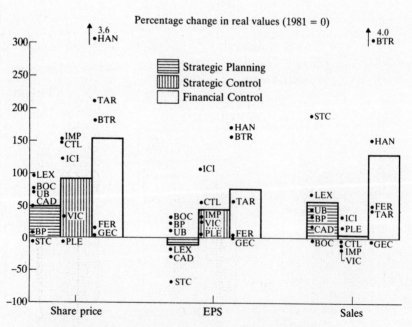

Figure A1.3 Four-year growth indices, 1981–5 (from Datastream[2]).

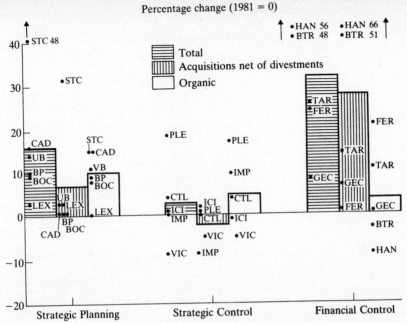

Figure A1.4 Average yearly fixed asset growth, 1981–5 (from Datastream, Annual Reports[3]).

in figures A1.1–A1.3 and table A1.1 have been drawn from Datastream and suffer from the definition problems associated with this data base. However, the numbers benefit from being comparable. Definitions are provided in the notes.

Notes

1 The profitability ratios have been drawn from Datastream using the following definitions:

Return on shareholders' equity	(RoE):	$\dfrac{\text{Earned for ordinary (fully taxed)}}{\text{Ord'y share capital plus reserves less goodwill plus deferred tax}}$
Return on capital employed (%)	(RoCE):	$\dfrac{\text{Pretax profits (incl. Assocs) + interest charges}}{\text{Total capital employed plus borrowing repayable within 1 year less goodwill}}$
Trading profit margin (%)	(RoS):	$\dfrac{\text{Trading profit}}{\text{Total sales}}$

Trading profit = Net profit before depreciation is deducted
Operating profit = Trading profit less depreciation
Pretax profit = Operating profit plus non-trading income less interest

2 The growth statistics have been drawn from Datastream using the following definitions:

Net earnings per share	(EPS)	$\dfrac{\text{Net earnings for ordinary}}{\text{Average weighted capital, fully adjusted}}$

Total sales

UK sales to third parties
PLUS exports from UK (incl. overseas subsidiaries if only described as exports in accounts – otherwise overseas sales excluded from exports)
PLUS overseas sales (overseas subsidiary sales to third parties – sometimes inclusive of intercompany sales if not defined in accounts)
LESS intercompany sales
LESS associate company sales
LESS VAT if included in turnover (mainly retail companies)
LESS other duties and taxes (excise and sales-related taxes paid)

3 Fixed asset data was drawn from Datastream. Acquisition growth is measured by calculating the average yearly growth due to acquisitions net of divestments. Organic growth is measured by subtracting net acquisition growth from total growth. Comprehensive data was available for 12 of the 16 companies. However, data on acquisitions of fixed assets was either absent or inconsistent for Vickers, Imperial, Courtaulds and GEC. We have estimated the data for these companies as follows:

1 Vickers: This company made significant acquisitions and disposals over the period. The extent of these was estimated by multiplying the total net expenditure on acquisitions during the year by the ratio of total fixed assets to total net current assets in that year (taken from the Vickers group balance sheet).
2 Imperial: For each year from 1981 to 1984 acquisitions and disposals of subsidiaries appear to balance. All growth is organic. In 1985 the company accounts indicate growth in total fixed assets of £421 million. However, this figure included a revaluation of retail property amounting to £588 million. Clearly it is inappropriate to include 'growth' by revaluation in our calculations and £588 million has therefore been subtracted from the 1985 year end total of fixed assets. The resulting picture of negative growth reflects the disposal during 1985 of Howard Johnson (fixed assets £338.4 million).
3 Courtaulds: Close examination of the Courtaulds accounts suggests that acquisitions and disposals of subsidiaries largely balanced out over the period, year by year. This was represented in our calculations by assuming that all their fixed asset increase resulted from organic growth.
4 GEC: Total change in fixed assets was multiplied by the average rate of the other firms in its style – Hanson, BTR, Ferranti and Tarmac. Knowledge of the company suggests that the behaviour of GEC closely mirrors the other financial control companies.

NB: In 1984 Tarmac acquired significant assets from Lone Star. These appear in their accounts as organic, yet are clearly in reality, acquisition. Therefore the acquired fixed assets figure for 1984 has been adjusted. The £74 million paid for these assets was multiplied by the ratio of total fixed assets to total net current assets for 1981, when Hoveringham (a US quarrying firm similar to Lone Star) was acquired, to give an indication of the fixed assets involved.

Table A1.1 Performance of UK industrial companies 1981–1984[a]

| | Profitability ratios (%)[b] | | |
	RoS	RoCE	RoE
1981	7.8	13.7	6.1
1982	8.2	14.2	6.7
1983	8.2	13.8	6.8
1984	9.0	15.2	8.9
1985	10.1	16.4	10.9
5-Year average	8.3	14.9	8.9

| | Growth ratios (real growth %) | |
	Share price	Sales
4-year averages 1980–84	67	25

[a] Drawn from Datastream excluding oils and financial companies.
[b] As at end January.

COMPANY SUMMARIES

The following descriptions of each company give business and financial information drawn from a variety of public sources.

Strategic Planning Companies

The Strategic Planning companies are: BOC, BP, Cadbury Schweppes, Lex Service, STC, United Biscuits (UB). They are described here in alphabetical order.

BOC Group

Chairman and chief executive: Richard V. Giordano

	Sales (£m)	Profit before interest & tax (£m)	Net assets (£m)	Employees
1985 results	1,901	237	2,009	36,936

Activities

Industrial Gases & related products
Healthcare: The manufacture and sale of equipment and systems for anaesthesia and critical care; a range of intravenous disposable products; pharmaceuticals; provision of home oxygen therapy.
Carbon and Carbide: The manufacture and sale of graphite electrodes, principally for electric furnace steel-making; a range of specialty graphite products; the sale of calcium carbide.
Special Products and Services: The manufacture of high vacuum pumps, instruments, systems, vacuum coating equipment; thermit welding.

Major Recent Events

1978	Airco majority acquired.
1979	Airco Ferroalloys disposal.
	Dick Giordano becomes chief executive officer.
1981–83	Major investment in Carbon Graphite Electrode business.
1977–82	Variety of smaller businesses sold.
1982	Current approach to strategic planning introduced.
1983	Computer Services division sold.
	Gases companies in Venezuela and Columbia acquired; and 43 per cent holding in Osaka Sanso Kogyo.
	Acquisitions of Glasrock Medical Services and 26 per cent of Mountain Medical (USA).
	Further divestments, including UK welding interests.
1984	Further divestments in welding, smaller businesses.
	Acquisitions in US home health care.
1985	Holding in Mountain Medical divested.
	Dick Giordano becomes chairman and chief executive officer.

Divisional Analysis

Division		Sales as % of total					RoCE			
		1979	1982	1985	1979–85 real growth of sales (% pa)		1979	1982	1985	1979–85 average
Gases		35	49	61	11.0		11.4	11.9	12.9	11.7
Health		11	16	21	14.0		11.7	20.7	25.9	18.3
Welding		18	16	–	N/A		8.4	(3.4)	–	N/A
Carbon		23	8	8	(16.0)		18.2	(1.1)	(1.7)	5.3
Other		13	11	10	(3.0)		11.7	9.3	19.6	10.1
Totals										
Sales (£m)		1,230	1,530	1,900	7.5	RoCE	12.0	10.6	12.2	11.0
Sales (1985 £m)		2,070	1,800	1,900	(1.4)	RoS	10.0	10.9	13.2	10.9

Geographical Analysis

% sales	1979	1982	1985
Europe	41	29	22
Americas	7	9	6
Asia/Pacific	41	41	47
Africa	11	21	25

£m	1979	1982	1985
Net cash flow	N/A	(77)	80
Investment in fixed assets[a]	N/A	84	40

[a] Included in ncf.

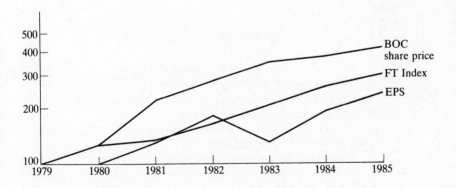

British Petroleum

Chairman: Sir Peter Walters

	Sales (£m)	Profit before interest & tax (£m)	Net assets (£m)	Employees
1985 results	40,986	4,189	21,510	129,450

Activities

Exploration: Prospecting, developing and producing oil and gas.
Gas: Supply, processing, trade and distribution of natural gas and LPG.
Oil International: Oil supply, trading, refining and marketing world wide.
Chemicals International: Manufacture and marketing of petrochemicals and plastics.
Minerals: Production and marketing of minerals from existing operations and identification and development of investment opportunities.
Coal: Exploration, production and marketing of coal.
Shipping: For BP and third parties.
Detergents: Production and marketing of household cleaning and personal care products.
Nutrition: Services the whole chain of animal husbandry from stock, through feeds to processing of meat.
Scicon: Computing services and information technology.
Ventures: Creation of businesses for the future based on modern technology and BP skills.
The Standard Oil Company: A diversified energy and natural resources group based in Cleveland, Ohio. BP has 55 per cent interest.

Major Recent Events

1979	Second oil shock.
1980	Selection Trust (Minerals) acquired for £407 million.
1981	Business streaming reorganization.
	Kennecott Corp. (US, copper) acquired for $1,770 million.
	Coal properties acquired from US Steel for $600 million.
	Sir Peter Walters becomes chairman.
1982–85	Rationalization of downstream oil activities.
	Refinery closures.
1984	Acquisition of Amoco's downstream oil interests in Australia for £136 million.
	Sale of 50 per cent interest in Mercury Communications to Cable and Wireless.
1985	Sohio acquisitions in US downstream oil from Chevron.
1986	Oil price collapse.

Divisional Analysis

Division (excl. Standard Oil)	Sales as % of total					RoCE			
	1979	1982	1985	1979–85 real growth of sales (% pa)		1979	1982	1985	1979–85 average
Exploration & Gas	18	16	19	3.4		}33.3	36.2	47.2	59.9
Oil International	72	73	69	1.9			1.2	14.3	6.9
Chemicals	7	5	6	(2.0)		6.6	(19.0)	7.2	(5.2)
Other[a]	3	6	6	14.2		5.1	(1.5)	(1.1)	(0.9)
Totals (incl. Standard Oil)									
Sales (£m)	22,700	34,580	47,156	13.0	RoCE	44.0	28.0	31.0	34.0
Sales (1985 £m)	37,900	40,268	47,156	3.7	RoS	21.0	16.0	14.0	18.0

[a] Minerals, Coal, Detergents, Nutrition, Scicon, Shipping, Ventures.

% sales	1985
United Kingdom[b]	48
Europe	30
Middle East & Africa	4
Americas	9
Australasia & F. East	9

£m	1979	1982	1985
Net cash flow	750	(1,160)	1,800
Investment in fixed assets[c]	1,390	1,470	270

[c] Included in ncf.

[b] Includes North Sea production, much of which is eventually sold elswhere.

Volume sales of petroleum products by competitors

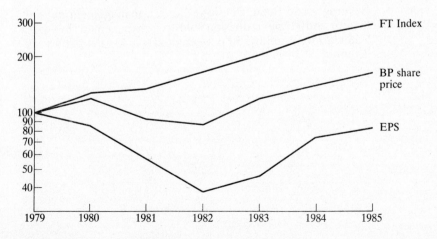

Cadbury Schweppes

Chairman: Sir Adrian Cadbury
Chief executive: N. D. Cadbury

	Sales (£m)	Profit before interest & tax (£m)	Net assets (£m)	Employees
1985 results	1,880	113	677	18,522

Activities

Confectionery
Drinks: Soft drinks.
Tea and Foods: Beverages, foods and catering.
Health and Hygiene

Major Recent Events

1977	Group objectives and Core Business strategy established.
1978	Peter Paul Inc. acquired for £30 million.
1981	Current strategic planning system established.
	66 per cent of Rioblanco SA (Spain) acquired for £17 million.
	Industrial supply operations of Reckitt and Colman acquired.
	Duffy Mott and Holland House (US) acquired for £39 million.
1983	Closure of Italian drinks business.
1984	Dominic Cadbury becomes chief executive.
	Acquisitions in Australia.
1985	Acquisition of Sodastream Holdings for £26 million.
	Agreement with Coca Cola to form joint UK soft drinks company.
1986	Beverages and Foods division sold to a management buy-out.
	Health and Hygiene division sold to a management buy-out.
	Canada Dry, Sunkist, 30 per cent stake in Dr Pepper's acquired.

Divisional Analysis

Division	Sales as % of total				RoS (%)			RoCE (%)
	1977	1981	1985	1977–85 real growth in sales (% pa)	1977	1981	1985	1985
Confectionery	41	47	41	0.5	8	9	7	14.4
Drinks	28	30	36	3.5	5	6	6	15.5
Tea and Foods	26	19	20	(2.7)	6	5	4	14.5
Health and Hygiene	5	3	3	(5.3)	3	7	2	5.2

Totals	1977	1981	1985	1977–85 real growth (% pa)		1979[a]	1981	1985
Sales (£m)	884	1,271	1,879	9.9				
Sales (£m) adj for inflation '85 values	1,811	1,608	1,879	0.5	Total RoCE	17.2	17.9	18.2

[a] 1977 N/A.

Geographical Analysis

Geographical area	Sales as % of total				RoCE (%)		
	1977	1981	1985	1977–85 real growth in sales (% pa)	1979	1981	1985
United Kingdom	60	58	51	(1.6)	18	20	18
Europe	8	9	13	7.2	14	11	28
Americas	7	14	19	13.8	11	12	(3)
Australia	12	12	12	0.0	13	21	29
Other	13	7	5	(10.9)	18	22	24

	1980[b]	1981	1985
Net cash flow (£m)	(5)	(59)	(20)
after investment of:	63	17	(45)

[b] 1977 N/A.

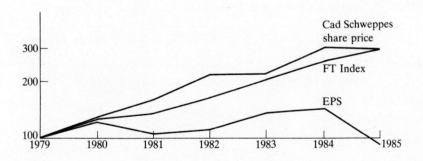

Lex Service

Chairman and chief executive: Trevor Chinn

	Sales (£m)	Profit before interest & tax (£m)	Net assets (£m)	Employees
1985 results	1,041	28.1	216	8,476

Activities

Automotive Distribution: Sole importer of Volvo cars and parts in the UK. Dealerships for Volvo cars, Austin Rover, Jaguar, Rolls–Royce and Leyland Vehicles.
Electronic Components Distribution: Distributor of electronic components and systems, computer and telecommunications products.
Full Service Leasing: Contract hire of cars, commercial vehicles and fork lift trucks.

Major Recent Events

1979	Acquisitions of Motor Rim & Wheel Service Inc., Chanslor & Lyon Inc. (50 per cent), Transfleet.
1980	Disposals of Heathrow & Gatwick Park Hotels, 50 per cent of Lex Vehicle Leasing, Crane Hire fleet of Harvey Plant.
1981	Disposals of more hotels, 50 per cent of Transfleet. Acquisition of Schweber Electronics Inc., Hawke Electronics Ltd, remaining 50 per cent of Chanslor & Lyon Inc.
1982	Acquired 19 per cent of David Jamison Carlyle Corp.
1983	Acquired Jermyn Holdings, Sasco Vertrieb Gmbh, Panel Electronics Gmbh.
1984	'Service Excellence' theme, move from 'Control to Commitment' approach to strategic decision-making begun. Acquired further 34 per cent of David Jamison Carlyle Corp.
1985	Divested Chanslor & Lyon Inc., 50 per cent of Harvey Plant Hire. Acquired Almac, E.I.S., remaining equity in David Jamison Carlyle Corp.
1986	Divested Wilkinson Transport. Acquired Celdis, two subsidiaries of Cargill Inc.

Divisional Analysis

Division	Sales as % of total				RoS (%)			
	1977	1982	1985	1977–85 real growth in sales (% pa)	1980	1982	1985	1980–85 average
Automotive Distribution	77	71	58	3.1	4.8	5.5	5.2	5.4
Electronic Components Dist.	–	20	35	N/A	–	(0.1)	(0.5)	1.9
Transport and Distribution	11	9	7	8.5	5.7	4.4	5.2	3.6
US & UK Hotels	8	–	–	–				
UK Others	4	–	–	–				
Totals								
Sales (£m)	300	664	1,041	16.8 RoS	4.5	4.5	3.0	4.4
Sales (1985 £m)	614	773	1,041	6.8 RoCE	14.5	19.0	15.1	17.6

Geographical Analysis

% sales	1977	1982	1984	1985
United Kingdom	96	77	54	69
United States	4	23	42	27
Europe	–	–	4	4

£m	1980	1982	1985
Net cash flow	15	6	50
Investment in fixed assets[a]	(16)	12	6

[a] Included in ncf.

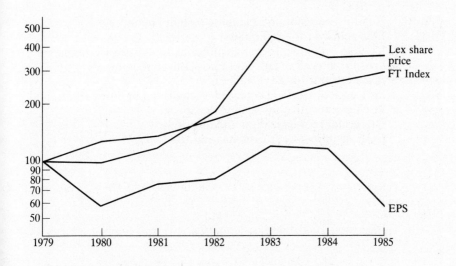

STC

Chairman: Lord Keith
Chief executive: Arthur Walsh

	Sales (£m)	Profit before interest & tax (£m)	Net assets (£m)	Employees
1985 results	1,997	92.7	736	48,021

Activities

Computers and Office Equipment: ICL office communication for voice, text and data.
Telecommunications: Network systems, end user systems; defence systems.
International Communications: IAL; STC Submarine Systems.
Components and Distribution: Electronic components, subsystems, modules and instrumentation.

Major Recent Events

1982	Separation from ITT as publicly quoted company. Sir Kenneth Corfield continues as chairman and chief executive of STC plc.
1982–84	Head office team and planning system created.
1983	IAL acquired for £60 million. Various investments and acquisitions to expand Components division internationally and into semi–conductors.
1984	ICL acquired for £411 million.
1985	Sir Kenneth Corfield replaced as chairman by Lord Keith, and as chief executive by Arthur Walsh.
1986	Divisional reorganization and disposals. CGE acquire 24 per cent stake in STC.

Divisional Analysis

Division	Sales as % of total 1985	RoS (%) 1984	RoS (%) 1985
International Computers	52	7.5	6.9
Telecommunications	13	20.5	9.8
International Communications and Services	11	13.2	4.5
Components and Distribution	14	7.1	(1.6)
Defence	5	14.3	12.0
Office Equipment and other activities	3	(6.0)	(20.3)
Discontinued activities	2	(11.8)	(20.9)

Totals

	1982	1984	1985	1982–5 growth (%)
Sales (£m)	629	1,967	1,997	47
Sales (1985 £m)	732	2,086	1,997	40

%	1982	1984	1985	1982–85 average (%)
RoS	10.5	9.2	5.0	9.1
RoCE	23.8	24.2	12.4	22.7

Geographical Analysis

% sales	1982	1984	1985
United Kingdom	77	65	64
Europe	7	11	13
The Americas	7	3	3
Rest of world	9	21	20

	1982	1984	1985
Net cash flow	38	(275)	(124)
Investment in fixed assets[a]	26	13	41

[a] Included in ncf.

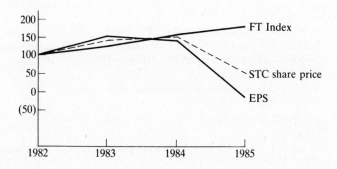

United Biscuits (Holdings)

Chairman: Sir Hector Laing
Chief executive: R. Clarke

	Sales (£m)	Profit before interest & tax (£m)	Net assets (£m)	Employees
1985 results	1,806	122.7	621	29,951

Activities

UK
Biscuits
Foods: Brand name KP.
Frozen Foods
D. S. Crawford: Baking and meat interests.
Restaurants: Restaurants other than Wimpy.
Wimpy International: Franchising of hamburger restaurants.
Distribution Services: Of food products.

United States
Keebler: Manufacture and sale of biscuits and snacks.
Speciality and other foods

Rest of World
Production of biscuits and snacks

Major Recent Events

1974	Acquired Keebler Co. in the US manufacturer of cookies.
1976	Acquired Wimpy International, a hamburger restaurant chain.
1977	Acquired Alverston Kitchens, frozen food manufacturers and TFC Foods, distributors.
1978	Acquired Associated Restaurants (Pizzaland).
1979	Central responsibilities devolved to divisions.
1980	Acquired Magic Pantry Foods Inc. and Johnston's Pie Crust Inc.
1982	Acquired Joseph Terry and Sons chocolate manufacturers.
1985	Bob Clarke appointed chief executive.
	Proposed merger with and subsequent bid for the Imperial Group. Defeated by Hanson Trust bid.

Divisional Analysis

Division	Sales as % of total					RoS (%)			
	1979	1982	1985	1979–85 real growth in sales (% pa)		1979	1982	1985	1979–85 average
United Kingdom									
Biscuits	28	25	21	2.4		9.3	10.0	11.0	10.2
Foods	18	16	14	3.1		8.9	8.7	9.6	8.9
Frozen Foods	10	6	6	(2.3)		(1.1)	0.8	1.8	(0.1)
Crawfords	7	4	4	(4.3)		4.9	0.9	1.1	1.8
Other	3	8	8	24.7		7.7	5.5	7.4	7.3
United States									
Keebler	29	32	39	12.1		6.2	7.8	4.2	4.2
Other	2	6	5	25.3		14,0	6.0	10.8	12.8
Rest of world									
Other	3	3	3	7.1		2.0	2.5	3.1	5.2
Totals									
Sales (£m)	791	1,205	1,907	15.8	RoS	6.7	7.8	7.1	7.2
Sales (1985 £m)	1,320	1,403	1,907	5.4	RoCE	17.9	20.0	19.8	18.7

Geographical Analysis

% sales	1979	1982	1985
UK	66	60	54
North America	31	37	43
Rest of world	3	3	3

£m	1979	1982	1985
Net cash flow	(28)	(33)	6
Investment in fixed assets[a]	66	(31)	(3)

[a] Included in ncf.

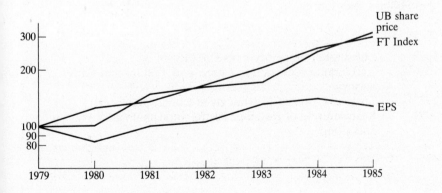

Strategic Control Companies

The Strategic Control companies are: Courtaulds, ICI, Imperial Group, Plessey, Vickers. They are described here in alphabetical order.

Courtaulds

Chairman and chief executive: Sir Christopher Hogg

	Sales (£m)	Profit before interest & tax (£m)	Net assets (£m)	Employees
1985/86 results	2,173	149	822	68,000

Activities

Fabrics: Production of apparel fabrics, domestic furnishings, technical and industrial fabrics, commission dyeing and printing.

Fibres: Production of Courtelle, viscose staple and acetate fibres. Manufacture of chemicals and plastics and carbon fibre. The production of dissolving woodpulp. Production of spun yarns.

Consumer Products: Manufacture of garments for men, women and children for sale as contract clothing and brand clothing.

International Paint: Worldwide production and sale of paints.

BCL: Production of Cellophane, polyethylene film and coextruded OPP (oriented polypropylene). Film printing, laminating and bag-making. Manufacture of dry-laid non-woven fabrics.

National Plastics: Manufacturers of closures, capsules, containers, mouldings and flooring.

Major Recent Events

1979	Christopher Hogg becomes chief executive.
1980–82	Accelerated reduction of capacity in Textiles and Fibres businesses.
1982	Current approach to strategic planning established.
1985	Restructuring of clothing, fabrics and spinning activities into one group.

Divisional Analysis

Division	Sales as % of total				RoCE			
	1979	1981	1986	1979–86 real growth in sales (% pa)	1979	1981	1986	1979–86 average
Fabrics	23	22	25	2.8	6	(2)	18	8.5
Fibres	41	36	35	(4.7)	8	0	27	15.7
Clothing	16	18	16	(2.1)	15	14	23	17.7
Paint	11	14	14	0.9	27	27	18	21.8
BCL	7	8	8	(0.8)	13	5	10	14.0
Nat Plastics	2	2	2	4.5	37	20	10	22.2
Totals								
Sales (£m)	1,662	1,710	2,173	3.9	RoCE	10.6	6.3	22	14.3
Sales (1986 £m)	2,713	2,294	2,173	(3.2)	RoS	5.5	2.3	6.9	5.5

Geographical Analysis

% sales	1979	1981	1986
United Kingdom	71	69	60
Europe	10	10	18
North America	9	10	12
Rest of world	10	11	10

£m	1980	1981	1986
Net cash flow	132	198	192
Investment in fixed assets[a]	78	64	74

[a] Included in ncf.

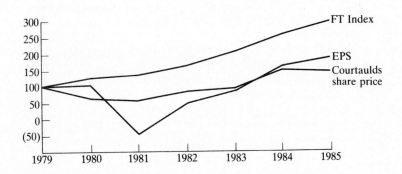

ICI

Chairman: Sir John Harvey-Jones (retired 1987)

	Sales (£m)	Profit before interest & tax (£m)	Net assets (£m)	Employees
1985/86 results	10,725	978	5,714	57,200

Activities

Petrochemicals and Plastics
Agriculture: The supply of fertilizers and agrochemicals.
General Chemicals
Oil: Oil production and exploration.
Organic and Speciality Chemicals
Pharmaceuticals
Fibres
Paint
Industrial Explosives

Major Recent Events

1982	Sir John Harvey-Jones becomes chairman.
1982–83	Rationalization in Fibres, Petrochemicals and Plastics divisions.
1983	Current strategic planning system established.
1985	Acquisition of speciality chemical interests from Beatrice Inc.
1986	Acquisition of Glidden Paints from Hanson Trust.
	ICI Chemicals and Polymers Group to be formed from Fertilizers, Fibres, Petrochemicals and Plastics, and Mond divisions.
1987	Sir John Harvey-Jones retires, and is replaced by D. H. Henderson

Divisional Analysis

Division	Sales as % of total					RoS (%)			
	1981	1983	1985	1981–85 real growth of sales (% pa)		1981	1983	1985	1981–85 average
Petrochemicals/plastics	23	25	24	7.3		(3.1)	0.0	3.3	(0.4)
Agriculture	17	16	17	6.1		14.6	11.5	9.1	11.7
General Chemicals	16	16	15	2.7		6.1	7.3	8.0	6.9
Oil	14	11	9	(4.6)		7.9	8.9	5.3	7.3
Organic/Speciality chemicals	8	9	11	17.1		(5.2)	1.2	4.4	(0.2)
Pharmaceuticals	5	7	8	16.1		22.1	31.2	29.0	28.0
Fibres	6	6	6	4.9		(8.1)	(1.2)	2.3	(1.8)
Paint	6	6	6	4.7		5.9	4.4	6.1	5.4
Industrial Explosives	3	3	3	3.4		13.6	8.6	9.1	10.9
Miscellaneous	2	1	2	4.1		0.0	4.5	0.0	2.1
Totals									
Sales (£m)	6,581	8,256	10,725	13.0	RoS	10.4	11.8	11.7	11.4
Sales (1985 £m)	8,325	9,193	10,725	6.5	RoCE	12.7	16.7	20.6	16.6

Geographical Analysis

% sales	1981	1983	1985
United Kingdom	56	53	48
The Americas	14	16	19
Europe	14	16	17
Other	16	15	16

£m	1981	1983	1985
Net cash flow	(200)	411	(368)
Investment in fixed assets[a]	414	(101)	99

[a] Included in ncf.

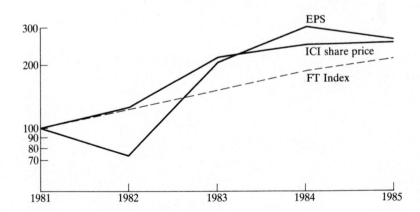

Imperial Group

Chairman and chief executive: Geoffrey Kent

	Sales (£m)	Profit before interest & tax (£m)	Net assets (£m)	Employees
1985/86 results	4,919	264	1,809	60,018

Activities

Tobacco

Brewing and Leisure: Courage Ltd, restaurants, retailing, hotels and catering.

Foods: Snacks, frozen foods, sauces and miscellaneous.

Major Recent Events

1980	Howard Johnson Inc. acquired for £280 million.
1981	Geoffrey Kent becomes chairman and chief executive.
1982	Current approach to strategic planning established. Divestitures of Poultry, Paper, Plastics, Eggs, Animal Feed and Meat Trading businesses.
1985	Howard Johnson sold for £219 million. Bid for United Biscuits launched. Hanson Trust bids for Imperial.
1986	United Biscuits bids for Imperial. Hanson Trust acquires Imperial.

Divisional Analysis

Division	Sales as % of total					RoS (%)			
	1980	1982	1985	1980–85 real growth of sales (% pa)		1980	1982	1985	1980–85 average
Imperial Tobacco Ltd	61	55	53	(1.3)		4.3	3.6	4.4	4.0
Imperial Brewing & Leisure	19	20	20	2.0		6.5	7.2	8.8	8.0
Imperial Foods Ltd	15	14	14	1.5		3.4	3.9	4.5	4.1
Howard Johnson Co.	3	10	12	32.3		10.7	3.9	2.1	4.8
Other activities	2	1	1	(19.9)		(10.3)	1.9	(1.1)	(1.3)
Totals									
Sales (£m)	3,215	4,098	4,919	8.9	RoS	4.4	5.0	5.4	4.8
Sales (1985 £m)	4,550	4,772	4,919	1.6	RoCE	10.4	17.3	13.8	15.5

Geographical Analysis

% sales	1980	1982	1985
United Kingdom	84	87	84
Europe	3	2	2
North America	12	10	13
Other	1	1	1

£m	1980	1982	1985
Net cash flow	(149)	33	(131)
Investment in fixed assets[a]	286	(101)	(43)

[a] Included in ncf.

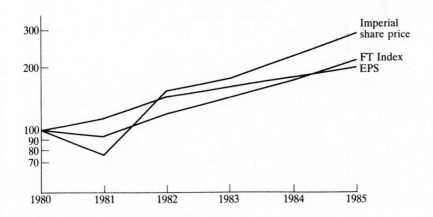

Plessey

Chairman: Sir John Clark
Chief executive: Sir James Blyth

	Sales (£m)	Profit before interest & tax (£m)	Net assets (£m)	Employees
1985 results	1,461	152.6	808	34,366

Activities

Telecommunications: System X, PABX, fibre optics.
Electronics Systems: Defence and other systems.
Aerospace and Engineering: Contractor to the aircraft industry; turbine generation systems.
Microelectronics and Components.
Computer Peripherals.

Major Recent Events

1978	Plessey Objectives Strategy and Tactics (POST) planning system introduced.
1979	24 per cent interest in ICL divested.
	Garrard Engineering Ltd divested.
1979–82	Various smaller divestments.
1982	Acquisition of Stromberg–Carlson Corp.
1985	Bid received from GEC: referred to MMC.
1986	MMC rule against GEC bid.

Divisional Analysis

Division	Sales as % of total				RoS (%)			
	1978	1982	1986	1978–86 real growth in sales (% pa)	1978	1982	1986	1978–86 average
Telecommunications	40	43	46	4.9	10.0	13.0	10.4	10.9
Electronic Systems & Equipment	26	29	34	6.7	7.8	7.9	7.8	7.7
Aerospace & Engineering	13	13	8	(3.9)	6.5	12.3	21.0	12.6
Microelectronics & Components	18	12	10	(5.4)	4.2	5.5	9.2	7.6
Computer Peripherals	3	3	2	(3.1)	(23.8)	(6.5)	0.6	(7.3)
Totals								
Sales (£m)	611	963	1,461	11.6	RoS 7.5	12.9	10.5	11.6
Sales (1986 £m)	1,214	1,177	1,461	2.3	RoCE 25.2	25.2	23.4	23.7

Geographical Analysis

% sales	1978	1982	1986
United Kingdom	47	61	71
North America	15	11	12
Europe	13	8	6
Africa	8	9	4
Other	17	11	7

£m	1981	1983	1986
Net cash flow	41	28	178
Investment in fixed assets[a]	27	44	16

[a] Included in ncf.

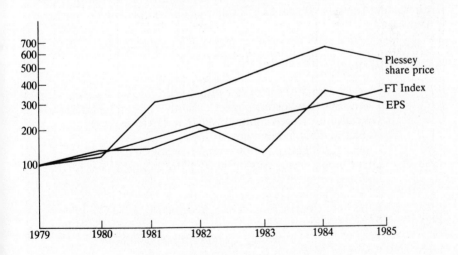

Vickers

Chairman and chief executive: Sir David Plastow

	Sales (£m)	Profit before interest & tax (£m)	Net assets (£m)	Employees
1985 results	611	50.3	276	15,800

Activities

Rolls–Royce Motors: Production and sale of Rolls–Royce cars.

Lithographic Plates and Supplies: Production and sale of lithographic printing plates and other supplies.

Defence and Aerospace: Manufacture of battle tanks and other military vehicles. Manufacture of components mainly for gas turbine engines.

Marine Engineering: Systems and electronic equipment, supplier of stablizers, steering gear, bearings, ships elevator systems, controllable pitch propellers.

Business Equipment: The production of office furniture.

Healthcare and Instruments: Design, development and manufacture of a wide range of advanced healthcare equipment such as incubators, pumps and microscopes.

Machine Tools: Manufacture and sale of machine tools.

Printing and Packaging Machinery: Manufacture of metal decorating equipment (now sold), paper printing machinery, packaging machinery (now sold).

Design and Projects: Work on various engineering projects.

Major Recent Events

1980	Merger with Rolls–Royce Motors Ltd. David Plastow becomes chief executive of combined group. Divestiture of International Machine Division of Roneo Vickers Office Equipment Group.
1981	Current strategic planning system established.
1983–85	Divestments of various businesses, including Diesel Engine Division, majority interest in Vickers Australia, Vickers South Africa, Vickers Dawson.
1983	Sofec Inc. (marine engineering) acquired for $3.2 million.
1985	Conforto Gmbh (office furniture) acquired for £15 million. Teca Corp. (healthcare) acquired for £11 million.
1986	Acquired Royal Ordnance Factory, Leeds. Acquired Airshields.

Divisional Analysis

Division	Sales as % of total				RoS (%)			
	80	*82*	*85*	1980–85 real growth in sales (% pa)	*80*	*82*	*85*	1980–85 average
Motor Cars	21	19	29	–	6.8	4.9	9.8	7.2
Lithographic Plates	11	12	19	4.5%	13.4	7.5	9.7	10.3
Business Equipment and Supplies	11	9	14	(0.8)%	2.2	5.3	7.3	4.4
Defence and Aerospace	11	8	11	(4.3)%	13.7	9.8	8.9	10.5
Marine Engineering	4	7	12	17.0%	8.3	7.7	6.4	8.1
Medical and Scientific Equipment	4	4	6	2.8%	2.3	3.8	11.6	6.4

Totals								
Sales (£m)	597	656	611	0.4	RoS	6.7	5.4	8.2	6.6
Sales (1985 £m)	842	760	611	(4.5)	RoCE	16.0	11.4	18.0	14.0

Geographical Analysis

% sales	1985
United Kingdom	33
North America	29
Europe	21
Rest of world	17

£m	1980	1982	1985
Net cash flow	(18)	(24)	20
Investment in fixed assets	(34)	1	(43)

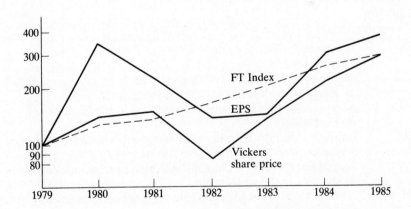

Financial Control Companies

The Financial Control companies are: BTR, Ferranti, General Electric Company, Hanson Trust, Tarmac. They are described here in alphabetical order.

BTR

Chairman: Sir Owen Green

	Sales (£m)	Profit before interest & tax (£m)	Net assets (£m)	Employees
1986 results	4,109	505	1,957	79,400

Activities

Construction: Manufacturer for and distributor to the construction industry.

Energy and Electrical: Electrical distribution; production of values, pipes and fittings, control systems, electronic point of sale equipment.

Industrial: A wide range of engineering products and projects.

Consumer Related Activities: Transportation, healthcare, paper, printing, sports and leisure.

Major Recent Events

1980	Acquired Huyck Corporation, manufacturers of drying equipment used in the paper-making process.
1981	Acquired the Serck Group, specialist engineers manufacturing valves, heat exchange equipment and water treatment plant.
1983	Acquired the Thomas Tilling Group including companies such as Tilcon, Cornhill Insurance and Pretty Polly.
1984	Acquired Nylex Corporate in Australia, manufacturers of plastic product.
1985	Acquired Dunlop Holdings, a diversified tyre and consumer products group.
	Sold Heinemann to Octopus Publishing in exchange for a 35 per cent stake in Octopus.
	Sold Dunlop Tire Corp (US) through a management buy-out.
	Sold Cornhill Insurance.
1986	Bid for Pilkingtons.

Divisional Analysis

Division	Sales as % of total				RoS (%)			
	1979	1982	1986	1979–86 real growth in sales (% pa)	1979	1982	1986	1979–86 average
Construction	N/A	1	22	N/A	N/A	10.7	11.5	N/A
Energy and Electrical	N/A	21	21	N/A	N/A	16.9	8.9	N/A
Industrial	N/A	34	19	N/A	N/A	13.2	14.9	N/A
Consumer Related	N/A	44	38	N/A	N/A	19.9	15.4	N/A
Totals								
Sales (£m)	433	725	4019	54	RoS 14.6	17.7	12.6	13.8
Sales (1986 £m)	682	796	4019	45	RoCE 30.2	24.1	25.5	23.8

Geographical Analysis

% sales	1979	1982	1986
European	66	55	60
Western	14	20	27
Eastern	20	25	13

£m	1980	1982	1986
Net cash flow	(100)	(13)	159
Investment in fixed assets[a]	50	55	34

[a] Included in ncf.

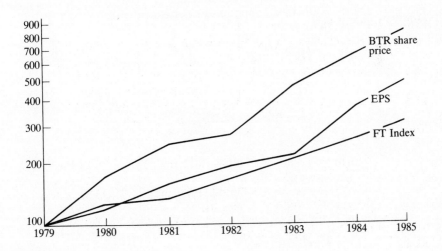

Ferranti

Chairman: B. Z. Ferranti
Chief Executive: J. D. Alun-Jones

	Sales (£m)	Profit before interest & tax (£m)	Net assets (£m)	Employees
1986 results	596	47.6	193	21,420

Activities

Computer Systems: Computers and data handling systems for civil and defence applications.
Defence Systems: Radar, navigation and display systems, electro-optics, product support.
Instrumentation: Specialized items for military and civil use combining electronic and mechanical techniques.
Electronics: Manufacture of semi-conductor products.
Ferranti GTE: PABX equipment.
Industrial Electronics: Commercial systems and precision components.

Major Recent Events

1974	Government rescue of Ferranti.
1975	Derek Alun-Jones appointed chief executive.
1978	Public share issue.
1980	ULA business began to grow rapidly.
1984	Acquired TRW Controls.

Divisional Analysis

Division	Sales as % of total					RoS (%)			
	1979	1982	1986	1979–86 real growth in sales (% pa)		1979	1982	1986	1979–86 average
Computer Systems	32	33	37	11.9		7.4	7.7	7.9	7.8
Scottish	38	40	50	14.3		9.2	10.5	8.	9.4
Instrumentation	7	7	9	14.1		5.1	5.8	5.5	6.5
Electronics	8	10	11	17.4		7.3	12.8	5.3	9.9
Engineering	9	3	–	N/A		(6.9)	23.2	–	N/A
Other	6	7	–	N/A		4.5	(5.8)	–	N/A
Totals									
Sales (£m)	192	307	596	17.7	RoS	6.8	8.3	8.0	8.3
Sales (1986 £m)	327	319	596	8.5	RoCE	16.0	19.1	22.9	20.0

Geographical Analysis

% sales	1979	1982	1986
United Kingdom	60	67	65
Europe	13	18	16
USA & Canada	15	6	10
Rest of world	12	9	9

£m	1980	1982	1986
Net cash flow	8	2	(2)
Investment in fixed assets[a]	11	18	37

[a] Included in ncf.

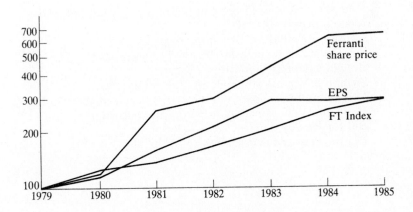

The General Electric Company

Chairman: Rt Hon James Prior
Managing director: Lord Weinstock

	Sales (£m)	Profit before interest & tax (£m)	Net assets (£m)	Employees
1986 results	5,253	714	3,400	164,536

Activities

Electronic Systems
Telecommunications and Business Systems
Automation and Control
Medical Equipment
Power Generation
Electrical Equipment
Consumer Products
Distribution and Trading

Major Recent Events

1979	Acquired Averys Ltd, manufacturer of weighing machines.
1981	Acquired Picker International, manufacturer of medical diagnostic imaging equipment.
1982	Sold Morphy Richard Ltd, manufacturer of consumer electrical products.
1983	Sold investment in Fisher Controls International Inc. and related investments.
1984	Considered a bid for British Aerospaces plc.
	Sold 50 per cent share in Hitachi Television Ltd.
1985	Bought £156.5 million of own shares.
	Acquired Yarrow Shipbuilders Ltd in Glasgow.
	Made an offer to acquire a minority interest in Westland Helicopters plc as part of a European consortium.
	Bid for Plessey plc.
1986	Bid for Plessey ruled against by MMC.

Divisional Analysis

Division	Sales as % of total 1986	RoS (%) 1986
Electronic Systems	34.7	10.4
Electrical Equipment	13.7	5.6
Telecom and Business	14.0	10.9
Power Generation	11.9	9.0
Medical Equipment	7.5	5.3
Automation and Control	8.5	10.4
Consumer Products	5.9	10.1
Distribution and Trading	3.8	6.3

	1979	1982	1986	1979–86 Growth (%pa) Average (%)	
Total sales (£m)	2,501	4,190	5,253	11.4	
Total sales (1985 £m)	4,383	5,120	5,253	2.7	
RoCE (%)	24	22	22		22.4
RoS (%)	15.1	13.9	13.6		14.2

Geographical Analysis

% sales	1979	1982	1986
United Kingdom	53	47	52.7
Europe	12	11	10.2
The Americas	7	19	16.8
Australasia	20	17	16.7
Africa	8	6	3.6

£m	1980	1982	1986
Net cash flow	(136)	406	635
Investment in fixed assets[a]	203	(282)	190

[a] Included in ncf.

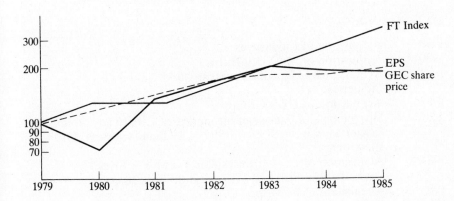

Hanson Trust

Chairmen: Lord Hanson (Hanson Trust plc)
 Sir Gordon White (Hanson Industries Inc.)

	Sales (£m)	Profit before interest & tax (£m)	Net assets (£m)	Employees
1985 results	2,674.5	252.8	1,946	29,000

Activities

Allders: Department stores, duty free shops, retailing.
British EverReady: Dry cell batteries.
Hanson Brick: Fletton bricks, non-fletton bricks.
Lindustries: Electrical, automative and gas products, yarns and threads.
Hanson Engineering: Engineering, machine tools, control systems and construction equipment services.
Carisbrook: Speciality fabrics and textile finishing machinery, yarns, soft furnishings and apparel.
Consumer Products: Footwear, housewares and artifical flowers.
Food Products: Meat processing.
Furniture and Furnishings: Office and home furniture and furnishings, kitchen cabinets, vanities, fasteners.
Hanson Building Products: Garden and industrial hand tools, wood mouldings, windows, building material and lumber.
USI Industrial: Manufacturing, energy equipment and engineering products and services.
USI Lighting: Lighting fixtures and fittings and control systems.

Major Recent Events

1979	Acquisition of Lindustries.
1980	Acquisition of McDonough Inc.
1982	Acquisitions of British EverReady and United Gas Industries.
1983	Acquisition of UDS Group. Divestments of European businesses of EverReady, John Collier Menswear, Richard Shops, William Timpson, Orbit Electronics.
1984	Acquisition of US Industries (Inc.), London Brick. Divestment of Seacoast (US), and other businesses.
1985	Acquisition of SCM Inc.
1986	Acquisition of Imperial Group. Disposal of Glidden Paints, Courage, Golden Wonder.

Divisional Analysis

Division	Sales as % of total				RoS (%)			
	1979	1982	1985	1979–85 real growth in sales (% pa)	1979	1982	1985	1979–85 average
United Kingdom								
Allders	–	–	17	N/A	–	–	6.4	N/A
British EverReady	–	14	5	N/A	–	8.6	24.1	N/A
Hanson Brick	4	2	7	30.1	21.5	20.8	28.2	22.2
Lindustries	9	7	6	10.0	6.8	9.6	13.9	10.1
Hanson Engineering	5	10	5	14.1	11.3	6.1	9.3	7.8
United States								
Carisbrook	11	11	7	6.8	6.8	9.9	8.1	8.7
Consumer Products	–	15	10	N/A	–	9.5	8.2	N/A
Food Products and Services	71	37	18	(8.3)	3.5	2.8	3.0	3.2
Furniture and Furnishings	–	–	5	N/A	–	–	11.6	N/A
Hanson Building Products	–	4	8	N/A	–	15.3	12.9	N/A
USI Industrial	–	–	6	N/A	–	–	10.7	N/A
USI Lighting	–	–	6	N/A	–	–	12.1	N/A
Totals								
Sales (£m)	658	1.148	2.674	26.3 RoS	6.1	9.5	13.9	9.4
Sales (1985 £m)	1.108	1.349	2.674	15.8 RoCE	22.0	19.4	15.8	18.5

Geographical Analysis

% sales	1979	1982	1985
United Kingdom	17.9	33.3	40.1
United States	82.1	66.7	59.9

£m	1980	1982	1985
Net cash flow	(1)	(125)	(143)
Investment in fixed assets[a]	15	86	194

[a] Included in ncf.

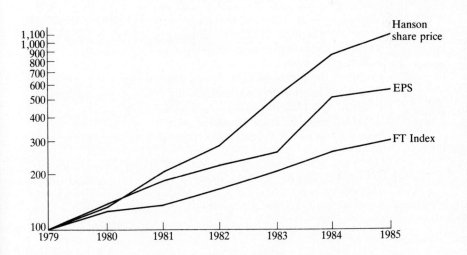

Tarmac

Chairman: Sir Eric Pountain

	Sales (£m)	Profit before interest & tax (£m)	Net assets (£m)	Employees
1985 results	1,536	156.7	597	25,748

Activities

Quarry Products: Stone, sand and gravel, concrete, asphalt, bricks and tiles.

Building and Industrial Products: Manufacture and installation of building materials, bitumen refining.

Construction: Construction, design and management for all forms of building work, civil engineering and gas and oil engineering.

Housing

Properties: Development of commercial and industrial property.

Major Recent Events

1979	Sir Eric Pountain became chief executive. Disposed of Cubitts International, including Cubitts Nigeria and the group's asphalt plants in Germany.
1980	Acquired the Concrete Products Co. of Tampa in the United States.
1981	Acquired the Hoveringham Group, started acquiring small quarrying companies and small building products companies.
1982	Acquired oil and gas interests of Candecca Resources, including Plascom Ltd.
1983–84	Acquired the assets of Lone Star Industries Inc. Continued small quarrying and building products acquisitions.
1985	Sold stake in Plascom Ltd.
1986	Acquired Ellis Transportation. Acquired 60 per cent holding in Tarmac Lonestar Inc.

Divisional Analysis

Division	Sales as % of total					RoS (%)			
	1979	1982	1985	1979–85 real growth of sales (% pa)		1979	1982	1985	1979–85 average
Quarry	30	35	38	7		9.1	11.3	14.3	11.5
Building	15	19	14	2.2		9.9	6.8	7.3	7.4
Construction	35	23	23	−2		0.4	2.8	2.6	2.2
Housing	10	14	19	14.4		11.5	7.6	11.5	9.8
Properties	1	2	2	10.7		23.3	8.9	11.4	15.8
Oil/Industrial	1	2	4	29.5		20.8	18.2	17.4	19.3
International	8	5	–	N/A		1.8	5.3	–	N/A
TOTALS									
Sales (£m)	788	989	1,536	11.8	RoS	5.4	7.4	10.2	7.5
Sales (1985 £m)	1,229	1,132	1,536	3.9	RoCE	21.1	23.5	26.3	23.0

£m	1979	1982	1985
Net cash flow	2	14	96
Investment in fixed assets[a]	13	(8)	61

[a] Included in ncf.

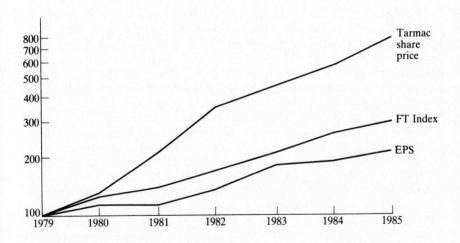

Appendix 2 Strategic Planning System Design

This appendix draws together and amplifies points made about the design of the strategic planning system throughout this book. It is intended to be of use to managers who are critically reviewing their current strategic planning processes. We believe that a poorly designed planning system can damage the quality of strategic decisions that get taken. However, a well-designed system is no guarantee of good strategies; this depends much more on how the system is used and on the quality of the general managers using it. We therefore regard the design of the strategic planning process as an important, but by no means the only, contributor to good strategy.

Purpose

A company's strategic planning system (SPS) can serve a variety of functions. At a minimum it should be designed to allow corporate, divisional and business management to identify and discuss strategy options, and it should create processes for arriving at decisions on them. To this end, it should bring together information and analysis which is relevant to the formulation of options and the choice between them, and it should build consensus around the chosen way forward.

In addition, an effective SPS provides a check on the quality of business-level thinking and a challenge to prevailing assumptions and strategy patterns. It can surface new views and ideas from a variety of sources in the company, and allow central themes, thrusts and suggestions to be put forward. It should also establish a framework within which differences of opinion can be argued through to a shared conclusion. The SPS can therefore play a role in coordinating thinking and actions of managers throughout the company.

The debate on strategy in the SPS can also have an educational role for managers. By exposing weaknesses in thinking and setting standards, it can deepen understanding of both the business and the strategy formulation process.

Lastly, the SPS can help in defining strategic control measures, and in determining how strategies should be implemented. Detailed objective-setting and the establishment of action programmes and strategic milestones should be the final stage of the strategic planning process.

This range and variety of purposes means that different companies will emphasize different aspects of the SPS. For example, Strategic Planning companies place considerable emphasis on their SPS, and view them as important means for influencing business strategy development. Strategic Control companies are also committed to their SPS, but are more concerned with the quality control aspects of the process than with making their own substantial contributions to business thinking. Financial Control companies tend not to operate a formal SPS, preferring to work through the capital appropriation system, the budgetary process, or informally.

In discussing the design of the SPS we will not therefore attempt to put forward a single 'right' detailed model,[1] but will try to get at the underlying factors that make for successful use of the SPS.

Design of Formal SPS

1   Guidelines/Formats

The process should be initiated with a set of guidelines to business units from corporate management. These should cover:

— formats to use, definitions of terms, accounting conventions, etc.;
— background economic and other assumptions;
— timetables, meetings, etc.;
— any issues that corporate management particularly wish to see addressed.

Standard formats and definitions ensure that each business unit's plans are drawn up in comparable form, and that specified headings are covered, ratios calculated and so forth. Elaborate formats and ratios cannot create good information, analysis and thinking, but they can direct attention to relevant matters and make the plans more easily digestible by corporate management.

There is no value to length and detail in plans *per se*. The more the planning exercise becomes an elaborate form-filling, paper-generating system, the less useful it is. If formats are specified, they should be flexible enough to allow the plan documents to be no longer than is necessary to get the relevant information on the table.

Background economic assumptions prevent duplication of efforts with, for example, each business attempting to make its own exchange rate forecasts. They also make it easier to compare results from different businesses since they will at least have built in the same background assumptions.

Timetables, meetings and other administrative details are needed to provide the framework for the work. Although there needs to be some agreed schedule for the process, rigidity and inflexibility should again be avoided as far as possible.

Guidelines that identify particular strategic issues allow corporate management to focus the work on matters that they see as most deserving of attention. These may have come out of previous planning rounds, budget discussions, industry developments or a wide variety of other sources.

2   Information and Analysis

Planning formats and guidelines can to some extent identify the nature and depth of information and analysis that corporate management wish to see. However, these formats and guidelines will inevitably allow some latitude of interpretation. Therefore the sort of questioning and probing that the centre pursues is an essential further determinant of expectations concerning information and analysis. A very common complaint of corporate management is that plans lack good information on external developments: markets, technologies and – particularly – competitors. Since the most effective way to remedy this defect is through corporate questioning in the review process, central management must share the blame for shortcomings of this kind.

There is no general answer to the question of how much information and analysis should be provided. The test is not the quantity of work done nor the amount of paper generated, but the value that is added. New insights may emerge from a few key pieces of information; or they may require very thorough analysis to get past the traditionally accepted conventional wisdoms. A sense that the strategy is not firmly based on a good understanding of the market, the technology, the competition, and the key success factors in the business signals the need for further information-gathering and analysis. Unfortunately, a lack of such a sense does not guarantee that no fresh insights would be derived from digging more deeply.

The quality of information and analysis suffers if business management filter or hold back information to prevent the centre getting too close to their businesses, in order to control corporate perceptions of how their businesses are doing. This practice prevents proper corporate understanding of the businesses, and needs resisting. One of Geoffrey Kent's early initiatives at Imperial was to institute an on-line Chief Executive Information System, which made available to a selected group of senior corporate managers information that had previously been jealously guarded at the divisional level. Prior to this, corporate management had simply not been aware of key trends and results, and had therefore lacked a basis for intervening strategically. Corporate management should insist on their right to have access to detailed, unprocessed information about each business, even if they do not normally delve into the details. It must be possible for them to peel back enough layers of the information onion to satisfy themselves on important or contentious points.

Mutual respect and common purpose prevent filtering of information from occurring.

3 Cycle

The design of the formal SPS cycle concerns:

— the number of steps in the process (e.g. strategy plan – development plan – operating plan is a three-step process);
— the frequency with which the cycle is carried out (e.g. annually, every 2 years, irregularly);
— the selectivity of focus on particular businesses.

Chapters 4 and 5 discussed and illustrated the cycle in several Strategic Planning and Strategic Control companies.

The number and nature of formal steps in the process is less material than the willingness and ability of corporate management to devote time to thinking through, with the businesses, the strategic issues. Lex and BOC have both been dismantling their formal planning structures in recent years, in the belief that formal timetables, reports and meetings can get in the way of strategic thinking. On the other hand, a formal process that clearly does not allow enough time or iterations to cover both strategy and tactics will tend to crowd strategy discussion out. For example, several companies feel that it is best to initiate the discussion of strategy on a qualitative basis only. This prevents getting tied up with numerical forecasts too early and stops the numbers crowding out the discussion of strategic issues. Plessey's more recent revisions to its planning system to separate the strategy, the medium-term forecasts and the budget reviews are an attempt to address this problem.

Several participant companies have encountered difficulty in finding time for corporate management to delve deeply enough into the strategies of each business on an annual basis. Indeed, an annual review cycle in diverse, multibusiness companies can force corporate management to give no more than superficial attention to each business. Accordingly BP, ICI and Lex have moved to 2-year cycles for strategy reviews; Cadbury Schweppes has introduced a degree of selective focus into their process by specifying three different levels of effort for business plans and deciding each year on which businesses to concentrate; and BOC have moved away altogether from formal, annual reviews of strategy.

Some companies therefore now rely much more on one-off, ad hoc efforts than on regular formal processes for addressing major issues. BOC's Intensive Strategy Reviews (ISRs) have been mentioned earlier; Cadbury Schweppe's redirection of strategy towards major, international brands in the core confectionery and drinks businesses arose from a similar, task-force-based intensive effort; and Courtaulds and Vickers have made much use of outside consultants to focus concentrated effort on to particular businesses.

4 Meetings

The timetable for meetings should be established, to allow for full discussions of strategy, as outlined above. In addition, it is important that the atmosphere of these meetings be constructive.

The SPS can also provide an excellent communication and commitment building vehicle for the organization at large; but is seldom used for this purpose. Involving a broad cross-section of managers in meetings to review presentations of strategy can play a useful role in building consensus around new strategies. The constitutional forum provided by these meetings allows lower levels of management to question emerging strategies, to put forward their points of view, and to satisfy themselves that senior management have thought through thoroughly the proposals they are putting forward. Few companies invest the time needed to make such meetings a success; those that do derive benefits in communicating new directions, and getting commitment to implementation.

Exclusive reliance on formal meetings is, however, insufficient both for the formulation and the communication of strategy. We shall return to this topic below.

5 Decisions

The formal SPS provides a visible due process whereby important decisions get discussed and taken. This can 'legitimize' hard decisions. It can also be valuable to have an unambiguous decision process, since otherwise there can be confusion about what has been decided.

6 Evolution

Routine is the enemy of good thinking and planning. A changeless annual cycle can be stultifying. Therefore some companies try consciously to modify the formats, timetables and meeting structures in their SPS year by year. This helps to preserve more freshness and interest in the process.

No formal SPS changes, however, can guarantee a good strategic decision-making process. At bottom, it must be recognized that, to get behind and challenge existing strategy patterns, or to perceive ways in which overlaps between businesses can be productively managed, typically requires the commitment of more senior corporate time and effort than many companies allow for the strategy review process; and, conversely, more superficial questioning across a large number of unconnected businesses in a standard annual planning review adds little value. It is the willingness to cross this threshold of effort rather than the formal design of the SPS that is the fundamental requirement.

Informal and Formal Systems

Formal and informal processes should complement each other. The formal SPS ensures due process, a structured information flow, the need to meet, discuss and decide together on strategic issues. But an exclusively formal process is not sufficient.

Casual, off-the-record meetings and discussions allow more open communication and give a 'feel' for what is going on in a business that by no means always emerges from formal documents. Often the only way to get behind the façade of the formal flows, and to isolate those areas that deserve real corporate focus, is therefore through informal channels. Furthermore, informal contacts allow earlier discussion of issues, before particular points of view have received 'sponsorship' within business management. They often allow a more open discussion of these issues, in the absence of the need to express views formally and publicly. And informal contacts can be pursued as frequently and extensively as needed, irrespective of the formal timetable for the SPS. This is the basis for the management by walking around (MBWA) theory of management that a number of CEOs such as Sir Hector Laing of UB regard as invaluable.

In building consensus for action, informal contacts and discussions are essential. In addition to providing clarification of individual requirements to implement the strategy, they allow fears concerning the personal repercussions of new strategies to be aired and resolved in ways that no formal process can achieve. Changes in strategy are seldom painless; but the pains can be eased by good informal communication about their implications, and by setting to rest the groundless concerns that often arise.

Ideally, therefore, formal due process works side by side with a more flexible communication system. Indeed, some companies, such as Vickers, feel that the existence of formal processes fosters the development of informal contacts. If business management know they must report and plan formally, they become more willing to enter into informal preliminary dialogue to ensure that their case receives the best possible hearing in due course.

Notes

1 Many writers have put forward suggestions concerning how to set up the strategic planning process. In *Corporate Planning: an Executive Viewpoint* (Prentice-Hall, 1980), Peter Lorange summarizes many of these views and proposes his own approach, which involves five stages, three organizational levels and 23 steps. Although such suggestions can be useful points of departure, we believe that the SPS needs to be tailored to the needs of each individual company, and that detailed design proposals are unlikely to be appropriate for all situations.

Appendix 3   The Strategic Change Process

Here we review the ways in which some leading authors have conceptualized the process of strategy change. Our purpose is to define the main steps or phases in the change process, in order to provide a framework within which to discuss the contribution to managing change made by the corporate centre.

One of the fullest recent accounts of the change process in organizations is given by James Brian Quinn in his book *Strategies for Change*.[1] Quinn carried out research with nine large companies in the United States and Europe, with the intention of understanding better how change was managed. Although the scope of his work included the corporate centre, his main focus was at the business level. Quinn's basic conclusion was that strategy changes occur 'incrementally'; that is to say, they consist of a series of individually small adjustments in direction, which are the result of the many varied forces operating in large companies. Major, one-time shifts in direction are hard to accomplish and seldom successful. The best course is to try to guide the incremental steps in accordance with some rational conception of how to move the business forward. Quinn calls this 'logical incrementalism'.

In his discussion of how logical incrementalism works Quinn distinguishes 14 'typical process steps'. Figure A3.1 (drawn from Quinn's book) illustrates these steps – 'highly simplified to help visualize a few basic relationships' as Quinn puts it. The variety of steps, the multiple feedbacks, the proliferation of tactical moves are indeed all part of what it takes to create change in the complex and political world of today's large companies. And Quinn is right to assert that his conceptualization is a simplification of reality, since each step could be broken down into further substeps and since the broadly sequential progress he assumes is often replaced by parallel activities on several steps simultaneously.

Even so, for our purposes, Quinn's account is too elaborate. We are more interested in the major phases of the change process than in a full representation of all the tactical steps involved. Any model should be

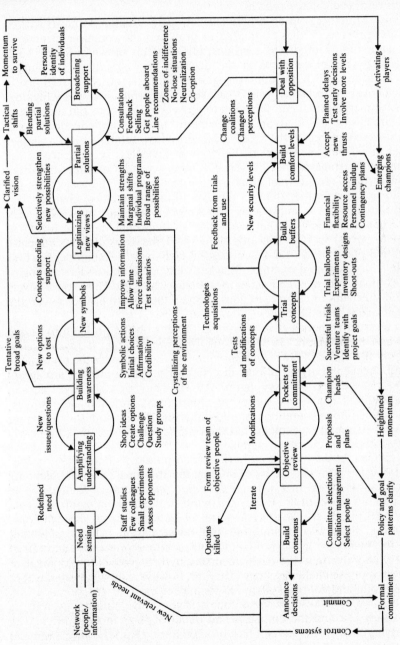

Figure A3.1 Some typical process steps in strategic decision-making.

Reprinted with permission from James Brian Quinn, *Strategies for Change: Logical Incrementalism,* © Richard D. Irwin Inc. 1980.

consistent with Quinn's, but should attempt to get more at the underlying structure of the change process.

Henry Mintzberg, in an article entitled 'The structure of unstructured decision processes',[2] has attempted to draw out the common 'structural' characteristics of important decisions. His model is shown in figure A3.2. Mintzberg groups the steps in the decision process into three phases: identification (which includes recognition and diagnosis), development (which covers search and design), and selection (which involves screening, evaluation and formal authorization to proceed). He points out that not all steps are always included, and that there are often multiple feedbacks and iterations to complicate the process. Nevertheless, Mintzberg's is a simpler model than Quinn's. However, his account gives less prominence to the crucial initial stage of 'need sensing' (Quinn's words) and the important follow through after formal authorization to proceed. The focus is on the decision process, rather than on the overall management of change.

Andrew Pettigrew, in his book *The Awakening Giant*,[3] provides a very full account of some of the changes in strategy that have occurred (or failed to occur) in ICI. Towards the end of the book he also adopts a simplified phase model for describing these changes.[4] The model has four phases – development of concern, acknowledgment and understanding of the problem, planning and acting, stabilizing changes. This model covers the full spectrum of change, as does Quinn's; but it emphasizes fewer and more broadly defined steps.

An alternative perspective is brought to bear on the problem by Irving Janis and Leon Mann.[5] In their book *Decision-Making: a Psychological Analysis of Conflict, Choice and Commitment* they consider the psychology behind changes in organizational direction. They, too, provide a diagram of the change process (see figure A3.3). They describe five steps – appraising the challenge, surveying alternatives, weighing alternatives, deliberating about commitment, and adhering. Their model is tied more closely into human psychology, but their phases of decision-making clearly relate to those in the other models.

Peter Lorange, a leading authority on corporate planning, approaches the management of change by examining the structure of formal planning and control systems. In *Corporate Planning: an Executive Viewpoint*[6] he talks about a model of the five cycles in the strategic planning process (see figure A3.4). These five cycles are objective-setting, strategic programming, budgeting, monitoring and rewarding. It is noticeable that these five cycles are less rich than Quinn's more comprehensive account of change, and also miss the early need sensing/recognition/development of concern/appraise challenge steps. They do, however, show how and where the planning and control system has its impact.

There is a parallelism in the accounts of these five authors, even if the words they use and the emphasis and detail of their models differ. The underlying themes are perhaps best brought out by Kurk Lewin. Writing in the 1950s,[7] he identified three fundamental steps in the change process: unfreeze – change – refreeze. This simple conception gets at the need to

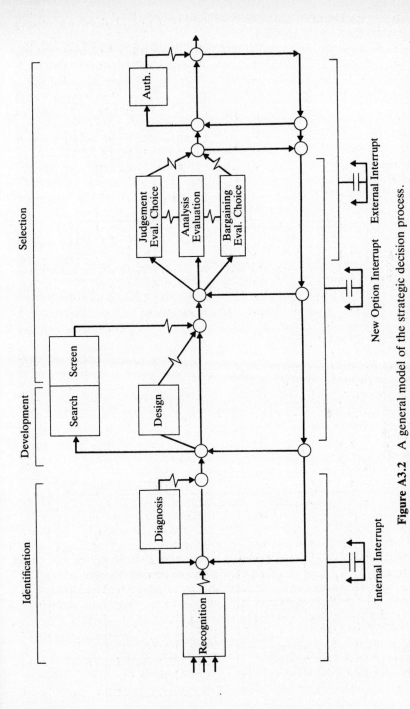

Figure A3.2 A general model of the strategic decision process.

Reprinted from 'The Structure of "Unstructured" Decision Processes' by Henry Mintzberg et al., published in *Administrative Science Quarterly* vol 21, no. 2 (June 1976), by permission of *Administrative Science Quarterly*.

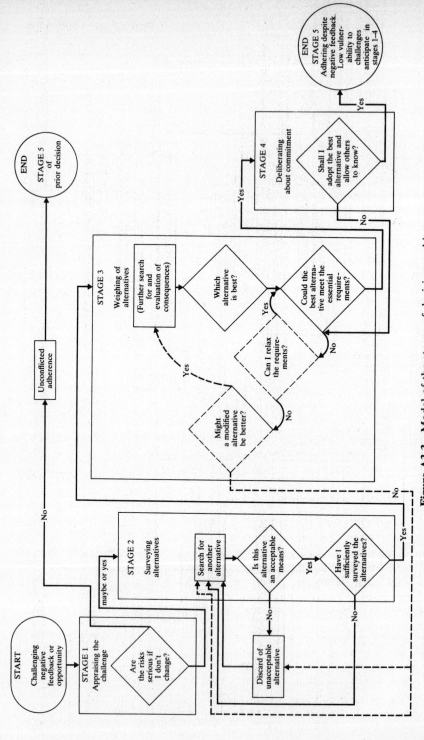

Figure A3.3 Model of the stages of decision-making.

Reprinted with permission of The Free Press, a Division of Macmillan, Inc., from *Decision Making: A Psychological Analysis of Conflict, Choice and Commitment* by Irving L. Janis and Leon Mann. Copyright © 1977 by The Free Press.

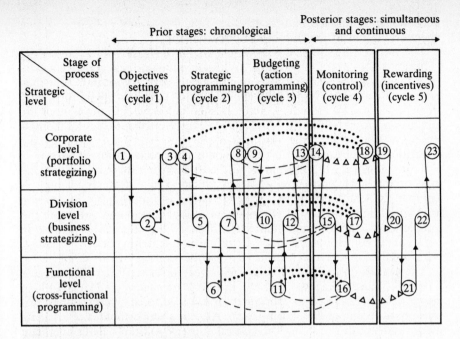

The basic information/communication flow: solid line
The tracking of actual vs planned performance: broken line
The corrective actions and modifications of plans: dotted line
The comparison of actual vs planned performance for incentives: triangle line

Figure A3.4 Conceptual model of the steps in the information flow of the strategic planning process.

Reprinted with permission from Peter Lorange, *Corporate Planning: An executive viewpoint*, © 1980, p. 55, Prentice-Hall, Inc., Englewood Cliffs, New Jersey.

break out of existing strategy patterns, to find a new and preferable strategy, and then to lock on to the new strategy. We like the term 'unfreeze' to describe the first step, but prefer 'search' to bring out the active nature of managed change in the second step, and 'consolidate' to stress the need for consensus building in the third step.

We have tried to draw these various change models together in figure 11.2, and to show the approximate relationships between the phases or steps that each describes. It can be seen, for example, that unfreezing describes a similar step to need sensing (Quinn), recognition (Mintzberg), development of concern (Pettigrew) and appraisal of challenge (Janis and Mann).

Our unfreeze – search – consolidate model shows exensive overlaps between steps. Unfreezing is necessary to begin the process, but must be rolled out to different levels and different individuals as a wider and wider consensus is built around the need for a new strategy. The search phase proceeds through different levels of detail, with the need to begin to consolidate around a broad conception of the new strategy often preceding the working out of the full implementation plan.

The value of the simple three-phase model is that it gets at fundamentally different stages in creating change. Without initial unfreezing, there will be no change. In the search phase many activities are appropriate, but they should all contribute to defining and evaluating new strategy options. And change will not be effectively accomplished unless people throughout the organization can be motivated to buy into and consolidate behind the new strategy. We believe that this is a useful framework for assessing the contribution to change of different people and processes in a company.

To demonstrate the usefulness of this framework we can consider the role of the strategic planning system in supporting strategic change. A company's 3- or 5-year plan is usually viewed as a mechanism for 'raising managers' sights', a way of getting them to look ahead and anticipate the problems or opportunities that may arise. By looking at the process in terms of the contribution it makes to unfreezing, searching or consolidating, we can develop a clearer picture of what the strategy plan is doing.

The planning process can help a manager unfreeze. Where the process involves 'multiple views', where business managers and function or geographic heads need to coordinate, it can lead to changed thinking and open questioning of the existing logic. Also, realistic estimates of financial performance can show that the current strategy will not deliver adequate results.

In many planning systems, however, the business manager produces an optimistic financial forecast, showing the normal 'hockey stick' perform-ance profile. He then strings some words together around the existing strategic logic. His boss probes some of the numbers and discusses imponderables like exchange rates; but he does not make any serious challenge to the strategy. In these circumstances the process contributes little to the unfreezing step.

The second stage is the search process. Planning systems are expected to provide a vehicle for developing new, more exciting, more profitable strategies. But if a major search for a better approach is to occur, it must be recognized that the process cannot be completed in the run-up to the annual strategy review. It is an activity that may take months or years and may need continued support from the centre.

In many companies the search for new strategies goes on informally, outside the planning process. In fact the formal process often gets in the way of the search, because managers are asked to complete a plan before they have completed the search. Moreover, the time frame for most annual planning cycles makes any real effort to search for a new logic unrealistic.

In some companies the unfreeze and search activity is enhanced by launching special reviews of particular businesses. These may be supported by outside consultants or they may be part of the periodic planning system. But their objective is to ensure that sufficient time is devoted to unfreezing the management team and searching for an alternative. In most companies, however, the formal strategic planning system provides little support to the unfreezing or search stages. Its major role is to help the consolidation stage. In a sense this is reasonable: planning is usually an annual activity and most businesses only need to change their basic strategy every 5 or 10 years.

Where the strategy of the business is basically sound, the focus should be on implementation and tactics. A 3- to 5-year plan is helpful in anticipating events before they arrive. It is also helpful in reinforcing the strategy in the minds of the management team and ensuring that their action programmes are focused on the important things rather than the urgent.

The strategic planning system is not, therefore, the solution to all of a company's planning problems. In fact it may get in the way of efforts to deal with the most urgent and critical problems. Managers need to recognize its limitations and develop additional mechanisms for tackling the locked-in management team and the failing strategy.

By reviewing the impact of the strategic planning system in terms of the unfreeze–search–consolidate steps, we have been able to expose both how it can contribute to strategy change, and how it may fail to do so. This is helpful in considering how the strategic planning system should be designed and operated (see appendix 2).

Notes

1 James Brian Quinn, *Strategies for Change* (Richard D. Irwin, 1980)
2 Henry Mintzberg, Duru Raisinghani and Andre Theoret, 'The structure of unstructured decision processes', *The Administrative Science Quarterly*, 21 (June 1976), 246–75.
3 Andrew Pettigrew, *The Awakening Giant* (Basil Blackwell, 1985).
4 Ibid., p. 473.
5 Irving L. Janis and Leon Mann, *Decision Making* (The Free Press, 1977).
6 Peter Lorange, *Corporate Planning: an Executive Viewpoint* (Prentice-Hall, 1980).
7 Kurt Lewin, 'Group decision and social change', in T. M. Newcombe and E. L. Hartley (eds), *Readings in Social Psychology* (Holt, Rinehart and Winston, 1958).

Appendix 4   Research Methodology

This study was designed to explore an aspect of management that is not well defined. Its main purpose was to generate models and hypotheses. It was not designed to test any formal propositions. With this objective, the methodology was purposely open-ended. However, it may still be useful to describe in some detail the steps we went through to generate a data base and develop our conclusions.

Sample Selection

The study was launched based on a sample of six large UK companies to which the researchers were able to gain good access. This initial sample was chosen almost entirely as a result of the existing management contacts held by the Centre for Business Strategy and the members of its Council. After about 6 months of discussion with these companies the sample was extended by a further ten companies. The second sample was chosen more carefully, using two criteria. First, we wanted to make the sample more representative by including all the major company types (e.g. consumer goods, industrial goods, high tech) in the UK. Secondly, we wanted the sample to include some of the best performing companies in the UK. Companies like BTR, Tarmac, Plessey, Courtaulds and United Biscuits were added to the sample at this stage.

Gaining access to this second set of companies proved to be difficult. There were, however, only two or three large companies that we would have liked to include where we were refused access. Admittedly we received access to Ferranti late in the research, and as a result our findings from the Ferranti interviews may have been influenced by the conclusions we had already drawn from the earlier interviews with other companies.

In addition to the 16 large companies, we originally planned to include some smaller companies in the sample; particularly companies with exceptional track records. We thought that these younger companies might have developed new approaches that were not used by the large concerns. However, we encountered even more serious problems of access with these companies, and after a limited amount of interviewing, we decided that the smaller companies would not add significantly to our findings and we therefore dropped them from the sample.

Our final sample is not scientifically representative, but we are confident that it includes companies broadly representative of management practice in the UK, that it includes state-of-the-art practitioners, and that they cover a range of manufacturing and service sectors. Their common characteristics are size, diversity and success. We purposely excluded financial services, the professional services, and retailing because we felt that these sectors would be likely to have different management processes and because we wanted to focus on the problems of decision-making in Britain's industrial heartland.

One possible bias that may exist in the sample is a geographic one. All of the companies except Tarmac have headquarters located in the south of England, mainly in and around London. Although this is probably representative of large companies in the UK, this geographical bias did not occur to us until after the work was complete and hence we have not carried out any test of its importance.

Interviews

We undertook interviews with between six and 20 managers in each of the participant companies. Typically the interview process began with an extended session with the head of planning to develop background on the history, strategy and decision-making processes of the company. A semi-structured questionnaire was used during these meetings. The major headings of the questionnaire are given on page 363. The interviews did however extend much more broadly than the topics covered in the questionnaire. These meetings lasted from about 3 up to 8 hours, in most cases split into two or three sessions.

After these initial meetings, we met with a cross-section of managers (line and staff) at the corporate level and in the divisions and businesses. In all companies we attempted to check and validate the perceptions of corporate managers with those of business level managers. In some companies we interviewed quite extensively in individual business areas in order to get a variety of views on how specific strategy decisions were taken. In almost all cases we met with the chief executive of the company during the interview process, often on several occasions. Individual interviews normally lasted 1½ to 2½ hours.

After each interview we wrote up detailed notes from the meeting, capturing points of fact, matters of opinion and specific quotes. We sent these notes to our interview partners to check their accuracy as a record of the interview, and to allow for the correction of any misunderstandings or factual errors. Interview partners were assured of the confidentiality of the meetings, and no views have been attributed publicly to individuals without their authorization. These interview notes form a large part of the raw material from which our conclusions were constructed.

We did not tape record interviews for two reasons. First, there was unwillingness on the part of several interviewees to talk freely with a tape recorder running. We judged that the sort of openness we sought in these meetings would not be encouraged by taping, even if the interviewee did not formally object to it. Secondly, we found that transcripts of tapes were not the most efficient way to capture the data we were collecting. By producing an interview summary soon after the meeting we were able to sort the data we had received into a five- to ten-page document which proved to be much easier to use when we began to analyse the results. We conducted more than 200 interviews and the data would have become unmanageable unless we had found a way of summarizing as we went along.

Company Analysis

In addition to interview data, files were assembled on each company. These files contained annual reports and press clippings going back 10 years, together with any other relevant articles or publications about the company and its markets. Financial and other data on the companies' competitors were also assembled. This published information was supplemented in some cases by unpublished in-company reports and data that were provided to us.

We analysed this information to develop a view on

— the major strategic issues that the company had faced during the period;
— the decisions that had been taken;
— the results (financial and non-financial) that had been achieved;
— the decision-making process employed by the company, and how it affected the decisions taken and the results achieved.

A detailed memorandum was written on each company and sent to our primary contact. Although these memoranda were specifically not for publication, they (and the company reactions to them) served in a more general sense as a further input to our overall conclusions.

From the files of company-specific information we were also able to compile the brief company summaries and the statistical comparisons that appear in appendix 1.

Progress towards Conclusions

Based upon the pilot sample of six companies, an initial set of hypotheses was generated during the summer of 1985. These hypotheses were discussed with representatives of participant companies, and were embodied in a paper for the Strategic Management Society Conference in Philadelphia in October 1984.

As the field work with the extended sample was drawing to a close at the end of 1985, a further summary paper was written. This served as a discussion paper at two dinner meetings attended by the chief executives of the participating companies in November 1985.

A full set of draft working papers was produced in the period December 1985 to March 1986, and was circulated to participant companies for comments and clearance of examples and quotes. These papers were revised in the light of comments received, and published by the Centre for Business Strategy in June 1986. A major conference at which the outline findings of the work were presented was held for about 120 senior managers both from the participating companies and from other companies, also in June 1986.

During the autumn of 1986 a series of workshop sessions, attended by participating companies and other interested managers, was held at the Centre for Business Strategy to discuss the research papers. A series of in-company and open presentations of findings was also made to a wide variety of management audiences. Comments on or criticisms of the work received during this process have influenced our thinking and helped to sharpen our findings. Hence, our conclusions in this book are more developed than those in the original research papers. We feel that by documenting our thinking at each stage of the work, and refining it as we have moved forward, we have been able to enrich the eventual findings. This procedure is in keeping with our view of the work as an attempt to generate models and hypotheses rather than to undertake scientific testing of propositions.

Major Headings of the Company Questionnaire

 1 Corporate portfolio strategy
 2 Corporate influence on development of SBU strategy proposals/ options
 3 Corporate role in setting SBU objectives (specific targets)
 4 What is corporate resource allocation process?
 5 Corporate role in control of strategy
 6 Formal planning system
 7 Formal and informal approaches to strategic decisions
 8 Performance appraisal and compensation systems
 9 Composition of corporate management
10 Corporate structure and SBU definition
11 History
12 Key problems

Index

Index

Index by Jacqueline McDermott